INTANGIBLE CULTURAL HERITAGE OF INDIA

INTANGIBLE CULTURAL HERITAGE OF INDIA (VOL. I)

INDIAN RELIGIOUS PRACTICES

A Selective Bibliography

(Fairs, Festivals, Customs, Beliefs, Ceremonies, Rites, Rituals, Manners, Traditions)

Kamal Kant Misra
Mohammad Rehan
Ravindra K. Gupta

Indira Gandhi Rashtriya Manav Sangrahalaya
(National Museum of Mankind)
Bhopal

GYAN

GYAN PUBLISHING HOUSE

Preface

A well-organized information system is a prerequisite for the growth and development of any discipline. It can efficiently and effectively serve the needs of the seeker of nascent information. Bibliography is one such useful information system, as it acquaints the scholars and research workers with the work already done in the past on a particular subject, region or place, author, etc. Quick and easy access to information is vital to the development of varies fields of knowledge. Therefore, it is essential that relevant information be brought to the attention of the professionals, administrators, and researchers who have urgent need of it. In this respect, bibliography plays an important role. There was a time in the past, when it was possible to a scholar to keep herself/himself up-to-date and well informed on current literature in her/his field of interest. But due to the increase in the amount of literature available, it has become more and more difficult now to do so. But for a bibliography a scholar may lose her/his way, wasting much time before he is able to read even a part of what he is required to study.

Much has been written on religious practices in India, fairs, festivals, customs, tradition, beliefs, rituals, rites, manners, etc. and the references are many and distributed over numerous journals, monographs, memoirs, internet database and other publications that are not easily accessible to research workers and the seekers of information. Keeping in view these facts, it has been considered useful to compile a bibliography available.

This bibliography on Intangible Cultural Heritage : A Selective Bibliography, Vol. 1: Religious practices in India, (Indian fairs, festival, custom, beliefs, ceremonies, rites, rituals, manners, etc.) indexes 2206 monographs (books), journal articles, research papers, thesis, notes, etc.

In the compilation of this comprehensive bibliography, varieties of sources have been used. They can be broadly classified as:

(a) Individual Journals
(b) Monographs (books)
(c) Bibliographies
(e) INTERNET database
(d) Indexing/ Abstracting services. (Local and International)

Structure of the Bibliography

Each entry in the bibliography contains the following information:

Books : Name of Author/editor (Surname, forename), Title of book (in double inverted comma), Place of publication, Name of publisher, Year of publication, and total pages of book.

Example: Pandey, R.P. "Pre-historic archaeology of Madhya Pradesh". New Delhi, Sandeep Prakashan, 1987, p. 296.

Journal Article: Name of Author (Surname, forename), Title (in double inverted comma), Name of Journals (in Italic), Volume No., Issue No., Year, and the pages.

Example: Mathpal, Y. "Rock art sites in India and problems of their preservation and management". Purakala, Vol. 2, No. 1, 1991, pp. 22-23.

The bibliography consists of full entries arranged alphabetically under authors. Each entry has been serially numbered. To facilitate quick references from any desired viewpoint three alphabetical indices, viz., Subject/Keyword Index, and Title Index, referring to the text by the serial number, have been appended.

We sincerely hope that this bibliography would be useful for scientists, research scholars, and other personnel related to the field of religious practices, fairs, festivals, customs, beliefs, ceremonies, rites, rituals, manners, etc.

K.K. Misra
Mohammad Rehan
Ravindra K. Gupta

Abbreviation Used

A.P.	:	Andhra Pradesh
AIOC	:	All India Oriental Congress
Annon.	:	Anonymous
CRM	:	Cultural Resource Management
D.C.R.I	:	Deccan College and Research Centre
GPS	:	Global Positioning System
IAHC	:	Indian Art History Congress
IAR	:	Indian Anthropological Review
IGNCA	:	Indira Gandhi National Centre for Arts
IGRMS	:	Indira Gandhi Rashtriya Manav Sangrahalaya
JAOS	:	Journal of the American Oriental Society
JRASB	:	Journal of Asiatic Society of Bengal
M.P.	:	Madhya Pradesh
Ph.d.	:	Doctor in Philosophy
PILC	:	Journal of Dravidic Studies
T. N.	:	Tamil Nadu
U.P.	:	Uttar Pradesh
UGC	:	University Grant Commission
UNESCO	:	United Nations Educational, Scientific and Cultural Organization

List of Journals

1. Acta Orientalia: Founded in 1922, is published annually under the auspices of the Oriental Societies of Denmark.

2. Akhand Jyoti: (Hindi–Monthly magazine) Akhand Jyoti Sansthan Gheeyamandi, Mathura – 281003 (UP) India.

3. American Anthropologist: Published by American Anthropological Association, Washington, USA.

4. American Ethnologist: Journal published by the The American Anthropological Association (AAA), the primary professional society of anthropologists in the United States since its founding in 1902, is the world's largest professional organization of individuals interested in anthropology.

5. American Journal of Physical Anthropology: (AJPA) is a Monthly peer-reviewed scientific journal and the official journal of the American Association of Physical Anthropologists. It was established in 1918 by Aleš Hrdlicka. ISSN, 0002-9483 (print) 1096-8644 (web)

6. American Studies: The American Studies Journal is published semiannually by the Center for United States Studies at Martin Luther University Halle-Wittenberg, Germany.

7. Ancient Science of Life: Ancient Science of Life has evolved into an online only, open access multidisciplinary journal in the field of Ayurveda serving as a platform to bridge

traditional knowledge and modern science. free download at, http://www.avpayurveda.com/downloads/cat_view/71-ancient-science-of-life.html

8. Anthropological Linguistics: A quarterly journal published by the American Indian Studies Research Institute and the Department of Anthropology at Indiana University, Bloomington, Indiana, USA. founded in 1959, provides a forum for the full range of scholarly study of the languages and cultures of the peoples of the world.

9. Anthropological Quarterly: is a quarterly publication of the George Washington University Institute for Ethnographic Research. www.aq.gwu.edu

10. Anthropologie: Anthropos Institute-Moravian Museum, Brno, Czechoslovakia.

11. Anthropology Today: Anthropology Today is a bimonthly publication which aims to provide a forum for the ap plication of anthropological analysis to public and topical issues, Published on behalf of Royal Anthropological Institute.

12. Anthropos: International Review of Anthropology and Linguistics (Anthropos Institute) St – Paul, P.O. 176, Perolles 42, CH-1705 Fribourg, Switzerland.

13. Antiquity, Antiquity Publication Limited, Oxford University Press, London, U.K.

14. Art Asia Pacific: Journal of Arts and Cultural Management is an online, free to air, fully peer reviewed academic journal. The journal publishes articles about arts and cultural management and cultural policy issues.

15. Art India: is India's premier art magazine: over the last eleven years, Mumbai, India.

16. Aryan Path: The Aryan Path was an Anglo-Indian theosophical journal. Bombay, India from 1930, publishedby Indian Institute of World Culture.

17. Asian Ethnology: Asian Ethnology is a peer-reviewed journal dedicated to the promotion of scholarly research on the peoples and cultures of Asia. Asian Ethnology is registered as an Open Access Journal ISSN 1882–6865.

18. Asian Folklore Studies : see Asian Ethnology : currently Asian Ethnology.

19. Asian Music : Bi-annual Journal of the Society for Asian Music Society Founded 1959, Journal Founded 1969.

20. Asian Quarterly of Culture and Synthesis.

21. Asian Theatre Journal: is dedicated to the performing arts of Asia.

22. Bionature : Affiliated as Official publication of The Society of Bionaturalists, Founder Editor: H. K. Goswami, 24, Kaushalnagar (Misrod), Bhopal, (M.P.)

23. BMJ: British Medical Journal: BMJ is a partially open-access, peer-reviewed medical journal. Originally called the British Medical Journal, the title was officially shortened to BMJ in 1988. The journal is published by the BMJ Group, a wholly owned subsidiary of the British Medical Association.

24. Breastfeeding Medicine: Published Bimonthly Breastfeeding Medicine is an authoritative, peer-reviewed journal created by physicians and dedicated to the advancement of breastfeeding worldwide. ISSN: 1556-8253. Online ISSN: 1556-8342.

25. Bulletin of the Anthropological Survey of India, Kolkatta, India.

26. Bulletin of the Cultural Research Institute: Published by the Cultural Research Institute, West Bengal (India). since 1980.

27. Bulletin of the Deccan College Research Institute, (D.C.R.I.) Poona, India.

28. Bulletin of the Department of Anthropology: Published by Department of Anthropology, Gauhati University, Assam, 1975.

29. Bulletin of the School of Oriental and African Studies: University of London, London, UK.

30. Bulletin of Tribal Research and Development Institute: (TRI), Bhopal, Madhya Pradesh.

31. Calcutta Historical Journal: Published by the Department of History, University of Calcutta. West Bengal, ISSN: 0254-9794, OCLC Number: 6744867

32. Calcutta Review: The Calcutta Review is a bi-annual periodical, now published by the Calcutta University Press, featuring scholarly articles from a variety of disciplines. The Calcutta Review was founded in May 1844, by Sir John William Kaye and Reverend Alexander Duff.

33. Caribbean Quarterly: is the flagship journal on culture of the University of the West Indies, Jamaica. The journal appears quarterly in March, June, September and December.

34. Ceramic Review: Ceramic Review is published six times a year. Each issue is printed in full colour, with a minimum of pages (300 x 220 mm) and includes regular columns and articles concerning all aspects of studio pottery, Ceramic Review, 63 Great Russell Street, London, WC1B 3BF, http://www.ceramicreview.com/contactus.asp

35. Chhayanat: A Monthly Hindi Magazine/Journal of the Sangeet Natak Academy, Lucknow, India.

36. Chomasa: A bi-lingual (Hindi and English) Journal of the Adivasi Lok Kala Prishad, Bhopal, Madhya Pradesh.

37. Comparative Studies of South Asia, Africa and the Middle East: Published by the Duke University Press, CSSAAME publishes articles from around the world, Frequency: Three issues annually, ISSN: 1089-201X, e-ISSN: 1548-226X.

38. Contemporary India: Journal of the Nehru Memorial Museum and Library, New Delhi, India.

39. Contributions to Asian Studies.

40. Contributions to Indian Sociology : Electronic access: Contributions to Indian Sociology is available electronically on SAGE Journals Online athttp://cis.sagepub.com

41. Cultural Forum (Delhi): Published by the Ministry of Education and Youth Services. and Ministry of Scientific Research and Cultural Affairs, Government of India.

42. Current Anthropology (Monthly) Published by the University of Chicago Press, Sponsored by the Wenner-Gren Foundation For Anthropological Research, Chicago, U.S.

43. Current Science: is a peer-reviewed scientific journal established in 1932 and published by the Current Science Association along with the Indian Academy of Sciences.

44. Daedulus: Quarterly (Winter/Spring/Summer/Fall) Dædalus was founded in 1955 as the Journal of the American Academy of Arts and Sciences.

45. Dharmayug (Bannet Colman and Company, Bombay) India.

46. Discover India.

47. East and West.

48. The Eastern Anthropologist: (Published Quarterly) Founded in 1947 by D.N. Majumdar, Published by Serial Publications, New Delhi on behalf of Ethnographic and Folk Culture Society, Lucknow (U.P.) www.efcsindia.com

49. Eco News: EcoNews is a free monthly newsletter, Editor 395 Conway Road, Victoria, BC CANADA V9E 2B9 Tel (250) 881-1304 www.earthfuture.com

50. Economic and Political Weekly: (Weekly) A Sameeksha Trust Publication, 320-21, A to Z Industrial Estate, Ganpatrao Kadam Marg, Lower Parel, Mumbai, Maharastra. www.epw.com

51. Economic Botany: is an academic journal that deals with the uses of plants by people, or economic botany. It covers fields such as ethnopharmacology as well as potential new crops. Economic Botany is a quarterly journal published by The New York Botanical Garden for the Society for Economic Botany.

52. Economic Development and Cultural Change: Frequency: 4 issues/year; University of Chicago Press, 1427 East 60th Street, Chicago, IL 60637, Telephone: (773) 702-8116, email: edcc@press.uchicago.edu

53. ELH: English Literary History is an academic journal established in 1934 and devoted to the study of major works in the English language, Publised by the Johns Hopkins University Press (United States).

54. Environment and History: Published four times a year by Oxford University Press on behalf of the American Society for Environmental History and the Forest History Society, the journal brings together scholars and practitioners from the humanities, sciences, and social sciences to explore the changing relationships between humans and the environment over time.

55. Environmental Ethics: Editorial Office: Department of Philosophy and Religion Studies, The University of North Texas, 1155 Union Circle #310980, Denton, TX 76203-5017. hargrove@unt.edu

56. Ethnobotany.

57. Ethnohistory: The journal of the American Society for Ethnohistory, Frequency: Quarterly, Editorial Office: Department of History Pennsylvania State University 108 Weaver Bldg. University Park, PA 16802 814-865-620 3814-863-7840 (fax), ethnohistory@psu.edu

58. Ethnology: Ethnology (ISSN 0014-1828) is published quarterly--with an additional issue published in October-by the University of Pittsburgh, Pittsburgh, PA 15260, and supported jointly by the Department of Anthropology and the University Library System.

59. Ethnomusicology: Published by: University of Illinois Press on behalf of Society for Ethnomusicology, 2110 Clarice Smith Center School of Music University of Maryland College Park, MD 20742-1620 Email: ethnomusicology@umd.edu

60. Ethos: Print ISSN: 0091-2131, Online ISSN: 1548-1352, is an interdisciplinary and international quarterly journal, Published by the American Anthropological Association on behalf of the Society for Psychological Anthropology.

61. Folklore : Folklore is the journal of The Folklore Society, ISSN : 0015-587X (Print), 1469-8315 (Online), Publication Frequency 3 issues per year.

62. Frontiers in Ecology and the Environment: issued 10 times per year, consists of peer-reviewed, synthetic review articles on all aspects of ecology, the environment, and related disciplines.

63. Harper's Monthly Magazine : Harper's Magazine was launched as Harper's New Monthly Magazine in June 1850, by the New York City publisher Harper & Brothers; who also founded Harper's Bazaar magazine.

64. Himbharti: A journal of Pahari Language of Himachal Pradesh, Published by Himachal Kala Sanskriti Bhasha Akadami, Sangarmal Bhawan, Cliff and Estate, Shimla, H. P. 171 001 India.

65. Himprastra: A monthly Hindi magazine, Himprastha, was published from Shimla by the Public Relations and Tourism Department and edited by Hari Krishna Mittoo and Ram Dayal Neeraj. It carried stories, poetry, articles and happenings in the state.

66. History of Religions: Published by the University of Chicago Swift Hall 005 1025 E. 58th Street Chicago, IL 60637.

67. Hrigandha: Published by the Haryana Sahitya Akadami.

68. Human Ecology.

69. Human Organization.

70. Human Science.

71. Humankind.

72. ICOM News: (International Council of Museums, ICOM) 1, Rue Miollis, 75732, Paris, France.

73. Indian and Foreign Review: (Semi-Monthly) Ministry of Information and Broadcasting, Government of India, New Delhi, India.

74. Indian Journal of History and Science: This journal is being published by Indian National Science Academy [INSA] since more than three decades now. Initially, the journal was launched in 1966 with two issues per year.

75. Indian Journal of Physical Anthropology and Human Genetics : Published/Hosted by The Ethnographic and Folk Culture Society, India. ISSN: 0378-8156. full text articles not currently available online.

76. Indian Journal of Social Development: Published by : serials Publications, ISSN: 0972-3692 Frequency : Bi-annual, IJSD is abstracted in the American Libraries of Congress Cataloguing.

77. Indian Journal of Social Work: (IJSW) is a pioneering publication of the social work profession in India, published by the Tata Institute of Social Sciences, The IJSW is published every January, April, July and October, and has entered its 72nd year of uninterrupted publishing, a record in journal publishing. The first issue of the IJSW was published in June 1940.

78. Indian Journal of Traditional Knowledge: (Quarterly) Published by the National Institute of Science Communication and Information Resources, CSIR Dr. KS Krishan Marg, New Delhi, India, www.niscair.res.in

79. Indian Museum Bulletin.

80. International Journal of Hindu Studies.

81. International Journal of Sociology of the Family: Published By : Serials Publications Frequency : Bi-Anuual ISSN : 0973-2039.

82. Jansatta: a daily newspaper from New Delhi (India [Hindi].

83. Journal of American Folklore: The Journal of American Folklore, the quarterly journal of the American Folklore Society since the Society's founding in 1888.

84. Journal of American Oriental Society: The Journal of the American Oriental Society is a quarterly academic journal published by the American Oriental Society since 1843.

85. Journal of Ancient Indian History: Calcutta (India). University. Dept. of Ancient Indian History and Culture, University of Calcutta. Dept. of Ancient Indian History and Culture, D.C. Sircar, 1969.

86. Journal of Anthropological Research : Published by the University of New Mexico in the interest of general anthropology since 1945, Department of Anthropology MSC01 1040 1 University of New Mexico, Albuquerque, New Mexico 87131-0001, U.S.A..

87. Journal of Asian Studies: Published in February, May, August, and November, The Journal of Asian Studies (JAS) has long been recognized as the most authoritative and prestigious publication in the field of Asian studies. Jeffrey N. Wasserstrom, University of California, Irvine, E-Mail: jas@journalofasianstudies.org, Phone: (949) 824-6521, Fax: (949) 824-2865.

88. Journal of Epidemiology and Community Health : is a leading international journal devoted to publication of original research and reviews, The journal aims to improve epidemiological knowledge and ultimately health worldwide, JECH is the official journal of the Society for Social Medicine.

89. Journal of Human Ecology: Monthly (12 issues 4 Vols. Per year) Published by Kamla Raj Enterprises, New Delhi, full text online available at www.krepublishers.com

90. Journal of Indian and Buddhist Studies: The Japanese Association of Indian and Buddhist Studies publishes the Journal of Indian and Buddhist Studies twice a year. It contains articles, essays, translations, and related news stories.

91. Journal of Indian Anthropological Society.

92. Journal of Indian Folkloristics: Published by Zooni Publictions, 1103, C-D Block, Udaya Ravi Road, Kuvempunagar, Mysore – 570 023. India.

93. Journal of Indian Museum.

94. Journal of Indian Philosophy.

95. Journal of Marriage and the family : Edited by: David H. Demo, Print ISSN: 0022-2445 Online ISSN: 1741-3737, Published on behalf of National Council on Family Relations.

96. Journal of Medicinal Aromatic Plants Science.

97. Journal of Oriental Research: (Kuppuswami Sastri Research Institute, Madras, Tamil Nadu).

98. Journal of Social Anthropology: Published by Serial Publications, New Delhi in June and December, 4830/24 Ansari Road, Darya Ganj, New Delhi, 110 002. India, www.serialpublications.com

99. Journal of Social Sciences: (12 issues 4 Vols. Per year) Published by Kamla Raj Enterprises, New Delhi, full text online available at www.krepublishers.com

100. Journal of the Anthropological Society of Oxford: JASO.
101. Journal of the Anthropological Survey of India.
102. Journal of the Asiatic society of Bengal (Quarterly) 1, Park Street, Calcutta, India.
103. Journal of the Asiatic Society of Bombay: (Town Hall, Bombay, India).
104. Journal of the Asiatic Society of Pakistan.
105. Journal of the Assam Research Society.
106. Journal of the Bihar Research Society: (Quarterly) Bihar Research Society Museum Building, Patna, Bihar, India.
107. Journal of the Bombay Branch of the Royal Asiatic Society.
108. Journal of the Economic and Social History of the Orient.
109. Journal of the Indian Anthropological Society: Published in three issues every year, March, July and November, Published by the Indian Anthropological Society, 27, Jawaharlal Nehru Road, Kolkata, 700 016 India.
110. Journal of the Oriental Institute : Editor, BHATT, G.H., M.S. University of Baroda, Baroda, Gujarat.
111. Journal of the Royal Asiatic society of Bengal: Calcutta, West Bengal.
112. Journal of the Royal Asiatic society of Great Britain : Royal Asiatic Society, London.
113. Journal of the Society of Architectural Historians: is a quarterly publication of the Society of Architectural Historians, ONLINE (JSAH online). Developed in partnership with University of California Press and JSTOR, and using software from Atypon Systems, JSAH online offers access to JSAH from the first volume published in 1941 through the present.
114. Journal of the University of Poona : Pune, Maharashtra.

115. Kala Deergha.

116. Kala Varta: Journal of the Madhya Pradesh Kala Parishad, Bhopal, India.

117. Kala: the journal of Indian art history congress.

118. Language in Society: Language in Society is a peer-reviewed academic journal of sociolinguistics. It was established in 1972 and is published five times a year by Cambridge University Press. The current editor in chief is Barbara Johnstone (Carnegie Mellon University).

119. Lipika: A Journal of the Performing Arts.

120. Madhya Bharti: Monthly, Dr. Hari Singh Gour University, Sagar, Madhya Pradesh, India.

121. Man (The Royal Anthropological Institute), 56, Queen Anne Street, London, England.

122. Man and Environment : Journal of the Indian Society for Prehistoric and Quaternary Studies, [Editor, V.N. Misra, P.P. Joglekar, Shanti Pappu].

123. Man and Life: (Quarterly) A journal of the Institute of Social Research and Applied Anthropology, Bidisa, P.O. Fulgeria, Dist. Paschim Medinipur, West Bengal – 721 437.

124. Man in India: A Quarterly Journal Founded in 1921 by Sarat Chandra Roy, Published by the Serial Publications, New Delhi, India.

125. Manav.

126. Mankind.

127. Marg: A quarterly journal, 34-38, Bank Street, Bombay, India.

128. Modern Asian Studies.

129. Museum (UNESCO): 7-9, Place de Fontenoy, Paris, France.

130. Nai Duniya: Daily news paper published from Bhopal, Madhya Pradesh, India.

131. National Geographic.

132. Natural History of Sociology and Natural History of Museum.

133. Nava Bharat Times : Daily News paper published from Bombay, India.

134. Numen: Numen is an academic journal on the history of religions, published by Brill Publishers in Leiden, The Netherlands. It publishes non-confessional articles on the history of all religions, of all regions and times, as well as papers discussing theoretical innovations in the study of religion and reflective studies on the history of the discipline.

135. Ojasvini: (Monthly) Published by Vasudha Publcations Pvt. Ltd. 103, Vasundhra Building, Near Barkatullah University, Bhopal, (M.P.)

136. Pahar (Peoples Association for Hill Area Research, Nainital, Uttaranchal, India.

137. Panchajagat.

138. Pashyanti.

139. PILC Journal of Dravidic Studies: A Bi-Annual Research journal published in English in January and July by the Puducherry Institute of Linguistics and Culture (PILC), PIPMET Campus, Lawspet, Puducherry India.

140. Population and Development Review

141. Prabuddha Bharat or Awakened India: Started by Swami Vivekanada in 1896, A monthly journal of the Ramakrishna Order, Advaita Ashram, PO Mayavati, via Lohaghat, Dist. Champawat, Uttarakhand, India. www.advaitaashrama.org

142. Prabuddha Bharat or Awakened India.

143. Prachya Pratibha.

144. Puratan: The Directorate of Archaeology Archives & Museums, Bhopal, Madhya Pradesh.

145. Purusartha.

146. Purvagrah.

147. Religions of South Asia: Publication: June and December ISSN 1751-2689 (Print) ISSN 1751-2697 (Online).

148. RES: Anthropology and Aesthetics.

149. Resarun: Journal of the Directorate of Research.

150. Roma.

151. Samkaleen Bhartiya Sahitya.

152. Sangeet Natak: Published since 1965 by Sangeet Natak Akademy – the National Academy of Music, Dance and Drama for India.

153. Shodh Samvet: A Quarterly Journal of Sri Kaveri Research Institute, 37, Keshavnagar, Gaughat, Ujjain (M.P.).

154. Sikh Review: Monthly, Published by Sikh Culture Centre.

155, Karnani Mansion, 25A, Park Street, Kolkata 700016, INDIA, www.sikhreview.org

156. Society and Natural Resources: Publisher Taylor & Francis, ISSN 0894-1920.

157. Sociological Bulletin: Sociological Bulletin is published thrice a year: January-April, May-August, and September-December. The journal was published biannually from 1952 to 2003, and became a triannual publication from 2004. Copyright © Indian Sociological Society, New Delhi.

158. Sociological Theory: Present Pub. by Wiley, Beginning January 1, 2012 Sociological Theory will be published by SAGE. Please visit their website for further information.

159. Somsi.

160. South Asia Research.

161. South Indian Folklorist.

162. Southwestern Journal of Anthropology.

163. Soviet Anthropology and Archeology: Published by: University of New Mexico, ISSN: 0038-4801.

164. Sruti: South Indian Classical Music and Dance Magazine.

165. Statesman: a daily newspaper published From Kolkata, India.

166. Studies of Tribes and Tribals: Published since 1933 (2 issues One Vols. Per yar) July-December, Kamla Raj Enterprises, New Delhi, full text online available at.

167. Sundaram: A magazine on contemporary art is a monthly magazine Published by Neeru Nanda 281, Muthiganj, Allahbad 211 003, India.

168. Swarajya.

169. Telegraph.

170. The Anthropologist: A quarterly International Journal of Contemporary and Applied Studies of Man, Published by the Kamla Raj Enterprises, Chawri Bazar, New Delhi, India.

171. The Drama Review: TDR provides scholarship on performances and their social, economic and political contexts. TDR:The Drama Review was founded in 1955 by Robert W. Corrigan as the "Carlton Drama Review", TDR is owned by New York University and is published in hard copy and online by the MIT Press.

172. The Eastern Anthropologist: A quarterly journal Founded in 1947 by Dr. D.N. Majumdar, Published by Serial Publications on behalf of Ethnographic and Folk Culture Society, Lucknow, India.

173. The Hindu: Daily English News Paper, Published From New Delhi, India.

174. The India Magazine.

175. The Indian Forester: The Indian Forester, a pioneer journal of forestry research, established in 1875, Forest Research Institute, (Indian Council of Forestry Research & Education), Post- New Forest, Dehra Dun – 248006, Uttarakhand, India.

176. The Journal of Asian Studies.

177. The Journal of Religious Ethics.

178. The Journal of the Royal Anthropological Institute.

179. The Journal of the Royal Asiatic Society of Great Britain and Ireland.

180. The Oriental Anthropologist: A Bi-Annaul Internatioan journal of the science of man, Published by MD Publication Pvt. Ltd., 11 Darya Ganj New Delhi, Journal is online at www.mdppl.com

181. The Pioneers: A daily News Paper, New Delhi, India.

182. Traveller in India.

183. Vanyajati: A Quarterly Journal in English and Hindi, Published by the Bhartiya Adimjati Sevak Sangh, New link road, Jhadewala, New Delhi, India.

184. Vishvesharanand Indological Journal.

185. Vivekananda Kendra Patrika, Madras.

186. Women and performance: A Journal of Feminist Theory.

187. World Archaeology.

188. Yearbook for Traditional Music.

189. Yojana: (Monthly) Publication Division, Govt. Of India, 538, Yojana Bhawan, Sansad Marg, New Delhi, www.yojana.gov.in, www.publicationdivision.nic.in

190. Journal of Sociology and Social Anthropology.
191. The Tribal Tribune, An E. Journal, Online at site www.etribaltribune.com.
192. Orissa Historical Research Journal.
193. Man in Society.

Introduction
Intangible Cultural Heritage of India: An Overview

Kamal K. Misra

The saga of human history and civilization is replete with examples that testify the fact that unprecedented technological sophistication and unswerving process of globalization of our times have not come without a price. They have a leveling effect on human culture, thus alarmingly shrinking the cultural diversity. The eco-specific cultural patterns and amazingly varied languages are now rushing towards greater uniformity, thus losing individual identities of peoples and their cultures. There is, therefore, a threat to the cultural heritage of the humankind.

But what is cultural heritage? The International Council on Monuments and Sites (ICOMOS) has defined that "Cultural Heritage is an expression of the ways of living developed by a community and passed on from generation to generation, including customs, practices, places, objects, artistic expressions and values." (2002). The process of globalization has not only reduced distance considerably, but also brought information and commodities much closer to the people. With the increase in buying power and easy availability of information and commodities, preferences are more towards those which look glamorous and fascinating. Examples of this trend are many;

the songs that marked beginning of a season, celebration of birth or marriage, or a mourning in rural and tribal India are now replaced by cinema songs. This is how the distinctiveness of identity is in peril and cultural heritage is threatened.

Cultural Heritage is a much wider concept. John Feather (2006) has aptly said that the driving force behind all definitions of cultural heritage is a human creation intended to inform. It informs all that is created and maintained by the people as a part of their distinct culture. It could be built environments, such as buildings, townscapes and archaeological remains; natural environments, such as rural landscapes; artifacts, such as manuscripts, documents, material objects or pictures; or the ideas and the skills behind all the above mentioned creations and innovations. Therefore, cultural heritage could be either tangible or intangible. In the UNESCO document it is stated that "Cultural heritage is not limited to material manifestations, such as monuments and objects that have been preserved over time. This notion also encompasses living expressions and the traditions that countless groups and communities worldwide have inherited from their ancestors and transmit to their descendants, in most cases orally." While the former is the tangible aspects of the cultural heritage that underlines the visible traces from human antiquity to the recent times, the latter connotes the intangible or "living heritage" representing the value systems, beliefs, traditions and lifestyles of the people that are mostly transmitted orally.

According to the Donald Horne Institute of Cultural Heritage at the University of Canberra, cultural heritage and its recognition and preservation were not taken seriously till recent times. As a field of scholarship, cultural heritage emerged over the past forty or fifty years when universities in the West diversified beyond the traditional disciplines into new fields of cross-disciplinary or multi-disciplinary enquiry. Simultaneously, collections in museums, archives, libraries and galleries became a topic of study in their own right, so too did national parks, sacred places, historic buildings and entire landscapes. When the National Trusts, National Parks Associations and activist citizens groups started propagating the value of cultural heritages and started protecting them, popular awareness about cultural heritage gained momentum. The UNESCO contributed to the recognition and protection of cultural heritages of nations in a big way. Many governments and non-government agencies also joined their hands in this process. Popular consciousness got heightened with the rapid pace of globalization, mono-culturalism and ruthless destruction of priceless cultural heritages all over the world.

India's cultural heritage is rich and diverse due to its civilizational past. It is represented by thousands of monuments, temples and other works of art, such as paintings, sculptures and handicrafts found across the length and breadth of this country. Besides these tangible heritages are the less visible forms of cultural heritages, pertaining to oral traditions, aesthetic and religious beliefs, rituals and festivals, arts, music, folk traditions, dances, theatre forms, performing arts and narrative styles of storytelling. They are the insignia of the rich and diverse, multi-cultural, multi–linguistic cultural heritage of India. These are also called traditional expressions and include oral literature, music, dance, games, mythology, rituals, costumes and crafts. Sometimes the cultural spaces, such as sites for story-telling, rituals and festivals, market places, where traditional cultural activities take place, are also included under the intangible cultural heritage.

Now we might question the relevance of understanding and protecting cultural heritage of the people and nations, particularly the intangible cultural heritage. The UNESCO document states that "While fragile, intangible cultural heritage is an important factor in maintaining cultural diversity in the face of growing globalization. An understanding of the intangible cultural heritage of different communities helps with intercultural dialogue, and encourages mutual respect for other ways of life. The importance of intangible cultural heritage is not the cultural manifestation itself but rather the wealth of knowledge and skills that is transmitted through it from one generation to the next. The social and economic value of this transmission of knowledge is relevant for minority groups and for mainstream social groups within a State, and is as important for developing States as for developed ones."

The UNESCO document suggests the following features of intangible cultural heritage or the living heritage:

(1) It is traditional, contemporary and living at the same time. This means that although inherited cultural traditions from the past are very important intangible heritages, it does not preclude the contemporary rural and urban cultural practices undertaken by diverse groups and communities as their heritage.

(2) It is inclusive or a shared expression that is similar to those practiced by many different groups and communities. Acculturation and spatial mobility are the hallmarks of human civilization. As a result, it is likely that similar practices may be observed in different villages, cities, and even in different corners of the world when the diasporic communities continue to practice them to express their origin and identity. These are all intangible cultural heritages, although they might have changed a bit due to their adaptation to the local environments. In any case they give a sense of identity and continuity, providing a link from our past, through the present, and into our future. It fosters social cohesion through the process of sharing of heritages.

(3) Intangible cultural heritage represents peoples and communities and depends upon those whose knowledge of traditions, skills and customs are transmitted to the rest of the community from one generation to the other or from one to other communities.

(4) Intangible cultural heritages have to be recognized as such by the groups, communities or individuals who create, maintain and transmit them. Without their recognition, none can decide them as heritages on their behalf.

Given the scope and spread of intangible cultural heritage or living heritage of India, there could be a huge list that includes many traditions, practices and customs as outlined earlier. For example, stories, family events, community gatherings, languages and dialects, songs, knowledge of natural and cultural spaces, healing traditions, food and beverages, recreation activities, beliefs and cultural practices, skills, performing arts, etc., which we inherit generationally and share between groups and communities. The Janapada Sampada Division of the Indira Gandhi National Centre of Art (IGNCA) has prepared an inventory of 30 elements (sic. items) under intangible cultural heritage of India. The list includes Buddhist chanting of Ladakh, Chaar Bayt, Dashavatar, the festival of Salhesh, Hingan paintings, Kalbelia dance and songs, and many more (http://www.ignca.nic.in/ich_inventory.htm).

Eastern India's Chhau dance, Kalbelia folk songs and dances of Rajasthan, and Mudiyettu ritual theater and dance drama of Kerala have already found place in the UNESCO representative list of intangible cultural heritage of humanity. The Indira Gandhi Rashtriya Manav Sangrahalaya had earlier made an attempt to include the Nacha folk theater of Chhatisgarh and the Vaishnav Satriya tradition of Majuli islands in Assam under the UNESCO list of intangible cultural heritages of India.

India undoubtedly is a rich repository of intangible cultural heritages due to its cultural diversity. But many of these heritages have already disappeared or are endangered due to the relentless sway of globalization and mono-culturalism. The need of the hour, therefore, is to document whatever little still exists and protect them for the posterity. The World Intellectual Property Organization (WIPO) based in Geneva has been making all out efforts to prepare international legal instruments for the protection of genetic resources, traditional knowledge and traditional cultural expressions including folklore, so that they could be protected from unethical piracy and those who innovate, practice and protect them could be benefited.

Realizing the importance of intangible cultural heritages of India and their documentation, Indira Gandhi Rashtriya Manav Sangrahalaya has undertaken the task of preparing selective bibliographies on various aspects of intangible cultural heritages to facilitate scholars and researchers in their pursuit of knowledge. It is proposed to be a multi-volume exercise due to enormous literature available on the subject. While the Volume I intends to cover fairs, festivals, customs, beliefs, ceremonies, rites, rituals, manners and traditions, the Volume II incorporates ethno-medical practices in India. Subsequent volumes on other aspects of intangible cultural heritage of India would follow these volumes soon. If these volumes indeed help and inspire scholars in the field of intangible cultural heritage, our efforts would be encouraging and productive.

References

Bhela, Anita (2001) Preserving India's Intangible Cultural Heritage: Issues and Challenges, International Journal of the Humanities, 8 (5), 207-214.

Feather, John (2006) Managing the Documentary Heritage: Issues from the Present and Future. In, Gorman, G.E. and Sydney J. Shep (eds.) Preservation Management for Libraries, Archives and Museums, 1-18, London: Facet.

http://www.unesco.org/culture/ich/doc/src/01851-EN.pdf.

http://www.canberra.edu.au/centres/donald-horne/cultural-heritage/what-is.

http://www.ignca.nic.in/ich_inventory.htm.

Bibliography

1. Abbe, J. A. Dubois "Hindu mannars and customs". Clarendan Press, London, 1906.

2. Abbott, J. "Indian ritual and belief: the keys of power". New Delhi, Usha, 1984. viii, 560 p.

3. Abbott, J. John "The keys of power: a study of Indian ritual and belief". [Microform], London, Methuen & Co., 1932. xxi, 560 p.

4. Abhedananda, Swami "Life beyond death". 2nd ed. Calcutta, Ramakrishna Vedanta math, 1948. 306 p., iii : front., plate; 21 cm.

5. Abraham, C. M. "The custom of polyandry as practised in Travancore". The Eastern Anthropologist, Vol. 12, No. 2, 1959, pp. 107-118.

6. Achyuteshananda "The car festival of lord Jagannatha". *Prabuddha Bharat*, Vol. 104, No.7, 1999, pp. 676-679.

7. Ackerley, J. R. "Hindoo holiday: an Indian journal". Harmondsworth, Middlesex, England ; New York, Penguin Books, 1983, 1932, 276 p. ; 20 cm.

8. Adam Hardy "Tradition and transformation: continuity and ingenuity in the temples of Karnataka". *Journal of the Society of Architectural Historians,* Vol. 60, No. 2 (Jun., 2001), pp. 180-199.

9. Adhikary, Ashim Kumar "Ritual and cosmology of the Birhor: A nomadic hunting and gathering tribe in India". *Jounran of the Indian Anthropological Society,* Vol. 38, No. 02-03, 2003 (July/ Novembe), pp. 207-214.

10. Agarwal, Vijay Lakshmi. "Jhunjhunu Mela" in Kulpali". Delhi: Rani Sati Temple, 1984. [Hindi]

11. Agoramorthy, Govindasamy and Hsu, Minna J. "Ritual releasing of wild animals threatens island ecology". Human Ecology, Vol. 35, No. 2, 2007 (April), pp. 251-254.

12. Agrawal, Ramnarayan "Raas ki manchiya parampara aur uska vartmaan swaroop". *Chhayanat,* No. 15, 1980 (Oct.-Dec.), pp. 16-23. [Hindi]

13. Agrawal, V. S. "Ancient Indian folk cults". Varansi, 1970.

14. Ahmad, N. L. "Some feasts and festivals at the court of Shah Jahan". In, 'Festivals in Indian society', 2 Vols., Edited by Usha Sharma, New Delhi, Mittal Publication, 1997, pp. 241-246.

15. Ahmad, Zakiuddin. "Sati in eighteenth century Bengal". *Journal of the Asiatic Society of Pakistan,* Vol. 13, No. 2 (August 1968), pp. 147-164.

16. Ahmed, Jmitiaz (ed.) "Family, kinship and marriage among muslims in India". Delhi, Manohar book service, 1976.

17. Ahmed, S. "Neem in sociocultural life in South Asia." In, 'The Neem Tree: Azadirachta indica A. Juss. and other Meliaceous Plants, Sources of Unique Natural Products for Integrated Pest Management, Medicine, Industry, and Other Purposes', ed. H. Schmutterer, New York, Weinheim, 1995, pp. 579-84.

18. Aiyar, A. Nataraja & Sastri, S. Lakshminarasmba "Traditional age of Sankaracharya and the Maths". Madras, 1962.

19. Aiyar, S. S. "Fetivals and legends of South India". *March of India,* No. 5, 1953.

20. Akundy, Anand "Ritual, narrative and the continuum: Anthropology of a Goddess festival". *The Eastern Anthropologist*, Vol. 58, No. 1, 2005, pp. 79-90.

21. Alahackoon, H. W. "Ceremonies observed by low-country Sinhalese: A girl attaining the age of puberty or maidenhood". *Modern Literacy Review: Notes and Queries for Ceylon,* Vol. 1. No.5. 1893, pp. 153-155.

22. Al-Beruni "On hindu belief". *Aryan Path*, Vol. 44, No. 9, 1973, pp. 379-83.

23. Alekshin, V. A. "Burial customs as an Archaeological source". *Current Anthropology*, Vol. 24, No. 2, 1983 (April), pp. 137-150.

24. Alexander, Bobby Chris "Televangelism reconsidered: Ritual in the search of human community". Atlanta, Scholar Press. 1994.

25. Alfred Gell "The Gods at play: Vertigo and possession in Muria religion". *Man, New Series*, Vol. 15, No. 2 June, 1980, pp. 219-248.

26. Ali, Meer Hassan "Observation on the mussulmauns of India: descriptive of their manners, customs, habits, & religious opinions made during a Twelve Year residence in their immediate society". 2nd ed., Bombay: Oxford University, Press, 1917. xvii, p. 442.

27. Ali, S. A. "The two 'Ids". In, 'Festivals in Indian Society', 2 Vols., Edited by Usha Sharma, New Delhi, Mittal Publication, pp. 45-50.

28. Ali, S. Z. "The Ajmer Urs". In, Festivals in Indian Society, 2 Vols., Edited by Usha Sharma, New Delhi, Mittal Publication, pp. 39-44.

29. Alimad, Imtiaz, (ed.) "Ritual and religion among Muslims in India". New Delhi, Manohar, 1984.

30. Allen, Judith "It is the custom in this village". *Folklore*, Vol. 92, No. 1, 1981, pp. 67-76.

31. Alley, Kelly D. "On the banks of the Gangā: when wastewater meets a sacred river". Ann Arbor, University of Michigan Press, 2002.

32. Alok, Ashwani Kumar "Lokparva: Sama-Chakeba". *Chaumasa,* Vol. 17, No. 52, 2000, pp. 60-64. [Hindi]

33. Alter, Joseph S. "Nag Panchami: snakes, sex, and semen." In, 'The wrestler's body: Identity and ideology in North India'. Berkeley, University of California Press, 1992. pp. 136-66.

34. Alter, Stephen "Sacred waters: a pilgrimage up the Ganges river to the source of Hindu culture". New York, Harcourt, 2001, 368 p. : Maps ; 24 cm.

35. Altheer, David "Roma festival". *Roma, issue,* No. 48-49, January-July 1998, p. 17.

36. Ambiye, D. A. "Some customs among the Goan Gavdas". In, Proceedings of the national seminar on 'Living customs and their ancient Indian sources', Edited by V. N. Jha, Pune, Centre of Advanced Study in Sanskrit, University of Poona, 1991, pp.119-123.

37. Amirthalingam, M. "Neem tree: a review." *The Indian Forester,* Vol. 127, No. 12, 2001. pp. 1336-1342.

38. Amirthalingam, M. "Sthala Vrikshas of Tamilnadu". In, 'The Ecological Traditions 557 of Tamil Nadu', eds. Nanditha Krishnan and Javanthi Prabhakaran, Chennai, C.P.R. Environment Educational Centre. 1998. pp. 83-100.

39. Amirthalingam, M. "Sacred trees of Tamil Nadu." *Eco News*, Vol. 4, No. 4, 1999. pp. 12-16.

40. Amitai Etzioni "Toward a theory of public ritual". *Sociological Theory*, Vol. 18, No. 1 (Mar., 2000), pp. 44-59.

41. Ammaman Tampuran, Keralavarmma "Kuttum kutiyattavum [microform]". Trssur, Keralodayam, 1939 xvi, 167 p.: ill. ; 19 cm. [In: Malayalam]

42. Anderson, Leona M. "Vasantotsava: the spring festivals of India: texts and traditions". (Series: Reconstructing Indian history and culture, no. 4), New Delhi, D.K. Printworld (P) Ltd., 1993, 254 p.: ill. ; 22 cm.

43. Andhra Pradesh. Superintendent of census operation "Census of India 1961: Andhra Pradesh fairs and festivals Warangal District". Vol. II, pt. VII-B, (18). Delhi, Manager of publication, 1965. Xi, 142 p.

44. Andhra Pradesh. Superintendent of census operation "Census of India 1961: Andhra Pradesh fairs and festivals Khammam District". Vol. II, pt.VII-B (19). Delhi, Manager of publication, 1965. Xi, p. 112.

45. Andhra Pradesh. Superintendent of census operation "Census of India 1961: Andhra Pradesh fairs and festivals Adilabad District Vol. II, pt.VII-B, (16). Delhi, Manager of publication, 1966. xi, p. 87.

46. Andhra Pradesh. Superintendent of census operation "Census of India 1961: Andhra Pradesh fairs and festivals Guntur District". Vol. II, pt.VII-B, (6), Delhi, Manager of publication, 1967. xiv, p. 210.

47. Andhra Pradesh. Superintendent of census operation "Census of India 1961: Andhra Pradesh fairs and festivals Krishna District". Vol. II, pt.VII-B, (5), Delhi, Manager of publication, 1966. xi, p. 74.

48. Andhra Pradesh. Superintendent of census operation "Census of India 1961: Andhra Pradesh-Fairs and Festivals West Godavari District". Vol. II, pt. VII-B (4).— Delhi: Manager of Publication, 1966. xi, 80 p. ill: maps, Plates p.

49. Andhra Pradesh. Superintendent of census operation "Census of India 1961: Andhra Pradesh Fairs and Festivals Nalgonda District". Vol. II, pt. VII-B (20). — Delhi: Manager of publication, 1965. xi, 65 p. ill: maps, plates p.

50. Andhra Pradesh. Superintendent of census operation "Census of India 1961: Andhra Pradesh-Fairs and Festivals Khammam District". Vol. II, pt.VII-B, (19). Delhi, Manager of publication, 1965. xi, p. 112.

51. Andhra Pradesh. Superintendent of census operation "Census of India 1961: Andhra Pradesh fairs and festivals Mahbubnagar District". Vol.II, pt.VII-B,(12). Delhi, Manager of publication, 1965. xii, p. 106.

52. Andhra Pradesh. Superintendent of census operation "Census of India 1961: Andhra Pradesh Fairs and Festivals Cuddapah District". Vol. II, pt. VII-B (9), Delhi, Manager of publication, 1965. xi, p. 199.

53. Andhra Pradesh. Superintendent of census operation "Census of India 1961: Andhra Pradesh Fairs and Festivals Medak District" Vol. II, pt.VII-B (14), Delhi, Manager of publication, 1965. xi, p. 171.

54. Andhra Pradesh. Superintendent of census operation "Census of India 1961: Andhra Pradesh Fairs and Festivals East Godavari District". Vol. II, pt. VII-(3). Delhi, Manager of publication, 1966. xi, p. 425. ill: maps.

55. Andhra Pradesh. Superintendent of Census Operations "Census of India 1961: Andhra Pradesh fairs and festivals Karimnagar District" Vol. ii, pt. vii-B (17), Delhi, Manager of Publications, 1966. xiv, 62.

56. Andrew Alter "Garhwali Bagpipes: syncretic processes in a North Indian regional musical tradition". *Asian Music*, Vol. 29, No. 1 (Autumn, 1997 - Winter, 1998), pp. 1-16.

57. Andrew L. Roth "Men wearing masks: issues of description in the analysis of ritual". *Sociological Theory*, Vol. 13, No. 3, Nov., 1995, pp. 301-327.

58. Annapoorna, L. "Music and temples: a ritualistic approach". New Delhi: Sundeep Prakashan, 2000. x, p. 245.

59. Anne Hardgrove "Sati worship and marwari public identity in India". *The Journal of Asian Studies,* Vol. 58, No. 3, Aug., 1999, pp. 723-752.

60. Annon. "Baruni Mahamela: A religious festival of a scheduled caste (Namasudra)". *Vanyajati*, Vol. 36, No. 1, 1988, pp. 17-18.

61. Annon. "Bhil tribal festivals". *India and Foreign Review*, Vol. 22, No. 1, 1984, pp. 15-17.

62. Annon. "Cultural heritage of Ladakh". *Our Cultural Fabric*, 1978, pp. 1-100.

63. Annon. "Deepawali : The festival of lights". *Indian and Foreign Review,* Vol. 25, No. 1, 1987, pp. 20-21.

64. Annon. "Dussehra of Kulu". *Traveller in India*, Vol. 6, No. 10, October 1962, pp. 17-24.

65. Annon. "Fairs and festivals". *Souvenir*, Shimla Summer Festivasl, 1974, p. 3.

66. Annon. "Far from peaceful: Nadars join the orgy of violence with thevars; dalits continue to suffer." New Delhi, *Frontline*, 13 June 1997.

67. Annon. "Festival of India: 1985-86". *Indian Foreign Review*, Vol. 22, No. 16, 1985, pp. 4-9, 20-25.

68. Annon. "Festivals Himachal Pradesh". Tourism and Travel, Vol. III, No. 2, March 1976, pp. 5-7.

69. Annon. "Hindu Marriage: More is meant than mere ritual". *Dowry Custom (Vivekananda Kendra Patrika, Madras),* Vol. 2. No. 2. 1973, pp. 198-202.

70. Annon. "Kishano ka mela: Mejar". *Himprastra,* Vol. 19, No. 5, Aug. 1973. pp. 65-66. [Hindi]

71. Annon. "Manamukha Sudhara" [microform]. Ambala, Khalasa Bhujangi Sabha, [1903] ii, 114 p.; 22 cm. [In: Panjabi]

72. Annon. "Mandi ki Shivratri". *Himprastra*, Vol. 2, No.1, 1956, pp. 34-35. [Hindi]

73. Annon. "The festival of India: its import and perspectives". *Museum (UNESCO)*, Vol. 34, No. 4, 1982, pp. 214-220.

74. Annon. "The festival of India: its import and perspectives". *Museum (UNESCO)*, Vol. 34, No. 4, 1982, pp. 214-220.

75. Annon. "The Madras festival season: Too much and too little". Sruti: South Indian Classical Music and Dance Magazine, Issue No. 4, 1984, pp. 9-12.

76. Annon. "The Pageant of marriage-through dowry and no dowry (Customs of different castes and communities)". *Dowry Custom (Vivekananda Kendra Patrika, Madras)* Vol. 2. No. 2. 1973, pp. 205-238.

77. Annon. "Aligning rituals". *Economic and Political Weekly*, Vol. 7, No. 49 Dec. 2, 1972, pp. 2349-2350.

78. Annon. "Apni mahan paramparaon ko khokar hi ham deen-heen bane hen". *Akhand Jyoti*, Vol. 70, No. 6, 2006, pp. 29-32. [Hindi]

79. Annon. "Das karma paddhati. [On Hindu rituals]". Nepali translation from Sanskrit, Varanasi, Hitaisi Co., 1950. 84 p. ; 17 cm. [Sanskrit]

80. Annon. "Deepawali: The festival of lights" Indian and Foreign Review, Vol. 25, No. 1, 1987, pp. 20-21.

81. Annon. "Essays in Indian folklore". Papers presented to the centenary festival of Rai Bahadur S. C. Roy. Calcutta: Indian, 1973. v, p. 200.

82. Annon. "Fairs and Festivals of India". New Delhi: Gyan Publishing, 2003. In 6. Vols. (seperate pages).

83. Annon. "Festival of India: in the United states 1985-1986". New York, Harry N. Abrams, 1985. 240 p.: Col. Plates p.

84. Annon. "Festivals in Indian society." New Delhi: Mittal Publications, 2008. 2 Vol. (ix, 253; vi, 263) p.

85. Annon. "Festivals of India". New Delhi, Publications Division, 1903. p. 25.

86. Annon. "Graha santi. [Rituals]". Varanasi, Hitaisi Co., 1947. 120 p. ; 17 cm. [Nepali]

87. Annon. "Guramata prakasha, arathata, Guramryada karana di bidhi [microform]. [Sikhism Rituals]". Ammritasara, Cifa Khalasa Diwana, [1915], 112 p. ; 23 cm. [Punjabi]

88. Annon. "India: specially published for the festival of India in the. S. S. R". New Delhi, Brijbasi, 1987. 235 p.: col. ill.

89. Annon. "Kalakshetra: festival of dance-dramas". Bombay, [s.n.], 1966.

90. Annon. "Koeshur rof". [Anthology of songs for marriage festivals]. Srinagar, Ghulam Muhammad Nur Muhammad, n.d. 32 p. ; 15 cm. [In: Kashmiri]

91. Annon. "Kuki customary law: Kukite Chondan (Kuki)". Manipur: Kuki Inpi, 2000. p. 66.

92. Annon. "Mopin: a festival of Adis of Arunachal Pradesh". Shillong, Director of Information and Public Relations, 1976. p. 9 : plates p.

93. Annon. "Paramparaon me chipe tark". *Akhand Jyoti*, Vol. 64, No. 7, 2001, July, pp. 43. [Hindi]

94. Annon. "Prakrati ke sang Hulsane ka parv". *Akhand Jyoti*, Vol. 65, No. 3, 2002 March, pp. 35-36 [Hindi]

95. Annon. "Religious beliefs and rituals: cross cultural studies". New Delhi, Cosmo Publications, 1998. p. 301.

96. Annon. "Ritual and religion among Muslims in India". New Delhi, Manohar, 1981. xv, p. 246.

97. Annon. "Sacred India". London, Lonely Planet, 2002, 1999, x, 166 p. : col. ill., 1 col. map, ports. (Some col.) ; 22 x 29 cm.

98. Annon. "Satyanarayan brata katha. [Puranic tale relating to ritualistic ceremony]". Varanasi, Hitaisi Co., 1950. 80 p. ; 17 cm. [In: Nepali]

99. Annon. "Shravani parv par karyakartaon ki riti-niti". *Akhand Jyoti*, Vol. 64, No. 8, 2001 August, pp. 45-50. [Hindi]

100. Annon. "Solung: a festival of the adis of NEFA". Shillong, North East Frontier Agency, 1969. p. 61.

101. Annon. "Tribal rituals: life cycle rituals and ceremonies in tribal societies". New Delhi, Cosmo Publications, 2002. p. 321.

102. Annon. "Uttar Kashi ke riti rivaz". *Vanyajati*, Vol. 27, No. 2, 1979 (April), pp. 16-18.

103. Annon. "Yog ki pawan punya parampara". *Akhand Jyoti*, Vol. 9, No. 3, 2001 Sept. pp. 5-7. [Hindi]

104. Anuradha Seneviratna "Pañcatûrya Nāda and the Hçwisi Pûjā". *Ethnomusicology*, Vol. 23, No. 1 (Jan., 1979), pp. 49-56.

105. Appadurai, Arjun "Topographies of the self: Praise and emotion in Hındu India". In, 'Language and the politics of emotion', edited by Lutz, Catherine A., Abu-Lughod, Lila, New York, Paris, NY, US, France: Cambridge University Press Editions de la Maison des Sciences de l'Homme, 1990. pp. 92-112.

106. Apte, V. M. "The Rg-veda mantras in their ritual setting in the grhya sutras". *Bulletin of the Deccan College Research Institute*, Vol. 1, No. 1- 4, 1940, pp. 14-36.

107. Apte, V. M. "Social and religious life of the Grihya sutras". Bombay, Popular Book Depot. 1954.

108. Apte, V. M. "Vedic rituals". In, 'The cultural heritage of India'. Calcutta, The Ramakrishna mission institute of culture, 1958.

109. Archana Shastri "Language of symbols: a project on south Indian ritual decorations of a semi-permanent nature". New Delhi, Crafts Council. 1981, 91 p. ill. p.

110. Archana, Barua "The traditional of religion in Assam: a philosophical study". Puthi Pustak, 1996.

111. Archer, W. G. "The Hill of flates: life, love and poetry in tribal India: a portrait of the Santal". London, George Allen & Unwin, 1974.

112. Archer, W. G. "Ritual friendship in santal society". *Man in India,* Vol. 27, No. 01, 1947 (March), pp. 71-75.

113. Archer, W. G. Miller, Barbara Stoler & Archer, Mildred "Songs for the bride: wedding rites of rural India". (Series: Studies in Oriental culture, no. 20.; UNESCO collection of representative works., Indian series), New York, Columbia University Press, 1985, xl, 181 p. : ill. ; 22 cm.

114. Arifur Zaman "An appraisal to the marriage system of the Karbis of Assam". *Stud Tribes Tribals*, Vol. 6, No. 2, 2008, pp. 93-97.

115. Arnett, Robert "India unveiled". Columbus, Atman Press, 2002, vii, 215 p. : col. ill. ; 32 cm.

116. Arora, U. P. "Motifs in Indian mythology". New Delhi, Munshiram Manohaarlal, 1981.

117. Arun, Narandra. "Mera Gao: Tatti re mela". Pahadi lekhamala, Himachal pradesh kala, sanskrati Bhasha Akadami, Shimla, 1975, pp. 127-134. [Hindi]

118. Arun, Narendra "Bsoaa: ek vivechan". Somsi, Vol. 12 No. 2, 1986, pp. 65-70. [Hindi]

119. Arun, Narendra "Solan Jile ke Teez tyohar (Pahari Bhasa)". Himbharati, Vol. 24, No. 2, 1991, pp. 1-18. [Hindi]

120. Arun, Rajendra "Raghukul Riti Sadaa". New Delhi, Prabhat Prakashan, 1997, p. 307. [Hindi]

121. Arunachalam, M. "Adup Perukku of adoration of the rivers". *Swarajya*, Vol. 21, No. 5, 1976, pp. 21-22.

122. Arunachalam, M. "The Adi-puran festival". *Swarajya*, Vol. 21, No. 3, 1976, pp. 21-22.

123. Arya, U. "Ritual songs and folksongs of the Hindus of Surinam". Leiden, E.J. Brill, 1968.

124. Ashton, Martha Bush "Spirit cult festivals in South Kanara". *The Drama Review*, Vol. 23, No. 2, 1979, pp. 91-98.

125. Ashton, Martha May Bush "Beauti and the Bhuta". *Illustrated Weekly of India*, 25 Feb., 1979.

126. Aslesha, Ram "Dancers and festivals of India: Selection system under scrutiny". *Sruti: South Indian Classical Music and Dance Magazine,* Issue No. 84, 1991, pp. 35-40.

127. Asokan, P. "Ritual in a Theyya Kavu". *The India Magazine,* Vol. 8, No. 2, 1988, pp. 44-48.

128. Assayag, Jackie "Ritual action of political reaction: the invention of Hindu nationalist processions in India during the 1980s". *South Asia Research* Vol. 18, No. 2, 1998 (autumn), pp. 125-146.

129. Asutosh Bhattacharyya "The Serpent as a folk-deity in Bengal. *Asian Folklore Studies*. Vol. 24, No. 1, 1965, pp. 01-10.

130. Annon. "Atha Pratistha sangraha prarambhah [microform]. [Hinduism Rituals]". Bombay, Venkatesvara Presa, 1907, 258 p.; 27 cm. [Sanskrit]

131. Athavale, Visnu Ramakrsna "Purusartha cintamanih". [Treatise on the Hindu festivals, their rituals and calendar]. Poona: Anandasram Press, 1909. xii, 594 p. ; 24 cm. [Sanskrit]

132. Atikal, Ilanko. "The tale of an Anklet: an epic of South India: the Cilappatikāram of Inakô Anika". Trans. R. Parthasarathy. New York, Columbia University Press. 1993.

133. Auboyer, Jeannine "Daily life in ancient India: from 200 BC to 700 AD". London, Phoenix, 2002, 344 p. : ill., map ; 22 cm.

134. Aurobindo, "The wedding of the eternal Lord and Spouse-In a new act of the drama of the world". *Dowry Custom (Vivekananda Kendra Patrika, Madras)* Vol. 2. No. 2. 1973, p. 256.

135. Avasthi, Asha. "Hindu marriage in continuity and change". Lucknow, 1979.

136. Awatara Singha "Khalasa dharama shasatra samsakarabhaga, arathata, Guru ke sikham lai guramata anusara janama tom laike anta prayanta de samskaramdi bidhi [microform] [Sikhism Rituals]. Lahaura : Arora Bamsa Presa, 1894, ii, 136 p. ; 23 cm. [Panjabi]

137. Ayachit, S. M., "Shri Satyanarayana: Thematic probe into history". In, Proceedings of the national seminar on 'Living customs and their ancient Indian sources', Edited by V. N. Jha, Pune, Centre of Advanced Study in Sanskrit, University of Poona, 1991, pp. 234 238.

138. Ayyar, P. V. Jagadisa "Chaitra Vishu: the Hindu new year day". In, 'Festivals in Indian Society', 2 Vols., Edited by Usha Sharma, A Mittal Publication, New Delhi, pp.103-108.

139. Ayyar, P. V. Jagadisa "Maha Sivaratri". In, 'Festivals in Indian Society', 2 Vols., Edited by Usha Sharma, A Mittal Publication, New Delhi, pp. 79-82.

140. Ayyar, P. V. Jagadisa "South Indian festivals". Madras, 1921.

141. Ayyar, P. V. Jagadisa "Sri Rama Navami". In 'Festivals in Indian Society', 2 Vols., Edited by Usha Sharma, A Mittal Publication, New Delhi, pp. 109-114.

142. Ayyar, P. V. Jagadisa "South Indian customs". New Delhi, Asian Educational Services. 1992.

143. Ayyar, P. V. Jagadisa "Principal Hindoo religious festivals of Southern India". In, 'Festivals in Indian Society', 2 Vols., Ed. Usha Sharma, A Mittal Publication, New Delhi, pp. 45-52.

144. Babar, Sarojini "Marathi Pradesh ke lokgeet aur Pooja Parva". *Folklore* Vol. 24, No. 4, 1983, pp. 1-7. [Hindi]

145. Babb, L. A. "Heat and control of Chattisgari ritual". *Eastern Anthropologist,* Vol. 26, No. 1, 1973, pp. 11-28.

146. Babb, L. A. "Monks and miracles: religious symbols and images of origin among Osval Jains". *The Journal of Asian Studies,* Vol. 52, No. 1. Feb., 199), pp. 3-21.

147. Babb, Lawrence A. "Absent lord: ascetics and kings in a Jain ritual culture". Berkeley, Calif., University of California Press, 1996, xi, 244 p. : ill., map ; 24 cm.

148. Babb, Lawrence A. "The divine hierarchy: popular Hinduism in central India". New York: Columbia University. 1975.

149. Badal, Shyam Sundar "Faag literature in Bundelkhand". *Folklore*, Vol. 17 No. 2, 1975, pp. 50-57.

150. Badhwar, Inderjit, "A Pagan Sacrifice". *India Today*, Vol. 12, No. 19 (October 15, 1987), pp. 58-61.

151. Badpagga, Chudamani "Mandi Janpad me Lohri ka tyohar". *Somsi*, Vol. 22, No. 79, 1996 (March), pp. 59-63 [Hindi]

152. Bagla, Pallava "The mask dances of Hemis". *Discover India*, Vol. 3, No. 10, 1990, pp. 56-61.

153. Bahulkar, S. S. "Magic and medicine". In, Proceedings of the national seminar on 'Living customs and their ancient Indian sources', Edited by V. N. Jha, Pune, Centre of Advanced Study in Sanskrit, University of Poona, 1991, pp. 278-288.

154. Bahulkar, S. S. "Medical ritual in the Atharavaveda tradition". Pune, Tilak Maharashtra Vidyapeeth, 1994.

155. Bakshi, Shashi "From dawn to dusk they dance with joy". *Discover India*, Vol. 3, No. 10, 1990, pp. 44-47.

156. Bakshi, Shashi "Rongali Bihu: The heady songs of spring". *Discover India*, Vol. 4, No. 4, 1991, pp. 66-69. [Hindi]

157. Bala Ratnam, L. K. "Serpent worship in Kerala." In, 'Through the vistas of life and lore: Folkloric reflections on traditional India', ed. R. M. Sarkar, Calcutta, Punthi Pustak, 2000. pp. 621-42.

158. Balapur, K. M., Maheshwari, J. K. and Tandan, R.K. "Plants of Ramayana". *Ancient Science of Life*, Vol. 7, No. 2, 1987, pp. 86-74.

159. Baldizzone, Tiziana and Baldizzone, Gianni "Wedding ceremonies: ethnic symbols, costume, and rituals". Paris, Flammarion, 2001, 224 p., col. ill. ; 32 cm.

160. Bali, Hemendra "Satluj ghati ri Shivraatar". *Himbharti*, Vol. 30, No. 111, 1998, pp. 26-28 [Pahari Language]

161. Balram "Pattan Ghati (Lahul) ke kuch mukhya mele tyohar". *Somsi*, Vol. 13, No. 4, 1987, pp. 21-27. [Hindi]

162. Balram. "Lahaul ke tyohar tatha mele". *Somsi*. Vol. 2. No. 4. Oct. 1976. pp. 28-32. [Hindi]

163. Balram. "Lahol mein Vivah pratha". *Somsi*, Vol. 2, No. 2, April 1976, pp. 35-39. [Hindi]

164. Balzani, Marzia "Modern Indian kingship: tradition, legitimacy and power in Rajasthan". (Series: World anthropology (Santa Fe, N.M.), Oxford, James Currey ; Santa Fe, N.M. : School of American Research Press, 2003, 204 p. : ill., maps ; 24 cm.

165. Balzani, Marzia "Pregnancy rituals amongst the Rajput elite in contemporary Rajasthan: Anthropology and the world of women". In, 'Playing for Real: Hindu Role Models, Religion, and Gender', eds. Jacqueline Suthren Hirst and

Lynn Thomas, New York: Oxford University Press. 2004, (pp. 141-160). p. 558.

166. Bandopadhyaya, Gita "The 'Anna Kali' of Bengal". *Dowry Custom (Vivekananda Kendra Patrika, Madras)* Vol. 2. No.2. 1973, pp. 156-157.

167. Baneerjee, Manabendu "Sanskrit inscriptions and the spitit of religious toleration". In, Proceedings of the national seminar on 'Living customs and their ancient Indian sources', Edited by V. N. Jha, Pune, Centre of Advanced Study in Sanskrit, University of Poona, 1991, pp. 308-322.

168. Banerjee, B. N. "Hindu culture custom and ceremony". Delhi, Agam Kala Prakashan, 1979, p. 219 : plates.

169. Banerjee, Biswanath "Sarbojonin Durgotsab in Calcutta: a preliminary report of the pujas in 1969". *Folklore*, Vol. 14, No. 9, 1973, pp. 347-353.

170. Banerjee, D.K. "Magico-religious beliefs about plants among some adibasis of India". *Journal of Myth and Society*, Vol. 65, No. 3, 1974, pp. 05-08.

171. Banerjee, G. "The Hindu law of marriage and stridhana". Calcutta, 1923.

172. Banerjee, H.N. "The Kora in the Pull of Hindu: great tradition". In, 'West Bengal Tribes, Socio -economic and Cultural Life' Edited by A.K. Das, R.N. Saha, R. Gupta and S.M. Chakraborty, *Bulletin of Cultural Research Institute, Special Series* No. 35, S.C. & S.T. Welfare Department, Govt. of West Bengal. 1991.

173. Banerjee, Madan Mohan "Vasant Utsav at Shantiniketan". *Indian and Foreign Review*, Vol. 22, No. 9, 1985, pp. 16-17, 23.

174. Banerjee, N. R. "Museums and the festivals of India: the search for a rationale". *Journal of Indian Museum*, Issue No. 43, 1987, pp. 1-15.

175. Banerjee, P. "The Nāga cult." In 'Early Indian Religions'. New York: John Wiley & Sons. 1973. pp. 94-116.

176. Banerjee, S. C. "Durga Puja in Bengal". *Journal of Orient. Inst.,* Vol. 39 No. 1-4, 1969-70, pp. 11-15.

177. Banerjee, Sudeshna "Durga Puja yesterday, today and tomorrow, Rupa & Co, New Delhi, 2004.

178. Banerjee, Sukumar "An ethnographic study of the Kuvi Kandha of Orissa". Calcutta: ASI, monography No. 24. 1968.

179. Banerji, Chitrita "Bengali cooking: seasons and festivals". London, Serif, 1997, 201 p. : ill. ; 20 cm.

180. Banerji, Chitrita "The hour of the Goddess: memoires of women, food and rituals in Bengal". New Delhi, Penguin Books, 2006. p. 144.

181. Banerjee, Madan Mohan "Durgotsava". *Indian and Foreign Review,* Vol. 24, No. 24, 1987, pp. 16-17.

182. Baron, Archie "An Indian affair". London, Channel 4, 2001, 254 p. : ill. (Some col.), ports. ; 26 cm.

183. Barrett, S.A. "Ceremonies of the Pomo Indians". (Series: University of California publications., American archaeology and ethnology; V. 12, No. 10), Berkeley, University of California press, 1917, 441 p. diagrs. 27 cm.

184. Basa, K. K. and Others "The Daroi Gonds of central India: A study on their intangible cultural heritage". Bhopal, Indira Gandhi Rastriya Manav Sangrahalaya & New Delhi; Pratibha Prakashan. (In Press).

185. Basa, Kishor K.; Pandey, Surya K.; Mohanta, Basanta K. and Khan, Riyaz A. "Mortuary practices of the Daroi Gonds: A study of their intangible cultural heritage". *Humankind*, Vol. 2. 2006, Ed. By Kishor K. Basa, Serials Publications, New Delhi, pp. 59-84

186. Basa, Kishor Kumar; Pandey, Surya Kumar; Basanta, Kumar Mohanta and Khan, Riyaz Ahmed. "Birth and

associated rituals of the Daroi Gonds: A study on intangible cultural heritage". *Humankind*, Vol. 3. 2007, Ed. By Kishor K. Basa, Serials Publications, New Delhi, pp. 127-140.

187. Baskaran, S. Theodore "Jallikattu in Tamil Nadu: Bull vaulting". *The India Magazine*, Vol. 5, No. 3, 1985, pp. 20-29.

188. Basu, Nirmal Kumar "The spring -festival of India". *Man in India,* Vol. 7, No. 2-3, 1927, pp. 6-55.

189. Basu, Ramsankar "The tribe 'Santals' and their sacred groves rituals". *Vanyajati*, Vol. 57, No. 3, 2009 (July), pp. 3-6.

190. Basu, Ramsankar and Mukherjee, Prasanta Kumar "Ethnobotany on the 'Soharai' festival of 'Mundas' in Purulia district West Bengal". *Man and Life*, Vol. 24, No. 3-4, 1998, pp. 217-219.

191. Basu, Srimati "Dowry and inheritance". (Series: Issues in contemporary Indian feminism, London, England), London, Zed Books ; New York, Distributed in the USA exclusively by Palgrave Macmillan, 2005, liii, 318 p. ; 23 cm.

192. Basu, Sunil Kumar "A note on important festivals among the major tribals of West Bengal". *Bulletin of the Cultural Research Institute,* Vol. 8, No. 3-4, 1969, pp. 17-33.

193. Basumatary, Sukumar "Boro Aiyen: customary law of Bodos". Barama, Renu Basumatary, 1995, p. 31.

194. Bauer, Jerome H. "Karma and control: The prodigious and the auspicious in Jaina canonical mythology", Ch. 5. Ph.D. diss, University of Pennyslvania, 1998.

195. Bauman, Martin. "Performing vows in diasporic contexts: Tamil hindus, Temples, and Goddesses in Germany." In, 'Dealing with deities: the ritual vow in South Asia', eds. Selva J. Raj and William P. Harman, Albany: State University of New York Press, 2006. pp. 129-44.

196. Bauman, Richard, (ed.) "Folklore, cultural performances, and popular entertainments: A communication centered handbook". Oxford, Oxford University Press. 1992.

197. Bawa, P. S. "Celebrating republic day". *Discover India*, Vol. 12, No. 1, 1999, pp. 12-14.

198. Bawa, P. S. "Diwali: Then and now". *Discover India*, Vol. 11, No. 10, 1998, pp. 28-31.

199. Bayly, C. A. "From ritual to ceremony: death ritual in Hindu North India." In 'Mirrors of Mortality: Studies in the social history of death'. Edited by J. Wahley, New York: St. Martin's Press, 1981.

200. Bebas, Chandra Sakhar "Dahashara kullu ka". Kullu dahashara sovinar, 1972. pp. 4. [Hindi]

201. Beck, Brenda E. F. "Colour and heat in a south Indian ritual". *Man*, Vol. 4, No. 4. 1969. pp. 553-572.

202. Beck, Brenda E. F. "The Goddess and the demon: A local South Indian festival in its wider context." *Purusartha*, No. 5, 1981. pp. 83-136.

203. Beck, Brenda "The symbolic merger of body, space and cosmos in Hindu Tamil Nadu". *Contributions to Indian Sociology*. Vol. 10, No. 2, 1976. pp. 213-245.

204. Beck, Guy "Sakta-tantra: sacred sound as the Goddess". In, 'Sonic theology: Hinduism and sacred sound'. Columbia, SC: University of South Carolina Press, 1993.

205. Beckwith, Martha Warren "Mandan-Hidatsa myths and ceremonies". (Series: Memoirs of the American folk-lore society, vol. 32), New York, American folk-lore Society, G.E. Stecherd [i.e. Stechert] & Co. [1938, 2 p. l., xviii p., 1 l., 327 p. front., illus., plates, ports. 25 cm.

206. Behera, Deepak Kumar "Marriage customs among the christians of clean caste origin in Cuttack town of Orissa". *Man and Life*, Vol. 16, No. 3-4, 1990, pp. 145-156.

207. Behera, Deepak Kumar and Sahoo, Ranju H. "Participation of the Telgu speaking immirgrants in the religious activities of the host society". *The Anthropologist*, Vol. 2, No. 2, 2000, pp. 69-76.

208. Behura, N. K. and Misra, K. K., "Religious rites and festivals among the tribes of Orissa". *Vission* Vol. 4, No. 4, April-September, 1985, pp. 66-86.

209. Behura, N. R. "Rajaparba: The festival of fertility cult in Orissa". *The Eastern Anthropologist*, Vol. 16, No. 3, 1963, pp. 186-190.

210. Beidelman, Thomas O. "A comparative analysis of the Jajmani system". *Monography of the Association for Asian Studies,* No. 8 Locust valley, New York, 1959, J.J. Augustin.

211. Bell, Catherine "Performance." In, 'Critical Terms for Religious Studies', ed. Mark C. Taylor, Chicago: University of Chicago Press. 1998, pp. 205-24.

212. Bell, Catherine "Ritual theory: ritual practice". New York: Oxford University Press, 1992.

213. Bell, Catherine "Ritual: perspectives and dimensions". New York, Oxford University Press. 1997.

214. Bellamy, Carla G. "Everyday healing: Hindus and others in an ambiguously 559 muslim place". Ph.D. dissertation, Columbia, Columbia University, 2007.

215. Bendann E. "Death customs: an analytical study of burial rites". 1st edn. London, Dawsons, 1969.

216. Bendavid, Kochevet "Ritual and sensuality". *Ceramic Review,* Vol. 251, 2011 (Sept-Oct), pp. 54-57.

217. Bentinck, William. "Minute on Sati". Speeches and Documents on Indian Policy, 1750-1921. Volume 1. London: Oxford University Press, 1922.

218. Bera, Gautam Kumar "The Dusshehra festival of Bastar: Understanding secularization and universalization". *The Oriental Anthropologist*, Vol. 7, No. 2, pp. 296-312.

219. Bhabagrahi Misra "Rice rituals of Orissa". *Asian Folklore Studies,* Vol. 25, 1966, pp. 235-246.

220. Bhagat, Ashrafi S. "Festival of colours". *Art India,* Vol. 16, No. 1, 2011, pp. 110-112.

221. Bhagwan, Singh. "Disposal of the dead by mutilation in spiti". *Man,* Vol. 33, No. 149, 1933.

222. Bhallaa, Sudarshan. "Chamba ki vivahik prampraye". *Jiriraj,* Vol. 2, No. 32, April 30, 1980, pp. 1-5. [Hindi]

223. Bhanawat, Mahendra "Rajasthan ki Holi". *Chayanat,* No. 9, 1979, pp. 27-28, 32. [Hindi]

224. Bhanawat, Tuttak "Udaipur ki Taziadari". *Chomasa,* Vol. 17, No. 54, 2001, pp. 37-41 [Hindi]

225. Bhandari, Bhagwat "Tribal marriage and sex relations: customary laws of marriage in bhil and Garasia tribes". Udaipur, Himanshu Publications, 1989. xix, p. 118.

226. Bhandari, M. M. "Feminine feeds in Rajasthan district". *Economic Botany,* Vol. 28, 1974, pp. 73-81.

227. Bharathi, S. Bhakthavatsala "Ritual healing: Metamedical discourse and discursive practices of a south Indian nomadic sub – caste". *Man in India,* Vol. 78, No. 3-4, 1998 (Sept. - Dec.), pp. 239-253.

228. Bharathi, S. Bhakthavatsala "Ritual healing: Metamedical discourse and discursive practices of a south Indian nomadic sub – caste". *South India Folklorist,* Vol. 1, No. 2, 1998 (January), pp. 23-43.

229. Bharati, Agehananda (Swami) "Great tradition and little traditions: Indological investigations in cultural anthropology". Varanasi, Chowkhamba Sanskrit Series Office, 1978, xvi, p. 384 ; 23 cm.

230. Bharati, Reddy Sunita "Beliefs and practices related to parturition among the Konda Reddis of Andhra Pradesh," *Man in India,* Vol. 83, No. 3 - 4, 2003, pp. 315-336.

231. Bharatiya, Rupkishore and Brahmcari, K. R. "Barahon mahine ke sampurna vrat aur tyohar". Mathura, Govardhan Prakahsn, 1974. [Hindi]

232. Bharatt, Agehananda. "Pilgrimage in the Indian Tradition". *History of Religions*, No. 3, 1963, pp. 135-167.

233. Bhardvaaj, Chatram. "Chamba ka lokpriya utsav". *Himbharti,* Vol. 6. No. 1, March 1974, pp. 23-27. [Hindi]

234. Bhardvaaj, Mathali prashad. "Chamba ka lokpriva lohadi nitya shastri adhan". *Himprasat,* Vol. 14, No. 10, Jan. 1970, pp. 25-29; No. 11, Feb 1970, pp. 35-39. [Hindi]

235. Bhardvaaj, Mathali Prashad. "Milan parv-Basoya". *Himprasta*, Vol. 8, No. 2, May, 1962, pp. 2-4. [Pahari Language]

236. Bhardvaaj, Mathali Prashad. "Rath rathni ra mela". *Himprasta,* Vol.16, No. 129, April 1966, p. 49. [Pahari Language]

237. Bhardvaaj, okar Lal. "Rali". *Himbharti*. Vol. 6, No. 3, Sept. 1974, pp. 20-22.

238. Bhardwaj, Bhagwati Charan "Mela Markand". Nalwari fair Bilaspur". Souvenir, 1971, p. 29.

239. Bharti, Sangat. "Mandi aari shivratra (mela)". *Himbharti,* Vol. 3, no. 4. Dec. 1971. pp. 10-11.

240. Bhasin, Mridula "Jaipur virasat festival explores different mediums of creativity". *Kala Deergha*, Vol. 4, No. 8, 2004, pp. 81-83.

241. Bhaskar, Manu "Family law and customary practices of Muslims in Southern Kerala". *The Eastern Anthropologist,* Vol. 49, No. 1, 1996, pp. 1-26.

242. Bhat, Shripad "Some typical vratas in Karnataka and their sources". In, Proceedings of the national seminar on 'Living customs and their ancient Indian sources', Edited by V. N. Jha, Pune, Centre of Advanced Study in Sanskrit, University of Poona, 1991, pp.146-151.

243. Bhate, Govinda Cimanaji "Samajasastravarila vyakhyane, athava, Hindusamajantila kahi caliritince samajasastradrshtya vivecana [microform]". Pune, Aryabhushana Chapakhana, 1914. viii, 128 p. ; 18 cm. [Marathi]

244. Bhatia, Mohan Swaroop "Baithan ki Holi". *Ojasvini,* 2008 (March), pp. 56-57 [Hindi]

245. Bhatla, N., Mukherjee, T. & Singh, G. "Plants: traditional worshipping". *Indian Journal of History and Science*, Vol. 19, No. 1, 1984, pp. 37-42.

246. Bhatnagar, Manju "The fun and frolic of Holi songs: a note of the festival in areas associated with Lord Krishna". *Folklore*, Vol. 28, No. 6, 1987, pp.139-141.

247. Bhatnagar, S. M. "Pagi ki phool yatra". *Punchajagat,* Vol.5, No. 10, Oct. 1966, pp. 11-12. [Hindi]

248. Bhatta, Lakshmichandra "Krityakalpataru, Rajadharama kanda". Baroda, 1943.

249. Bhattacarya, Snehalata "Amar bihu". [On Bihu - a national festival of Assam]. Calcutta, The author, 1927. vi, 56 p. ; 17 cm. [Assamese]

250. Bhattacharjee, Priyabrata "Tribal pujas and festivals in Tripura". Agartala, Tripur a State Tribal Cultural Research Institute and Museum, 1994, 151 p. ill. p.

251. Bhattacharya, A. "Cult of the tree deities of Bengal." *Indian Folklore,* Vol. 1, No. 4, 1958, pp. 26-46.

252. Bhattacharya, Ashutosh. "The sun and the serpent lore". Calcutta, Firma KLM Pvt. Limited, 1977.

253. Bhattacharya, Batuknath "Festivals and sacred days". In, 'Festivals in Indian Society', 2 Vols., Ed. Usha Sharma, A Mittal Publication, New Delhi, pp. 159-176.

254. Bhattacharya, Bholanath "The Car festival of West Bengal". *Folklore*, Vol. 13, No. 6, 1972, pp. 201-209.

255. Bhattacharya, Birendra Kumar. "The Assamese Bihu festival". *United Asia*, Vol. 12. No. 2, March-April 1963, pp. 115-117.

256. Bhattacharya, Manibrata "A study of village through ritual analysis". *Bulletin of Cultural Research Institute*, Vol. 10 No. 3-4, 1974, pp. 76-91.

257. Bhattacharya, Nandini and Das, Ashis KIumar "Economy and persistence of rituals: Observation in two settings". *Journal of Indian Anthropological Society,* Vol. 39, No. 03, 2004 (November), pp. 291-295

258. Bhattacharya, Tithi "Tracking the Goddess: religion, community, and identity in the Durga Puja Ceremonies of 19th century Calcutta". *Journal of Asian Studies,* Vol. 66, issue 4, November 2007, pp. 919-962.

259. Bhattacharyya, Asutosh "Folk festivals of Bengal". In, 'Festivals in Indian Society', 2 Vols., Ed. Usha Sharma, New Delhi, A Mittal Publication, pp. 85-92.

260. Bhattacharyya, N. N. "History of the Tantric religion: a historical, ritualistic and philosophical study". New Delhi, Manohar Publication, 1982. xviii, p. 507.

261. Bhattacharyya, Swapan Kumar "Farmers rituals and modernization: a sociological study". Calcutta, Minerva Associates, 1976. xiv, p. 316.

262. Bhattachryya, Narendra Nath "Ancient Indian rituals and their social contents". Delhi, Manohar Book Service, 1975. xvi, p. 184.

263. Bhomik, Mmiya "Khariya Janjati ke vishwas, mele aur tyohar". *Manav*, Vol. 19, No. 2, 1991, pp. 85-102 [Hindi]

264. Bhowmic, Sarita "A short note on the Festival of the Jhargram sub-division, Midnapur, West Bengal, *Folklore*, Vol. 23, No. 11, 1982, pp. 221-225.

265. Bhowmick, P. K. "Annual festivals of the Lodhas of west Bengal". *Man in India*, Vol. 37, No. 3, 1957, pp. 208-216.

266. Bhowmick, P. K. "The Bandana festival of midnapore". *Man in India*, Vol. 37, No. 1, 1957, pp. 49-53.

267. Bhowmick, Sarita "A study of the festivals of the Kisans and Birjhias of Netarhat". *Folklore*, Vol. 22, No. 8, 1981, pp. 193-200.

268. Bhowmick, Sarita "Folk belief behind a festival: A case study in Midnapur". *Folklore*, Vol. 19, No. 1, 1978, pp. 22-25.

269. Bhowmick, Sarita "Sarhul festival at Netarhat, Bihar". *Human Science*, Vol. 34, No. 1, 1985, pp. 17-25.

270. Bhowmick, Sarita "Paraber Anginay: In the courtyard of festivals in Bengali". Calcutta: Janashiksha prachar kendra, 1985.

271. Bhowmik, P. K. and Chowdhury, B. "Some aspects of magico-religious beliefs and practices of Mundes". *Folklore*, Vol. 7, 1966, pp. 100-107.

272. Biardeau, Madeleine "Stories about posts: Vedic variations around the Hindu Goddess". Trans. Alf Hiltebeitel, Marie-Louise Reiniche, and James Walker; eds. Alf Hiltebeitel and Marie-Louise Reiniche. Chicago: Chicago University Press. 2004.

273. Bijlani, S. K. "A non-conformist's view of the dowry custom". *Dowry Custom (Vivekananda Kendra Patrika, Madras)* Vol. 2. No. 2. 1973, pp. 141-145.

274. Bilimale, Purushuthama "Siddavesa - an interpretation". *Man in India*, Vol. 68, No. 1, 1988, 112-120.

275. Biswas, Debanjali "Her body, her story: situating the Maibis in the ritual- performance of Lai Haraoba. *Journal of the Indian Anthropological Society*, Vol. 47, No. 1, 2012 (March), pp. 29-38.

276. Biswas, Suhas Kumar "Annual hunting festival of the Pauri Bhuiyas: and significance of the annual hunt among the Tribes of Cent". *Bulletin of the Cultural Research Institute,* Vol. 3, No. 3-4, 1964, pp. 38-44.

277. Blachburn, Stuart "Oral performance: narrative and ritual in Tamil tradition". *Journal of American Folklore*, Vol. 94, 1981, pp. 207-27.

278. Blackham, Robert James "Incomparable India [microform] : tradition, superstition, truth". (with a foreword by Sir William Birdwood). London, Sampson Low, Marston & Co., [19—] xviii, 302 p. : ill., maps ; 22 cm.

279. Bloomfield, Maurice. "The Dohada or craving of pregnant women: a motif in Hindu fiction". *Journal of American Oriental Society*, Vol. 40, No. 1, 1920, pp. 1-24.

280. Boal, Barbara M. "The Konds: human sacrifice and religious change". Warminster, Wilts, England, Aris & Phillips; Atlantic Highlands, N.J., Distributors in USA and Canada, Humanities Press, 1982, xiv, 294 p., [1] folded leaf of plates: ill. ; 24 cm.

281. Bock, F.G. "A descriptive study of the dramatic function and significance of the clown during Hopi Indian public ceremony". University of Southern California). ProQuest Dissertations and Theses, 1971, p. 373, Access Online at, http://search.proquest.com/docview/302549037? accountid =43898.

282. Bodding, Paul Olaf "The Santals and Disease". *Memories of Asiatic society of Bengal, Calcutta,* Vol. 10, No.1, 1925, pp. 1-132.

283. Bodewitz, H.W. "The Jyotisma ritual: Jaiminia Brahmana, 1, Introduction translation and commentary". Leiden, E.J. Brill, 1991.

284. Bodewitz, H. W. "The daily evening and morning offering (Agnihotra) according to the Brahmanas". Leiden, E.J. Brill, 1976.

285. Bokhare, Narendra "Celebration of life: Festivals in Jhauba". In, 'Fairs and Festivals of Indian Tribes'. Ed. by Robin David Tribhuwan, Discovery Publishing House, New Delhi, 2003, pp. 63-73.

286. Bombay. Maharashtra census office "Census of India 1961: Maharashtra - fairs and festivals in Maharashtra".l vol. X, pt. VII-B, Delhi: The Manager of Publication, 1969. xvii, p. 542.

287. Borah, Sadhana. "Bihu: festival of Assam". *Illustrated Weekly India.* Vol. 83. No. 30, 29 July 1962, p. 69.

288. Borden, Carla M. (Ed.) "Contemporary Indian Tradition", Washington DC, Smithsonin Institution Press, 1989.

289. Bose, Bipaschit "A splash of colour". *Discovery of India*, Vol. 2, No. 3, 1989, pp. 50-55.

290. Bose, J. K., "Garo kinship terminology", *Man in India*, 36, 1935, pp. 203-215.

291. Bose, Mandakranta "Confrontation, transgression, and submission: ideals of womanhood in the Manasāmangala." In, 'Playing for real: Hindu role models, religion, and gender', eds. Jacqueline Suthren Hirst and Lynn Thomas, New York: Oxford University Press. 2004. pp. 102-16.

292. Bose, N. K. "Hindu method of tribal absorption", *Man in India*, Vol. 27. 1941.

293. Bose, Phanindra Nath. "Snake worship in Bengal." In, 'Through the vistas of life and lore: folkloric reflections on traditional India', ed. R.M. Sarkar, Calcutta: Punthi Pustak. 2000 pp. 605-608.

294. Bose, Sunil K. "Music the soul of spiritual ecstasy". *Lipika: A Journal of the Performing Arts,* Vol. 1, No. 1, 1972, pp. 7-12.

295. Bouissac, P. "Circus and culture: A semiotic approach". J/Deely and B. Williams (eds.). University Press of America, 1985.

296. Boul, Barbara M. "Kond rituals practices and prayers". *Journal of Indian Folkloristics*, Vol. 2, No. 3-4, 1979.

297. Bradford, Nicholas J. "Transgenderism and the cult of Yellamma: heat, sex, and sickness in South Indian ritual."

Journal of Anthropological Research, Vol. 39, 1983. pp. 307-22.

298. Brahma, K. "Aspects of social customs of the Bodos". Assam: Chiranjib Brahma, 1989. p. 81 : plates p.

299. Brahmavarchas (ed.) "A manual of Hindu marriage". Translated by T.N. Sahai, Haridwar, Shantikunj, 1997, p. 56.

300. Brandon, S. G. F. "Man and god in art and ritual: a study of iconography, architecture and ritual action as primary evidence of religious belief and practice". New York: Charles Scribner's Sons, 1975. xiv, p. 514 : plates p.

301. Brar, Bharpur Singh. "Social change and marriage pattern in the North Western Himalayas (i.e. Churah, Pangi and Ladakh). London Doctoral disseration, 1971.

302. Brav, Aaron. "The evil eye among the Hebrews". In, 'The evil eye: a folklore casebook', ed. by Alan Dundes. New York and London: Garland Publishing, Inc. 1981. pp. 44-54.

303. Breuilly, Elizabeth and Others "Religions of the world: the illustrated guide to origins, beliefs, traditions and festivals". New York, Facts on File, 1997, 160 p. : Col. ill., Col. maps ; 29 cm.

304. Brian K. Smith "Ritual, knowledge, and being: Initiation and Veda study in ancient India". *Numen*, Vol. 33, Fasc. 1 (Jun., 1986), pp. 65-89.

305. Briffault, R. "Festivals" In, 'Encyclopaedia of the social sciences', Ed. E.R.A. Seligman, Vol. 5, New York, 1951, p.198.

306. Brooks, Douglas Renfrew "Auspicious wisdom: the texts and traditions of Srividya Sakta Tantrism in South India". Albany: State University of New York Press, 1992.

307. Brooks, Douglas Renfrew "The secret of the three cities: An introduction to Hindu Sakta Tantrism". Chicago: The University of Chicago Press, 1990.

308. Brown, W. J. "Effects of "hum log", a television soap opera, on pro-social beliefs in india". University of Southern California). Pro Quest database - Dissertations and Theses, 1988. Acess online at, http://search.proquest.com/docview/303693900? accountid= 43898.

309. Brown, W. Norman. "Glass and cultural tradition in India". *Journal of American folklore*, Vol. 10, 1958, pp. 35-39.

310. Bruckner, Heidrun, Lothar Lutze and Aditya Malik, (eds.) "Flags of fame: studies in South Asian folk culture". Delhi, Manohar. 1993.

311. Brunton, Paul "A search in secret India". York Beach, Me. : S. Weiser, 1985, 312 p., [16] p. of plates : ill. ; 21 cm.

312. Buch, C. H. "Hindu festivals". In, 'Festivals in Indian Society', 2 Vols., Ed. Usha Sharma, A Mittal Publication, New Delhi, pp.1-20.

313. Buch, C. H. "Mahabharata". Berkeley, University of California Press. 1917.

314. Buck, C. II. "Faiths, fairs and festivals of India". Calcutta: Spink and Co. 1917.

315. Buck, C. H. "Muslim festivals and fasts". In, 'Festivals in Indian Society', 2 Vols., Ed. Usha Sharma, A Mittal Publication, New Delhi, pp. 7-12.

316. Buck, C. H. "Parsee Festivals". In, 'Festivals in Indian Society', 2 Vols., Ed. Usha Sharma, A Mittal Publication, New Delhi, pp. 53-54.

317. Buck, C. H. "Faiths, fairs and festivals of India". New Delhi, Asia Publication Services, 1977. ix, 262; Map.

318. Buddhadeb Chaudhuri "Fire-walking the tribal way. A rejoinder". *Anthropos*, Vol. 62, No. 3-4, 1967, pp. 552-554.

319. Buhnemann, Gudrun "The worship of Mahaganapati according to the Nityotsava". Wichtrach, Intitute fur Indologie, 1988.

320. Buhnemann, Gudrun "The heavenly bodies in Hindu ritual". *Sambhasa*, Vol. 11, 1989, pp. 01-09.

321. Buhnemann, Gudrun "Puja: a study in Smarta ritual". Vienna: University of Vienna (Publication of the DeNobili Research Library). 1988.

322. Burbank, Vitoria K. The Mirrir as ritualized aggression. *Oceania*, Vol. 56, No. 1, 1985 (September), pp. : 47-55

323. Burkhart, Geoffrey "A note on customs of naming and south Indian genealogies". *Man in India*, Vol. 53, No. 2, 1973 (April - June), pp. 188-191.

324. Burling Robbins "Garo Avuncular authority and matrilineal cross-cousin marriage". *American Anthropologist*, Vol. 50, 1958, pp. 743-749.

325. Bush, R. S. "Festivals, rituals and ethnicity among east Indians in Trinidad". The Ohio State University. ProQuest Dissertations and Theses, 1997, p. 218, http://search.proquest.com/docview/304403172? accountid= 43898.

326. Busquet, Gerard "An abode in the Aravallis: the secret world of Gracias". *The India Magazine*, Vol. 5, No. 5, 1985, pp. 36-43.

327. Busquet, Gerard "Jhampan: A conference of snake charmers". *The India Magazine*, Vol. 4, No. 8, 1984, pp. 56-63.

328. Butalia, Urvashi "Fairs and festivals of India". *Indian Foreign Review*, Vol. 23, No. 4, 1985, pp. 25-28.

329. Byebas, Chandra Shakar. "Kullu janpad mein vivah sanskar sambandhi sabdo ka shanskratik dharatal". *Somsi*, Vol. 2, No.1, Jan. 1976, pp. 26-29. [Hindi]

330. Bynum, Caroline Walker "Women's stories, women's symbols: A critique of Victor Turner's theory of liminality". In, 'Anthropology and the Study of Religion', eds. Robert L. Moore and Frank E. Reynolds, Chicago: Center for the Scientific Study of Religion, 1984, pp. 105-25.

331. Calvert, H. "Notes on the customs and beliefs in Spiti". *Indian Antiquary*, Vol. 38, 1909, pp. 49-51.

332. Campatrāj. "Tradition of South India: Karakam". [Audio recording]. Chennai, Giri Trading Agency. 2007.

333. Campbell, A. "Superstitions of the Santals". *Journal of the Bihar and Orissa Research Society, Patna*, Vol.1, No. 2, June 1915, pp. 213-238.

334. Campbell, J. Gabriel "Saints and householders: a study of Hindu ritual and myth among the Kangra Rajputs". Kathmandu, Ratna Pustak, 1976 xiv, p. 175: plates p.

335. Candidasa (Son of Durgadatta) "Ahnika-paddhati [microform]: daily routine for princes". [Hinduism Rituals], Srinagar, Director of Archaeology and Research, J. & K. Govt. and Harabhatta Shastri, 1929. xiv, 74 p. ; 24 cm. [In: Sanskrit]

336. Cantwell, C. M. "An ethnographic account of the religious practice in a Tibetan Buddhist refugee monastery in northern India". University of Kent at Canterbury (United Kingdom)). Pro Quest Dissertations and Theses, 1989, p. 698, Online at, http://search.proquest.com/docview/303784509?accountid=43898.

337. Capoor, Indu and Mehta, Sonal "Talking about Love and Sex in Adolescent health fairs in India". *Reproductive Health Matters,* Vol. 3, No. 5, Pregnancy, Birth Control, STDs and AIDS: Promoting Safer Sex (May, 1995), pp. 22-27.

338. Carasvati, K. N. "Rāku Pakavān". Chennai, Kadalangudi Publications, 1995. [Tamil]

339. Carasvati, K. N. "Rāku Pakavān". Chennai, Kadalangudi Publications, 1995. [Tamil]

340. Carberry, F. (ed.) "History of the rise and progress of the operations for the suprression of human sacrifice and female infanticide in the hill tracts of Orissa". Selections from the records of the GOI (Home dep.) no. V. Calcutta: Bengal Military Orphan press. 1854.

341. Carrithers, Michael "Ritual and emotions". *Journal of the Anthropological Society of Oxford: JASO*, Vol. 11, No. 3, 1980 (Michaelmas), pp. 172-180.

342. Carstairs, G. M. "Patterns of religious observance in three villages in Rajasthan". *Journal of social research* 4, 1961, pp. 59-113.

343. Celvanayakam, Israyel "Tamil Nadu: confrontation, complementarily, compromise". (Series: Gospel and cultures pamphlet, 7.), Geneva : WCC Publications, 1996, 57 p. ; 21 cm.

344. Census of India 1961 "Fairs and Festivals, Chandigarh". Vol. 13, Punjab, Part, 8 B, 1961.

345. Census of India 1961 "Fairs and Festivals of Punjab". Delhi: Government of India, 1961.

346. Census of India 1961 "Fairs and Festivals, Shimla". Vol. 20, Himachal Pradesh, Part 8-B, 1967, p. 437.

347. Census of India 1961 "Maharashtra-fairs and festivals in Maharashtra". Vol. x, pt. vii-B, Delhi: Controller of Publications, 1969. xvii, p. 542 : plates p.

348. Chaitanya, Krishna "Vasant Panchami: The spring festival through the ages". *Indian Foreign Review*, Vol. 23, No. 8, 1986, pp. 25-26, 28.

349. Chakrabarty, Falguni "Agricultural rituals of the Santals of Ajodhya hills: Techno - ecological perspective". *Man in India*, Vol. 67, No. 2, 1987 (June), pp. 99-123.

350. Chakrabarty, P. B. "Arunachal Pradesh: Apa Tanis and Myoko festivals". *Himalaya: Man and Nature*, Vol. 16, No. 3, 1992, pp. 26-28.

351. Chakrabarty, P. B. "Arunachal Pradesh: Apa Tanis and Myoko festivals". *The India Magazine*, Vol. 4, No. 7, 1984, pp. 62-69.

352. Chakraborty, Jyotirmoy "Marriage customs of the Siddis". *Journal of the Anthropological Survey of India,* Vol. 43, No. 1-2, 1994 (March-June), pp. 17-23.

353. Chakraborty, Uday K. "Ganga Sagar mela: A tryst with the truth" *Discover India*, Vol. 6, No. 1, 1993, pp. 70-74. [Hindi]

354. Chanda, Keshaw "Mandi-Rivalsar re mele tuhaar". *Himbharti*, Vol. 29, No. 109, 1997 pp. 50-55. [Pahari Language]

355. Chanda, Sudhendu "Tanaha: A traditional festival of Car Nicobar". *Bulletin of the Anthropological Survey of India,* Vol. 19, No. 3-4, 1970, pp. 247-257.

356. Chandra, Subhash "Keral ka bada din". *Discover India*, Vol. 2, No. 12, 1989, pp. 12-16. [Hindi]

357. Chandra, Sudhir. "Sati: the Dharmic fallacy". *New Quest*, No, 68 (March-Arpil 1988). pp. 111-114.

358. Chandrakanta "Nirjan me utsav". *Sakshatkaar*, No. 339, 2008 March, pp. 20-27. [Hindi]

359. Chandran, M. D. Subhash and Hugesh, J. Donald "Sacred groves and conservation: The Comparative History of traditional reserves in the mediterranean area and in South India". *Environment and History*, Vol. 6, No. 2, May 2000, pp. 169-186.

360. Changikija, S. & Kumar, Y. "Ethnobotanical folk practices and beliefs of the Ao Nagas in Nagaland, India". *Ethnobotany*, Vol. 8, 1996, pp. 26-30.

361. Chapentier, "The meaning and etymology of puja". *The Indian Antiquary,* May-June 1927, pp. 93-99, 130-36.

362. Charukeshi and Janaki, S. "Sattriya from ritual to performing art". *Sruti: South Indian Classical Music and Dance Magazine*, No. 180, 1999, pp. 39-41.

363. Chaterji, Kapila, "Dowry custom barbarous and anti-Hindu". *Dowry Custom (Vivekananda Kendra Patrika, Madras)* Vol. 2, No. 2, 1973, pp. 149-151.

364. Chatterjee, C. K. "Studies in the rites and rituals of Hindu marriage in ancient India". New Delhi, 1978.

365. Chatterjee, Gautam "Under the celestial umbrella. *Discover India*, Vol. 12, No. 10, 1999, pp. 24-27.

366. Chatterjee, Malay "Contemporary Indian architecture at the Festival of India, Paris". *Inside Outside*, Issue No. 47, 1986, pp. 21.

367. Chatterjee, Sita "The dowry custom". *Dowry Custom (Vivekananda Kendra Patrika, Madras)* Vol. 2. No. 2. 1973, pp. 40-42.

368. Chatterji, Tapan Mohon "Alpona: ritual decoration in Bengal". Calcutta, Orient Longmans, 1948. iv, 62 p. : illus.; 19 cm.

369. Chattopadhaya, Kamladevi "Socio Kalis religious Kalis ritualistic Kalis: Kerala's lesser known dances". *The India Magazine,* Vol. 4, No. 2, 1984, pp. 70-74.

370. Chattopadhyay, Gauranga and Biswas, Suhas "An annual festival of the Hos". *Man in India*, Vol. 35, No. 3, 1955, pp. 185-194.

371. Chattopadhyay, Kumara-Nanda. "Rites and rituals: media of rural integration". *Eastern Anthropologist*, Vol. 23, No. 3. Sep-Dec. 1970, pp. 217-233.

372. Chattopadhyay, Pampa and Jana, A. K. "Impact of some Hindu rituals among the Mundas of Midnapore". *Vanyajati*, Vol. 43, No. 3, 1995 (July), pp. 3-6.

373. Chattopodhyay, Paulami "Changing festivals of the Santals in Jharkhand". *Vanyajati*, Vol. 51, No. 4, 2003, pp. 13-19.

374. Chaturvedi, B. K. "Navagrahas (Nine Planets)". Delhi, DK Publishers. 1998.

375. Chaturvedi, Deepak Krishna "Kang-Dali". *Discover India*, Vol. 13, No. 4, 2000, pp. 52-53.

376. Chaturvedi, P. S. "Bhartiya Vratotsava". Varansi, 1961. [Hindi]

377. Chaudhary, N. D. and Vyas, N. N. and Mann, R. S. (eds.) Rajasthan Bhils. Udaipur: Tribal Research Institute. 1978.

378. Chaudhuri, A.B. "The Santals: religion and rituals". New Delhi, Ashish Publishing House, 1987. p. 229.

379. Chaudhuri, Jatindra Bimal "The position of women in Vedic ritual". Calcutta: Pracyavani, 1945. Vol.; 18 cm.

380. Chaudhuri, Roma, "Dowry old order and the new". *Dowry Custom (Vivekananda Kendra Patrika, Madras)* Vol. 2. no. 2. 1973, pp. 1-4.

381. Chaudhury, B.N. "Marriage custom and Vivaha Mantras of the Bengalee Buddhists". In, Proceedings of the national seminar on 'Living customs and their ancient Indian sources', Edited by V. N. Jha, Pune, Centre of Advanced Study in Sanskrit, University of Poona, 1991, pp. 101-109.

382. Chaudhury, Rai H. N. and Pal, D.C. "Plnats in folk religion and mythology". In, Glimpses in Indian ethnobotany. Edited by S.K. Jain, New Delhi, Oxford & IBH, 1981.

383. Chaudhury, Sushil "Medieval Indian society, state and social custom: Sati as a case study". *Calcutta Historical Journal,* Vol. 7, No. 1-2, July 1983-June 1984, pp. 38-60.

384. Chauhan, Brij Raj. "A study of a social institution in Indian villages". *Ritual sociology* 26, 1961, pp. 191-197.

385. Chekki, D. A. "Mate selection, age at marriage and propinquity among the lingayats of India". *Journal of Marriage and the family* 30, 1968, pp. 707-711.

386. Chemen, Jeevendiren "Socio-cultural aspects of Kavati festivals in Mauritius". *PILC Journal of Dravidic Studies,* Vol. 11, No. 1-2, 2001, pp. 121-131.

387. Cherian, Dilip "At the Trocadero: A celebration of India". *The India Magazine*, Vol. 5, No. 8, 1985, pp. 14-16.

388. Chib, S. S. "This beautiful India: Himachal Pradesh". Delhi, 1977.

389. Chirmade, S. R. "Hindu scriptual system and economic development in India". In, Proceedings of the national seminar on 'Living customs and their ancient Indian sources', Edited by V. N. Jha, Pune, Centre of Advanced Study in Sanskrit, University of Poona, 1991, pp. 329-342.

390. Chitrabhanu Sen "A dictionary of the Vedic rituals based on the Śrauta and Grhya Sūtras". *The Journal of the Royal Asiatic Society of Great Britain and Ireland*, No. 1 1979, pp. 64-65.

391. Chitrav, Siddheshwar "Puja". Poona, Bhartiya Charitrakosha Mandala, 1977.

392. Chitrav, Siddheshwar "Dharmik Samskara va nityakarma". Poona, Bhartiya Charitrakosha Mandala, 1965. [Hindi]

393. Chobey, Ajay Kumar "Tharu Aadivasiyon ki pujaa evam tyohar". *Vanyajati*, Vol. 53, No. 2, 2005 (April), pp. 32-37. [Hindi]

394. Chohan, Mohan Singh, "Mahare kuthaha". *Himprasta*, Vol. 16, No. 2 May 1970, pp. 39-41. [Pahari language]

395. Chohan, Ratan Singh "Sirmor ke mele aur tyohar". *Somsi*, Vol. 4, No. 89, 1998, pp. 58-73. [Hindi]

396. Chopra, Pran "Customs, rites and ceremonies". Shiva lal Agarwala & Co. (P) Ltd. Publishers, Agra, UP, 1992.

397. Choube, Omprakasha "Kartik Snan". *Chomasa*, Vol. 18, No. 55, 2001, pp. 114-117. [Hindi]

398. Choube, Omprakasha and Shukl, Shushma "Jhagde ki phagen". *Chomasa*, Vol. 17, No. 54, 2001, pp. 75-78. [Hindi]

399. Choudhury, Nishipada Deva "Serpent worship and manasa icons in Assam." In, 'Aspects of history and culture: Ananda Chandra Agarwala Commemoration Volume', eds. R.D.

Choudhury and Shri Bhagwan Singh, Delhi, Ramanand Vidya Bhawan, 1991, pp. 207-213.

400. Chowfla, Kuldeep "Minjar fair". Souvenir, 1976, pp. 09-14.

401. Chudawat, Laxmi Kumari "Rajasthan ke riti rivaaz: Devgarh thikane ka manavshastriya adhyayan". Jaipur, Publication Scheme, 2002, p. 184. [Hindi]

402. Cinnasvamisastri, A. "Yajna tattva prakasa [microform]". [Hinduism Rituals]. Edited by A.M. Ramanatha Dikshita. Madras: Madras Law Journal Press, 1953. xiv, 132, 2 p. : ill. ; 24 cm. [In Sanskrit]

403. Citrava, Siddhesvarasastri "Puja [microform] [Hindu rituals]. Avrtti 6. Pune, Sankara Ramacandra Date, [1941] xiv, 29 p. ; 19 cm. [In Marathi]

404. Citrava, Siddhesvarasastri "Sraddhaprayoga [microform] [Sraddha Hindu rite]". Avrtti 2. Poona, S. R. Date, 1936. xxx, 88 p. ; 19 cm. [Marathi]

405. Citrava, Siddhesvarasastri "Vivahasaskara [microform]". Pune, Sankara Ramacandra Date, [1927] xlii, 64 p. ; 18 cm. [Marathi, Sanskrit]

406. Clarence Maloney "Religious beliefs and social hierarchy in Tamil Nādu, India". *American Ethnologist,* Vol. 2, No. 1, Intra-Cultural Variation (Feb., 1975), pp. 169-191.

407. Clark-Decès, Isabelle "No one cries for the dead: Tamil dirges, rowdy songs, and Graveyard petitions". Berkeley: University of California Press. 2005.

408. Clark-Decès, Isabelle "Religion against the self: ethnography of Tamil rituals". New York, Oxford University Press, 2000, xi, 230 p. ; 25 cm.

409. Clark-Decès, Isabelle "The encounter never ends: A return to the field of Tamil rituals". Albany: State University of New York Press. 2007.

410. Clarke, Sathianathan "Re-viewing the religion of the Paraiyars: Ellaiyamman as an Iconic symbol of collective resistance and emancipatory mythography". In, 'Religions of the Marginalised: Towards a Phenomenology and the Methodology of Study', ed. Gnana Robinson, Bangalore: United Theological College. 1998. pp. 35-53.

411. Claus, Peter J. "Medical anthropology and the ethnography of spirit possession". In Judy Pugh and valentine Daniel, ed. Contributions to Asian Studies, Vol. 18, 1984. pp. 60-72.

412. Claus, Peter J. "Spirit possession and spirit mediumship from the perspective of Tulu oral traditions". *Culture, Medicine and Pyschiatry.* Vol. 3, No. 1. 1979, pp. 29-52.

413. Claus, Peter J. "Ritual transforms a Myth". *South Indian Folklorist,* Vol. 1, No. 1, 1997 (January), pp. 37-57.

414. Clothey, Fred W. "Rhythm and intent: ritual studies from South India". Madras, Blackie & Son Publishers, 1983, xiii, 200 p. : ill. ; 22 cm.

415. Clothey, Fred W. "The Yaga: a fire ritual in South India". In, 'Experiensing Siva: encounter with a hindu deity', Edited by Fred W. Clothey and J. Bruce Long, Coloumbia, South Asia Books, 1983.

416. Clothey, Fred W. "Ritualizing on the boundaries: continuity and innovation in the Tamil diaspora". Columbia, S.C., University of South Carolina Press, 2006, xiii, 248 p. : ill., maps ; 24 cm.

417. Clothey, Fred W. and J. Bruce Long, (ed.) "Experiencing Siva: encounters with a Hindu deity". New Delhi, Manohar, 1983.

418. Cole, W. O. and Sambhi, Piara Singh. "The Sikhs, their religious beliefs and practices". London, Routledge. 1978.

419. Coccari, Diane M. "The Bir Babas of Banaras: an analysis of a folk deity in North India". Ph.D. thesis, submitted in University of Wisconsin, 1986.

420. Collier, John & Moskowitz, Ira "Rites and ceremonies of the Indians of the Southwest". New York, Barnes & Noble Books, 1993, xvii, 222 p. : ill. ; 29 cm.

421. Coomaraswamy, A. K. "Myths of Hindus and the Budhists". New York, 1967.

422. Cooper, Ilay "The awakening of spring: Holi in Rajasthan". *The India Magazine*, Vol. 5, No. 4, 1985, pp. 20-27.

423. Corbett, Jim "My India". London, New York, Oxford University Press, 1952, 190 p. illus. 20 cm.

424. Cormack, Margaret "The Hindu woman [microform]". New York, Bureau of Publications, Teachers College, Columbia University, 1953. xiv, 207 p. ; 23 cm.

425. Cort, John E. "Murtipuja in Svetambar Jain temples". In, 'Religion in India'. Edited by T. N. Madan. Oxford, Oxford University Press. 1991.

426. Courtright, Paul "Ganesa and the Ganesa festival in Maharashtra: a study in Hindu religious celebration". Ph.D. thesis Princeton University, 1974.

427. Courtright, Paul B. "Ganeœa: Lord of obstacles, Lord of beginnings. New York, Oxford University Press. 1985.

428. Courtright, Paul B. "Sacrifice and regeneration in the ritual of Sati". *Paper presented to the Thirteenth Annual Conference on South Asia*, University of Wisconsin, Madison, 1984, pp. 5-7.

429. Courtright, Paul B. "The iconographies of Sati". In, 'Sati: the blessing and the curse the burning of wives in India', Edited by John Stratton Hawley, Oxford University Press, New York, 1994, pp. 27-48.

430. Courtright, Paul B. "Sati, sacrifice, and marriage: The modernity of tradition". In, 'From the margins of Hindu marriage: Essays on gender, religion and culture', pp. 184-203, New York, Oxford University Press. 1995.

431. Coward Harold and Goa, David "Mantra: hearing the divine in India". Chambersberg, Anima Publications, 1991.

432. Cozad, Laurie A. "The snake in the grass-roots movement: Orthodox texts and the preservation and transformation of snake worship rituals." *Paper presented* at Lund University, Lund, Sweden. 2004.

433. Craddock, Elaine "The Anatomy of devotion: The life and poetry of Karaikkal Ammaiyar". In, 'Womans lives, womans rituals in the Hindu tradition'. Edited by Tracy Pintchman, New York: Oxford University Press, 2007, pp. 131-148.

434. Craddock, Norma Elaine "Anthills, split mothers, and sacrifice: conceptions of female power in the Mariyamman tradition". Ph. D. dissertation, Berkeley, University of California, 1994.

435. Craddock, Norma Elaine "Reconstructing the split Goddess as Śakti in a Tamil Village." In, 'Seeking Mahādevī: Constructing the Identities of the Hindu Great Goddess', ed. Tracy Pintchman, Albany: State University of New York Press. 2001, pp. 145-69.

436. Crawford, C. "Ram Mohun Ray on sati and sexism". *Indian Journal of Social Work* Vol. 41, No. 1 (April 1980), pp. 73-90.

437. Cronk, L. E. "Mesoamerican and Indian fire gods and ceremonies. University of Calgary (Canada)). 1973, ProQuest Dissertations and Theses, 1. http://search.proquest.com/docview/302676334?accountid= 43898

438. Crooke W. "Primitive rites of disposal of the dead, with special reference to India". *Journal of the Anthropological Institute of Great Britain and Ireland,* 29, 1899, pp. 271–294.

439. Crooke, W. "Indian pilgrimage". In, 'Encyclopaedia of Religion and Ethics', Vol. 10, New York, Charles Scribners and Sons, 1956.

440. Crooke, W. "Some ritual festivals and ceremonies". In, 'Festivals in Indian Society', 2 Vols., Ed. Usha Sharma, A Mittal Publication, New Delhi, pp.183-204.

441. Crooke, William "The popular religion and folklore of Northern India". 2 Vols. London, A Constable & Co., 1896.

442. Culshaw, W. J. "Tribal heritage: A study of the Santals". London, Lutterworth Press, 1949.

443. Dalmia, Vasudha "The Nationalization of Hindu traditions: Bhartendu Harishchandra and 19th centuary Benaras". Delhi, Oxford University Press, 1999.

444. Dalmia, Vasudha, and Stietencron, Heinrich von, (eds.), "Representing Hinduism: The construction of religious traditions and National identity". New Delhi, Sage Publications, 1995.

445. Dalmia, Yashshodhara "The painted world of the Warlis: art and rituals of the Warli tribes of Maharashtra". New Delhi, Lalit Kala Akademi, 1988. p. 239.

446. Dalton, Jacob "The development of perfection: The interiorization of Buddhist ritual in the eighth and ninth centuries". *Journal of Indian Philosophy,* Vol. 32, No. 1, 2004 (February), pp. 1-30.

447. Dandekar, V. M. "India's sacred cattle and cultural ecology". *Economic and Political Weekly*, Vol. 4, No. 39 (September 27, 1969), pp. 1559, 1561-1566.

448. Dange, S. A. "Encyclopaedia of Puranic beliefs and practices". *Navrang*, Vol. 1, New Delhi, 1986.

449. Dange, Sadashiv A. "Medhi and the Torana". In, Proceedings of the national seminar on 'Living customs and their ancient Indian sources', Edited by V. N. Jha, Pune, Centre of Advanced Study in Sanskrit, University of Poona, 1991, pp.187-191.

450. Dange, Sadashiv Ambadas "Images from Vedic hymns and rituals". New Delhi, Aryan Books International, 2000. xix, p. 374.

451. Dange, Sindhu S. "Aspects of speech in Vedic ritual". New Delhi, Aryan Books international, 1996. xxi, p. 269.

452. Dange, Sindhu S. "A rite for the Suvasin and the Vedic Puranic tradition". In, Proceedings of the national seminar on 'Living customs and their ancient Indian sources', Edited by V. N. Jha, Pune, Centre of Advanced Study in Sanskrit, University of Poona, 1991, pp. 110-113.

453. Dange, Sindhu S. "Some non-vedic rituals in the vedic tradition". *Haryana Sahitya Akademi Journal of Indological Studies*, Vol. 2, No. 1-2, 1987, pp. 1-7.

454. Daniel, Sheryl B. "The tool box approach of the Tamil to the Issues of moral responsibility and human destiny." In 'Karma: An Anthropological Inquiry', eds. E. Valentine Daniel and Charles F. Keyes, Berkeley: University of California Press. 562 p. 1983. pp. 27-62.

455. Daniel, Valentine E. "Fluid Signs: Being a Person in the Tamil Way". Berkeley, University of California Press, 1984.

456. Das, Bhabesh "Botor Kikur: a folk festival of the Karbis for Rair". *Folklore*, Vol. 30, No. 8, 1989, pp. 181-183.

457. Das, Bhabesh "Khari song and dance of the Bodos of Assam: a festival of farewell and well-coming a New Year, *Folklore*, Vol. 28, No. 1, 1987, pp. 11-13.

458. Das, Bhabesh "Khuksi: the folk-festival of the Rabhas, an outline of the worship pattern". *Folklore*, Vol. 29, No. 3, 1988, pp. 67-68.

459. Das, Bhagavan, "Science of social organisation or the Laws of Manu in the light of Atmavidya Vols. 3". Theosphical Publishing House, Adyar, Madras, 1980.

460. Das, D. N. "Karam festival in a Munda village". *Vanjayati*, Vol. 2, No.1, Jan, 1954, pp. 22-25.

461. Das, D. R. "Archaeological evidence on cremation and post-cremation burial in India". *Journal of Ancient Indian History,* Vol. 3, No. 1-2, 1969-70, pp. 50-71.

462. Das, Frieda Mathilda Hauswirth "A marriage to India". New York, Vanguard Press, 1930, 4 p. l., 3-306 p. incl. fronts. (Mounted port.) 24 cm.

463. Das, Manmatha Nath "Movement to suppress the custom of femaale infanticide in the Punjab and Kashmir". *Man in India*, Vol. 37, No. 04, 1957 (Oct. - Dec.), pp. 280-293.

464. Das, Manoj, "Sita's marriage". *Dowry Custom (Vivekananda Kendra Patrika, Madras)* Vol. 2, No. 2, 1973, pp. 82-85.

465. Das, Nirmal Chandra "Social importance of ritual kinship in the "Godaba" society in Koraput district of Orissa". *Folklore*, Vol. 19, No. 2, 1978 (Feburary), pp. 45-51.

466. Das, Prabin Chandra "Mare puja and Deodha dance of Assam: a note on a type of serpent worship." *Folklore* (September) 1987. pp. 216-19.

467. Das, Prabin Chandra. "Mare puja and deodha dance". *The Sunday Sentinel,* 10 August, Guwahati, India. 1986.

468. Das, Prodeepta "In an Indian village". New York, Benchmark Books/Marshall Cavendish, 2002, 32 p. : Col. ill. ; 22 x 28 cm.

469. Das, Rajatkanti "Rituals in maring social life". *Man and Life*, Vol. 8, No. 1-2, 1982, pp. 29-38.

470. Das, Sudhir Ranjan "Folk religion of Bengal". Calcutta, S. C. Sarkar, 1953.

471. Das, Veena "The language of sacrifice". *Man*, Vol. 18, 1992, pp. 445-462.

472. Das, Veena "Critical events: an anthropological perspective on contemporary India". (Series: Oxford paperbacks), Delhi, New York, Oxford University Press, 1995, viii, 230 p. : ill. ; 22 cm.

473. Das, Veena "Structure and cognition: aspects of Hindu caste and ritual". Delhi: Oxford University Press, 1982. xiii, p. 171.

474. Das. M. N. "The suppression of the Meriah system among the hill tribes of Orissa". Ch. 10 in his studies in the economic and social development of modern India, 1848-1856, Calcutta: Firma KLM. 1959.

475. Dasa, Vraja Ratna "Vrataraja vratotsava-manjari [microform] [Hindu fast and festivals]". Agara, Gayaprasada enda Sansa, 2002 [1945] xx, 220 p. ; 19 cm.

476. Dasgupta Samira and Amitabha Sarkar "Synthesis of tribal region and hindu cults in Bastar" In, 'Culture, Religion and Philosophy: Critical studies in syncretism and Inter-Faith Harmony', N. K. Das (ed.) Jaipur: Rawat Publications. 2003.

477. Dasgupta, Atis "The bauls and their heretic tradition". *Social Scientist*, Vol. 22, No. 5-6, 1994, pp. 70-83.

478. Dasgupta, Shashi Bhushan "Obscure religious cults". Calcutta, Firma KLM, 1995 (first pub. 1946.)

479. Dasgupta, Biman Kumar "A note on the Rajbanshi (Rajbansi) of Eastern India with special reference to Social Movements". *Bulletin of the Anthropological Survey of India,* Vol. 18, No. 1, 1969, pp. 1-44.

480. Das-Gupta, Hem Chandra. "A short note on polyandry in Jubbal State (Simla)". *Indian Anitquary*, Vol. L, 1921, pp. 146-148.

481. Dasgupta, Samira "On Dussehra festival". *Journal of the Anthropological Survey of India,* Vol. 40, No. 1-2, 1991, pp. 101-102.

482. Dasgupta, Samira and Sarkar, Amitabha "Ritual value of Paddy in Bengal". *Folklore*, Vol. 229, 1979 (March-April), pp. 60-63.

483. Dash, Subas Chandra, "Jananasauca and Maranasuca: The past and present practice". In, Proceedings of the national seminar on 'Living customs and their ancient Indian sources', Edited by V. N. Jha, Pune, Centre of Advanced Study in Sanskrit, University of Poona, 1991, pp. 7-17.

484. Dass, G. S. "The festival of a Voyage to the island of Bali held at Cuttack". In, 'Festivals in Indian Society', 2 Vols., Ed. Usha Sharma, A Mittal Publication, New Delhi, pp.149-152.

485. Datar, B. N. "Himalayan pilgrimage". Delhi, 1961, p. 103.

486. Date, R. S. "Living customs regarding Jatakarma". In, Proceedings of the national seminar on 'Living customs and their ancient Indian sources', Edited by V. N. Jha, Pune, Centre of Advanced Study in Sanskrit, University of Poona, 1991, pp. 1-06.

487. Date, Ranjana Shrikant "Development of domestic rites (Satyasadha School)". Delhi, New Bhartiya Book Corporation, 2006.

488. Datta, Bhupendranatha "Dialectics of Hindu ritualism [microform] Calcutta, Gupta Press, 1956, Vol. 2, 22 cm.

489. Datta, Indra Nath "Vedic funeral customs and Indus valley culture". *Man in India*, Vol. 6, No. 4, 1926, pp. 223-307.

490. Datta, V. N. "Sati: A historical, social and philosophical enquiry into the Hindu rite of widow burning". New Delhi: Manohar, 1987.

491. Davane, G. V. "The Rāhu-Ketu Myth." *Vishveshvaranand Indological Journal,* Vol. 13, No.1-2, 1975, pp. 88-95.

492. David Pinault "Shia Lamentation rituals and reinterpretations of the doctrine of Intercession: two cases from modern India". *History of Religions*, Vol. 38, No. 3, Feb., 1999, pp. 285-305.

493. Davidson, Robyn "Desert places". New York : Viking, 1996, 279 p., [16] p. of plates : col. ill., maps ; 24 cm.

494. Davies, Nigel "Human sacrifice in history and today". London: MacMillan. 1981.

495. Davis, Richard H. "Cremation and liberation: therevision of a Hindu ritual". *History of Religions*, Vol. 28, No. 1, 1988, pp. 37-53.

496. Davis, Richard H. "Ritual in an oscillating universe: worshiping Śiva in medieval India". Princeton, N.J., Princeton University Press, 1991, xvi, 200 p. : ill. ; 25 cm.

497. Deb, D. & Malhotra K.C. "Conservation ethos in local traditions: The West Bengal heritage". *Society and Natural Resources*, 14, 2001. pp. 711-724.

498. Deb, D., Deuti K., Malhotra, K.C. "Sacred grove relics as bird refugia". *Current Science*, No. 73, 1997, pp. 815-17.

499. Debnath, Debashis "Ecology and rituals in tribal areas". New Delhi, Sarup & Sons, 2003, p. 215.

500. Deheja, Vidya "Yogini cult and temples: a tantric tradition". New Delhi, National Museum, 1986.

501. Dehejia, Vidya "The body adorned: dissolving boundaries between sacred and profane in India' art". New York, Columbia University Press, 2009.

502. Deodhar, Lalita, "Secular customs in the Upanayana ceremony". In, Proceedings of the national seminar on 'Living customs and their ancient Indian sources', Edited by V.N. Jha, Pune, Centre of Advanced Study in Sanskrit, University of Poona, 1991, pp. 23-27.

503. Derraugh, Pat and Bill. "Wedding etiquett". London, Foulsham, 1998.

504. Derygk O. Lodrick "Man and Mongoose in Indian Culture". *Anthropos,* Vol. 77, No. 1-2, 1982, pp. 191-214.

505. Desai, Anita "Fasting, feasting". New York, Houghton Mifflin Company. 1999.

506. Desai, Valaji Govindaji "Draupadinam cira [microform]: Gandhijikrta prastavana sahita - Avrtti 1. Amadavada: Navajivana Mudranalaya"., 1987 [1930] viii, 103 p. ; 18 cm. [In: Gujarati].

507. Deshpande, Maitreyee Rangnekar "The concept of time in Vedic ritual". Delhi, New Bharatiya Book Corporation, 2001. xx, p. 302.

508. Deshpande, Ragini "A festival to sita: in praise of the devoted wife, the ideal bahu, the wronged woman, at Deval". *The India Magazine*, Vol. 5, No. 2, 1985, pp. 56-63.

509. Deuri, R. K. "Festivals of Kameng: a few selected". Shillong, Directorate of Research, 1983. p. 48 : plates.

510. Dev, Bimal "Lushai customs and ceremonies". Delhi, Mittal Publications, 1983. xivi, p. 172.

511. Devadoss, T. S. "Socio-ethical and legal aspects of dowry". *Dowry Custom (Vivekananda Kendra Patrika, Madras)* Vol. 2. No. 2. 1973, pp. 75-81.

512. Devendra, Toyajakshi "Some reflections on dowry custom". *Dowry Custom (Vivekananda Kendra Patrika, Madras)* Vol. 2. No. 2. 1973, pp. 33-35.

513. Devi, E. H. "The medieval society of Kerala as reflected to the customs and practices of the Ballads of North Malabar". *Folklore*, Vol. 207, 1977 (April), pp. 105-123.

514. Devi, Indira and Roy, Dilip Kumar "Kumbha-why did they come". In, 'Festivals in Indian Society', 2 Vols., Ed. Usha Sharma, A Mittal Publication, New Delhi, pp. 61-64.

515. Devi, Indira Kumari "Buffalo fight of Himachal Pradesh". *Traveller in India*, Vol. 5, No. 4, May 1961, pp. 14-15.

516. Devi, Oinam Ronibala and Gangadhar, M. R. "Ritual practices among the Kaniyas of Karnataka". *Man and Life,* Vol. 37, No. 3-4, 2011 (July-Dec.), pp. 55-60.

517. Devi, Ragini "Festivals of the goddess Bhagavati in Kerala". *Marg*, Vol. 19, No. 2, 1966, pp. 46-48.

518. Dhakal, Nilhari "Juthe sutak nirnay". [On Hindu customs], Varanasi, Nepali saubhagya pustakalay, 1952. 32 p.; 17 cm. [Nepali]

519. Dhar, Bibhash "Chhos kor: the festival of the monpa and the sherdukpen" *Journal of Indian Anthropological Society,* Vol. 17, No. 3, 1982, pp. 265-268.

520. Dharampal "A Marhatta Brahmin ambassador explains hindu manners and customs". In, Some Europian narrations on India, Vol. 1, Ashram Pratishtan, Sevagram 2000. pp. 32-38.

521. Dharampal "Ancient manners of the Indian still existing in Bissenpour". In, Some Europian narrations on India, Vol. 1, Ashram Pratishtan, Sevagram 2000. pp. 23-25.

522. Dharampal "Jesuit narration of manners and customs in south India". In, Some Europian narrations on India, Vol. 1, Ashram Pratishtan, Sevagram 2000. pp. 17-19.

523. Dharampal "Manners and customs of Hindus". In, Some Europian narrations on India, Vol. 1, Ashram Pratishtan, Sevagram 2000. pp. 21-23.

524. Dharampal "On gomukh and Indian customs and manners". In, Some Europian narrations on India, Vol. 1, Ashram Pratishtan, Sevagram 2000. pp. 25-27.

525. Dharmadhikari, T. N. "Women's right to perform religious rites". In, Proceedings of the national seminar on 'Living customs and their ancient Indian sources', Edited by V. N. Jha, Pune, Centre of Advanced Study in Sanskrit, University of Poona, 1991, pp.181-186.

526. Dharmendra Maharaj "Hindu ki Divya Sati Parampara evam Vartaman Sandarbh". Delhi: Rani Sati Temple, n.d. [Hindi].

527. Dhiman, Prakash Chandra "Mhachala ri lohri hor Khohdi". *Himbharti*, Vol. 20, No, 4, 1988, pp. 41-43. [Pahari Language]

528. Dhiman, Ramesh "The festival of Rali". *Indian Express*, April 4, 1988. p. 3.

529. Dhingra K. "The Andaman and Nicobar Islands in the Twentieth Century: A Gazetteer". Oxford University Press, New Delhi, 2005.

530. Diamond, Jared "Anatomy of a ritual". *Natural History*, Vol. 110, No. 6, 2001 (July-August).

531. Diane P. Mines "Hindu Nationalism, untouchable reform, and the ritual production of a South Indian Village". *American Ethnologist*, Vol. 29, No. 1 (Feb., 2002), pp. 58-85.

532. Dickey, Sara "Anjali's prospects: class mobility in urban India." In, 'Everyday Life in South Asia', eds. Diane P. Mines and Sarah Lamb, Bloomington, IN: Indiana University Press. 2002. pp. 214-26.

533. Diehl, Carl Gustav "Instrument and purpose; studies on rites and rituals in South India. *Dissertation*: Inaug. Lund, CWK Gleerup, 1956, 394 p. 25 cm.

534. Dimock, Edward C. Jr. "The Goddess of Snakes in medieval Bengali literature." *History of Religions*, Vol. 1, No. 2, 1962. pp. 307-321.

535. Dimock, Edward C. Jr. and A. K. Ramanujan. "The Goddess of snakes in medieval Bengali literature, Part II." *History of Religions*, Vol. 3, No. 2, 1964. pp. 300-322.

536. Dionisopoulos-Mass "The evil eye and bewitchment in a peasant village". In, 'Regina-In the evil eye', edited by Maloney, Clarence, New York: Columbia UP, 1976, pp. 42-62.

537. Dipankar Gupta "Whither the Indian village: culture and agriculture in 'rural' India". *Economic and Political Weekly*, Vol. 40, No. 8 (Feb. 19-25, 2005), pp. 751-758.

538. Disuza, Nora S. "Goa ki dayamayi maa". *Discover India*, Vol. 5, No. 12, 1992, pp. 32-33. [Hindi]

539. Dixit, G. "Fire sacrificial plants". Geobios News Reports, Vol. 16, No. 8, 1997, pp. 47-48.

540. Dixit, L. D. "Samanvit prayas hi parampara ko bachayenge". *Kalavarta*, Vol. 23, No. 107-08, 2004, pp. 26-28. [Hindi]

541. Dixit, Pradeep "Parampara me vikas ke naye aayaam". *Kalavarta*, Vol. 23, No. 107-08, 2004, pp. 45-47.

542. Dixon, Benjamin Y. "Furthering their own demise: How Kansa Indian death customs accelerated their depopulation". *Ethnohistory*, Vol. 54, No. 3, 2007 (Summer), pp. 473-508.

543. Dobois, Abbe, J. A., "Description of the character, manners and customs of the people of India". Longman, Hurst, Rees, Orme and Borwn, Paternoster-Row (1817), London.

544. Dogra, Ramesh Chander "Hindu and Sikh wedding ceremonies: with salient features of Hindu and Sikh rituals". New Delhi, Star Publications, 2000. p. 192.

545. Dogra, Sudarshan "Barsat ke teen tyohar". *Somsi*, Vol. 12, No. 2, 1986, pp. 71-77. [Hindi]

546. Dogra, Sudarshan "Dhagon ka tyohar Rakshabandhan". *Somsi*, Vol. 13, No. 2, 1987. pp. 78-80. [Hindi]

547. Dogra, Sudarshan "Maaghi". *Somsi*, Vol. 15, No. 1, 1989, pp. 58-63. [Hindi]

548. Doniger, W. "The symbolism of black and white babies in the myth of parental impression" *Social Research*, Vol. 70, No. 1, 2003, pp. 1-44.

549. Doniger, Wendy "Put a bag over her head!': Beheading mythological women." In, 'Off with her head!: The Denial of Women's Identity in Myth, Religion, and Culture', eds. Howard Eilberg-Schwartz and Wendy Doniger, Berkeley: University of California Press. 1995. pp. 15-31.

550. Doshi, S.L. "Bhils: between social self awareness and cultural Synthesis". New Delhi, Sterling Publishers, 1997.

551. Dramnarayan, V. "Dance festival with a difference". *Sruti: South Indian Classical Music and Dance Magazine,* Issue No. 1, 1983, pp. 14-16.

552. Draper, Allison Stark "India: a primary source cultural guide". New York, PowerPlus Books, 2003, 128 p. : ill. (some col.), col. maps ; 25 cm.

553. Duarah, D. K. "Nyokum Yullo: A festival of the Nishis" *Yojana*, Vol. 26, No. 14-15, 1982, pp. 110-111.

554. Duary, Naba K. "Mortuary practices of the Lodhas of West Bengal". *Humankind*, Vol. 2, 2006, Edited by Kishor K. Basa, Serials Publications, New Delhi, pp. 37-46.

555. Duary, Nabakumar "Disuasendra in Santhal Society". In, 'Fairs and festivals of Indian tribes', Edited by Robin David Tribhuwan, Discovery Publishing House, New Delhi, 2003, pp. 47-52.

556. Dube, S. C. "Indian village". London, Routledge and Kegan Paul, 1955.

557. Dube, S. C. "Myths, religion and ritual of the Kamars". *The Eastern Anthropologist,* Vol. 1, No. 1, 1947, pp. 27-42.

558. Dube, S. C. "Ritual friendship in Chhattisgarh". *Man in India,* Vol. 29, No. 2, 1949 (April - June), pp. 98-102.

559. Dubey, G., Sahu, P. & Sahu, R. "Role of plants in differents religious ceremonies common to Bundelkhand region of Madhya Pradesh". *Journal of Medicinal Aeromatioc Plants Sci,* Vol. 22-23, 2001-2002, pp. 542-45.

560. Dubey, K. C. "Tribal legends and customs and tribal history". *Vanyajati*, Vol. 17, No. 2, 1969 (April), pp. 46-48.

561. Dubey, K. C. and M. G. Mohril Durkheim, E. "Fairs and festivals of Madhya Pradesh, Cenus of India. 1954 "Elementary forms of the religious life, trans. By Joseph Ward Swain, Glencoe III: The Free Press. 1961.

562. Dubey, S.N. "Celebration on Diwali among the Gonds of Tamia". *Bulletin of Tribal Research and Development Institute (Bhopal),* Vol. 4, No. 1, June, 1964, pp. 37-43.

563. Dubey, Ved Prakash "Bhartiya Samajik paramparaon me manvadhikaron ki shashavat anugunj". *Madhya Bharti,* Vol. 1, 2009, pp. 198-202. [Hindi]

564. Dubios, J. A. "Character, manners and customs of the people of India; and of their institutions, religion and civil". Delhi, Daya Publishing House, 1817. xxvii, p. 565.

565. Dubois, Abbe J. A. "Hindu manners, customs and ceremonies". 3rd ed. Delhi, Oxford Uiversity Press, 1906. xxxiv, p. 738.

566. Dudley, A. M. "Indigenous forest use practices and sustainability: A case study of the adivasis of the nilgiri biosphere region, south India". Saint Marys University, Canada, Pro Quest Dissertations and Theses, 1999. p. 148, Access online at, http://search.proquest. com/docview/304575287?accountid=43898

567. Duff, Alexander "Goomsur, the late war there-the Khonds or Hill tribes". *CR* Vol. 6 (Jan-March) 1846. pp. 1-85.

568. Duff, Alexander "The first series of government measures for the abolition of human sacrifice among the Khonds". *CR*, Vol. 06 (July-Sept.) 1846. pp. 45-108.

569. Duff, Alexander "The Khonds-abolition of human sacrifice". *CR,* Vol. 10, 1848, pp. 273-341.

570. Dumont, Louis, "Dowry in Hindu marriage as a social scientist sees it". *The Economic and Political Weekly* No. 11, 1959, pp. 519-520.

571. Dumont, Louis, "Hierarchy of marriage alliance in South Indian kinship". *Occasional papers of the royal anthropological institute*, No.12, London, 1957, Royal Anthropological Institute.

572. Duncan, Marion H. More harvest festival dramas of Tibet. London, Mitre Press, 1967. p. 123 : ill.

573. Dunin, Elsie Ivancich "Continuities and changes: Interrelationships of ritual and social dance contexts in Dubrovnik-area villages". Yearbook for Traditional Music, Vol. 33, 2001, pp. 99-107.

574. Durah, D. K. "Festival of the Nishis of Arunachal Pradesh". *Resarun*, Vol. 11, No. 2 Autumn-Winter, 1985, pp. 29-31.

575. Durga Bhagvat "Tribal gods and festivals in central India". *Asian Folklore Studies*, Vol. 27, No. 2, 1968, pp. 27-106.

576. Durga, P. S. Kanaka "Identity and symbols of sustenance: explorations in social mobility of medieval South India". *Journal of the Economic and Social History of the Orient,* Vol. 44, No. 2, 2001, pp. 141-174.

577. Durham, M. E. "Some tribal origins". London, Laws and customs of the Balkans, 1928.

578. Durrans, Brian & Knox, Robert "India: past into present". London, Published for the Trustees of the British Museum by British Museum Publications, 1982, 96 p. : ill. ; 25 cm.

579. Dutta, P. C. and Duarah, D. K. "Aspects of culture and customs of Arunachal Pradesh". Itanagar: Directorate of Research, 1990. p. 243.

580. Duvignaud, Jean "Festivals: a sociological approach". *Cultures*, Vol. 3, No. 1, 1976, pp. 13-25.

581. Duvvury, Vasumathi K. "Play, symbolism, and ritual: a study of Tamil Brahmin women's rites of passage". New York, P. Lang, 1991, x, 251 p.: ill. ; 24 cm.

582. Dvivedi, Vrajavallabha "Having become a God, he should sacrifice to the Gods". In, 'Ritual and speculation in early Tantrism', Edited by Teun Goudriaan, Albany, State University of New York Press, 1992.

583. Dwivedi, H. P. "Cultural significance of fairs". In, Census of India, 1961, Vol. 13, Punjab, Part VII B, Delhi: Government of India. 1965.

584. Dwivedi, Prem Krishn "Gonda janpad ke Danguria Tharu aadivasiyon ke riti-rivaj". *Vanyajati*, Vol. 30, No. 4, 1982, Oct. pp. 17-20. [Hindi]

585. Dwyer, Graham "The divine and the demonic: supernatural affliction and its treatment in North India". London; New York, Routledge Curzon, 2003, xiii, 190 p. : ill., maps ; 23 cm.

586. Dymock, W. "On the uses of turmeric in Hindoo ceremonial." *The Journal of the Anthropological Society of Bombay* Vol. 2, (1890-1892), 1891, pp. 441-48.

587. Eck, Diana L. "The sacrifice of religion, and the Sakta Pithas". Paper presented to the American Academy of Religion". Atlanta, November 1986.

588. Eck, Diana L. "Banaras: cosmos and pilgrimage in the Hindu imagination". In, 'The world and the world: fantacy, symbol and record', Edited by Veena Das, New Delhi, Sage Publications, 1986.

589. Eck, Diana L. "Darœan: seeing the divine image in India". New York: Columbia University Press. 1998.

590. Edwardes, Michael "Everyday life in early India". London, Batsford; New York, Putnam, 1969, xiv, 176 p. 97 illus., map. 23 cm.

591. Edwards S. Haynes "Rajput ceremonial interactions as a mirror of a dying Indian state system, 1820-1947". *Modern Asian Studies*, Vol. 24, No. 3 (Jul., 1990), pp. 459-492.

592. Egnor, Margaret Trawick "The changed mother, or what the smallpox Goddess did when there was no more smallpox." *Contributions to Asian Studies* Vol. 18, 1983, pp. 24-45.

593. Egnor, Margaret. "On the meaning of Śakti to women in Tamil Nadu" In, The powers of Tamil Women. Edited by Susan Wadley, Syracuse: Syracuse University, 1980. pp. 1-34.

594. Ehmore, W. T. "Dravidan gods in modern Hinduism". Lincoln, University of Nebraska, 1915.

595. Eidlitz, Walther "Unknown India [microform]: a pilgrimage into a forgotten world". London; New York, Rider and Co., 1952. 192 p.: ill. ; 21 cm.

596. Einoo, Shingo "From material to deity: Indian rituals of concecration". New Delhi, Manohar, 2005.

597. Einoo, Shingo "The formation of puja ceremony". *Studien zur Indologie und Iranistik* (Festschrifts fur Paul Thieme) Vol. 22, 1996, pp. 73-87.

598. Ekadasi "Mahatmya". [On observation of rituals]". Darjeeling, Jivanath Kaphle, 1935. 147 p.; 17 cm. [In: Nepali]

599. Ekka, William "Clan and some customs of the Nagbansi". *Journal of Indian Anthropological Society*, Vol. 16, No. 3, 1981 (November), pp. 197-201.

600. Elamon, Suresh "Boats, boat builders and carnivals: The Kerala regatta". *The India Magazine*, Vol. 4, No. 9, 1984, pp. 40-46.

601. Elizabeth English "Vajrayogini: her visualizations, rituals and forms: a study of the cult of Vajrayogini in India Boston, Wisdom Publications, 2002, xxxi, 563 p. : col. ill. ; 23 cm.

602. Elson, Vickie C. "Dowries from Kutch: a women's folk art tradition in India: [exhibition and catalogue]". Los Angeles, Calif., Museum of Cultural History, University of California, 1979, 127 p.: ill. ; 26 cm.

603. Elwin, V. "Beads among the Juangs of India". *Beads*, Vol. 8, 1943.

604. Elwin, Verrier "Maria murder and suicide". Bombay, Oxford University Press, 1943.

605. Elwin, Verrier "Myths of middle India". Bombay, Oxford University Press, 1949.

606. Elwin, Verrier "The Muria and their ghotul". Bombay, Oxford University Press, 1947.

607. Elwin, Verrier "Tribal myths of Orissa". Bombay, Oxford University Press, 1954.

608. Elwin, Verrier "Punerary customs in Bastar state". *Man in India,* Vol. 25, No. 2, 1945 (June), pp. 91-174.

609. Emeneau, M.B. "A century of Toda studies. reviewed work(s): The Toda of South India: A New Look by Anthony R. Walker; M.N. Srinivas, *Journal of the American Oriental Society,* Vol. 108, No. 4 (Oct. - Dec., 1988), pp. 605-609.

610. Emerson, H. W. "The historical aspect of some Himalayan customs" *Journal of the Punjab Historical Society*, Vol. VIII, No. 2, 1921. pp. 185-197.

611. Emile, Durkheim "The elementary forms of religious life", trans by J. W. Swain, Glencoe, 111: Free Press, 1954, See Jean Duvignaud Ibid.

612. Encyclopedia Britannica, "Ritual". Chicago, The University of Chicago Press, 1947.

613. Epstein, T. S. "Economic development and peasant marriage in South India". *Man in India,* Vol. 40, 1960, pp. 192-232.

614. Erndl, Kathleen. "Victory to the mother: The Hindu Goddess of Northwest India in myth, ritual, and symbol. New York: Oxford University Press, 1993.

615. Eschmann, A. H. "Hinduization of tribal deities in Orissa: The 'Sakta and Saiva typology". Ch. 4 In Eschmann et al. eds. Cult of Jagannath. 1978.

616. Esehmann, A. H. Kulke and G. C. Tripathi eds. "The cult of Jagannath and the regional tradition of Orissa". The South Asia Institute, Delhi: Manohar, 1978.

617. Esme "The Garos, their customs and mythology". *Calcutta Review*, LXXX, 1885, pp. 47-71.

618. Euter-Haimendorf, Christoph von. "The After life in Indian tribal belief". *Journal of Royal Anthropological Society*, London, Vol. 83, No.1, Jan-June 1953, pp. 37-49.

619. Evalyn Jacobson Michaelson and Walter Goldschmidt "Family and land in peasant ritual". *American Ethnologist,* Vol. 3, No. 1 (Feb., 1976), pp. 87-96.

620. Evison, G. "Indian death rituals: the enactment of ambivalence". University of Oxford (United Kingdom)). ProQuest Dissertations and Theses, 1. 1989.http://search.proquest.com/docview/303748301?accountid= 43898

621. Evison, Gillian "Indian death rituals: the enactment of Ambivalence (India, Hinduism, Brahmin)". London, University of Oxford (United Kingdom), 1989.

622. Fakhliyal, Hayat and Seepal, Chandr "Chodas ka mahaparva". *Pahad,* Vol. 3-4, 1989, pp. 108-111. [Hindi]

623. Farooqui, M.I.H. "Plants of the Quran". Luchnow, Sidrah Publisher, 1989.

624. Fazalbhoy, Nasreen "Rituals of protection in a Muslim community. *The Eastern Anthropologist,* Vol. 53, No. 3-4, 2000, pp. 443-455.

625. Feldhaus, Anne "Connected places: region, pilgrimage, and geographical imagination in India". New York, Palgrave Macmillan. 2003.

626. Feldhaus, Anne "Water and womanhood: religious meaning of rivers in Maharashtra". New York, Oxford University Press. 1995.

627. Fergusson, J. "Tree and serpent worship". New Delhi, Indological Book House, 1971.

628. Ferrari, Fabrizio M. "Love me two times'. from smallpox to AIDS: contagion and possession in the cult of Ǘîtalā." *Religions of South Asia,* Vol. 1, No. 1, 2007, pp. 81-106.

629. Figueira, Dorothy M. "Die Flambierte Frau: Sati in European Culture". In, Sati: The blessing and the curse-The burning of wives in India, Edited by John Stratton Hawley, Oxford University Press, New York , 1994, pp. 55-71.

630. Fischer, Eberhard "Art and rituals: 2500 years of Jainism in India". New Delhi, Stering Publishers, 1977. viii, 80 p.: plates p.

631. Fischer, Eberhard "Murals for goddesses and gods: the tradition of Osakothi ritual painting in Orissa, India". New Delhi, Indira Gandhi National Centre for the Art, 1996. p. 224 : ill. p.

632. Fisher, Fred Bohn & Williams, Gertrude M. "India's silent revolution". New York, Macmillan Co., 1919, 6 p. l., 192 p. plates. 20 cm.

633. Fleming, L "Name taboos and rigid performativity". *Anthropological Quarterly* 84, 1, 2011, pp. 141-164.

634. Flueckiger, Joyce Burkhalter "In Amma's healing room: gender and Vernacular Islam in South India". Bloomington, Indiana University Press. 2006.

635. Flueckiger, Joyce Burkhalter "Wandering from 'Hills to Valleys' with the Goddess: protection and freedom in the Matamma tradition of Andhra." In 'Women's Lives, Women's Rituals in the Hindu Tradition', ed. Tracy Pintchman, 2007. pp. 35-54.

636. Fogelin, Lars "The archaeology of religious ritual". *American Journal of Physical Anthropology*, Vol. 36, 2007, pp. 55-71.

637. Fontaine, Jean La "Invisible custom: public lectures as ceremonials". *Anthropology Today*, Vol. 2, No. 1-6, 1986, pp. 3-9.

638. Forth, Gregory "Blood, milk and coconuts: A study of intra-cultural ritual variation". *Man*, Vol. 18, No. 4, 1983 (December), pp. 654-668.

639. Francis X. Clooney "Finding one's place in the text: A look at the theological treatment of caste in traditional India". *The Journal of Religious Ethics,* Vol. 17, No. 1 (Spring, 1989), pp. 1-29.

640. Frank J. Korom "Holy Cow! The apotheosis of Zebu, or why the cow is sacred in Hinduism". *Asian Folklore Studies*, Vol. 59, No. 2, 2000, pp. 181-203.

641. Frank J. Moore "A note on rural debt and control of ceremonial expenditure in India". *Economic Development and Cultural Change,* Vol. 2, 1954, pp. 408-415.

642. Fred W. Clothey "Rhythm and Intent: ritual studies from South India. The play of the Gods: Locality, Ideology, Structure and Time in the Festivals of a Bengali Town". *History of Religions*, Vol. 25, No. 3 (Feb., 1986), pp. 284-288.

643. Fredericksen, Linwood "Feast and festival". The New Encyclopaedia Britannica, Chicago: Encyclopaedia Britannica, 1981, pp. 197-202.

644. Freed, Ruth S. Freed, Stanley A. "Ghosts: life and death in North India". (Series: Anthropological papers of the American Museum of Natural History, v. 72), New York, American Museum of Natural History, 1993, 396 p. : ill. ; 26 cm.

645. Freed, Ruth S. & Freed, Stanley A. "Rites of passage in Shanti Nagar". (Anthropological papers of the American Museum of Natural History, v. 56, pt. 3), New York, American Museum of Natural History, 1980, pp. 323-554 : ill. ; 26 cm.

646. Freed, Stanley A. and Ruth S. Freed "Guga naumi." In Hindu festivals in a North Indian Village. *Anthropological Papers of the American Museum of Natural History 81 (November)*. Seattle, University of Washington Press, 1998. pp. 45-55.

647. Freeman, James, "The Ladies of lord Krishna: rituals of middle-aged women in eastern India". In Unspoken worlds: Women's religious lives in non-western cultures, ed. Nancy falk and rita gross. San Francisco, Harper and Row. 1980.

648. Freeman, John R. "Purity and violence: sacred power in the Teyyam worship of Malabar: Ph.D. Diss., University of Pennsylvania. 1991.

649. Freeman, Richardson J. "Performing of northern Kerala". In Flags of fame. Studies in South Asian folk culture, ed. Heidrun Bruckner, Lothar Lutze, and Aditya Malik, Delhi, Manohar, 1993, pp. 109-138.

650. Freitag, Sandria "Religious rites and riots: From community Identity to communalism in North India, 1870-1940". Ph.D. dissertation, University of California, Berkeley, 1980.

651. Frere, Mary "Old deccan days". London, John Murrey, 1868.

652. Friend-Pereira J. E. "Marriage customs of Khonds". *JASB*, Vol. 70, No. 3, 1902. pp. 18-28.

653. Friend-Pereira J. E. "Totemism among the Khonds". *JASB*, Vol. 72, No. 3, 1904, pp. 39-56.

654. Fruzzetti, Lina and Ostor, A□kos "Kinship and ritual in Bengal: anthropological essays". New Delhi, South Asian Publishers, 1984, x, 244 p ; 23 cm.

655. Fruzzetti, Lina "The gift of a virgin: women, marriage, and ritual in a Bengali society". New Brunswick, N.J. : Rutgers University Press, 1982, xi, 178 p : ill. ; 24 cm.

656. Fuchas, Mother "Fairs and festivals of Bengal". Folklore, Vol. 17, No. 10, 1975, pp. 333-361.

657. Fuchas, Mother "Bengali customs and traditions". *Folklore*, Vol. 17, No. 9, 1975 (September), pp. 293-327.

658. Fuchs, S. "The marriage rites of the Bhils". *Anthropos*, Vol. 46, 1951.

659. Fuller, C. J. "The 'Vinayaka Chaturthi' festival and hindutva in Tamil Nadu". *Economic and Political Weekly*, Vol. 36, No. 19, 2001, pp. 1607-1616.

660. Fuller, C. J. "The renovation ritual in a South Indian temple: The 1995 Kumbhābhīeka in the Mīnākī Temple, Madurai". *Bulletin of the School of Oriental and African Studies, University of London*, Vol. 67, No. 1 (2004), pp. 40-63.

661. Fuller, Christopher "The camphor flame: Popular Hinduism and society in India". Princeton: Princeton University Press. 1992.

662. Fuller, Jason "Re-membereing the tradition: Bhaktivinoda Thakura's Sajjantosani and the construction of a middle class Vaisnava sampradaya in 19th centuary Bengal". In, 'Hinduism in publis and private: reform, hindutva, gender and sampradaya', Edited by Anthony Copley, Oxford, Oxford University Press, 2003, pp. 173-210.

663. Fuller, Mary "Nag-Panchami." *Man in India* Vol. 24 (June). 1944, pp. 75-81.

664. Fuller, Mary "The naming of names' in Indian folk belief. *Asian Folklore Studies*, Vol. 24, No. 1, 1965, pp. 63-79.

665. Funso, Aiyejina and Rawle, Gibbons "Orisa (Orisha) tradition in Trinidad". *Caribbean Quarterly*, Vol. 45, No. 4 (December 1999), pp. 35-50.

666. Furer-Haimendorf, Christoph von "Beliefs are concerning human sacrifice among the Hill Reddis". MII No. 24, 1944. pp. 15-41.

667. Furer-Haimendorf, Christoph von "The naked Nagas [microform]". London, Methuen & Co., 1939. xvi, 243 p. : ill., map ; 22 cm.

668. Gabriella Eichinger Ferro-Luzzi "Hindu rites in modern Tamil literature". *Anthropos*, Vol. 98, No. 2, 2003, pp. 361-377.

669. Gadgil, D. P., "Bhojonavidhi: a living custom as reflected in Ayurvedic treatises". In, Proceedings of the national seminar on 'Living customs and their ancient Indian

sources', Edited by V.N. Jha, Pune, Centre of Advanced Study in Sanskrit, University of Poona, 1991, pp. 214-217.

670. Gai, Moti Lal, "Mandi ka Lohadi". *Himprasta*, Vol. 16, No. 11., Feb. 1971, pp. 35-38. [Pahari language]

671. Gai, Moti Lal, "Mela kutha". *Himprasta*, Vol. 16, No. 2, May 1970, pp. 39-41. [Pahari language]

672. Gai, Moti Lal. "Mandi ka Shar tohar". *Himprasta*, Vol. 18, No.7, Oct. 1977. [Pahari language]

673. Galbraith, Catherine Atwater and Mehta, Rama "India: now and through time". New York, Dodd, Mead, 1971, 320 p. illus. 23 cm.

674. Ganambal, L. "Festivals of India", Calcutta. Anthropological Survey of India. 1967.

675. Ganapathy, B. D. "Kodavas their customs and culture". Mysore: B.D. Ganapathy, 1967. p. 224.

676. Gandhi, Raj, S. "Sati as altruistic Suicide in India". Jaipur: Publication Scheme, 1989.

677. Ganeri, Anita "Hindu festivals throughout the year". North Mankato, MN: Smart Apple Media, 2004, 30 p: Col. ill. ; 28 cm.

678. Ganeri, Anita "Journey's end: death and mourning". London, Evans Bros., 1998, 30 p : ill. ; 28 cm.

679. Ganeri, Anita "New beginnings: celebrating birth". New York, Peter Bedrick Books, 1998, 30 p : ill. (some col.) ; 28 cm.

680. Ganesh, J. Sankar "Music rituals of Srinivasamangapuram". *Sangeet Natak*, Vol. 44, No. 4, 2010, pp. 35-46.

681. Ganguly, Swagata "Tarnetar fair: Let's go husband hunting". *Discover India*, Vol. 6, No. 8, 1993, pp. 70-73.

682. Ganodwale, Rahjesh "Paraya hota parampara ka saaj". *Kala Samay*, 2010 (Aug-Sept), pp. 18-20. [Hindi]

683. Gardner, D. S. "Performativity in ritual: The mianmin case". *Man*, Vol. 18, No. 2, 1983 (June), pp. 346-360.

684. Garg, Shivdat. "Himachal pradesh ka ek pramparik purav: Kullu dasahara". *Giriraj*, Vol. 1, No. 52, Sept. 1979, p. 5.

685. Gathering Hopewell "Society, ritual, and ritual interaction". New York, Springer, 2006. xxi, p. 807 : ill.

686. Gaur, Meena "Sati and social reforms in India". Jaipur: Publication Scheme, 1989.

687. Gaurhari Sarma, Hanjabam "Sradha paddhati". [Religious rituals after death]. Imphal: State Press, 1930. 60 p. ; 18 cm. [Manipuri]

688. Gaurhari Sarma, Hanjabam "Vesasraya bidhi". [Rituals regarding Sannyas dharma]. Imphal: Krsnamani Sarma, 1952. 55 p. ; 18 cm. [Manipuri]

689. Gautam, Chamanlal "Vrat aur tyohar". Bareilly, Sanskrit Samsthan, 1975. [Hindi]

690. Gawankar, Gauri "Koli festival among the Kolies". *Vanyajati*, Vol. 3, No. 4, 1955, pp. 172-174.

691. Gennep, Arnold van "The Rites of passage, trans. by M.B. Veyedom and G.L. Chafee, London: Routledge, 1960.

692. George F. Mclean "Traditional and contemporary life: Hormeneufica of perennial wisdom and social change". Radhakrishnan Inst. for Advanced Study in Philosophy, 1986

693. George, Anita "The ritual of bathing". *Inside Outside*, No. 128, 1995, pp. 190-193.

694. Ghai, Moti "Lal Mandi ri lohri". *Himbharti*, Vol. 29, No. 109, 1997, pp. 63-67. [Hindi]

695. Ghatak, N. K. and Mukherjee, D. P. "Baruni: a folk festival of Thakurnagar: organised by the Namasudra community for onward movement". *Folklore*, Vol. 27, No. 11, 1986, pp. 241-247.

696. Ghate, V. S. "Plants in Patra Pooja: notes on their identity and utilization". *Ethnobotany*, Vol. 10, 1998, pp. 6-15.

697. Ghosh, Abhik and Sinha, Kishore "The Charak festival in India: A review and a case study from Delhi". *The Anthropologist,* Vol. 3, No. 4, 2001, pp. 231-246.

698. Ghosh, Dipali "Post-funeral ritual in a Dimasa Kachari village". *Man in India*. Vol. 44, No. 3. July-September 1964, pp. 247-251.

699. Ghosh, Leila and Roys, Daha "Festivals of India". India Book House, Spain prints Pvt. Ltd. Mumbai, 1986

700. Ghosh, S. L. "Urban morals in ancient India [microform]". 1st ed. Calcutta, Susil Gupta, 1944. vii, 71 p. ; 18 cm.

701. Ghosh, Swati "Creating New Myths: Post - Puja Reflections". *Economic and Political Weekly*, Vol. 35, No. 3, 2000, pp. 94-96.

702. Ghosha, Pratapachandra "Dugra Puja: with notes and illustration". Calcutta, The Hindoo Patriot Press, 1871.

703. Ghosha, Pratapachandra "The vāstu yāga and its bearing upon tree and serpent worship in India." *Journal of the Asiatic Society of Bengal*, Vol. 39, No. 164 (Part 1, No. 3), 1870, pp. 199-232.

704. Ghosha, Sisirakumara "Pictures of Indian life [microform]". Foreword by Rash Behary Ghose, Madras, Ganesh & Co., Madras, 1917. viii. 267 p. : ill. ; 18 cm.

705. Ghoshal, Subhas C. "A brief survey on the festivals of Nalkantha area of Gujarat". *Vanyajati*, Vol. 31, No. 1, 1983, pp. 21-26.

706. Ghulam Dastgir Rashid "Islami taqarib". [Essays on Islamic festivals]. Hyderabad (Dn.): Idara-i-shaat Islamiyat, 1945, 332 p. ; 18 cm. [In: Urdu]

707. Gidwani, Asha G. "Marriage, Dowry system and their implications". *Dowry Custom (Vivekananda Kendra Patrika, Madras)* Vol. 2. No. 2. 1973, pp. 127-130.

708. Gilbert, William Harlen "Peoples of India". (Series : War background studies, no. 18.; Publication Smithsonian Institution, 3767.), City of Washington, Smithsonian Institution, 1944, iv, 86 p., 21 p. of plates : ill., maps (1 folded) ; 23 cm.

709. Gill, Harjit singh "A phulkari from Bhatinda". New Delhi, Department of Anthropological Linguistics. Punjabi University Patiala. 1977.

710. Gill, Kamal "Vist India Year 1991: Sportlight on culture". *Discover India*, Vol. 4, No. 4, 1991, pp. 40-45.

711. Gleach, Frederic W. "The ritual world of Pocahontas". *Natural History*, Vol. 115, No. 9, 2006 (November), pp. 40-46.

712. Gluckman, Max. (ed.) "Essays on the ritual of social relations". Manchester: University Press. 1962.

713. Gnanambal, K. "Festivals on an all India basis". In, 'Festivals in Indian Society', 2 Vols., Ed. Usha Sharma, A Mittal Publication, New Delhi, pp. 65-84.

714. Gnanambal, K. "Festival of India". Calcutta, Anthropological Survey of India. p. 104.

715. Gnanambal, K. "The funeral customs of the Urali". *Bulletin of the Department of Anthropology*, Vol. 4, No. 1, 1955, pp. 29-40.

716. Godden, Jon & Godden, Rumer "Two under the Indian sun". New York, Knopf, 1966, x, 240 p. ; 22 cm.

717. Gode, P.K. "Some notes on the history of Diwali festival" *Annals of the Bhandarkar Oriental Research Institute*, Poona, Vol. 26. 1986.

718. Gogoi, P. & Borthakur, S. K. "Plants in religious cultural beliefs of the Kahamtis of Assam (India)". *Ethnobotany*, Vol. 3, 1991, pp. 89-93.

719. Gogoi, Padmeswar "Tai-Ahom religion and customs". Assam: Publication Board, 1976. p. 117.

720. Gold, Ann Grodzins "Fruitful journeys: The ways of Rajasthani pilgrims". Prospect Heights, IL: Waveland Press, 2000.

721. Gold, Ann Grodzins and Bhoju Ram Gujar "In the time of trees and sorrows: nature, power, and memory in Rajasthan". Durham, NC, Duke University Press, 2002.

722. Gold, Ann Grodzins. "Spirit possession perceived and performed in rural Rajasthan". *Contributions to Indian sociology,* Vol. 22, No. 1, 1988, pp. 35-63.

723. Gombrich, Richard F. (Ed.) "Oxford University papers on India. Vol. 2, pt. 1: Indian ritual and its exegesis". Delhi, Oxford University Press, 1988.

724. Gonda, Jan "Change and continuity in Indian religion". New Delhi, Munshiram Manoharlal, 1985.

725. Gonda, Jan "The Aghara ritual of Vaikhanasas". Torina, Idologica Taurinesia, 1981.

726. Gonda, Jan "Vedic ritual: the non-Solemn rites". Leiden-Koln, E.J. Brill, 1980.

727. Gonda, Jan "The ritual sutras". Wiesbaden, Otto Harrassowitz, 1977.

728. Gonda, Jan "Visnuism and Sivaism: a comparison". New Delhi, Munshiram Manoharlal, 1976.

729. Gondal, Ram Pratap "Changes in customs and practices among some lower agricultural castes of the of the Kotah state". *The Eastern Anthropologist*, Vol. 1, No. 4, 1948, pp. 21-28.

730. Good, Anthony "The female bridegroom: a comparative study of life-crisis rituals in South India and Sri Lanka". Oxford, Clarendon Press; New York, Oxford University Press, 1991, xii, 281 p.: ill. ; 23 cm.

731. Gopalakrishnan, M. S. "Mother Goddess and snake worship." *Journal of the Madras University,* Vol. 1, No. 1-2, 1974. pp. 53-56.

732. Gopalan, G. V. "The marriage ritual among the Nagar Brahmins of Gujarat". *Folklore*, Vol. 21, No. 2, 1980 (Feburary), pp. 29-36.

733. Gopalapilla, En. "Lokaranjanam [microform]". Tiruvanantapuram Gopakumar Braders, 1938. vi, 48 p. ; 18 cm. [In: Malayalam]

734. Gordon, Helen Cameron "Hindu life and customs". New Delhi, Mittal Publications, 2000. p. 220.

735. Goslinga, Gillian Marie "The ethnography of a South Indian God: virgin birth, spirit possession, and the prose of the modern world". Ph.D. diss., University of California at Santa Cruz. 2006.

736. Goswami, M. C. and Kamkhenthang, H. "Ritual experts (Siampi) in Paite society". *Bulletin of the Department of Anthropology,* Vol. 5, 1976, pp. 48-69.

737. Goswami, P. "Assamese marriage customs: Pre-nuptial". *The Eastern Anthropologist*, Vol. 4, No. 3-4, 1951, pp. 133-149.

738. Goswami, Satyanarondra Narayan "Snake worship: Goddess Manasā cult in Assam." *Journal of the Assam Research Society* Vol. 25, No.1979–1980, 1979, pp. 26-31.

739. Gotam, Pramlata. "Baadiya ra mela". *Himbharti*, Vol. 9, No. 35, Sept. 1977, pp. 61-63. [Pahari Language]

740. Gough, E. Katheleen. "Female initiation rites on the Malabar coast (Curl Bequest prize essay for 1953). *Journal of Royal Anthropological Institute,* Vol. 85, 1955, pp. 45-80.

741. Gould, Harold, "The Hindu Jajmani system: A case of economic particularism". *Southwestern Journal of Anthropology*, Vol. 14, 1958, pp. 428-437.

742. Gould, Harold. "The Jajmani system of North India: Its structure, magnitude and meaning". *Ethnology,* Vol. 3, 1964, pp. 297-300.

743. Goudriaan, Teun (Ed.) "Ritual and speculation in early Tantrism: studies in honour of Andre Padoux". Albany, State Uiversity of New York Press, 1992.

744. Goudriaan, Teun "Vaikhanasa daily worship: according to the handbook of Atri, Bhrgu, Kashyapa, and Marici". *Indo-Iranian Journal*, Vol. 12, 1970, pp. 161-215.

745. Govardhan, Singh. "Himachal ka pahari Jubal: Beshakhi ke mela mein nacati talvar". *Dharmayug*, Vol.14, no.16, April 21, 1963, pp. 10-11. [Hindi]

746. Gover, Geoffrey "Oracles and dreams among the Lepchas". In, 'Internatioanal encyclopaedia of tribal religion' Vol. 9. Edited by S.M. Channa, New Delhi, Cosmo Publications, 2000, pp. 139-148.

747. Govinda Samanta Raya, Kavibhusana "Surisarvasvam". [Manual of Brahmanic rituals]. Calcutta, Asiatic Society of Bengal, 1912-1914. 288 p. ; 23 cm. [In: Sanskrit]

748. Gowdra, G.K. "Ritual circles in a Mysore village". *Sociological Bulletin*, Vol. 20, No. 1, 1971, pp. 24-38.

749. Goyal, Kuntal "Sarguja: Aadivaasiyon ke Vrat aur tyohar". *Vanyajati*, Vol. 24, No. 4, 1976 (October), pp. 01-04. [Hindi]

750. Granoff, P. "Other people's rituals: ritual eclecticism in early medieval Indian religious". *Journal of Indian Philosophy,* Vol. 28, No. 4, 2000 (August), pp. 399-424.

751. Granoff, Phyllis "My rituals and my gods: Ritual exclusiveness in medieval India". *Journal of Indian Philosophy,* Vol. 29, No. 1-2, 2001 (April), pp. 109-134.

752. Grunebaum, G. E. von "Muhammadan festivals". London: Curzon Press, 1976. viii, p. 107.

753. Gubil, L. N. "The Dasara at Mysore". In, 'Festivals in Indian Society', 2 Vols., Ed. Usha Sharma, A Mittal Publication, New Delhi, pp. 171-174.

754. Guha, Anima "Kherai- the national festival of the Boro - Kachari". *Journal of Indian Anthropological Society*, Vol. 23, No. 1, 1988, pp. 95-98.

755. Guile, Melanie "Culture in India". Chicago : Raintree, 2005, 32 p. : chiefly Col. Ill., Map ; 28 cm.

756. Guinee, William "Suffering and healing in Trinidadian Kali worship ". Ph.D. diss., Indiana University. 1992.

757. Gujarat. Superintendent of Census Operations "Census of India 1961: Gujarat Fairs and Festivals". Vol.v, pt.VI-B. Delhi, Manager of Publication, 1965. vi, p. 292. : plates.

758. Gujarat. Superintendent of Census Operations "Census of India 1961: Gujarat Fairs and Festivals". Vol. v, pt. VII-B. Delhi, Manager of Publications, 1965. xix, p. 630 : plates.

759. Gunsai, Suman Singh, Bangwal, K. K. and Nayal, Rakesh "Uttarakhand ki Jaad Bhotia Janjati me 'Losar tyohar' ka mahatwa". *Vanyajati*, Vol. 55, No. 4, 2007 (October), pp. 44-47. [Hindi]

760. Gupt, Laxminarayan "Akti parv". *Chomasa*, Vol. 15, No. 47, 1998, pp. 64-67. [Hindi]

761. Gupt, Narmada "Samaj Nirman aur Lolkotswa". *Chomasa*, Vol. 14, No. 44, 1997, pp. 08-13. [Hindi]

762. Gupta, Ayodhya Prasad "Bundelkhand me Fago ke vividh roop". *Chomasa*, Vol. 19, No. 58, 2002, pp. 75-78. [Hindi]

763. Gupta, B. A. "Hindu holidays and ceremonies". Calcutta, 1916.

764. Gupta, Brij Mohan "Ritual and belief of Jaunsaris". *Vanyajati*, Vol. 5, No. 2, 1957 (April), pp. 70-73.

765. Gupta, Charu S. "Ganjifas, the tradition of gambling in India". *Discover India*, Vol. 11, No. 10, 1998, 62-64.

766. Gupta, Giri Raj "Family and social changes in India". Vikas Publishing House Pvt. Ltd. New Delhi (1976).

767. Gupta, Giri Raj "Religiosity, economy and patterns of Hindu marriage in India". *International Journal of Sociology of the Family,* Vol. 2, 1972. pp. 43-53.

768. Gupta, Gupteshwar Prasad "Bundeli sanskriti ka prateek Mamuliya". *Chomasa*, Vol. 11, No. 36, 1995, pp. 117-121. [Hindi]

769. Gupta, Latika "Ritual and routine objects". *Art India*, Vol. 11, No. 4, 2006, pp. 107-108.

770. Gupta, Narmada Prasad "Diwari Mahotsav". *Chaumasa*, Vol. 12, No. 37, 1995, pp. 31-34. [Hindi]

771. Gupta, S. P. "Disposal of the dead and physical types in ancient India". Delhi, [s.n.] 1972.

772. Gupta, S. S. "Tree symbol worship in India". Calcutta, [s.n.], 1965.

773. Gupta, Sanjukata "The Mandala s an image of man". In, Oxford paper of India Vol. 2, Pt. 1: Indian ritual and its exegesis', Edited by Richard F. Gombrich, Delhi, Oxford University Press, 1988, pp. 32-41.

774. Gupta, Sanjukta "Women in the Saiva/Sakta ethos". In, 'Roles and rituals for Hindu women', Edited by Julia Leslie, London, Pinter, 1991, pp. 195-209.

775. Gupta, Shakti M. "Festivals, fairs and fasts of India". New Delhi, Clarion Books, 1991, 228 p. : Col. ill. p.

776. Gupta, Sudha "Akhti". *Chomasa*, Vol. 10, No. 33, 1994, pp. 38-41. [Hindi]

777. Gupta, Sudha "Balikaon ka parv 'Suata". *Chomasa*, Vol. 9, No. 29, 1992, pp. 37-44. [Hindi]

778. Gupta, Sudha "Bundeli Lokotsava Mamulia". *Chomas*, Vol. 11, No. 36, 1995, pp. 122-124 [Hindi]

779. Gupte, B. A. "Harvest festivals in honour of Gauri and Ganesh". In, 'Festivals in Indian Society', 2 Vols., Ed. Usha Sharma, A Mittal Publication, New Delhi, pp.153-160

780. Gupte, B. A. "Hindu holidays and ceremonials with dissertations on origin, folklore, and symbols [microform]". 2nd ed. rev. Calcutta, Thacker, Spink & Co., 1919. lii, 285 p. : ill. (Some col.) ; 21 cm.

781. Gupte, B. A. "Hindu holidays and ceremonies with dissertations on origin, folklore and symbols". New Delhi: Asian Educational Services. 1994.

782. Gupte, B. A., and Rai Bahadur "Hindu holidays and ceremonials". Calcutta, Thacker, Spink & Co. 1919.

783. Gurmeet and Thukral, Elizabeth "Of faith and sacrifies: The village of Devi Dhura". *The India Magazine*, Vol. 4, No. 7, 1984, pp. 62-69.

784. Gurumurthy, K. G. "Eclipse ritual in South India." In, Through the Vistas of Life and Lore: Folkloric Reflections on Traditional India, ed. R.M. Sarkar, Calcutta: Punthi Pustak. 2000. 153-64.

785. Gurumurthy, K. G. "Eclipse ritual in south India". *Man in India,* Vol. 61, No. 4, 1981 (December), pp. 246-355.

786. Guy R. Welbon; Glenn E. Yocum "Religious festivals in South India and Sri Lanka". *History of Religions,* Vol. 25, No. 3 (Feb., 1986), pp. 284-288.

787. Hagen, Kurtis "The propriety of Confucius: A sense of ritual". *Asian Philosophy*, Vol. 20, No. 1, 2010 (March), pp. 1-25.

788. Hajarika, Ganescandra "Bihu aru tar prakrtik citra". [On Bihu, the festival of Assam, and its natural background]. Calcutta, Upendranath Das, 1918. ix, 41 p. ; 18 cm. [Assamese]

789. Hajra, R.C. "Studies in Puranic records on Hindu rites and customs". Dacca, Dacca University, 1940.

790. Hakim, Roxanne "Changing religion and ritual in a Vasava Bhil community impacted by involuntary resettlement". *The Eastern Anthropologist*, Vol. 56, No. 2-4, 2003 (April-Dec.), pp. 271-309.

791. Hallegua, Samuel H. "The marriage customs of the Jewish community of Cochin". *Marg*, Vol. 54, No. 2, 2002, pp. 9-16.

792. Hamlal, Dhaniram. "Chamba ki Lohadi". *Himprasta*, Vol. 13, No. 10, Jan. 1969, pp. 38-43. [Pahari Language]

793. Hanchett, Suzanne Lorraine "Changing economic, social and ritual relationships in a modern South Indian village". A Ph.D. thesis submitten in Columbia University, Columbia 1970.

794. Hanchett, Suzanne, "Coloured rice, symbolic structure in Hindu family festivals". Delhi: Hindustan Publishing Crop. 1988.

795. Hancock, Mary Elizabeth "Womanhood in the making: domestic ritual and public culture in urban South India". Boulder, Westview Press, 1999, xv, 286 p. : ill. map ; 24 cm.

796. Hancock, Mary Elizabeth "Women at work: ritual and cultural identity among Smarta Brahmans of Madras". Ph.D. diss., University of Pennsylvania, 1990.

797. Handa, O. C. "Festivals, fairs and customs of the Himachal Pradesh". Edited by Main Goverdhan Singh, Indus Publishing Company, New Delhi, 1992.

798. Handa, Om Chanda. "Pahado mein Shivratri". *Himprasta*, Vol. 18, No.12, March 1973, pp. 38-43. [Pahari Language].

799. Hansen, Kathryn "Ritual enactments in Hindi Mythological': Betab's Mahabharat in Parsi theatre". *Economic and Political Weekly*, Vol. 41, No. 48, 2006(December), pp. 4985-4991.

800. Haque, Enamul "The Manasā images of Bengal." *Bangladesh Lalit Kalā,* Vol. 1, No. 2, 1975, pp. 135-44.

801. Harcourt, A. F. P. "Himalayan district of Kooloo, Lahul and Spiti". London, 1871, pp. 381.

802. Hardenberg, Roland "Visu's sleep mahisa's attack. Durga's victory: Conceptss of royalty in a sacrificial drama" *Journal of Social Sciences*, Vol. 4, No. 4, 2000, pp. 261-276.

803. Hardenberg, Roland "Ritual representation of political change: The case of the Puri king". *Journal of Indian Anthropological Society,* Vol. 33, No. 1, 1998 (March), pp. 87-104.

804. Hardgrave, Robert "When stars displace the gods: The folk culture of cinema in Tamil Nadu". [Austin]: Center for Asian Studies, University of Texas. 1975.

805. Hardiman D. "The coming of the Devi: Adivasi assertion in Western India". Oxford University Press, Delhi. 1987.

806. Hardwarewala, A. H. "Bhil Janjati ke samajik sanrachna evam unke riti rivaj". *Vanyajati*, Vol. 46, No. 3, 1998 (July), pp. 06-08. [Hindi]

807. Hariharan, Jayasree "Eclipses in Hindu life and thought". Madras, The Kuppuswami Sastri Research Institute. 1995.

808. Harlan, Lindsey and Paul B. Courtright, (eds.) "From the margins of Hindu marriage: Essays on gender, religion, and culture". New York, Oxford University Press. 1995.

809. Harman, William P. "Negotiating relationships with the Goddess." In, 'Dealing with Deities: The Ritual Vow in South Asia', eds. Selva J. Raj and William P. Harman, Albany: State University of New York Press. 2006. pp. 25-41.

810. Harman, William P. "Taming the fever Goddess: transforming a tradition in Southern India". *Manushi*, No. 140 (January–February) 2004, pp. 2-13.

811. Harman, William P. "The sacred marriage of the Hindu Goddess". Delhi: Motilal Banarsidass. 1992. p. 567.

812. Harman, William Pulliamthe "Sacred marriage of Maturai: myth, ritual, and devotion in a South Indian temple". The University of Chicago, (T-27943). 1981.

813. Harmon, William "The sacred marriage of a hindu goddness". Bloomington, Indiana University Press. 1989.

814. Harold A. Gould "A Jajmani system of North India: Its structure, magnitude, and meaning". *Ethnology*, Vol. 3, No. 1 (Jan., 1964), pp. 12-41.

815. Harper, Edward, R. "Ritual pollulation as a integrator of caste and religion". *The Journal of Asia Studies* 2, 1964, pp. 151-197.

816. Harper, Katherine "Seven Hindu Goddesses of spritual transformation: the iconography of the Saptamatrikas". Lewiston, NY, Edwin Mellon Press, 1979.

817. Harper, Katherine and Brown, Robert "The roots of tantra". Albany, State University of New York Press, 2002.

818. Harrer, Heinrich "Ladakh: Gods and mortals behind the Himalaya". New Delhi, Himalayan Books, 1988.

819. Harris, Marvin "The cultural ecology of India's sacred cattle". *Current Anthropology*, Vol. 7, No. 1. 1966.

820. Hart, George L. "Sati Just a form of human sacrifice". Statesman, March 29, 1988.

821. Hart, George L. "Women and the sacred in ancient Tamil Nadu." *Journal of Asian Studies*, Vol. 32, No. 2, 1973, pp. 233-50.

822. Hartland, E. S. "Death and disposal of dead: Introduction and primitive". *ERE*, Vol. 4, 1971.

823. Hawley, John Stration. "Afterword: the mysteries and communities of Sati". In, 'Sati: The blessing and the curse,

The burning of wives in India', Edited by John Stratton Hawley, Oxford University Press, New York, 1994, pp. 175-186

824. Hawley, John Stratlon (ed.) "The Blessing and the curse, the burning of wives in India". New York, Oxford University Press, 1994.

825. Hawley, John Stratton, (ed.) "Sati: The blessing and the curse". New York, Oxford University Press. 1994.

826. Haxlehurst, L. "Ceremony and social structure in 19th centuary Punjab". *Economic and Political Weekly*, Vol. 11, No. 35, 28 Aug. 1976, pp. 1430-35.

827. Hay, Stephen, ed. "Source of Indian tradition". Vol. 2. New York, Columbia University Press, 1988

828. Hazra, Amit, S. K. Paul and Kakali Mitra "Santal rituals and Agro-ecosystem". *Bulletin of the Cultural Research Institute*, Vol. 19, No. 1, 1997. pp. 64-67.

829. Heather Elgood "Exploring the roots of village Hinduism in South Asia". *World Archaeology*, Vol. 36, No. 3, The Archaeology of Hinduism (Sep., 2004), pp. 326-342.

830. Heesterman, J. C. "Tradition in modern India". Bijdragen tot de Taal-, Land- en Volkenkunde, Deel 119, 3de Afl., *Anthropologica*, Vol. 5, 1963, pp. 237-253.

831. Heesterman, J. C. "The broken world of sacrifice: an essay in ancient indian ritual". London: The University of Chicago Press, 1993. x, p. 296.

832. Heesterman, J.C. "The case of the severed head." *Wiener Zeitschrift fur die Kunde Sud-und Ostasiens und Archiv fur indische Philosophie* Vol. 11, 1967, pp. 22-43.

833. Heiderer, Tony "Sacred space, sacred time: India's Maha Kumbh Mela draws millions *National Geographic*, Vol. 177, No. 5, 1990, pp. 106-117.

834. Hein, Morvin. "The miracle plays of Mathura". New Haven, Yale University Press, 1972.

835. Henderson, Carol E. "Culture and customs of India". (Culture and customs of Asia.), Westport, Conn. : Greenwood Press, 2002, 1 online resource (xxv, p. 210) : ill., map.

836. Henry Orenste "Death and kinship in Hinduism: structural and functional Interpretations". in *American Anthropologist,* New Series, Vol. 72, No. 6 (Dec., 1970), pp. 1357-1377.

837. Hichinson, Walter, "Customs of the world: A popular account of the manners, rites and ceremonies of man and women in all countries". 2 Vols, Concept, 1990.

838. Hickey, William. "The Tanjore Mahratta Principality in Southern India; The Land of the Chola the Eden of the South". New Delhi: J. Jetley for Asian Educational Service, 1873.

839. Hillebrandt, A. "Death and disposal of dead: Hindu". *ERE*, Vol. 4, 1971.

840. Himachal Pradesh, Directorate of Tourism. "Kulu Dussehra". Simla, Tourism Department, H.P. N.D. pp. 8.

841. Himachal Pradesh. Superintendent of Census Operations "Census of India 1961: "Himachal Pradesh-fairs and festivals". Vol. V, pt. VII - B. Delhi, Manager of Publications, 1967. p. 437 : plates.

842. Hobsbawm, E. J. & Ranger, T. O. "The Invention of tradition". Cambridge ; New York : Cambridge University Press, 1992, vi, 322 p. ; 22 cm.

843. Hodon, T. C. "Some Naga customs and superstitions". *Folklore*, Vol. 21, 1910, pp. 296-312.

844. Hodson, T. C. "Tree marriage." In, 'Through the Vistas of Life and Lore: Folkloric Reflections on Traditional India', ed. R.M. Sarkar, Calcutta: Punthi Pustak. 2000. pp. 527-44.

845. Hoens, Dirk Jan. "Mantra and other constituents of Tantric practice". In, Hindu Tantrism, ed. Sanjukta Gupta,

Dirk Jan Hoens and Teun Goudriaan. Leiden: E.J. Brill, 1979.

846. Houben, Jan E. M. "The ritual pragmatics of a Vedic Hymn: The "Riddle Hymn" and the Pravargya Ritual". *Journal of the American Oriental Society*, Vol. 120, No. 4, (Oct. - Dec.), 2000, pp. 499-536.

847. Housden, Roger "Travels through sacred India". London, San Francisco, Calif., Thorsons, 1996, xix, 316 p. : ill. ; 20 cm.

848. Hubert, Henri, and Marcel, Mauss, "Sacrifice: Its nature and function". Chicago: University of Chicago Press, 1964.

849. Hudson, D. Dennis "Violent and fanatical devotion among the Nāyanārs: A study in the Periya Purāam of Cēkkilār." In, 'Criminal Gods and Demon Devotees: Essays on the Guardians of Popular Hinduism', ed. Alf Hiltebeitel, Albany: State University of New York Press, 1989. pp. 373-404.

850. Hughes, Monica "My Divali". (Series: Festivals (Raintree Publishers), Chicago, IL : Raintree, 2004, 24 p.: col. ill. ; 23 cm.

851. Hugo, Victor "Phransana jagavikhyata navalakathakara Viktara Hyugoni amara krti La mijharebala [microform]". Gujaratimam utaranara, Mulasankara Mo. Bhatta. 2. Avrtti. Bhavanagara: Samskara Sahitya Mandira, 1953-1956. 2 v. ; 19 cm. In: Gujarati.

852. Humphrey, Caroline & Laidlaw, James "The archetypal actions of ritual: a theory of ritual illustrated by the Jain rite of worship". Oxford, Clarendon Press, New York, Oxford University Press, 1994, x, 293 p. : ill. ; 22 cm.

853. Hunter, W. W. "The annals of rural Bengal". Delhi: Cosmo Publication, 1975.

854. Hutchinson, H. N. "Marriage customs of the world". New Delhi: Classical Publications, 1978, v, p. 348.

855. Hutchinson, H. N. "Marriage rites, customs and ceremonies of the World". New Delhi: Logos press, 2009. p. 349.

856. Hutten, C. "Dreams and omens among the Nagas". In, 'Internatioanal encyclopaedia of tribal religion' Vol. 9. Edited by S. M. Channa, New Delhi, Cosmo Publications, 2000, pp. 23-32.

857. Hutton, J. H. "The significance of head-hunting in Assam". In, 'Internatioanal encyclopaedia of tribal religion' Vol. 1. Edited by S. M. Channa, New Delhi, Cosmo Publications, 2000, pp. 119-136.

858. Huyler, Stephen P. "Painted prayers: women's art in village India". New York : Rizzoli, 1994, 203 p. : Col. Ill., Maps ; 30 cm.

859. Ikramullah, Shaista Suhrawardy "Ceremonies customs and colour: behind the veil". Oxford: Oxford University press, 1992. xxvii, p. 191 : ill. p.

860. Inamdar, V. B., "Customs relating to the selection of Bride in Maharashtra and their Ancient Sources". In, Proceedings of the national seminar on 'Living customs and their ancient Indian sources', Edited by V. N. Jha, Pune, Centre of Advanced Study in Sanskrit, University of Poona, 1991, pp.72-83.

861. Inamdar, Vijalakshmi, Chimmad, Bharati and Naik, Rama "Nutrient composition of traditional festival foods of North Karnataka". *Journal of Human Ecology*, Vol. 18, No. 1, 2005, pp. 43-48.

862. Inamdar, Vijalaxmi and Chimmad, Bharati V. "Traditional festive cuisine of North Karnataka". *Journal of Human Ecology,* Vol. 17, No. 3, 2005, pp. 233-236.

863. India. Dept. of Tourism "Festivals of India". New Delhi, Publications Division, Ministry of Information and Broadcasting, 1960, 44.

864. India. Office of the Registrar General "Census of India 1961: India-study of customary rights and living and

working conditions of scavengers in two towns". Vol. 1, pt. xi-D / Office of the Registrar General. Delhi: Manager of Publications, 1966. p. 58.

865. India. Office of the Registrar General "Census of India 1961: Kerala-Onam a festival of Kerala". Vol. 1, pt. vii-B.— Delhi: Manager of Publications, 1966 ix, p. 51 : plates p.

866. India. Office of the Registrar General Census of India 1961: India-Ugadi the New Year's festival of Andhra Pradesh, Vol. 1, pt. vii-B. Delhi, Manager of Publications, 1971. 59 p.

867. Ingalls, Daniel "The Brahmin tradition". *Journal of American folklore* 71, July-Sept. 1958, pp. 1-9. Also in, 'Traditional India: Structure and change', Edited by Milton Singer, Jaipur, Rawat Publication, 1975.

868. Ingalls, Daniel H. H. "Dharma and Moksa". *Philosophy East and West,* Vol. 7, No. 1-2, 1957, pp. 41-48.

869. Irani, Threety "Navroze". *Our Cultural Fabric*, 1977, pp. 40-45.

870. Irwin, John "Asokan Pillars: a reassessment of the evidence". Part 5, Symbolism, Burmington Magazine, Vol. C XVIII, Nov. 1976.

871. Irwin, John C. "The sacred anthill and the cult of the Primordial Mound." *History of Religions*, Vol. 21, No. 4, 1982. pp. 339-360.

872. Isabelle Clark-Decès "How Dalits have changed the mood at Hindu funerals: A view from South India". *International Journal of Hindu Studies*,.Vol. 10, No. 3, Dec., 2006, pp. 257-269.

873. Isar, R. F. "Culture and the arts festival of the twentieth century". *Cultures*, Vol. 3, No. 2, pp. 125-145.

874. Israel J. Ross "Ritual and music in South India: Syrian Christian Liturgical Music in Kerala". *Asian Music*, Vol. 11, No. 1 (1979), pp. 80-98.

875. Isvari, S. R. "Tîccanni". [Audio Recording] Madurai: Ramji Folk Songs esearch Centre. 1995. [Tamil]

876. Iyer, V. R. Krishna. "Sati: Political paralysis". *Illustrated Weekly of India,* November 8, 1987, pp. 26-27.

877. Jackson, Ken "The Ganesh festival". *Discover India*, Vol. 12, No. 9, 1999, 51-53.

878. Jacob, N. S. "Parenting children with visual impairments in rural south India: Exploring contexts of maternal beliefs and behavior". University of California, Berkeley). Pro Quest Dissertations and Theses, (2002). p. 186, Access online at, http://search.proquest.com/docview/251737699?accountid=43898.

879. Jacobi, H. "Death and disposal of dead: Jaina". *ERE*, Vol. 4, 1971.

880. Jacobsen, Peter Otto & Kristensen, Preben Sejer "A family in India". (Series: Families around the world (New York, N.Y.), New York : Bookwright Press, 1984, 32 p. : Col. Ill. ; 20 x 22 cm.

881. Jaer, Oyvind "Pilgrimage as a source of knowledge: The Kumbh mela of Prayag Raj 1989" *The Eastern Anthropologist,* Vol. 47, No. 1, 1994, pp. 15-38.

882. Jafa, Jyoti "Honouring lord Venkateshwara". *Discover India,* Vol. 8, No. 3, 1995.

883. Jafa, Jyoti "Mohurrum: Requiem to a martyr". *Discover India,* Vol. 8, No. 3, 1995, 74-75.

884. Jafar Sharif "Islam in India, or, the Qanun-i-Islam [microform]: the customs of the Musalmans of India)". Composed under the direction of, and translated by G.A. Herklots; new edition, revised and rearranged with additions by William Crooke. New York, Humphrey Milford; Oxford University Press, 1921. xl, 374 p. : ill. ; 18 cm.

885. Jagadguru, Kanchi Kamakoti, "Sacrifice dowry for Dharma". *Dowry Custom (Vivekananda Kendra Patrika, Madras)* Vol. 2. No. 2. 1973, pp. 166-167.

886. Jagadisa Ayyar, P. V. "South Indian festivities [microform]". With a foreword from F.W. Thomas. Madras: Higginbothams Ltd., 1921. vii, 202 p. : ill. ; 25 cm.

887. Jagadisha Singha "Sade rasama riwaja [microform]". Lahaura, Jagadisha Singha, 1937. x, 227 p. ; 19 cm. [Panjabi]

888. Jagat, Bandu. "Suskar-Kinnar kaa prasida tohar". *Himprasta*, Vol. 8, No. 2, May 1962, pp. 28-30. [Pahari Language]

889. Jagdalpuri Lal. "Bastar-Lok (Kala-Sanskriti Prasangha), Jagdalpur: Akrati Sansthan, 2003.

890. Jagdisa Ayyar, P.V. "South Indian festivities". Madras, Higginbothams & Co., 1921.

891. Jai Prabhakar, S. C. and Gangadhar, M. R. "Baluvu: a ritual among Kadu Kuruba tribe of Karnataka". *Stud Tribes Tribals*, Vol. 9, No, 2, 2011, pp. 129-132.

892. Jai, Hemangini V. "Dipa-Garbha to Rasa-Garba an enchanting evolution of a fascinating festival-Navaratri". In, Proceedings of the national seminar on 'Living customs and their ancient Indian sources', Edited by V. N. Jha, Pune, Centre of Advanced Study in Sanskrit, University of Poona, 1991, pp. 239-244.

893. Jain, Bhurchand "Dharmik sanskritik, etihasik evam naitik paramparaon ka prateek raksha bandhan parv". *Sanskriti*, Vol. 23, No. 1-2, 1981, p. 19. [Hindi]

894. Jain, J. M. "Co-existing in two cultures: Parental beliefs and childrens activities in an Indian immigrant community". University of Illinois at Chicago). Pro Quest Dissertations and Theses, 1999, p. 203, Access online at,

http://search.proquest.com/docview/304560258? accountid =43898

895. Jain, Jyotindra "Jaina iconography: the tirthankara in Jaina scriptures art and rituals". Netherlands: Leiden E.J. Brill, 1978. x, p. 34 : ill. p.

896. Jain, Jyotindra "Painted myths of creation: Art and rituals of an Indian tribe". New Delhi: Lalit Kala Akademi, 1984. p. 99.

897. Jain, Kajri. "Gods in the Bazaar: the economies of Indian calendar art". Durham & London: Duke University Press. 2007.

898. Jain, Madhu "Diwali: The legend and its celebration". *Indian Foreign Review*, Vol. 22, No. 1, 1984, pp. 20-23.

899. Jain, Minu, "Sati or Murder". *Sunday Observer*, January 18, 1988.

900. Jain, S. K. "Magico-religious beliefs about plants among the tribal of Bastar, Madhya Pradesh". *Quarterly Journal of Mythology and Society,* Vol. 54, No, 3, 1963, pp. 73-94.

901. Jain, S. K. "Some magico-religious beliefs about plants among Adibasis of Orissa". *Adibasi*, Vol. 12, 1971, pp. 39-44.

902. Jamal, Kahan Singh "Mela Jagara". *Somsi*, Vol. 2, No.1, Jan. 1976, pp. 82-85.

903. James Heitzman "Ritual polity and economy: The transactional network of an imperial temple in Medieval South India". *Journal of the Economic and Social History of the Orient,* Vol. 34, No. 1-2, 1991, pp. 23-54.

904. Jamison, Stephanie W. "The ravenous hyenas and the wounded sun: myth and ritual in ancient India". Ithaca and London, Cornell University Press, 1991.

905. Jamison, Stephanie W. "Sacrificed wife/ sacrificer's wife: women, ritual, and hospitality in ancient India". New York, Oxford University Press, 1996, xvi, 340 p. ; 24 cm.

906. Jamous, Raymond & Scott, Nora "Kinship and rituals among the Meo of Northern India: locating sibling relationship". (Series: French studies in South Asian culture and society.), New Delhi ; New York : Oxford University Press, 2003, xiv, 198 p. : ill., map ; 23 cm.

907. Janaki, S., Vasan, Jan and Rao, Ranga "The mad Madras season of 1999-2000: An update". *Sruti: South Indian Classical Music and Dance Magazine*, Issue No. 186, 2000, pp. 15-29.

908. Jash, Pranabananda "The cult of Manasā in Bengal." *Proceedings: Indian History Congress*, 1986. pp. 169-77.

909. Jasrotia, Ramesh "Aise manaee Jati he Chamba me Lohdi". *Somsi*, Vol. 11, No. 1, 1985. pp. 11-14. [Hindi]

910. Jasrotia, Ramesh "Saach Jaatar va Jukaru tyohar". *Somsi*, Vol. 15, No. 4, 1989, pp. 89-92. [Hindi]

911. Jasta, Hari Ram "Lavi Mela". *Himprasta*, Vol. 13, No.8, Nov. 1968, pp. 13-14.

912. Jasta, Hariram "Himachal ke riti-rivaaj". *Himprasth*, Vol. 17, No. 10, 1972, January, pp. 48-51. [Hindi]

913. Jaswal, Balak Ram "Sirmor ka prasidh Maghi tyohar". *Somsi*, Vol. 9, No. 2, 1983, pp. 77-79 [Hindi]

914. Jatia, Kailash "Shree Rani Satiji is our ancestor. We workship her as our family Goddess". Delhi: Rani Sati Temple, n.d.

915. Jayakar, Pupul "The earth mother: Legends, ritual art, and goddesses of India". Revised edition of the earthern drum: An introduction to the ritual arts of rural India, 1990.

916. Jayakar, Pupul "The earther drum: an introduction to the ritual arts of rural India". New Delhi: National Museum, Publication Division, 1981, 304 p. (Some col.); 29 cm.

917. Jayaram, K. V. "In pursuit of rituals". *The India Magazine*, Vol. 14, No. 5, 1994, pp. 80-81.

918. Jayarāman, G. "Nāka Pañcami Pājai". *Tina Mani,* 21 July. 2006. [Tamil]

919. Jayawardena, Chandra "Religious belief and social change: aspects of the development of Hinduism in British Guiana". *Comparative Studies in Society and History,* Vol. 8, No. 2, 1966, pp. 211-40.

920. Jayaraman, R. "The Kaman festival among the Tamilian estate labourers in Ceylon". *The Eastern Anthropologist,* Vol. 19, No. 1, 1966, pp. 43-54.

921. Jayrath, Ashok "Jagar Utsav: ek manovishleshan". *Somsi,* Vol. 24, No. 3, 1991, pp. 40-46. [Hindi]

922. Jean-Robert Pitte "A short cultural geography of death and the dead". *GeoJournal*, Vol. 60, No. 4, Confronting Geographic Complexity: Contributions from some Latin Countries (2004), pp. 345-351.

923. Jethwani, Aruna Arjan, "Dowry-An obsolete custom". *Dowry Custom (Vivekananda Kendra Patrika, Madras)* Vol. 2. No. 2. 1973, pp. 86-87.

924. Jha, Balakrsna "Cauth candra puja". [Moon worship ritual in the 4th day of Bhadra observed in Mithila]. Darbhanga, The author, 1953. 16 p. ; 18 cm. [Maithili]

925. Jha, Bhesanath "Vyavahar vijnan. Darbhanga" [Social customs of Mithila] 945. 722 p. ; 18 cm. [Maithili]

926. Jha, Damodara "The Mantrartha chandrodaya [microform] [Hindi, Mantras for the rituals in Hinduism]". Benares, Jyotish Prakash Press, 1941. xxviii, 412 p. ; 24 cm. [In: Sanskrit, Hindi]

927. Jha, Hemanta K. "Hindu-Buddhist festivals of Nepal". New Delhi, Nirala, 1996. p. 40.

928. Jha, Pitambar "Prachalit Riti-Rivaj tatha yog evam tantra". In, Proceedings of the national seminar on 'Living customs and their ancient Indian sources', Edited by V. N. Jha, Pune, Centre of Advanced Study in Sanskrit, University of Poona, 1991, pp. 300-307. [Hindi]

929. Jha, V. N. "The Pratice of collective enterprise". In, Proceedings of the national seminar on 'Living customs and their ancient Indian sources', Edited by V. N. Jha, Pune, Centre of Advanced Study in Sanskrit, University of Poona, 1991, pp. 349-352.

930. Jha, V.N. "Proceedings of the national seminar on living customs and their ancient Indian sources". Poona: University of Poona, 1991. p. 352.

931. Jhala, J. "Marriage, hierarchy and identity in ideology and practice: An anthropological study of Jhala Rajput society in western India, against a historical background, 1090-1990 A. D." Harvard University). Pro Quest Dissertations and Theses, 1991 , p. 937, http://search.proquest.com/docview/303928772? accountid=4 3898

932. Jijnasu, "Temple festivals". In. Festivals in Indian Society, 2 Vols., Ed. Usha Sharma, A Mittal Publication, New Delhi, pp.193-198.

933. Jill Jepson "Urban and Rural Sign Language in India". *Language in Society*, Vol. 20, No. 1 (Mar., 1991), pp. 37-57.

934. Jimutavahana "Kalaviveka". [treatise on Hindu law and rituals]. Calcutta, Aisatic Society of Bengal, 1905. xiv, 544 [74] p. ; 22 cm. [In: Sanskrit]

935. Jinaprabhu Suri "Vividha-Tirtha-Kalpa". Bombay, 1944.

936. Jog, K. P. "Raksabandhana". In, Proceedings of the national seminar on 'Living customs and their ancient Indian sources', Edited by V. N. Jha, Pune, Centre of Advanced Study in Sanskrit, University of Poona, 1991, pp.192-200.

937. Jogta, Pannalal "Upari Mahasoo kshetra me Bishu ka tyohar". *Somsi*, Vol. 9, No. 1, 1983, pp. 68-71. [Hindi]

938. John Dixon Hunt "Muddle and Mystery in a passage to India". *ELH*, Vol. 33, No. 4 (Dec., 1966), pp. 497-517.

939. John E. Cort "The Svetambar Murtipujak Jain Mendicant". *Man, New Series*, Vol. 26, No. 4 (Dec., 1991), pp. 651-671.

940. John, S. Simon "Sacred folk festivals of Tamil Nadu". *Journal of Social Anthropology*, Vol. 3, No. 1, 2006, pp. 39-49.

941. John, S. Simon "Kaniyan: ritual performers of Tamil Nadu, South India". *Asian Ethnology*, Vol. 67, No. 1 (2008), pp. 123-135.

942. John, Usha "Onam". *Our Cultural Fabric*, 1977, pp. 46-54.

943. Jolly, J. "Hindu law and customs". Tr. By B. K. Ghosh: Greate India Society, Calcutta, 1928.

944. Jolly, M. C. "The sirmur marriage, with an intro. by H.H. Mandi". Ambala, Upper Indian Press, 1936, pp. 30.

945. Jones, Cliffford R. "A Kerala village temple festival: rituals and folk art forms as communications of traditional culture". Ann. Orient Res. (Silver Jubilee Number), 1975, pp. 399-420.

946. Jones, Clifford, "Kalam elluttu: Art and ritual in Kerala". In Yocum, New Delhi, Manobar, 1982.

947. Jonsari, Shyam Dutt "Jonsar Babar me Magh tyohar". *Vanyajati*, Vol. 5, No. 1, 1957 (January), pp. 8-11. [Hindi]

948. Jordan, Michael "Eastern wisdom: the philosophies and rituals of the East". New York, Marlowe & Co., 1998, 224 p. : col. ill. ; 28 cm.

949. Joseph M. Dye "Ways to Shiva: life and ritual in Hindu India Philadelphia, Pa., Philadelphia Museum of Art, 1980, 95 p. : ill. (Some col.) ; 31 cm.

950. Joshi, A. "Need for consolidating the gains of Chandigarh Roma festival". *Roma, Issue* No. 24, 1986, pp. 9-11.

951. Joshi, Dinesh Chandra. "Himachal Pradesh ka prasedha renuka mela". *Himprastra*, Vol. 18, No. 8, Nov. 1972, pp. 32-34.

952. Joshi, Dinesh Chandra. "Mejar ek Vijaya Prava". *Panchajagar*, Vol.1, No.8, Aug. 1962, pp. 30-31.

953. Joshi, Mahadeva Shastri "Puja Vidhana". Poona, Jnanaraj Prakashan, 1968. [Hindi]

954. Joshi, Prabhash. "Divarala ki sati". *Jansatta*, September 18, 1987.

955. Joshi, Rita "Festival of the desert". *Indian Foreign Review*, Vol. 23, No. 12, 1986, pp. 22-23.

956. Joshi, Tara Chand "Nanda Raj Jat Yatra". *Discover India*, Vol. 13, No. 7, 2000, pp. 71-73.

957. Justice, Christopher "Dying the good death: the pilgrimage to die in India's Holy City". Albany, State University of New York Press, 1997, 1 online resource (xx, p. 268) : ill., maps.

958. Jyoti, Surinder K. "Marriage practices of the Sikhs: a study of intergenerational differences". New Delhi, Deep & Deep, 1983, xi, 256 p. ; 22 cm.

959. Kabiraj, Shibnarayan "Bhadu festival of West Bengal: a glance of the pattern of Bhadu songs". *Folklore*, Vol. 30, No. 9, 1989. pp. 208-213.

960. Kabiraj, Sibnarayan "Significance of Durga worship: its antiquity and present development in Bengal". *Folklore*, Vol. 32, No. 10, 1991. pp. 169-176.

961. Kachroo, Mira. "The Goddess and her powers: the tantric identites of the Saundarya Lahari. Montreal: McGill University, 2005.

962. Kahyap, Satish "Khichadi Ri Saji". *Him Bharati*, Vol. 25, No. 96, 1992, pp. 9-12. (Pahari Bhasa)

963. Kailash Chandra Dash "A Study of the Origin of Ratha Yātrā in the Puruottama Ketra". *East and West*, Vol. 46, No. 1/2 (June 1996), pp. 117-125.

964. Kain, W. D. "International Roma festival reportage". *Roma*, Vol. 2, No. 2, 1976, pp. 14-25.

965. Kalantri, S. P., Cyrus A. Abbasian and Raguram, R. "Temple Healing". *BMJ: British Medical Journal*, Vol. 325, No. 7370 (Oct. 26, 2002), pp. 968-969

966. Kalelkar, Dattatraya Balakrishna "Jivata tahevaro [microform]". Dattatreya Valakrshna Kalelakara Sudharelivadhareli 4. Avrtti. Amadavada: Navajivana Prakasana Mandira, 1949. x, 301 p. ; 18 cm. [In: Gujarati]

967. Kalman, Bobbie "India. The people". (Lands, peoples, and cultures series.), New York, Crabtree Pub. Co., 2001, 32 p. : Col. ill. ; 29 cm.

968. Kamleshwar "Sanskritik samanvaya ki lokdharmi parampara". *Pashyanti*, 2005 (Janwari-March), pp. 15-18.

969. Kanitkar, V. P. "(Hemant) Hindu festivals and scriptures". London, 1984.

970. Kannadaasan "Artthamulla Inthu Matam". 10 volumes. Vaanathi Pathippakam: Chennai. 1973. [Tamil]

971. Kanwar, Dharmendar "Victory of good over evil". *Discover India*, Vol. 2 No. 3, 1989, pp. 56-60.

972. Kanwar, Pamala "Shivratri in Mandi". Souvnir, Shivratir Fair Mandi, 1972, p. 2.

973. Kapadia, K. M. "Marriage and family in India". Bombay, Oxford University Press, 1958.

974. Kapadia, K. M. "Bharatvarsh me vivah evam parivaar (Trans. From English by Hari Krishan Rawat)". Delhi, Motilal Banarasidasa, 1977. [Hindi]

975. Kapadia, Karin "Siva and her sisters: gender, caste, and class in rural South India. Boulder, CO: Westview Press. 1995.

976. Kapoor, Kamala "Daily rituals: Rekha Rodwittiya's rebellion". *Art Asia Pacific*, Vol. 17, 1998, pp. 60-65.

977. Kapoor, Lalni. "Mandi ka prashidha va pramparik Shivratri mela". *Giriraj*, Vol. 2, No.20, Feb. 13, 1980, pp. 7. [Hindi]

978. Kapoor, M. L. "Economic base of polyandry in the hill region of India-conflicting values and their socio-economic implications". Xth international congress of anthropological sciences and tribal development. Delhi, Government of Inida, Ministry of home affairs, 1979, pp. 22-34.

979. Kapoor, Navratna "Bal Kalyan ka puneet parv Ahoi". *Sanskriti (Bal Visheshank)*, Vol. 21, No. 2-4, 1979, pp. 104-107.

980. Kapoor, Navratna "Hasi Khusi Ka Parv: Teez". *Sanskriti (Bal Visheshank),* Vol. 25, No. 4, 1983, pp. 20- 24.

981. Kapoor, Nina "The ritual murder". *Seminar*, No. 331, 1987 (March), pp. 28-32.

982. Kapur, B. L. "Shivratri of Mandi". *Express Week* End., March 25, 1989, p. 3.

983. Kapur, M. L. "Himachal: A land of fairs and festivals". Mandi Shivratri Samarika 1975. pp. 3.

984. Karaka, Dosabha Framji "Important Parsi Festivals". In. Festivals in Indian Society, 2 Vols., Ed. Usha Sharma, A Mittal Publication, New Delhi, pp. 55-60.

985. Karan, Mahendra Nath "A short history and ethnology of the cultivating Pods". Diamond Harbour, Rai Charan Sardar, The All Bengal kshattriya samiti, 1919. viii, 82 p. : front. ; 18 cm.

986. Karandikar, S. V. "Hindu exogamy [microform]". Bombay, Advocate of India Press, 1928. vi, 290 p. ; 21 cm.

987. Karar, Arnab "Imapct of pilgrim tourism at Haridwar". *The Anthropologist*, Vol. 12, No. 2 2010, pp. 99-105.

988. Karnad, Girish "Nāga Mandala: play with a Cobra". Delhi: Oxford University Press. 1990.

989. Karsten, R. "The custom of couvade." *Folklore*, Vol. 42, No. 2, 1931, pp. 193-197.

990. Karunakaran, K. K. "Variety of Theyyams of Kerala: some descriptive notes about the performance and performer". Folklore, Vol. 29, No. 11, 1988, pp. 245-247.

991. Karve, Iravati "On the road: a Maharashtrian pilgrimage". In, 'The experience the Hinduism', Edited by Eleaner Zelliot and Maxine Bernsten, Albany, Suny Press, 1988.

992. Kashyap, Shyam "Parampara aur aadhunikta". *Madhya Bharti (Humanities)*, No. 47, 1999, March, pp. 11-14. [Hindi]

993. Kaudinya "Deuri Janjatiyo ke Dharmik evam Samajik parvotsav". *Manav*, Vol. 7, No. 2, 1979, pp. 87-104. [Hindi]

994. Kaur, Raminder "Rethinking the public sphere: The Ganapati festival and media competitions in Mumbai". *South Asia Research*, Vol. 21, No. 1, 2001, pp. 23-50.

995. Kaushal, Rajendra "Poorvani Ra Bishu (Pahar Bhasa)". *HimBharati*, Vol. 29, No. 109, 1997, pp. 56-62. [Pahari language]

996. Kaushik, Jay Narayan "Teej hi Tyohar" *Hrigandha*, Vol. 23, 1989, pp. 30-33. [Hindi]

997. Kaushik, Meena "The symbolic representation of death". *Contribution to Indian Sociology*, Vol. 10, No. 2, 1976, pp. 265-92.

998. Kayastha, S. L. "The Himalayan Beas basin: A study in Habitat". *Economy and Society*". Varanasi, 1964, pp. 346.

999. Kaye, John William "Dewali". In, 'Festivals in Indian Society', 2 Vols., Ed. Usha Sharma, A Mittal Publication, New Delhi, pp. 175-176.

1000. Kayeth, Krishan Chandra "Himachal Pradesh ki samajik paramparayen". *Somsi*, Vol. 15, No. 3, 1989 (July), pp. 17-19. [Hindi]

1001. Kayeth, Krishan Chandra "Mahasuvi Lok-Kavya me pushp-tyohar ki mahima". *Somsi*, Vol. 12, No. 2, 1986 (April), pp. 41-45 [Hindi]

1002. Kearns, J. F. "Marriage and family in India". Bombay, 1955.

1003. Keass, Morton, "Marriage rules in Bengal". *American Anthropologist* 68, 1966, pp. 951-970.

1004. Keesing Felix, M. "Cultural Anthropology: The Science of Custom". New York, Holt, Rinehart and Winston, 1962.

1005. Kelly, John D. and Kaplan, "Martha history, structure, and ritual". *Annual Review of Anthropology*, Vol. 19, 1990, pp. 119-150.

1006. Kennedy, Jean Wilson & Schalek, Alice "Here is India". New York, C. Scribner's Sons, 1945, 154 p. illus. (incl. maps) 24 cm.

1007. Kerala. Superintendent of Census Operations "Census of India 1961: Kerala Fairs and Festivals of Kerala Statements". Vol vii, pt. vii B (ii). Delhi: Manager of Publications, 1968. vi, p. 646.

1008. Kerala. Superintendent of Census Operations "Census of India 1961: Kerala-Fairs and festivals of Kerala". Vol.VII, pt.VII B (i). Delhi: Manager of Publications, 1966. iv, 434 p. : plates p.

1009. Kesari, Arjundas "Sonbhadra ke Janjatiya parv" *Chhayanat*, Issue No. 72, 1995, pp. 33- 36. [Hindi]

1010. Khalsa Tract Society, Amritsar "Das Patsahiam de Gurparab". [Religious festivals]. Amritsar : The Society, n.d. 48 p. ; 20 cm. [Panjabi]

1011. Khan, E. "The evolution of religious life and social life of man". New Delhi, Bait-At-Hikmat Trust, 1989.

1012. Khare, R. S. "Hindu rites of food", Vikas Publishing House Pvt. Ltd., New Delhi, 1977.

1013. Khare, R. S. "The changind Brahmana: association and elites among the Kanya Kubja of North India". Chicago, The University of Chicago Press, 1970.

1014. Khare, R. S. "Ritual purity and pollution in relation to domestic sanitation". *The Eastern Anthropologist*, Vol. 15, No. 2, 1962, pp. 125-139.

1015. Khare, R. S. "The Hindu hearth and home". New Delhi: Vikas Publishing House. 1976.

1016. Khativada, Subba Homnath "Asauc nirnay". [Religious rituals in verse]. Varanasi: Hitaisi Co., 1951. 32 p. ; 17 cm. [Nepali]

1017. Khedekar, Vinayak "Ritualistic theatre of Goa: with special reference to Jagar". *Folklore*, Vol. 28, No. 8, 1987 (August), pp. 193-194.

1018. Khokar, Mohan "Chaitra parva rituals chhau dances". *Marg*, Vol. 34, No. 2, pp.74-87.

1019. Khokar, Mohan "Dancing for themselves: folk, tribal and ritual dance of India". New Delhi, Himalayan Books, 1987. 173 p., Col. ill. p.

1020. Khullar, Sangeeta "Pongal: Shubh or sumangal". *Discover India*, Vol. 5, No. 1, 1992, pp. 46-48.

1021. Khushal, G. C. "Nalwari fair, its unique importance". Nalwari Fair Bilaspur 1971, Souvenir, 1 p.

1022. Kilambi, Jyotsna S. "Toward an understanding of the Muggu: Threshold drawings in Hyderabad". Res Oxford University Press, Vol. 10, 1985. pp. 71-100.

1023. Killingley, Dermot, Verner Mensky and Shirley, Firth "Hindu society and rituals". Newcastle upon Tyne, S. Y. Killingley, 1991.

1024. Kincaid, C. A. (Charles Augustus) "Our Hindu friends [microform]". [On the rites and practices]. Bombay, Times of India Press, 1930. xii, 69 p. ; 19 cm.

1025. Kingsland, Venika "The simple guide to customs and etiquette in India". (Simple guides., Series 1,, Customs & etiquette.), Folkestone, Kent, England : Global Books New York, NY, Distributed in the USA & Canada by Talman Co. Inc., 1996, 64 p. : ill., map ; 21 x 11 cm.

1026. Kinsley, David "Through the looking glass: divine madness in the Hindu religious tradition". *History of Religions,* Vol. 13, No. 4, 1974, pp. 270-305.

1027. Kinsley, David "The sword and the flute. Kali and Krisna: dark visions of the terrible and the sublime in Hindu mythology". Berkley, University of California Press, 1975.

1028. Kinsley, David "Hindu Goddesses: vision of the divine feminine in the Hindu religious tradition". Berkley, University of California Press, 1986.

1029. Kinsley, David. "Tantric visions of the divine feminine; the Ten Mahàvidyàs". Berkeley, University of California Press, 1997.

1030. Kishor, Yugal "Kangde de Janane parv tyohar (Pahari Bhasa)". *Himbharti*, Vol. 24, No.1, 1991, pp. 16-20. [Pahari Language]

1031. Kisku, Amit Kumar, Bhakat, Ram Kumar and Guha, Abhijit "A Santal Jaher: Rituals and biodiversity conservation". *Journal of Indian Anthropologial Society,* Vol. 45, No. 2, 2010 (July), pp. 143-151.

1032. Kleen, Tyra De "Mudras: the ritual hand poses of the Budha priests and the Shiva priests of Bali". Delhi: Ess Ess, 1975. 42 p. : plates p.

1033. Knipe, David M. "Hinduism: experiments in the sacred". New York, Harper Collins, 1991.

1034. Knipe, David M. "In the image of fire: Vedic experience of the heat". Delhi, Motilal Banarasidass, 1972.

1035. Knipe, David M. "Night of the growing dead: A cult of Virabhadra in coastal Andhra". In, 'Crimical gods and demon devotees. Essays on the guardians of popular Hinduism', ed. Alf Hiltebeitel, pp. 123-156. Delhi, Manohar. 1990.

1036. Knipe, David M. "Sapindikarana: the Hindu rite of entry into heaven". In, 'Religious encounters with death, Incite from the history and anthropology of the religions', Edited by Franck E. Raynolds and Earle H. Waugh, London, Pennsylvania State University Press, 1977, pp. 111-24.

1037. Knipe, David M. "Softening the cruelty of God: folklore, ritual and the planet Œani (Saturn) in Southeast India." In Syllables of Sky: Studies in South Indian Civilization: In Honour of Velcheru Narayana Rao, ed. David Shulman, Delhi: Oxford University Press. 570 p. 1995. pp. 206-48.

1038. Knipe, David M. "When a wife dies first: The Mūsivāyanam and a female Brahman ritualist in Coastal Andhra." In 'The Living and the Dead: Social Dimensions of Death in South Asian Religions', ed. Liz Wilson, Albany: State University of New York Press. 2003. pp. 51-93.

1039. Kochar, V.K. "Family spirits and deities among the Santals and associated rituals". *Journal of the Asiatic society of Bengal, Calcutta*, Vol. 5, No. 3-4, 1963, pp. 59-71.

1040. Kochar, V. K. "Village Deities of the Santal and associated rituals". *Anthropos*, Vol. 61, No. 1.2, 1966, pp. 241- 257.

1041. Koduveliparambil, J. J. "Construction practices in traditional dwellings of Kerala, india". Canada, McGill University. Pro Quest Dissertations and Theses, 1997, 180 p., Access online at, http://search.proquest.com/docview/304402589?accountid=43898

1042. Kolanad, Gitanjali "Culture shock: a guide to customs and etiquette". Singapore: Times Books International, 2003. 304 p.

1043. Kolenda, Pauline "Pox and the terror of childlessness: images and ideas of the smallpox Goddess in a North Indian village."In, 'Mother Worship: Themes and Variations', ed. James J. Preston. Chapel Hill: University of North Carolina Press. 1982.

1044. Komal Mehra "Festivals of India". New Delhi, Sterling Publishers Pvt. Ltd, 2001.

1045. Kondinya, Bikshu "Mishing Janjatiyon ke paramparagat dharmik utsav evam parv". *Manav*, Vol. 4. No. 2, 1976 (June-Dec.), pp. 35-47. [Hindi]

1046. Koppers, L and Jungblut, L., "Betrothal rites among the Bhil, of North-Western Central India". *Artibus Asiae*, Vol. 11, No.1, 1946, pp. 5-33.

1047. Koppers, L and Jungblut, L., "Wedding rites among the Bhil of North-Western Central India". *Anthropos*, Vol. XLVI, 1951, pp. 113-139.

1048. Korom, F. J. "Holy cow! the apotheosis of Zebu or why the cow is sacred in Hinduism". *Asian Folklore Studies* 59 2 2000, pp. 181-203.

1049. Korom, Frank J. "To be happy': ritual, play, and leisure in the Bengali Dharmaraj puja". *International Journal of Hindu Studies,* Vol. 3, No. 2, 1999 (August), pp. 113-164.

1050. Kosambi, D.D. "Myths and reality". Bombay, Popular Press, 1962.

1051. Koshy, Ashok "Of piety and gaiety". *Discover India*, Vol. 12, No. 10, 1999, pp. 60-62.

1052. Kothare, Balaji Sitaram. "Hindu holidays". Bombay: The Times Press, 1904.

1053. Kramrisch, Stella "Unknown India: ritual art in tribe and village". In, 'Exploring India's sacred art', ed. Barbara S. Miller, pp. 85-120. Reprint, 1968, Philadelphia: University of Pennsylvania Press, 1983.

1054. Krishana, Nanita "Festival of the 63 Saints". *Illustrated Weekly India,* Vol. 97, No. 36, 1976, pp. 32-35.

1055. Krishanalal "Grhya Mantra aur unka Viniyoga". Delhi, National Publishing House, 1970. [Hindi]

1056. Krishna, Nandita "The Mylapore festival". *The India Magazine*, Vol. 8, No. 6, 1988, pp. 36-43.

1057. Krishnamurthy, K. "Festivals of ancient India as gleaned from the Indian Literature-Festival as an important aspect of social life". In. Festivals in Indian Society, 2 Vols., Ed. Usha Sharma, A Mittal Publication, New Delhi, pp.199-206.

1058. Krishnamurthy, Radha, "Dowry: Scourge on society". Dowry Custom (Vivekananda Kendra Patrika, Madras) Vol. 2. No.2. 1973, pp. 121-124.

1059. Kroeber, A. L. "Disposal of dead". *American Anthropologist,* Vol. 29, 1927, pp. 308-315.

1060. Krsnasarma, Betageri "Karnataka janajivana [microform]". Dharavada, Karnataka Vidyavardhaka Sanghada Suvarnamahot savada prakatane, 1939. xvi, 164 p. ; 22 cm. In: Kannada.

1061. Kruber, Aarther R. "Durga Aagman Samaroh". *Discover India*, Vol. 2, No. 10, 1989, pp. 16-21.

1062. Kruber, Arther R. "Durga Pooja: Devi ki shaktishali Talwar". *Discover India*, Vol. 5, No. 9, 1992, pp. 54-58.

1063. Kshirsagar, V. M. "Sastyabdisanti: Its origin and nature extent today". In, Proceedings of the national seminar on 'Living customs and their ancient Indian sources', Edited by V. N. Jha, Pune, Centre of Advanced Study in Sanskrit, University of Poona, 1991, pp. 114-118.

1064. Kshirsagar, Vinaya M. "Use of ritual-motifs by Kalidasa". *Bulletin of Deccan College and Post Graduate Institute,* Vol. 53, 1993, pp. 219-222.

1065. Kulkarni, Nirmala, "Interpretation of dream through the eyes of moderns and ancients". In, Proceedings of the national seminar on 'Living customs and their ancient Indian sources', Edited by V. N. Jha, Pune, Centre of Advanced Study in Sanskrit, University of Poona, 1991, pp. 343-348.

1066. Kumar, Anil and Yadav, D. K. "Significance of Sacred Plants in Shraddh ritual (Pindadan) in Gaya, Bihar". *Ethnobotany*, Vol. 16, No. 1-2, 2004, pp. 103-107.

1067. Kumar, Baldev "Kuluyi utsav, Tyohar or parv". *Somsi*, Vol. 4 No. 4, 1978, pp. 48-58. [Hindi]

1068. Kumar, Krishna "People at the Kodungallur festival: A phtographer's portfolio". *The India Magzine*, Vol. 8, No. 12, pp. 8-16.

1069. Kumar, Prem "Roma festival comes of age". *Roma*, Vol. 8, No. 1&2, 1984, pp. 35-37.

1070. Kumar, Rajeev K. and Kapoor, A. K. "Religious festivals of Parhaiya: A tribal community of Jhakhand" *Vanyajati*, Vol. 52, No. 3, 2004, pp. 1-7.

1071. Kumar, Ram "Aanad or ullas ka parv Pongal". *Sanskriti*, Vol. 25, No. 4, 1983, pp. 33. [Hindi]

1072. Kumar, Ram "Sampradayik Sadbhav ke aadhar: Bharat ke Vividh tyohar". *Sanskriti*, Vol. 26, No. 4, 1984, pp. 23-25.

1073. Kumar, S., Gajrani, S. "Traditions and customs in Indian society". Faridabad: Om Publications, 1999. vii, 270 p.

1074. Kumar, Vinay "Santhal Jajjati dwara Manaye Janevala parv 'Sohray evam Geet'". *Vanyajati*, Vol. 58, No. 2, 2010, pp. 34-39.

1075. Kumari, Devindra "Himachali lokparampara me parv evam tyohar". *Somsi*, Vol. 24, No. 89, 1998, pp. 74-81.

1076. Kumari, Prathibha "Asur festivals". In, 'Fairs and Festivals of Indian tribes', Ed. by Robin David Tribhuwan, Discovery Publishing House, New Delhi, 2003, pp. 31-38.

1077. Kumari, Pratibha "Festivals of Sauria Paharia". In, 'Fairs and Festivals of Indian tribes', Ed. by Robin David Tribhuwan, Discovery Publishing House, New Delhi, 2003, pp. 39-46.

1078. Kumari, Pratibha "Fairs in the tribal Bihar". In, 'Fairs and Festivals of Indian tribes', Ed. by Robin David Tribhuwan, Discovery Publishing House, New Delhi, 2003, pp. 195-200.

1079. Kunugo, Alok Kumar "Folk dance in the season of fairs and festivals amongst Juangs". In, 'Fairs and Festivals of Indian tribes', Ed. by Robin David Tribhuwan, Discovery Publishing House, New Delhi, 2003, pp. 201-207.

1080. Kurian, Mini Chandran "Nag Panchami: The day of the cobra". *Discover India*, Vol. 3, No. 11, 1990, pp. 42-47.

1081. Kurian, Mini Chandran "The Tusker Parade: Colour and pageantry". *Discover India*, Vol. 4, No. 1, 1991, pp. 53-58.

1082. Kuriyan, Mini Chandran "Gaj Samaroh ki rangeen shobha". *Discover India*, Vol. 4, No. 1, 1991, 53-58. [Hindi]

1083. Kuriyan, Mini Chandran "Nag Panchami: Bhay or Bhakti". *Discover India*, Vol. 3, No. 11, 1990, 44-47. [Hindi]

1084. Kuruknetra "Dying before the Mahābhārata war: Martial and transsexual body-building for Aravān." *Journal of Asian Studies,* Vol. 54, No. 2, 1995, pp. 447-73.

1085. Kuruknetra "Hair like snakes and mustached brides: crossed gender in an Indian folk cult." In, 'Hair: Its Power and Meaning in Asian Cultures', eds. Barbara D. Miller and Alf Hiltebeitel, Albany: State University of New York Press. 1998. pp. 143-76.

1086. Kuruknetra "Kûttānnavar: The divine lives of a severed head." In, 'Ways of Dying: Death and Its Meaning in South Asia', eds. Elisabeth Schmbucher and Claus Peter Zoller, Delhi: Manohar. 1999. pp. 276-310.

1087. Kurup, A. M. "The sociology of Onam". *Indian Anthropologist,* Vol. 7, No. 2, 1977, pp. 95-111.

1088. Kurup, C. G. R. "Onam: The festival of fraternity" *Indian Foreign Review*, Vol. 21, No. 21, 1984, pp. 12-13, 30.

1089. Kurup, K. K. N. "Rural protests as reflected in the ritual songs: analysis of the Teyyam cult of Kerala". *Folklore,* Vol. 30, No. 7, 1989 (July), pp. 144-149.

1090. Kuruvilla, M. C. "Reaf the harvest and rejoice". *Discover India*, Vol. 3, No. 8, 1990, pp. 40-43.

1091. La Fontaine, J. S. "The interpretation of ritual". *Eastern Anthropologists*, Vol. 29, No. 2, 1976, pp. 219-21.

1092. Lady, Lawrence "Indian embers". Palo Alto, Trackless Sands Press, 1991, 397 p. : ill., map ; 23 cm.

1093. Lahiri, Dilip K. and Dev, Bimal J. "Customs of a few Naga Tribes: some accounts derived from the old files". *Folklore*, Vol. 24, No. 10, 1983 (October), pp. 195-198.

1094. Laksmidharabhatta "Krtyakalpataru [microform]. [Hinduism Rituals]. Lahore, University of the Panjab, 1942- v. 11; 24 cm. [In: Sanskrit]

1095. Laksminarasimhamu, Setti "Pandugu Kathalu. [Stories of religious festivals]. Eluru, Laksminarasimha pracuranalu, 1952. iv, 50 p. ; 18 cm. [In: Telugu]

1096. Lal, S. K. "Rivers in Hindu mythology and ritual". Delhi: Bharatiya Kala Prakashan. 2007.

1097. Lal, V. N. "Hindu Parv Mimansa". Azamgarh, 1969. [Hindi]

1098. Lalit, C. R. V. "Mahasu-mela aur tohar". *Somsi*, Vol. 3, No. 3, July 1977, pp. 17-32. [Hindi]

1099. Lalpuri "Kumbh parv ka vegyanik vishleshan". *Ojasvini*, 2004 (April), pp. 25-26 [Hindi]

1100. Lalye, P. G., "Funeral rites (Antyesti) and secular practices". In, Proceedings of the national seminar on 'Living customs and their ancient Indian sources', Edited by V. N. Jha, Pune, Centre of Advanced Study in Sanskrit, University of Poona, 1991, pp. 124-130.

1101. Lama, Santabir "Tamba kaiten hvai rimthim. (On traditional customs, culture and folklore of Tamang people)". Tindhariya (Darjeeling), Santa Bhavan, 1953. 113 p. ; 17 cm. [Nepali]

1102. Lamb, Sarah "White saris and sweet Mangoes: aging, gender, and body in North India". Berkeley: University of California Press, 2000.

1103. Lamb, Sarah. "Aging, gender and widowhood: perspectives from rural West Bengal." *Contributions to Indian Sociology,* Vol. 33, No. 3, 1999, pp. 541-570.

1104. Lang, Andrew "Myth, ritual and religion". New Delhi, Aryan Books International, 1993. 2v. (xxxix, 339; vii, 380) p.

1105. Lapoint, Elwyn C. "Solar contagion: ritual in a North Indian village." In, 'Through the Vistas of Life and Lore: Folkloric Reflections on Traditional India', ed. R. M. Sarkar, 131-52. Calcutta: Punthi Pustak. 2000.

1106. Lariviere, Richard W. "Dharmasastra, custom, 'real law' and 'apocryphal' smritis". *Journal of Indian Philosophy,* Vol. 32, No. 5-6, 2004 (December), pp. 611-627.

1107. Laroia, N., & Sharma, D. "The religious and cultural bases for breastfeeding practices among the Hindus. *Breastfeeding Medicine*, Vol. 1, No. 2, 2006. pp. 94-98.

1108. Layard, I. "Labyrinth ritual in South India: Threshold and tattoo designs". *Folklore*, Vol. 48, 1937. pp. 115-186.

1109. Layard, I. Hosting the divine: The Kolam in Tamil Nadu". In, 'Mud, mirror and thread: folk traditions in rural India'. Ed. Nora Fisher. Santa Fe: Museum of International Folk Art. 1993. pp. 192-203.

1110. Leach, Edmund R. "A critique of Yalman's interpretation of Sinhalese Gill's puberty ceremonial". In, 'Echanges et communications: Melanges offers a Claude Levi-Strauss a l' occasion de son 60 Anniversaire'. Ed. by Jean Pouillon and Pierre Maranda, eds. Hagues: Mouton, 1970, pp. 819-828.

1111. Leach, Edmund R. "Ritual". In, 'International Encyclopedia of Social Sciences'. D. L. Sill et al. (eds.) New York, MacMillan, 1968, pp. 520-526.

1112. Lean, Phylles S. "The value of rituals". *Theosophist*, Vol. 97, No. 12, 1976, pp. 207-09.

1113. Leelaram, Sunanda and Ramsundar, S. "The custom of marriage and its longevity in modern society". *Indian Journal of Social Development*, Vol. 10, No. 2, 2010 (Dec.), pp. 595-612.

1114. Lele, Jayant "Community, discourse and critique in Jnaneswar". In, 'Tradition and modernity in Bhakti tradition', Edited by Jayant Lele, Leiden, E.J. Brill., 1981.

1115. Lele, Jayant "The Bhakti movement in India: a critical introduction". In, 'Tradition and modernity in Bhakti tradition', Edited by Jayant Lele, Leiden, E.J. Brill., 1981.

1116. Lele, Kasinatha Sastri "Samskaradarsa [microform] [Hinduism Rituals]. Mumbai, Kasinatha Vamana Lele, 1915- v. 1; 18 cm. [Marathi].

1117. Lele, V. R. "Teacher taught relationship past and present". In, Proceedings of the national seminar on 'Living customs and their ancient Indian sources', Edited by V. N. Jha, Pune, Centre of Advanced Study in Sanskrit, University of Poona, 1991, pp. 289-299.

1118. Leo Howe "Risk, ritual and performance". *The Journal of the Royal Anthropological Institute,* Vol. 6, No. 1 (March., 2000), pp. 63-79.

1119. Lepowsky, Maria "The way of the ancestors: Custom, innovation, and resistance". *Environmental Ethics*, Vol. 30, No. 3, 1991 (July), pp. 217-233.

1120. Leslie C. Orr "Identity and divinity: Boundary crossing Goddesses in medieval South India". *Journal of the American Academy of Religion,* Vol. 73, No. 1 (Mar., 2005), pp. 9-43.

1121. Leslie, Julia, (ed.) "Roles and rituals for Hindu women. New Delhi, Motilal Banarsidass, 1991.

1122. Leuva, K. K. "The Asur". New Delhi Bharitya Adimjati Sevak Sangh, 1963.

1123. Levy, Gina "The Jagra festival". *The India Magazine*, Vol. 9, No. 12, 1989, pp. 66-75.

1124. Lewis, Gilbert "Problems of ritual in general". In, 'International encyclopedia of tribal religion' Vol. 7. Edited by S. M. Channa, New Delhi, Cosmo Publications, 2000, pp. 199-248.

1125. Linton, Ralph "Purification of the sacred bundles, a ceremony of the Pawnee". Chicago, Field Museum of Natural History, 1923, (Series: Field museum of natural history. [Anthropology leaflet, No. 7),11 p., pl. 22 cm.

1126. Listova, T. A. "A programme for collection of material on the customs and rituals associated with childbirth". *Soviet Anthropology and Archeology*, Vol. 30, No. 2, 1991, pp. 53-66.

1127. Lochtefeld, James. "Suicide in the Hindu tradition: varieties, propriety and practice". Unpublished M.A. essay, University of Washington, 1987.

1128. Logan, Penelope "Domestic worship and the festival cycle in the South Indian city of Madurai". Ph.D. Thesis, University of Manchester, 1980.

1129. Long, I. B. "Festivals of repentance, a study of Mahashivratri". *Journal of the Oriental Institute (M.S. University Baroda)*, Vol. 22, 1972.

1130. Longhurt, A. M. "The marriage of tree in South India". *Antiquity*, Vol. 29, 1955, pp. 36-37.

1131. Lorenzon, David "Traditions of non-caste Hinduism: the Kabir Panth". *Contribution to Indian Sociology*, Vol. 21, No. 2, 1987, pp. 263-83.

1132. Luschinsky, Mildred Stroop "The life of women in a village of North India: a survey of role and status". Unpublished Ph. D. Dissertation, Cornell University, 1962.

1133. Luthra, Chandni "Let's go fly a kite (Aao Patang udayen)". *Discover India*, Vol. 3, No. 3, 1990 (March), pp. 6-10. [Hindi]

1134. Luthra, Indira "Festive rituals". *Discover India*, Vol. 7, No. 11, 1994, pp. 22-23.

1135. Lyngdoh, Mary Pristilla Rina "The Festivals in the History and Culture of the Khasi". New Delhi: Har-Anand Publications /Vikas Pub. House in New Delhi, 1991, pp. 146-171.

1136. M.S.A. (Mahabir Sanskrutik Anusthan) "Maa Manikeswari-the Tutelary deity of Kalahandi". M.S.A. Bhawani Patana, Orissa, 1991.

1137. MacCormack, Carol P. "Ethnography of fertility and birth". London: Academic Press. 1982.

1138. Macdonald, Sarah "Holy Cow: an Indian adventure". New York, Broadway Books, 2003, 291 p. ; 21 cm.

1139. MacDorman, M. F. "Contemporary marriage practices in north India: evidence from three Uttar Pradesh villages". The Australian National University (Australia)). ProQuest Dissertations and Theses, 1986, 1. Access online at, http://search.proquest.com/docview/303542195?accountid=43898

1140. Madhu Kishwar "Toiling without rights: Ho women of Singhbhum". *Economic and Political Weekly,* Vol. 22, No. 3 (Jan. 17, 1987), pp. 95-101.

1141. Madras. Superintendent of Census Operations "Census of India 1961: Madras fairs and festivals". Vol. IX, pt. VII-B. Delhi: Manager of Publication, 1968. p. 718.

1142. Magan "Gorkha sampraday me Dashahra utsav". *Somsi*, Vol. 13, No. 3, 1987 (July), pp. 23-26. [Hindi]

1143. Maggi, Wynne "Our women are free: gender and ethnicity in the Hindukush". Ann Arbor: The University of Michigan Press, 2001.

1144. Mahadevan, Manu "Veneshwar mela: a Bhil celebration". *The India Magazine*, Vol. 9, No. 9, 1989, pp. 66-72.

1145. Mahajan, Jagmohan "The eternal Ganga". New Delhi, Spantech Pub., 1989.

1146. Mahajan, Ved Bhushan, "Kulu's Dussehra tradition". Kulu's colorful Dussehra 1970, Souvenir, p. 4.

1147. Mahanta, Dipjyoti and Goswami, M. C. "Ritual and secular role of a Duonia monastery". *Bulletin of the Department of Anthropology,* 2, 1973: 32-40 .

1148. Mahapatra, L. K. "Ritual kinship in Orissa". *Bulletin of The Deccan College Research Institute* 32, 1972: 89-105

1149. Mahapatra, Shyam Sunder "Flowers in the Santal festival: an interpretation of Baha festival". *Folklore*, Vol. 24, No. 12, 1983, pp. 241-243.

1150. Mahapatra, Sitakant "Modernization and ritual: Identity and change in Santal Society". Calcutta: Oxford University Press, 1986, p. 170.

1151. Mahato, Pashupati Prasad "Hunting festival of the tribal people of Jharkhand". *Folklore*, Vol. 22, No. 8, 1981, pp. 179-192.

1152. Mahato, Pashupati Prasad "Impact of Brahminical culture on the Tribes of Chhotanagpur, Indian Festival - a case study". *Folklore*, Vol. 13, No. 11, 1972, pp. 452-460.

1153. Mahavar, Niranjan "Gora Puja evam Deepavali parv". *Chomasa*, Vol. 19, No. 58, 2002 (March-June), pp. 38-44. [Hindi]

1154. Mahavar, Niranjan "Parampara itihas bodh aur sanskriti". *Chomasa*, Vol. 10, No. 32, 1993 (July-Oct.), pp. 57-63. [Hindi]

1155. Maheta, Bharatarama Bha (Bharatarama Bhanusukharama) "Pracina Hindamam sanghajivana [microform]". Amadavada, Gujarata Varnakyulara Sosayati, 1934. xxiv, 355 p. ; 19 cm. [Gujarati]

1156. Mahohar Lal. "Kaagada ke Mukhaya sanskar". *Somsi*, Vol. 2, No. 2, April 1997, pp. 39-49. [Hindi]

1157. Maiti, Sameera "Political organization and customary laws of the Bhotia of Uttaranchal". The Oriental *Anthropologist*, Vol. 3, No. 2, 2003, pp. 138-144.

1158. Maitra, A. "The Maithil Brahmin festival of Jursital". *Man in India,* Vol. 62, No. 4, 1982, pp. 420-424.

1159. Maity, P. K. "A note on the festivals of mediaeval Bengal: in the light of Bengali literature and folklore". *Folklore*, Vol. 23, No. 6, 1982, 119-126.

1160. Maity, P. K. "Children protecting Deities and rituals of Bengal: A Study". *Folklore*, Vol. 22, No. 4, 1981, pp.77-89.

1161. Maity, P. K. "Folk rituals of eastern India". New Delhi, Abhinav, 1988.

1162. Maity, Pradyot Kumar "Historical Studies in the Cult of the Goddess Manasa: A Socio-Cultural Study". Kolkata: Punthi Pustak. 2001.

1163. Majumdar, D. N. "Ritual life and communication". *The Eastern Anthropologist,* Vol. 11, No. 3-4, 1958, pp. 175-80.

1164. Majumdar, D. N. "A note on Hajong marriage customs". *Bulletin of the Anthropological Survey of India*, Vol. 17, No. 2, 1968 (April), pp. 79-82.

1165. Majumdar, Dhirendre Nath "The custom of burning human effigies of straw on the last day of the Bengali month Kartik (October-November) -in some parts of Bengal". *Man in India*, Vol. 03 No. 01-02, 1923 (March & June), pp. 92-96 .

1166. Majumder, Dhirendra Nath "Customs and taboos observed by east women from pregnancy to childbirth". *Man in India,* Vol. 03, No. 03-04, 1923 (Sept.- Dec.), pp. 232-242.

1167. Malabari, Behramji M. (Behramji Merwanji) "Gujarat and the Gujaratis [microform]: pictures of men and manners taken from life". 3rd ed. Bombay, Ford Print. Press, 1889. xxii, 358 p. ; 19 cm.

1168. Malabari, Behramji M. (Behramji Merwanji) "The Indian eye on English life or rambles of a pilgrim reformer [microform]". 3rd ed. Bombay Apollo Print. Works, 1895. vii, 287 p. ; 22 cm.

1169. Malhotra, Y. N. "Facets of Mandi Shivratri festival". Mandi Shivratri Souvenir, Shimla, (H.P.) 1974, p. 2.

1170. Malinowski, Bronislaw "Crime and custom in savage society". London: Rutledge and Kegan Paul, 1926. xii, 132 p.

1171. Malkani, Naraindas Ratanmal "Mirani Sindhuri". [Account of the life and customs of Sindhis during the reign of Mirs who ruled Sind before the advent of the

British.], Hyderabad (Sind), National Printing Press, 1936. xiii, 200 p. ; 19 cm. [Sindhi]

1172. Mallo, Indra "Nyokum: The festival of the Nyishis of Arunachal Pradesh". In, 'Fairs and Festivals of Indian tribes', Ed. by Robin David Tribhuwan, Discovery Publishing House, New Delhi, 2003, pp. 94-96.

1173. Malurkar, S. L. "Determination of seasons and equinoxes in Old India and related festivals". In, 'Festivals in Indian Society', 2 Vols., Ed. Usha Sharma, A Mittal Publication, New Delhi, pp. 177-182.

1174. Mamdani, Shelby "Traditions from India". (Series: Cultural journeys (Raintree Steck-Vaughn Publishers), Austin, Tex., Raintree Steck-Vaughn, 1999, 48 p. : Col. ill. ; 28 cm.

1175. Mamgai, Kesava Nand "Himachal ke ye mela". *Himprasta*, Vol. 71 No. 109-110, April-May, 1979, pp. 68-71. [Hindi]

1176. Mandal, Debabrata and Bagchi, Tilak "Customary law of marriage among the Jamatia tribe of Tripura". *Vanyajati*, Vol. 44, No. 2, 1996 (Arpil), pp. 8-11.

1177. Mandal, Sujit Kumar and Mukherjee, Ambarish "An Ethnobotanical envision into Santhali festivals in Purulia district, West Bengal". *Ethnobotany*, Vol. 15, No. 1-2, 2003, pp. 118-124.

1178. Mandlik, Rao Saheb Vishvanath Narayan "Serpent worship in Western India: The Nāga-panchamî holiday as it is now observed; serpent worship, the Nāgās and Sarpās." *Journal of the Bombay Branch of the Royal Asiatic Society*, Vol. 36, No. 9, 1869, pp. 169-200.

1179. Mani, Lata "Contentious traditions: the debate on SATI in colonial India". Cultural Critique (fall 1987), pp. 119-156. Reprinted in Recasting Women: Essays in Colonial History, ed, by K. Sangari and S. Vaid, New Delhi: Kali for Women, 1988, pp. 88-126.

1180. Manikpuri, Naaz "Nazeer Akbaraabadi aur basant ke tyohar". *Sanskriti*, Vol. 23, No. 1-2, 1981 (Jan.-June), pp. 14-15 [Hindi]

1181. Manipur. Superintendent of Census operations "Census of India 1961: Manipur-fairs and festivals". Vol. XXII, pt. VII-B. Delhi: The Manager of publication, 1969. viii, 56 p. : plates p.

1182. Mankada, Bhagavanalala La "Saurashtrana Sumara [microform Mankada. Amadavada, Gujarata Vidyasabha, 1951. vi, 42 p. : ill. ; 18 cm. In: Gujarati

1183. Mann, R. S. "Religious attributes of Bhils". In 'Rajasthan Bhils'. N. N. Vyas; R. S. Mann & N. D. Chaudhary (eds.) Udaipur: Tribal Research Institute, 1978.

1184. Mansfield, Stephen "Lao hill tribes: traditions and patterns of existence". Shah Alam, Selangor Darul Ehsan, Malaysia, New York, Oxford University Press, 2000, x, 91 p., [16] p. of plates: ill. (some col.), maps ; 20 cm.

1185. Mansukhani, H. L. "A custom law and procures: a reference book". Vikas, 1972.

1186. Manuel, Laitha "The dowry cult". *Dowry Custom (Vivekananda Kendra Patrika, Madras)* Vol.2. No.2. 1973, pp. 24-32.

1187. Mao, John "Customary law, dispute and litigation among the Garos". *Man and Life*, Vol. 16, No. 3-4, 1990, pp. 187-190.

1188. Marak, J. L. "Garo customary laws and practices: sociological study'. New Delhi: Akansha Publishing House, 2000. p. 244.

1189. Marak, Julius "Garo customary laws and practices: a sociological study". Calcutta: Firma KLM Private Limited, 1986 xi, p. 221.

1190. Marathe, N. B. "The living custom of Bodana and its ancient Indian sources". In, Proceedings of the national seminar on 'Living customs and their ancient Indian sources', Edited by V. N. Jha, Pune, Centre of Advanced Study in Sanskrit, University of Poona, 1991, pp. 51-55.

1191. Marcia Ascher "The Kolam tradition: A tradition of figure-drawing in southern India expresses mathematical ideas and has attracted the attention of computer science". *American Scientist*, Vol. 90, No. 1, January-Februaru, 2002, pp. 56-63.

1192. Marfatia, M. J. "Dowry system - A social evil". *Dowry Custom (Vivekananda Kendra Patrika, Madras)*, Vol. 2. No. 2. 1973, pp. 8-11.

1193. Martin, Nancy M. "Rights, roles and reciprocity in Hindu dharma". In, 'Human rights and responsibilities in the world religions', Edited by Joseph Runzo, Nancy M. Martin and Arvind Sharma, Oxford, One World, 2003, pp. 267-82.

1194. Martinez, D. P. "The dead: Shinto aspects of Buddhist ritual". *Journal of The Anthropological Society of Oxford: Jaso,* Vol. 21, No. 2, 1990, pp. 199-209.

1195. Marvin Harris "The cultural ecology of India's sacred cattle". *Current Anthropology*, Vol. 33, No. 1, Supplement: Inquiry and Debate in the Human Sciences: Contributions from Current Anthropology, 1960-1990 (Feb., 1992), pp. 261-276.

1196. Masilamani-Meyer, Eveline "Guardians of Tamil Nadu: folk deities, folk religion, and Hindu themes". Halle, 572 Germany: Franckeschen Stiftungen zu Halle, 2004.

1197. Masilamani-Meyer, Eveline "The changing face of Kāttavarāyan." In, 'Criminal Gods and Demon devotees: essays on the Guardians of popular Hinduism', ed. Alf Hiltebeitel, Albany: State University of New York Press. 1989, pp. 69-104.

1198. Mastana, Ramash Chand "Kagada Ghati main Jagrata". *Somsi*, Vol. 5, No. 2, April 1979, pp. 68-71. [Hindi]

1199. Mathias, T. "Bori dek [microform]". [Manners and customs]. Bombay, L. M. Furtado & Co., 1910. V, 61 p. ; 18 cm. [Konkani]

1200. Mathur Shobha "Raksha bandhan: prem aur suraksha ki pratigya". *Discover India*, Vol. 4, No. 8, 1991 (August), pp. 72-73. [Hindi]

1201. Mathur, K. S. "Festivals of the Chroes". *The Eastern Anthropologist,* Vol. 6 No. 2, 1953, pp. 116-118.

1202. Mathur, K. S. "Caste and ritual in a Malva village". New York: Asia Publishing House, 1964. ix, 215 p. : ill. p.

1203. Mathur, Madhu "Holi-er in spring". *Discover India*, Vol. 12, No. 3, 1999, pp. 72-73.

1204. Mathur, Nihal "Why we celebrate". *Discover India*, Vol. 11, No. 10, 1998, pp. 16-19.

1205. Mathur, Shobha "Raksha Bandhan: The bond of protection". *Discover India*, Vol. 4, No. 8, 1991, pp. 72-73.

1206. Maulīsvaran, Jōtinar "Nāka Pañcami! Karuna Pañcami! *Tina Mani,* 17 August, 4. Murukappiriyan. n.d. Rāku Kçtu Parikāra Vinakkankan. Chennai, Om Muruga Publications. 2007. [Tamil]

1207. Maurer, K. "Trinkaus mortuary ritual and mortuary remains". *Current Anthropology*, Vol. 25, No. 5 (Dec., 1984), pp. 674-679.

1208. Mauss, Mrcel "The gifts, forms and functions of exchange in Archaic" Societies, trans by Ian Cunnison (New York: W. W. Norton 7 Co., 1967, p. 128.

1209. Mayer, Adrian C. "The Holi festival among the Indians of Fiji". *The Eastern Anthropologist*, Vol. 6, No. 1, 1953, pp. 3-17.

1210. Mayilvaganan, V. "A village where Dalits can't wear footwear or ride bikes". New Delhi, The Times of India, 3 May, 2011.

1211. Mazumdar, Rochona "Self sacrifice' versus 'Self interest': a non-historicist reading of the history of women's rights in India". *Comparative Studies of South Asia, Africa and the Middle East* Vol. 22, No. 1-2, 2002, pp. 20-35.

1212. McDaniel, June "Does Tantric ritual empower women? renunciation and domesticity among female Bengali Tantrikas". In, 'Womans Lives, womans Rituals in he Hindu Tradition'. Ed. Tracy Pintchman, New York: Oxford University Press, 2007, pp. 159-176.

1213. McDaniel, June "Making virtuous daughters and wives: an introduction to women's Brata rituals in Bengali Folk religion". Albany: State University of New York Press. 2003.

1214. McDaniel, June "Offering flowers, feeding skulls: Popular Goddess worship in West Bengal. New York: Oxford University Press. 2004.

1215. McDermott, Rachel F. "Encountering Kali: in the margins, at the centre, in the west". Berkeley: University of California Press, 2003.

1216. McGavran, D. A. "Education and the beliefs of popular Hinduism; a study of the beliefs of secondary school boys in central provinces, India, in regard to nineteen major beliefs of popular Hinduism". (Columbia University). Pro Quest Dissertations and Theses, 1937, p.179, Access online at, http://search.proquest. com/docview/ 301761831?accountid=43898

1217. Mcgee, Mary "Ritual rights: the gender indications of Adhikara". In, 'Jewels of authority: women and textual tradition in Hindu India', Edited by Laurie L. Patton, Oxford, Oxford University Press, 2002, pp. 32-50.

1218. Mcgee, Mary "Feasting and fasting: the Vrata tradition and its significance for Hindu women." Ph.D. dissertation, Harvard University, Cambridge, MA. 1987.

1219. Mckenna, T. "Food of the Gods: the search for the original tree of knowledge". New York, Bantam, 1992.

1220. McKenzie, Michael C. & Others "Mythologies of the world: the illustrated guide to mythological beliefs and customs". New York, Checkmark Books, 2001, 160 p. : ill. (some col.), Col. Maps ; 29 cm.

1221. Meena Bhargava "Forests, people and state: continuities and changes. *Economic and Political Weekly*, Vol. 37, No. 43 (Oct. 26 - Nov. 1, 2002), pp. 4440-4446.

1222. Meer Hasan Ali & Crooke, William "Observations on the Mussulmauns of India". Karachi, Oxford University Press, 1974, xxvi, 442 p. illus. 19 cm.

1223. Mehendale, M. A., "The custom of Sahagamana, some early references". In, Proceedings of the national seminar on 'Living customs and their ancient Indian sources', Edited by V. N. Jha, Pune, Centre of Advanced Study in Sanskrit, University of Poona, 1991, pp. 159-171.

1224. Mehra, J. D. "Snake worship among the Nayars of South India." In, 'Through the Vistas of Life and Lore: Folkloric Reflections on Traditional India', ed. R.M. Sarkar, Calcutta: Punthi Pustak. 2000. pp. 609-20.

1225. Mehta, Dipaka "Work, ritual, biography: a Muslim community in North India". Delhi; New York: Oxford University Press, 1997, 283 p. ; 22 cm.

1226. Mehta, Ramesh "Parampara". *Samkaleen Bhartiya Sahitya,* Vol. 22, No. 100, 2002 (March-April), pp. 92. [Hindi]

1227. Mehta, Saudamini and Mehta, Gaganvihari L. "Garba". In, 'Festivals in Indian Society', 2 Vols., Ed. Usha Sharma, A Mittal Publication, New Delhi, pp. 141-144.

1228. Mehta, Tania "Tradition, modernity and the landscapes of belief and ritual: Nirmal Verma's "The burning bough" and U.R. Anantha Murthy's "why not worship in the Nude?" *Indian Literature*, Vol. 47, No. 1, 2003 (Jan-Feb.), pp. 174-184.

1229. Meighan, Clement W. "Mortuary customs in Southern India". *The Eastern Anthropologist*, Vol. 5, No. 4, 1952, pp. 143-164.

1230. Meister, Michael W. "Regional variation in Matrka conventions". *Artibus Asiae*, Vol. 47, No. 3, 1986, pp. 233-62.

1231. Mene, Tarun and Chaudhuri, Sarit K. "Festival and emerging social reality: Perspectives on the Idu Mishimis of Arunachal Pradesh". *The Oriental Anthropologist,* Vol. 10, No. 1, 2010, pp. 33-51.

1232. Menon, C. Karunakara "Serpent worship in Malabar." *Calcutta Review* Vol. 113, 1901. pp. 19-25.

1233. Menon, K. P. "Padmanabha". In, 'Festivals in Indian Society', 2 Vols., Ed. Usha Sharma, A Mittal Publication, New Delhi, pp.117-124.

1234. Menon, Subhadra "The Hemis festival". *Discover India*, Vol.4, No. 5, 1991, pp. 34-36.

1235. Menon, Subhadra "Hemis ka Parv: dusht aatmaon ki parajay". *Discover India*, Vol. 4, No. 5, 1991 (May), pp. 34-36. [Hindi]

1236. Menski, W. F. "Role of ritual in the Hindu marriage". University of London, Ph.D. thesis. 1984.

1237. Menski, W. F. "Change and continuity in Hindu marriage rituals". London, 1991

1238. Mesnil, Marianne "The masked festival: disguise or affirmation?" *Cultures*, Vol. 3, No. 2, 1976, pp. 11-29.

1239. Metcalf, L. L. "Saintly householders: religious beliefs and practices among the Varkaris of Maharashtra, India". The University of Rochester. ProQuest Dissertations and Theses, 1991, p. 212, http://search.proquest.com/docview/303915807? accountid=43898.

1240. Meyer, J. J. "Sexual life in ancient India, etc". (Translated from authors original German), Indian Reprint, Delhi, 1971.

1241. Michael Tobias & Rai, Raghu "A day in the life of India". San Francisco, Calif. : Collins Publishers, 1996, 191 p. : col. ill., map ; 37 cm.

1242. Michael, Prafulla. "The origin of the Ganapati cult". *Asian Folklore Studies* Vol. 42, No. 1, 1983. pp. 91-116.

1243. Middleton, L. "Customary law of the Kangra district (excluding Kulu)". Lahore, superintendent Govt. Printing Press, 1919, vol. IV, pp. 183.

1244. Midya, Dipak K. "A study on the ritual actions in Ho festivals". *Journal of Indian Anthropological Society,* Vol. 31, No. 2, 1996, pp. 161-170.

1245. Mines, Diane P. "Fierce Gods: Inequality, ritual, and the politics of dignity in a South Indian village". Bloomington, IN: Indiana University Press. 2005.

1246. Mines, Diane P; Parish, Steven M. "Fierce gods: inequality, ritual and the politics of dignity in a South Indian village". *American ethnologist*, 34. 2 (May 2007): 247.

1247. Mishra, Jayashankar "Munda janjati ka dharmik parv-tyohar". *Vanyajati*, Vol. 29, No. 2, 1981 (April), pp. 12-17. [Hindi]

1248. Mishra, Krishn Bihari "Kalptaru ki utsav leela: Ramkrishan Paramhans". New Delhi, Bhartiya Gyanpeeth, 2004, p. 596.

1249. Mishra, Madhusudan, "Customs regarding hospitality and their sources". In, Proceedings of the national seminar on 'Living customs and their ancient Indian sources', Edited by V. N. Jha, Pune, Centre of Advanced Study in Sanskrit, University of Poona, 1991, pp. 225-233.

1250. Mishra, Mahendra Kumar "Toki Parab: a Kondh-Paraja festival of Kalahandi". *Folklore*, Vol. 32, No. 1, 1991, pp. 11-20, 24.

1251. Mishra, Neelmani "Kolhon ke ullasmaya tyohar". *Sanskriti Sangam*, Vol. 2, 1987, pp. 5-12. [Hindi]

1252. Mishra, Nihrranjan "Farmers festivals: A case from eastern Orissa". *Journal of Indian Anthropological Society*, Vol. 40, No. 1, 2005, pp. 75-85.

1253. Mishra, Shyam Manohar "Customs of sati: Probable causes of its origin". *The Eastern Ant,* Vol. 51, No. 3, 1998, pp. 269-274.

1254. Mishra, Srikant "Ancient Hindu marriage law and scriptures". New Delhi, 1994.

1255. Mishra, Vibhuti Bhushan "Religious beliefs and practices of North India during the early mediaeval period". Leiden, Brill, 1973, xx, 191 p., 25 cm.

1256. Misra, Gitanjali "Gadaba festivals". *Vanyajati*, Vol. 30, No. 2, 1982, pp. 33-36.

1257. Misra, Gitanjali "Puspunei: a festival of the Juangs: of the hills of Keonjhar district of Orissa". *Folklore*, Vol. 24, No. 10, 1983, pp. 211-214.

1258. Misra, Jaishree "Ancient promises". London, Penguin, 2000, 309 p. ; 20 cm.

1259. Misra, K. K. "Trees in the religion and folklore of the Konda Reddi of South India". *Journal of Human Ecology*, Vol. 9, No. 3, 1998, pp. 257-62.

1260. Misra, Om Prakash "Mother Goddes in central India". Delhi, Agam Kala Prakashan, 1985.

1261. Misra, Shyam Manohar "Origin and antiquity of the custom of sati in ancient India". *The Eastern Anthropologist,* Vol. 47, No. 4, 1994, pp. 379-386.

1262. Mistry, Pramod "Tarnetar fair: Out on a husband hunt" *Discover India*, Vol. 4, No. 8, 1991, pp. 68-71.

1263. Mitra, A. "Fairs and festivals of West Bengal". Alipore, (West Bengal), 1953.

1264. Mitra, Aditi & Knottnerus, J. David "Sacrificing women: A study of ritualized practices among women volunteers in India". *Voluntas: International Journal of Voluntary and Nonprofit Organizations,* Vol. 19, No. 3 (September 2008), pp. 242-267.

1265. Mitra, Bijitendra Mohan "Customary law as the corner-stone of legal framework." *Journal of Indian Anthropological Society,* Vol. 34, No. 1, 1999 (March), pp. 57-60.

1266. Mitra, S. C. "On the cult of Jujube tree". *Man in India,* Vol. 5, 1925, pp. 115-131.

1267. Mitra, S. C. "On the cult of tree Goddess in Eastern Bengal". *Man in India,* Vol. 2, 1922, pp. 228-41.

1268. Mitra, Sarat Chandra "Snake-worship in eastern Bengal, and western and Southern India". In, 'Festivals in Indian Society, 2 Vols., Ed. Usha Sharma, A Mittal Publication, New Delhi, pp. 125-138.

1269. Mitra, Ved "Happy married life in ancient India". New Delhi, 1965.

1270. Mnyampala, Mathias E. "Gogo: history, customs and traditions". Armonk: M. E. Sharpe, 1995. xiv, p. 149 ; maps.

1271. Modi, (Sir) Jivanji Jamshedji "The religious ceremonies and customs of the Parsees". (Series: Oriental religions, 7), New York, Garland Pub., 1979, ii, 484 p., [1] fold. leaf of plates : ill. ; 23 cm.

1272. Modi, J. J. "Symbolism in the marriage ceremonies of different nations". Bombay, Caxton Printing, 1909.

1273. Mohan "The dowry system in India". *Dowry Custom (Vivekananda Kendra Patrika, Madras)* Vol. 2. No. 2. 1973, pp. 48-49.

1274. Mohan Rao, K. "The ceremonial friendship among the tribal people of Andhra Pradesh, *Main in India* Vol. 68, No. 1 March, 1988, pp. 93-104.

1275. Mohanta, Basanta Kumar "Birth rituals of the Ho tribe". *The Tribal Tribune,* An E. Journal, site www.etribaltribune.com. Vol. 3. Issue 4, February 2008. (ISSN:2249-3433).

1276. Mohanta, Basanta Kumar "A Study of syncretism in the Ho rituals and festivals". *Man in Society,* Vol. 14 &15, 2001-2002, pp. 94-100.

1277. Mohanta, Basanta Kumar "Bandana festival of Kudmis of eastern India". *The Tribal Tribune* An E. Journal, site www.etribaltribune. com. Vol. 2. Issue 11, 2006. (ISSN:2249-3433).

1278. Mohanta, Basanta Kumar "Cult of Bongaism, linguistic synthesis and religious syncretism in the Ho society". In, 'Culture, Religion and Philosophy: Critical Studies in Syncretism and Inter- Harmony' edited by N. K. Das. Jajpur, Rawat Publication, 2003, pp. 325-371. (ISBN: 81-7033-820-4).

1279. Mohanta, Basanta Kumar "Death rituals of the Ho tribe: An anthropological observation". *Orissa Review,* Vol. 59, No. 10-11, 2003, pp. 61-63 (ISSN: 0970-8669).

1280. Mohanta, Basanta Kumar "Mortuary practices of the Hos: an Ethno archaeological study". Kolkata; Anthropological Survey of India (Govt. of India). 2010.

1281. Mohanta, Basanta Kumar "Syncretism in the Ho rituals and festivals: A study". *The Tribal Tribune* E. Journal, site www.etribaltribune.com. Vol. 2, Issue 2, 2006. (ISSN:2249-3433).

1282. Mohanta, Basanta Kumar "The Ho: a glimpse of tribal life in transition". *The Tribal Tribune.* An E. Journal, site www.etribaltribune.com. Vol.1, Issue 1, 2004. (ISSN:2249-3433).

1283. Mohanta, Basanta Kumar "Tusu festival of the Kudumis of Northern Orissa: Origin and Causes". *Journal of Sociology and Social Anthropology,* Vol. 2, No. 1, 2011, pp : 23-29. (ISSN: 0976-6634).

1284. Mohanta, Basanta Kumar and Mahato, S. "Bandana Parab: a thanks giving ceremony of the Kurmis". *Orissa Historical Research Journal,* Vol. 46, No. 3, 2004, pp. 74-86.

1285. Mohanta, Basanta Kumar, Duary, N. & Das, P. "Death ritual of the Ho: a study in Kolhan Area". In, 'Dimensions of Researches in Indian Anthropology, Oriental Anthropologist Series II, edited by Vijoy S. Sahay, Pradip K. Singh and Gautam K. Bera. Allahabad; The Oriental Institute of Cultural and Social Research and New Delhi, Serial Publication. 2004, pp. 293-304. [ISBN 81-86771-80-8].

1286. Molley, O. "Modern India and the west: a study of the interaction of their civilization". Oxford University Press", London, 1941.

1287. Momim, A. N. "Burashavar ka Mela". *Himprasat,* Vol. 4. No. 2, May, 1958, pp. 9-10. [Hindi]

1288. Monger, George "Marriage customs of the world: from henna to honeymoons". Santa Barbara, Calif., ABC-CLIO, 2004, xiii, 327 p. : ill. ; 26 cm.

1289. Monika Saxena "Ganikas in early India: its genesis and dimensions. *Social Scientist,* Vol. 34, No. 11/12 (Nov. - Dec., 2006), pp. 2-17.

1290. Monteil, Pascal "Festival colours". *Art India,* Vol. 11, No.3, 2006, pp. 88-89.

1291. Mookerjee, Ajit "Ritual art of India". London: Thames and Hudson, 1985. 176 p., Col. ill. p.

1292. Mookerjee, Ajit "Tantric way: art, science, ritual". Boston, New York Graphic Society, 1977. 208 p. : ill. p.

1293. Mookerjee, Ajit "Tantra asana". Basel, Paris, and New Delhi, Ravi Kumar Books. 1971.

1294. Mookherjee, Harcha N. "Ritual structure of a village in West Bengal, India". *Man and Life,* Vol. 11, No. 1-2, 1985, pp. 1-16.

1295. Mookherjee, Harsha Nath and Dasgupta, Satadal "Caste status and ritual observances in a west Bengal Village". *Man in India*, Vol. 50, No. 04, 1970 (Octo. - Dec.), pp. 390-402.

1296. Morinis, E. A. "Pilgrimage in the Hindu tradition: a case study of West Bengal". Delhi: Oxford University Press, 1984.

1297. Morris E. Opler "Further comparative notes on the Hijarā of India". *American Anthropologist,* New Series, Vol. 63, No. 6 (Dec., 1961), pp. 1331-1332.

1298. Morris, Ian "Death ritual and social structure in classical antiquity". New York, Cambridge University Press, 1992. xviii, p. 264.

1299. Moses, S. T. "Ants and folk-beliefs in South India." In, 'Through the Vistas of Life and Lore: Folkloric Reflections on Traditional India', ed. R. M. Sarkar, Calcutta: Punthi Pustak. 2000. pp. 709-14.

1300. Motwani, K. "Manu: A study in Hindu Social theory". Ganesh & Co.' Madras, 1937.

1301. Muhammad Abdul Qadir, S.S. "Isattul hasanat". [On some Islamic customs]. Vellore: Baqiyat salihat Arabic kalluri, 1932. xii, 269 p. ; 19 cm. In: Tamil.

1302. Muhammad Shamsuddin Siddiqi "Khairo barkat ki shadi vagherah. [Marriage customs]. Hyderabad (Dn.), Shamsul-Islam Press, 1931. 80 p. ; 18 cm. [Urdu]

1303. Muirhead-Thomson, R. C. "Assam valley [microform]: beliefs and customs of the Assamese Hindus" London: Luzac & Co., 1948. 96 p. : ill. ; 21 cm.

1304. Mujjundar, Anuja Arun "Gujarat's tribal fairs". In, 'Fairs and Festivals of Indian tribes', Ed. by Robin David Tribhuwan, Discovery publishing house, New Delhi, 2003, pp. 208-213.

1305. Mukerjee, Bhabanda "Machong among the Garos of Assam", *Eastern Anthropologist*, 09, 1957, pp. 112-116.

1306. Mukerjee, Bhabanda "Mother in law marriage and kinship Organisation". *Anthropologist* (Delhi University), III, 1956 (b), pp. 48-55.

1307. Mukerjee, Bhabanda: "Garo family", *Eastern Anthropologist,* 11, 1935, pp. 25-30.

1308. Mukerji, Sankarananda "Mak' Monre (Mak' Mode)-A Santal Festival in Calcutta: A study in tradition and change". Bulletin of the Cultural Research Institute, Vol. 7, No. 1-2, 1968. pp. 144-147.

1309. Mukherjea, Charulal "Baba: the Santhal Sal-Blossom festival". In, 'Festivals in Indian Society', 2 Vols., Ed. Usha Sharma, A Mittal Publication, New Delhi, pp.145-148.

1310. Mukherjee, B. M. and Khatua, Nilanjan "Mahua: A trai-complex in the kamar tribe of gariband" *Journal of Human Ecology*, Vol. 8, No. 3, 1997, pp. 217-218.

1311. Mukherjee, S. N. "The Bhadraloks of Bengal." In, 'Elites in South Asia', edited by E. Leach. England: Cambridge University Press. 1970.

1312. Mukherjee, Santa and Mandal, Debabrata "Customary rites and festivals in Santal society". *Vanyajati*, Vol. 45, No. 4, 1997, pp. 7-8.

1313. Mukherjee, Sumita and Tribhuwan, Robin D. "Influence of Kali Puja festival on tribals of West Bengal". In, 'Fairs and Festivals of Indian tribes', Ed. by Robin David Tribhuwan, Discovery publishing house, New Delhi, 2003, pp. 116-120.

1314. Mukherji, A. C. "Hindu fasts and feasts". 2nd. Ed. Delhi, Vintage Books, 1989.

1315. Mukhopadhyay, A. "Sati as a social institution in Bengal". Bengal Past and Present 76 (1957), pp. 99-115.

1316. Mukhopadhyay, Asutos "Meyer bratakatha". [Legendary tales concerning girls' customs and rituals], 6th ed. Calcutta: The author, 1927. 164 p. : illus. ; 19 cm. [Bengali].

1317. Mukhopadhyay, Bandana "Notes on some popular festivals in ancient India: with special reference to Pali literature". *Folklore*, Vol. 29, No. 5, 1988, 114-116.

1318. Mundkur, Balaji "The Serpent as sexual symbol." In, 'The Cult of the Serpent: An Interdisciplinary Survey of Its Manifestations and Origins. Albany: State University of New York Press. 1983. pp. 172-208.

1319. Murali, D. "Fighting evil and frightening visitors". *The Hindu: Property Plus-Chennai.* September 18, 2004.

1320. Muralitaran, Mitra "Celvam kolikkum cina vastu". Chennai: Sri Hindu Publications. 2003. [Tamil]

1321. Murdoch, J. "Hindu and Mohammadan festivals". London, 1907.

1322. Murthy, A Satyanarayana, Vijayalakshmikumari, M. and Moorthy, B Rama "Caste and ritual in an Andhra Village". *Bionature*, Vol. 19, No. 5, 1978 (May), pp. 146-150.

1323. Murty, M. L. K. "A cattle festival". *The India Magazine*, Vol. 9, No. 7, 1989, pp. 36-41.

1324. Muthiah, S. "Pongal: The blessings of the pot that boiled over". *Indian Foreign Review*, Vol. 23, No. 7, 1986, pp. 24-25, 28.

1325. Nag, Narendra Gopal. "Family and marriage in Lahul Valley". *Eastern Anthropologist*, Vol. XIII, No. 4, June-Aug., 1960, pp. 261-275.

1326. Nagar, Mahendra Singh, "Marwar Ki Sanskritik Virasat". Jodhpur, Rajasthani Granthagar, 2001. [Hindi]

1327. Nagaraj, K. "Fertility decline in Tamil Nadu: Social capillarity in action?" Chennai: Madras Institute of Development Studies. 2000.

1328. Nagarajan, Vijaya Rettakudi "The earth as Goddess Bhū Devī: Toward a theory of 158 'Embedded ecologies' in folk Hinduism." In 'Purifying the Earthly Body of God: Religion and Ecology in Hindu India', ed. Lance E. Nelson, Albany: State University of New York Press, 1998. pp. 269–95.

1329. Nagarajan, Vijaya, "Hosting the divine: The Kolam in Tamil Nadu". In, 'Mud, Mirror and thread: Folk traditions in rural India'. ed. Nora Fisher, Santa Fe: Museum of international folk art. 1993. pp. 192-203.

1330. Nagendra, S. P. "The concept of rituals in modern sociological theory". *Eastern Anthropologist*, Vol. 26, No. 2, 1973, pp. 214-16.

1331. Nagendra, S. P. "The nature and significance of ritual". *The Eastern Anthropologist*, Vol. 15, No. 01, 1962, pp. 2-20.

1332. Nagpal, Kavita "Holi: The festival of rainbow colours". *Indian Foreign Review*, Vol. 22, No. 11, 1985, pp. 23-27.

1333. Naidu, N Y "Dashara in Bastar: A study of Raja tribal relationship". *Folklore*, Vol. 17, No. 3, 1975, pp. 82-86.

1334. Naik, T. B. "Aboriginal festivals in Gujarat". *The Eastern Anthropologist,* Vol. 2, No. 1, 1948, pp. 16-21.

1335. Naipaul, V. S. "An area of darkness". New York, Vintage Books, 1981, 1964, 281 p. ; 21 cm.

1336. Nair, Janaki "The Devadasi, Dharma and the state". *Economic and Political Weekly*, Vol. 29, No. 50 (Dec. 10, 1994), pp. 3157-3159+3161-3167.

1337. Nakane, Chie. "Garo and Khasi-A comparative study in matrilineal systems". Parism Monton & Co. 1967.

1338. Nakassis, Constantine. "Youth and status in Tamil Nadu, India". University of Pennsylvania, Department of Anthropology Ph.D. thesis. 2010.

1339. Nambiar, A. K. "The ritual accessories of Teyyam". *The India Magazine*, Vol. 13, No. 9, 1993, pp. 6-15.

1340. Nambiar, Balan "Gods and ghosts Teyyam and bhuta rituals". *Marg*, Vol. 34, No. 02, pp. 63-73.

1341. Nanda, Neeru "Flowers and festivals". *Sundaram: A magazine on contemporary art*, Vol. 3, No. 1-2, 1990, pp. 5-7.

1342. Nandwana, Shobha "Customary laws, marriage among Bhils". *Vanyajati*, Vol. 42, No. 01, 1994 (January), pp. 20-24.

1343. Nandy, Ashis. "Sati as profit versus Sati as a spectacle: The public debate on Roop Kanwar's death". In, 'Sati: The blessing and the curse. The burning of wives in India', Edited by John Stratton Hawley, Oxford University Press, New York, 1994, pp. 131-148.

1344. Narain, Dhirendra "Hindu character". Bombay, University of Bombay Publications, 1957.

1345. Narain, Tewari Udai "India: A cultural voyage" Chapt. On "festivals: Accents on truer lights". Gian Offset Printers, Old Rohatak Road, Delhi, 1987, pp. 135-144.

1346. Narana Duraikkannan "Velaikkari. [On social customs]". 3rd ed. Madras: M. Cakravarti Nayanar, 1953. iv, 90 p. , 18 cm. [Tamil]

1347. Narasimhan, Shakuntala "The brightest moonless night". *Discover India*, Vol. 2, No. 11, 1989, pp. 51-53.

1348. Narayanan, Vasudha "Religious vows at the Shrine of Shahul Hamid." In, 'Dealing with Deities: The Ritual Vow in South Asia, eds. Selva J. Raj and William P. Harman Albany: State University of New York Press. 574 p., 2006, pp. 65-85.

1349. Narayanan, Vasudha "Water, wood, and wisdom: ecological perspectives from the Hindu traditions." *Daedulus*, Vol. 130, No. 4, 2001, pp. 179-206.

1350. Narendra Nath Bhattacharyya "Ancient Indian rituals and their social contents". *The American Historical Review,* Vol. 81, No. 5 (Dec., 1976), 1206 p.

1351. Naresh "Hamare riti-rivaaz". Chandigarh, Haryan Sahitya Akadami, 1990, 71 p.

1352. Narsingh, Shakuntala "Jagmagaati Amavasya". *Discover India*, Vol. 2, No. 11, 1989 (November), pp. 47-53. [Hindi]

1353. Naruka, Devi Singh "Holi: rangon ka tyohar". *Sanskriti*, Vol. 23, No. 1-2, 1981 (Jan. -June), pp. 16-17. [Hindi]

1354. Natarajan, S. "Swati Tirunal festival in Trivandrum: Interesting new features". *Sruti: South Indian Classsical Music and Dance Magazine,* Issue No. 18, 1985, pp. 6-7.

1355. Natesa Sastri, S. M. "Cradle tales of Hinduism". Calcutta: Advaita Ashrama. North Indian Notes and Queries. 1917.

1356. Nath, Pandit Amar "Local festivals of Ladakh". In 'Festivals in Indian Society', 2 Vols., Ed. Usha Sharma, A Mittal Publication, New Delhi, pp. 111-122.

1357. Nath, S. C. "Mopin festival in Arunchal Pradesh". *Soc. Welfare,* Vol. 23, No.1, 1976, pp. 14-15.

1358. Nath, Sujatha "Fasting, a lesson in restraint". *Discover India,* Vol. 11, No. 10, 1998, pp. 54-56.

1359. Nath, Y. V. S. "Bhils of Ratanmal: an analysis of Western India community. Baroda: Maharajah Sayajirao University. 1960.

1360. Nayak, Kunj Bihari "Festivals of India: A theoretical consideration". In, 'Fairs and Festivals of Indian tribes', Ed. by Robin David Tribhuwan, Discovery Publishing House, New Delhi, 2003, pp. 121-144.

1361. Nayak, Kunj Bihari "Tribal festivals in Kalhandi, Orissa". In, 'Fairs and Festivals of Indian tribes, Ed. by Robin David Tribhuwan, Discovery Publishing House, New Delhi, 2003, pp. 97-115.

1362. Neema Caughran "Fasts, feasts, and the slovenly woman: Strategies of resistance among North Indian potter women". *Asian Folklore Studies,* Vol. 57, No. 2 (1998), pp. 257-274.

1363. Neff, Deborah. 1987. "Aesthetics and power in Pambin Tullal: A possession ritual of rural Kerala". *Ethnology* Vol. 26, pp. 63-71.

1364. Negi, Thakur Sen "Kinnnor ke tyohar mele". *Himbharti,* Vol. 1, No. 4, 1979, December, pp. 26-31. [Hindi]

1365. Neher, Andrew "A physiological explanation of unusual behaviour in ceremonies involving drums". *Human Biology,* Vol. 34, 1962, pp. 151-60.

1366. Neog, Maheswar "Bhaona: the ritual play of Assam". New Delhi: Sangeet Natak Akademi. p. 65 : plates p.

1367. Nepali, Gopal singh, "The Newars: An ethno-sociological study of a Himalayan community". Bombay: United Asia Publications, 1965.

1368. Neurgavker, H. B. P. & Keshav, Sadashiv "Palkhi Sohala". Pune, Utkasrsh Prakasha, 1984. [Marathi]

1369. Newell, W.H. "Inter caste marriage in Kugti village, upper Budl Nadi Brahmaur Tehsil, Chamba District, Himachal Pradesh, India". *Man,* Vol. LXIII, No. 59, April 1963, pp. 55-57.

1370. Newman, R. S. "Faith is all! emotion and devotion in a Goan Sect". *Numen.* Vol. 28, Fasc. 2 (Dec., 1981), pp. 216-246.

1371. Nicholas, Ralph W. "Fruits of worship: practical religion in Bengal". New Delhi, Chronicle, 2003.

1372. Nicholas, Ralph W. "The Goddess Sitala and epidemic smallpox in Bengal." *Journal of Asian Studies,* Vol. 41, No. 1, 1981. pp. 21-44.

1373. Nicholas, Ralph W. "The village mother in Bengal." In, 'Mother Worship, Themes and Variations, ed. James J.

Preston, Chapel Hill: University of North Carolina Press. 1982. pp. 192-209.

1374. Nicholson, Louise "When Paris went to town: The festival of India opens". *The India Magazine*, Vol. 6, No. 1, 1985, pp. 56-67.

1375. Nieuwsma, J. A. "Depression beliefs in Northern India and the United States: A cross-cultural study. University of Wyoming). ProQuest Dissertations and Theses, 2009. http://search. proquest.com/docview/518740156?account id=43898

1376. Nilakantha, K. A. "Traditional cultures in South-East Asia". Orient Longmans, 1958.

1377. Niraj Jaisingh. "Rajasthan Ki Sanskritik parampara". Jaipur, Maharaja Mansingh Pustak Prakash Sodh Kendra, 1994. [Hindi]

1378. Nirmohi, M. L. "Utsavon Ka samajshastra". New Delhi, Radha Publications, 2008, p. 184. [Hindi]

1379. Nishimura, Yuko "Gender, kinship and property rights: Nagarattar womanhood in South India". Delhi ; New York, Oxford University Press, 1998, xii, 343 p. : ill., map ; 22 cm.

1380. Nivedita, Sister "The Durga Puja". *Folklore*, Vol. 20, No. 10, 1979, pp. 219-220.

1381. Niyogi, Tushar K "Sacred bath ceremony and myth-ritual complex at Gangasagar". *Journal of the Anthropological Survey of India,* Vol. 47, No. 1, 1998, pp. 25-47.

1382. Noble, Pepita "Panchavadyam, thyambaka, percussion of Kerala: From stirring beats to soft and fragile notes". *The India Magazine*, Vol. 5, No. 8, 1985, pp. 44-49.

1383. Noble, Pepita "The Trichur Pooram: A ritual, a ceremony and a parade". *The India Magazine*, Vol. 3, No. 6, 1983, pp. 24-34.

1384. Nolson, T.S. "The origin of popular superstitions and customs". London, T. Warner Lorry Ltd., 1930.

1385. Northey, W. Brook "Gurkhas: their manners, customs and country". New Delhi, Cosmo, 1976. xxxvii, p. 282 : ill.; maps.

1386. Note on magico-relious beliefs about plants among Lodhas of Midnapur, West Bengal". *Vanyajati*, Vol. 23, Now 2-3, 1975, pp. 20-22.

1387. Novetzke, Christian Lee "The tongue makes a good book: history and performance in the Namdev tradition in Maharashtra". Ph.D. Dissertation, Columbia University, 2003.

1388. Novetzke, Christian Lee "Bhakti and its publics". *International Journal of Hindu Studies*, Vol. 11, No. 3, 2007, pp. 255-72.

1389. Novetzke, Christian Lee "Religion and public memory: a cultural history of Saint Namdev in India". New York, Columbia University Press, 2008.

1390. Ntha, Pratibha "Kullu Dussehra: devtaon ki shradhanjali". *Discover India*, Vol. 4, No. 9, 1991 (September), pp. 70-72. [Hindi]

1391. Nur Yalman "The structure of Sinhalese healing rituals". *The Journal of Asian Studies*, Vol. 23, Aspects of Religion in South Asia (Jun., 1964), pp. 115-150.

1392. Nur, Yalman "Under the Bo tree". The University of California Press, Berkeley and Los Angeles, 1967.

1393. O'Flaherty, Wendy Doniger "Siva: the erotic ascetic". Oxforad, Oxford University Press, 1973.

1394. O'Flaherty, Wendy Doniger "The origins of evil in Hindu mythology". Berkeley: University of California Press. 1976.

1395. O'Flaherty, Wendy Doniger, (trans.) "Hindu myths: A sourcebook translated from the Sanskrit". London: Penguin Books. 1975.

1396. Oaten, Edward Farley "Travel and travelers in India, A.D. 1400-1700". New York, AMS Press, 1971, xiv, 274 p., 19 cm.

1397. O'Flaherty, Wendy Doniger. "Hindu myths". Harmondsworth: Penguin Books, 1980.

1398. Ogle, Carol & Ogle, John "Through the year in India". London: Batsford Academic and Educational, 1983, 72 p., : ill. ; 26 cm.

1399. Oki, Morihiro "India fairs and festivals". New Delhi, Gakken Co., 1989. p. 160, Col. ill. p.

1400. Oldenberg, Hermann & Muller, F. Max "The Grihya-sutras: rules of Vedic domestic ceremonies". (Sacred books of the East..., v. 29-30, UNESCO collection of representative works: Indian series.), Delhi, Motilal Banarsidass, 1964, 2 v. ; 23 cm.

1401. Oldenburg, Veena Talwar "Comment: the continuing invention of the Sati tradition." In, 'Sati, the Blessing and the Curse: The Burning of Wives in India', ed. John Stratton Hawley, New York: Oxford University Press, 1994. pp. 159-73.

1402. Oldham, C. F. "The Nāgas: a contribution to the history of serpent worship." Cambridge: Cambridge University Press for the Royal Asiatic Society. 575 p. *Journal of the Royal Asiatic Society of Great Britain and Ireland*, 1901. pp. 461-73.

1403. Oldham, C. F. "The Sun and the serpent: a contribution to the history of serpent worship. New Delhi: Asian Educational Services. 1988.

1404. O'Malley, L. S. S. (Lewis Sydney Steward) "India's social heritage [microform]". Oxford, Clarendon Press, 1934. 194 p. ; 18 cm.

1405. O'Malley, L. S. S. "Indian caste customs". Cambridge [Eng.] University Press, 1932, x, 190 p. 19 cm.

1406. Oman, John Campbell "Cults, customs, and superstitions of India; comprising studies and sketches of interesting peculiarities in the beliefs, festivals and domestic life of the Indian people; also of witchcraft and demoniacal possession, as known amongst them". Delhi, Vishal Publishers, 1972, xiii, 336 p. illus. 22 cm.

1407. Oman, John Campbell "Religious festivals and caste system in India during 19th century". New Delhi, Khama Publishers, 2003. p. 302.

1408. Oman, John Campbell "The Brahmans, theists, and Muslims of India [microform]: studies of goddess-worship in Bengal, caste, Brahmaism and social reform, with descriptive sketches of curious festivals, ceremonies, and faquirs". London, T. Fisher Unwin, 1907. xv, 342 p. : ill. 22 cm.

1409. Orans, Martin, "The Santal: a tribe in search of a great tradition". Detroit: Wayne state university press, 1965.

1410. Oraon, Karma "Dimension of religion, magic and festivals of Indian tribe: the Munda". New Delhi, Kanishka, 2002. p. 140.

1411. Orenstein, H. "The structure of Hindu caste values, a preliminary study of hierarchy and ritual defilement, ethnology". Princeton, Princeton University Press, 1965.

1412. Orr, Leslie C. "Women in the temple, the palace, and the family: The construction of women's identities in pre-colonial Tamil Nadu." In, 'Structure and Society in Early South India', ed. Kenneth R. Hall, New Delhi: Oxford University Press. 2001. pp. 198-234.

1413. Orr, Leslie C. "Domesticity and difference/woman and men: religious life in medieval Tamil Nadu". In, 'Woman's lives, woman's rituals in the Hindu tradition'. Ed. Tracy Pintchman, New York: Oxford University Press, 2007. pp. 109-130.

1414. Ortner, Sherry B. "Sherpa through their rituals". New Delhi, Vikas, 1979. ix, p.195 : ill. p.

1415. Osada, Toshiki "A view of nature of the Munda people in eastern India: rice, ancestor and nature". *Tropics*, Vol. 8, No. 1-2, 1998, pp.147-58.

1416. Osborn, Martin "The Gods of India: their history, character and worship". 1913, reprint Delhi and Varansi, Indological Book House, 1972.

1417. Osella, Filippo; Osella, Caroline. "From transience to immanence: consumption, life-cycle and social mobility in Kerala, South India". *Modern Asian Studies,* Vol. 33, No. 4, (Oct 1999), pp. 989-1020.

1418. Osella, Fillippo, and Caroline Osella. "Articulation of physical and social bodies in Kerala". *Contributions to Indian Sociology*, Vol. 30, No. 1, 1996, pp. 37-68.

1419. Ostor, Akos "On the ethnographic study complex Bengali pujas festivals". *Journal of Indian Anthropological Society,* Vol. 13, No. 3, 1978, pp. 215-264.

1420. Ostor, Akos "The play of the gods: locality, ideology, structure and time in the festivals of a Bengali town". Chicago: University of Chicago. 1980. p. 201.

1421. Ostor, Akos "Puja in society". Lucknow, Ethnographic and Folk Culture Society, 1982.

1422. Ostor, Akos "Culture and power: legend, ritual, bazaar, and rebellion in a Bengali society". New Delhi, Beverly Hills, Sage Publications, 1984, 224 p.: ill. ; 23 cm.

1423. Padel, Felix "The sacrifice of human being: British rule and the Konds of Orissa". Delhi, New York, Oxford University Press, 1995, xvii, 428 p. : maps ; 23 cm.

1424. Padfield, J. E. "Hindu festivals (Parvani). In, 'Festivals in Indian Society', 2 Vols., Ed. Usha Sharma, A Mittal Publication, New Delhi, pp. 27-44.

1425. Padhi, Anjali "The Dalkhai ritual of Western Orissa". *Jounral of Indian Folkoristics*, Vol. 10, No. 1/2, 2008 (Jan-Dec.), pp. 79-92.

1426. Padhy, Sachindananda "Ethnobiological analysis from myth to science: XII. Pancha Yajnya (five sacrifices)-A welcome episode of the Human community for rainy season exhibited through festivals, Journal of Human Ecology, Vol. 24, No. 1, 2008, pp. 1-6.

1427. Padmanabhan, S. "Onam: the national festival of Kerala". *Swarajya*, Vol. 21, No. 10, 1976, pp. 14-15.

1428. Paeet, Panindra "Aali aaye Linga". *Vanyajati*, Vol. 31, No. 4, 1983 (October), pp. 6-9. [Hindi]

1429. Paige, Karen Ericksen; Paige, Jeffery "The politics of reproductive ritual". M. Berkeley: University of California Press, 1981.

1430. Pal, Anjali, "Quaint marriage customs of a primitive people". *Indian Express*, March 11, 1973, p. 3.

1431. Pal, D.C. "Magico-religious beliefs about plants among Adibasis of Bihar". *Folklore*, Vol. 13, No. 12, 1972, pp. 479-83.

1432. Pal, D. C. "Plants associated with Durga puja ceremony in West Bengal". *Natuaral History of Sociology and Natural History of Museum*, Vol. 36, 1970, pp. 61-67.

1433. Pālakumāran "Munnakakkanni: Oru Pēcum Teyvam. Tinakaran, *Ānmika Cinppu Malar,* 14 July, No. 2-3. 2007. [Tamil]

1434. Palat, Ramchandra "Rajasthan ke sahariya ke riti rivaaz". *Vanyajati*, Vol. 34, No. 3, 1986 (July), pp. 15-24. [Hindi]

1435. Palat, Ramchandra "Rajasthan ki aadim jaatiyon me tyohar aur pritibhoj". *Vanyajati*, Vol. 35, No. 3, 1987 (July), pp. 1-9 [Hindi]

1436. Palathara, J. C. "Snake-worship in India." *Asian Quarterly of Culture and Synthesis,* Vol. 2, No. 5, 1952. pp. 45-48.

1437. Palinisami, R. "Festival of Mahaliathal and Muniappans". *Soc. Welfare*, Vol. 22, No. 3, 1975, pp. 26-27.

1438. Palit, P. K. "India celebrates a festival of science in the USA". *Journal of India Museums,* Issue No. 40, 1984, pp. 190-191.

1439. Palita, Haridasa "Adyera Gambhira [microform] : Bangalara dharmma o samajika itihasera eka adhyaya [Account of Gambhira festival of Bengal]. Haridasa Palita. Maladaha: Maladaha-Jatiyasikshasamiti; Kalikata, Ejentas, Cakrabarti Cyatarjienda Kom., 1319 [1912] xxiii, 326 p. ; 18 cm. [Bengali]

1440. Palrovali, Pram. "Kullu ka prasidha devoustav dashahara". *Himprastra*, No. 147, Oct. 1967, pp. 20-23. [Pahari language]

1441. Palsikar, S. M., "Sukharpuda: Custom and it's sources". In, Proceedings of the national seminar on 'Living customs and their ancient Indian sources', Edited by V. N. Jha, Pune, Centre of Advanced Study in Sanskrit, University of Poona, 1991, pp. 84-87.

1442. Panchal, Chinu. "1,500 Witness 'Sati' ritual". *Times of India*, October 6, 1986.

1443. Panda, Ganesh Prasad, "Living manners at the time of taking meals in Orissa and their sources". In, Proceedings of the national seminar on 'Living customs and their ancient Indian sources', Edited by V. N. Jha, Pune, Centre of Advanced Study in Sanskrit, University of Poona, 1991, pp. 201-210.

1444. Panda, N. C. "Suliya Jatra: a folk festival of Kondhs: A survey". *Folklore*, Vol. 31, No. 3-4, 1990, pp. 94-99.

1445. Panda, P. "Karama: A Binjhal festival-its socio-religious significance". *The Eastern Anthropologist*, Vol. 34, No. 2, 1981, pp. 141-150.

1446. Panda, Sadhu Charan "Naga cult in Orissa". Delhi, B.R. Publishing Corporation. 1986.

1447. Pande, T. "Tree worship in ancient India". *Folklore*, Vol. 5, No. 6, 1964, pp. 213-18.

1448. Pandey, Asha "The mela of Deva Sharif". *Sundaram: A Magazine on contemporary art,* Vol. 2, No. 3, 1989, 37-40.

1449. Pandey, Ashok "Kandali utsav: Barahven sal phir". *Pahad,* Vol. 11, 2000, pp. 103-109. [Hindi]

1450. Pandey, B. B. "Festivals of Subansiri". Shillong, Directorate of Research, 1981. p. 78.

1451. Pandey, Indu Prakash "Avadhi vrat kathayen". New Delhi, Bhartiya Gyanpeeth, 1967. [Avadhi]

1452. Pandey, Om Prakahs "Tantrik vichar parampara ke vedik aadhar". *Madhya Bharti (HUMANITIES),* Vol. 42, 1996 (November), pp. 28-35 [Hindi]

1453. Pandey, R. B. "Hindu Samskaras". Banaras, Vikram Publications, 1949.

1454. Pandey, R. B. "Hindu Samskara-samajik tatha dharmik adhyayan" (Revised Hindi version of authors original English) 2nd ed., Varansi, 1966. [Hindi]

1455. Pandey, Rajbali "Hindu Sanskāras: Socio-Religious Study of the Hindu Sacraments". Delhi: Motilal Banarsidass, 2002.

1456. Pandey, Tripti "Jumbo jamboree". *Discover India*, Vol. 6, No. 3, 1993, pp. 70-73.

1457. Pandey, Tripti "Swinging in the rain". *Discover India*, Vol. 3, No. 7, 1990, pp. 69-71."

1458. Pandey, Tripti "Traditional themes and haunting melodies". *Discover India*, Vol. 5, No. 2, 1992, pp. 40-41.

1459. Pandey, Tripti "Gangor: vevahik such aur sampannata ka parv". *Discover India*, Vol. 4, No. 3, 1991 (March), pp. 40-43. [Hindi]

1460. Pandey, Tripti "Paramparik prasang gunjte geet". *Discover India*, Vol. 5, No. 2, 1992 (Feb.), pp. 40-41. [Hindi]

1461. Pandian, Anand. "Crooked stalks; cultivating virtue in South India". Durham and London: Duke University Press. 2009.

1462. Pandian, E. T. Jacob "Nadu Veedu rituals and family shamanism in Tamil society: A cult institution of hinduism". *Man in India*, Vol. 55, No. 2, 1975 (Jan. - March), pp. 67-77.

1463. Pandya, Vishvajit "Above the forest: a study of Andamanese ethno-anemology, cosmology, and the power of ritual". Delhi, Oxford University Press, 1993. xxxi, p. 319 : ill p.

1464. Pandya, Vishvajit "Spirits, politics and rituals in the History of Nicobar Islands". *Journal of Social Sciences,* Vol. 4, No. 4, 2000 (October), pp. 243-260.

1465. Panikkar, K. M. "Religion and magic among the Nayars". *Man*, 18 (1918): 104-110.

1466. Panikkar, Shivaji K. "Saptmatrika worship and sculptures: an iconological interpretation of the conflicts and resolutions in the storied Brahmanical Icons". New Delhi, D. K. Printworld, 1997.

1467. Pannell, Sandra "Carving the palm: The role of metaphor in Mayamo marriage rituals". *Mankind*, Vol. 19, No.), 1989 (August), pp. 160-169.

1468. Panse, Ujjwala, "Omens: past and present". In, Proceedings of the national seminar on 'Living customs and their ancient Indian sources', Edited by V. N. Jha,. Pune, Centre of Advanced Study in Sanskrit, University of Poona, 1991, pp. 251-258.

1469. Pant, Arun "Night of Mandaan". *The India Magazine*, Vol. 7, No. 9, 1987, pp. 46- 51.

1470. Pant, Rajanikant "History of Rāhu and Ketu." *Vishvesharanand Indological Journal*, Vol. 19, No. 1-2, 1981, pp. 277-83.

1471. Panwar, Chatar Singh "Sipi ka Mela". *Himprasth*, Vol. 3, No. 3 June 1957, pp. 23-24. [Hindi]

1472. Panwar, Dashrath "Maharashtra me banjara samaj ka teej parv". *Shodh Samvet*, Vol. 20, No. 2, 2011 (July-Sept), pp. 64-68. [Hindi]

1473. Pappaport, Roy A. "Ritual and religion in the making of humanity". London, Cambridge University Press. 1999. xxiii, p. 535.

1474. Paranjpe, Sucheta, "Customs at the time of taking meals in Maharashtrian families". In, Proceedings of the national seminar on 'Living customs and their ancient Indian sources', Edited by V. N. Jha, Pune, Centre of Advanced Study in Sanskrit, University of Poona, 1991, pp. 221-213.

1475. Parekh, Neha "Festival of art". *Art India*, Vol. 9, No. 3, 2004, pp. 95-99.

1476. Paricha, R. N. "Kulu Dussehra". *Indian and Foreign Review*, Vol. 24, No. 24, 1987, pp. 24-26.

1477. Parihar, Shriman "Lokotsava: Gangore". *Chomasa*, Vol. 20, No. 62, 2003 (July-October), pp. 106-109. [Hindi]

1478. Parker, Victoria "We're from India". (Series We're from.), Chicago, Ill. : Heinemann, 2005, 32 p. : chiefly col. ill., map ; 23 cm.

1479. Parmar, Shyam "Madhya Pradesh: lok Sanskrit aur Sahitya". New Delhi, National Book Trust, 1975. [Hindi]

1480. Parmar, Y. S. "Kulu Dussehra becomes international festival". Kulu Dussehra Souvenir 1974, p. 3.

1481. Parmar, Yashwant Singh, "Polyandry in the Himalayas". Delhi, Vikas Publishing House, 1975, Vol. XV. p. 195.

1482. Parpola, Asko "Bangles, sacred trees, and fertility: interpretations of the Indus 576 script relating to the cult of Skanda-Kumāra." In, 'South Asian Archaeology' 1987: *Proceedings of the Ninth International Conference of the Association of South Asian Archaeologists in Western Europe* (Serie Orientale Roma 66:1), ed. Maurizio Taddei with P.F. Callieri, 1987. pp. 263-84.

1483. Parratt, Saroj Nalini "Religion of Manipur: beliefs, rituals and historical development". Calcutta: Firma Klm, 1980. p. 218 : plates.

1484. Parry, Jonathan "The Aghori ascetics of Benaras". In, 'Indian religion', edited by Richard Burghart and Audry Cantlie, London, Curzon Press, 1985, pp. 51-78.

1485. Parry, Jonathan "Death and the digestion: the symbolism of food and eating in North Indian mortuary rites". *Man*, Vol. 20, 1985, pp. 612-30.

1486. Parry, Jonathan "Sacrificial death and the macrophages ascetic". In, 'Death and the regeneration of life', Edited by Mourice Blouch and Jonathan Parry, Cambridge, Cambridge University Press, 1982, pp. 74-110.

1487. Parry, Jonathan "Death and cosmogony in Kasi". In, 'Way of life: King, householder, renounces. Essays in honour of Louis Dumont', Edited by T. Madan, New Delhi, Vikas Publishsing House, 1981, pp. 337-65.

1488. Parry, Jonathan "Ghosts, greed and sins: the occupational identity of the Benaras funeral priests". *Man*, Vol. 15, 1980, pp. 88-111.

1489. Parry, Jonathan P. "Death in Banaras". Cambridge ; New York : Cambridge University Press, 1994, xxvi, 314 p. : ill., maps ; 24 cm.

1490. Parry, N. E. "Monograph on Lushai customs and ceremonies". Mizoram: Firma Klm, 1928. p. 130.

1491. Parry, N. E. "Lushai custom: a monograph on lushai customs and ceremonies". Aizawl: Firma KLM Private Limited, 1976. iv, p. 130.

1492. Parshad, Ram, Munshi "Hindu teoharon ki asliyat aur un ki jughrafiyai kaifiyat [microform] [On Hidu festivals]. Munshi Ram Parshad. Lahaur : Mufid-i Am Pres, [19—] 128 p. ; 18 cm. [Urdu]

1493. Partap C. Aggarwal "Islamic revival in modern India: The case of the Meos". *Economic and Political Weekly,* Vol. 4, No. 42 (October 18, 1969), pp. 1677, 1679-1681.

1494. Parthasarathy, Y. G. "Dowry system today". *Dowry Custom (Vivekananda Kendra Patrika, Madras)* Vol. 2. No. 2. 1973, pp. 125-126.

1495. Parton, Margaret "The leaf and the flame". New York, Knopf, 1959, 277 p. 22 cm.

1496. Pasayat, Chitrasen "The Nuakhai tradition of West Orissa". *The Eastern Anthropologist,* Vol. 61, No. 2, 2008, pp. 253-262.

1497. Pasayet, Chitra Sen and Seth, Radhakanta "Nuakhai: a tradition of Western-Orissa: oath-taking to live a peaceful and happy life". *Folklore,* Vol. 28 No. 2, 1987, pp. 34-36, 37.

1498. Pataskar, Bhagyalata, "Custom of Gudhi Padava and its sources". In, 'Proceedings of the national seminar on 'Living customs and their ancient Indian sources', Edited by V. N. Jha, Pune, Centre of Advanced Study in Sanskrit, University of Poona, 1991, pp. 259-270.

1499. Pate, Suman Y. "Bonded Labour or Dasa Pratha". In, Proceedings of the national seminar on 'Living customs and their ancient Indian sources', Edited by V. N. Jha, Pune, Centre of Advanced Study in Sanskrit, University of Poona, 1991, pp. 323-328.

1500. Patel, M. L. "Customary laws among the Gond of Madhya Pradesh". *Human Science,* Vol. 34, No. 1, 1985, pp. 5-16.

1501. Patel, Y. S. "Children's appropriation of their teacher's beliefs about the "purpose of reading: An exploratory study in an Indian setting. University of California, Los Angeles). ProQuest Dissertations and Theses, 1994, p. 192. http://search.proquest.com/docview/304093985? accountid=43898

1502. Patel-Amin, N. "Relationship of modernity and childrearing practices among Guajarati Hindu families living in India". University of Pittsburgh). ProQuest Dissertations and Theses, 1996, p 112. http://search.proquest.com/docview/304256839? accountid= 43898

1503. Pathak, Manjushree "Tribal customs law and justics: a teleological study of Adis". 2nd ed. New Delhi, Mittal Publications, 2005. xiv, p. 426.

1504. Pathak, V. S. "Vows and festivals in early medieval inscriptions of Northern India". In 'Festivals in Indian Society', 2 Vols., Ed. Usha Sharma, A Mittal Publication, New Delhi, pp. 217-230.

1505. Pathy, Dinanath "Art: regional traditions the temple of Jagannatha architecture sculpture painting ritual". New Delhi: Sundeep Prakashan, 2001. p. 246.

1506. Patil, Ashok D. "Korku Janjati ke parv". *Chomasa*, Vol. 11, No. 3), 1994 (March - June), pp. 105-111. [Hindi]

1507. Patil, Shyamrao Mane "Funeral ritual (Dak Vidhi) in Potter community: of Maharastra and its importance". *Folklore*, Vol. 28, No. 8, 1987 (August), pp. 191-193.

1508. Patnaik, U. N. "Religious ceremonies, ordeals amd legends about Oriya infiltration in Kondh Hill". *Adibasi*, Vol. 11, No. 4, January 1970, pp. 76-84.

1509. Pattanayaka, Padmacarana "Hindu acarara bicara. [On the Hindu customs and manners]". Cuttack, The author, 1951, Vol. 1 (ii, 100 p.); 18 cm. [Oriya]

1510. Patton, Laurie L. (Ed.) "Jewels of authority: women and textual tradition in Hindu India". Oxford, Oxford University Press, 2002.

1511. Patyal, H. C. "Role of Barber in the religious ceremonies". In, 'Proceedings of the national seminar on 'Living customs and their ancient Indian sources', Edited by V. N. Jha, Pune, Centre of Advanced Study in Sanskrit, University of Poona, 1991, pp. 44-50.

1512. Patyal, Hukam Chand "Tortoise in the Vedic mythology and ritual". *Bulletin of The Deccan College Research Institute,* Vol. 38, No. 1-4, 1979, pp. 107-115.

1513. Paul Younger "A temple festival of Māriyamma". *Journal of the American Academy of Religion,* Vol. 48, No. 4 (Dec., 1980), pp. 493-517.

1514. Paul, C. T. "The economic aspects of tribal rituals: a case study of Paniyas in Wynad district of Kerala". *Folklore,* Vol. 29, No. 6, 1988 (June), pp. 121-126.

1515. Paul, Kakali (Mitra) "Kora religious belief: A fusion of traditional tribal faith and Hinduism". *Stud. Tribes Tribals,* Vol. 2, No. 2, 2003, pp. 81-87.

1516. Paul, Radha Kanta "Sacrificing the Mithun: Baru puja: fertility rite of the Kabui Nagas". *The India Magazine,* Vol. 6, No. 5, 1986, pp. 20- 27.

1517. Pauline Kolenda "Woman as tribute, woman as flower: images of "Woman" in weddings in North and South India". *American Ethnologist,* Vol. 11, No. 1 (Feb., 1984), pp. 98-117.

1518. Pawar, Shubhangi and Patil, D.A. "Identities and utility of botanicals used in religious worship and festivals in Khandesh region of Maharashtra". *Ethnobotany,* Vol. 22, No. 1-2, 2010, pp. 102-106.

1519. Pazili, Gowhar "Another autumn in Kashmir". *Economic and Political Weekly,* Vol. 46, No. 38, 2011, pp. 28-29.

1520. Pearson, Anne Mackenzie "Because it gives me peace of mind: rituals fasts in the religious lives of Hindu Women". Albany: State University of New York Press. 1996.

1521. Pemberton, C. "Masti aur umangon bhara, Christmas dhoop me khila". *Discover India*, Vol. 3, No. 12, 1990 (December), pp. 24-27. [Hindi]

1522. Pemberton, Christine "Ganesh Chaturthi: When the lord comes to town". *Discover India*, Vol. 3, No. 9, 1990, pp. 22-27.

1523. Pemberton, Christine "Join the Easter parade". *Discover India,* Vol. 5, No. 4, 1992, pp. 70-73.

1524. Penner, Hans H. "Rituals". The New Encyclopedia Britannica. Chicago: Encyclopaedia Britannica, 1981. pp. 865–866.

1525. Pentuker, Ramchander "A promise fulfilled". *Discover India,* Vol. 2, No. 2, 1989, pp. 28-31.

1526. Pentuker, Ramchander "Korivi: A festival of faith". *Discover India*, Vol. 6, No. 5, 1993, pp. 43-46.

1527. Pertierra, Raul "Ritual and the constitution of social structure". *Mankind*, Vol. 17, No. 3, 1987 (December), pp. 199-211.

1528. Pervez, K. "Borders & beliefs: ethics, actor hood, and the India Pakistan conflict". The American University. ProQuest Dissertations and Theses, 2009. http://search.proquest.com/docview/304843699? accountid=43898

1529. Peter J. Claus "The Siri myth and ritual: a mass possession cult of South India". *Ethnology,* Vol. 14, No. 1 (Jan., 1975), pp. 47-58 (article consists of 12 pages)

1530. Peter, H.R.H. Prince, "Study of polyandry". The Hague, Mounton and Co., 1963, p. 602.

1531. Pfaffenberger, Bryan "Social communication in Dravidian Ritual". *Journal of Anthropological Research,* Vol. 36, No. 2, 1980 (summer), pp. 196-219.

1532. Phadke, Narayan Sitaram "Sex problems in India [microform]: a scientific exposition of sex life and some curious marriage customs prevailing in India from time immemorial to the present day". Foreword by Margaret Sanger. 2nd ed. Bombay, D.B. Taraporevala Sons & Co., 1929. xviii, 322 p. ; 19 cm.

1533. Phul, Sudhil Kumar "Kulu Dussehra". *Home life (Bombay)*, Vol. 2, No. 10, October, 1977, pp. 17-18.

1534. Pice, Stanely, "Hindu customs and their origins". Daya Publishing House, 1986.

1535. Pika Ghosh "Tales, tanks, and temples: The creation of a sacred center in Seventeenth-Century Bengal". *Asian Folklore Studies,* Vol. 61, No. 2 (2002), pp. 193-222.

1536. Pinault, David "Horse of Karbala: Muslim devotional life in India". New York, St. Martin's Press, 2000, xii, 257 p. ill. ; 22 cm.

1537. Pinch, W. R. "Being Vaishnava, becoming Kshatriya: culture, belief, and identity in north India, 1800-1940. University of Virginia). Pro Quest Dissertations and Theses, 1990, p. 346, http://search.proquest.com/docview/303900084?accountid=43898

1538. Pingle, Pratibha "Toys, Ayurvedic texts and ritual". *Bulletin of The Deccan College Research Institute*, Vol. 44, 1985, pp. 137-140.

1539. Pingle, Pratibha, "Bodana-Motana". In, 'Proceedings of the national seminar on 'Living customs and their ancient Indian sources', Edited by V.N. Jha, Pune, Centre of Advanced Study in Sanskrit, University of Poona, 1991, pp. 56-63.

1540. Pintchman, Tracy (ed.) "Seeking Mahadevi: constructing the Identities of the Hindu Great Goddess. Albany: State University of New York Press. 2001.

1541. Pintchman, Tracy "Guests at God's wedding: celebrating Kartik among the women of Benares. Albany: State University of New York Press. 2005.

1542. Pintchman, Tracy "Women's live, women's rituals in the Hindu tradition". New York: Oxford University Press, 2007.

1543. Pisharoti, K. Rama "Naga worship in Kerala." *Journal of the Bombay Branch of the Royal Asiatic Society*, 1925. pp. 259-261.

1544. Pitrè, Giuseppe. "The Jettatura and the evil eye". In, 'The evil eye: a folklore casebook, ed. by Alan Dundes. New York: Garland Publishing, Inc. 1981. pp. 130-142.

1545. Pocock, David Francis "Mind, body and wealth; a study of belief and practice in an Indian village". (Pavilion series), Oxford, Basil Blackwell, 1973, xv, 187 p. map. 22 cm.

1546. Pondicherry. Superintendent of Census Operations "Census of India 1961: Pondicherry State Fairs and Festivals". Vol. xxv. pt. vi. Delhi, Manager of Publication, 1969. p. 267 : plates p.

1547. Pondicherry. Superintendent of Census Operations "Census of India 1961: Pondicherry-Fairs and Festivals". Vol. XXV, pt. VI. Delhi, Manager of Publications, 1969, p. 262 : plates p.

1548. Ponnaiah, James "Rituals and ritual power of the broken people: A debate over strategies". *South Indian Folklorist,* Vol. 9, 2010, pp. 17-40.

1549. Poornima, "Beating out the cash for a dowry". *Dowry Custom (Vivekananda Kendra Patrika, Madras)* Vol. 2. No. 2. 1973, pp. 88-89.

1550. Pousin, Louis de la Vallee "Death and disposal of the dead: Buddhist". ERE, Vol. 4, 1971.

1551. Povinelli, Daniel J; Giambrone, Steve. "Reasoning about beliefs: A human specialization?" *Child development*, Vol. 72, No. 3, 2001, pp. 691-695.

1552. Powle, Madhu "Festival of colours: introducing the primary and secondary colours". New Delhi, National Book Trust, 1990, p. 16: col. ill. p.

1553. Prabhakar, V. P. "Marriage are simpler quieter". *The Tribune* 4, 1976, p. 7.

1554. Prabhakar, V. P. "The Kulu beat, Dussehra with a difference". *The Sunday Tribune*, October 3, 1976, p. 5.

1555. Prabhu, Ramachandra Krishna "Novena and Navaratri". *Prabuddha Bharat or Awakened India*, Vol. 106, No. 10, 2001, pp. 498-503.

1556. Pradip Kumar Bose "Stratification among tribals in Gujarat". *Economic and Political Weekly*, Vol. 16, No. 6 (Feb. 7, 1981), pp. 191-196.

1557. Prakash, Gyan "Another reason: science and imagination of modern India". Princeton, Princeton University Press, 1999.

1558. Pramod Kumar "Folk icons and rituals in tribal life". New Delhi: Abhinav, 1984. viii, p. 85.

1559. Pramukh, K. E. Raj "Jatapus ritual and belief concerned with the physical phenomena". *Vanyajati*, Vol. 23, No. 4, 1975 (October), pp. 25-27.

1560. Prarthi, Lal Chand. "Kulu Dussehra, than and now'. Kulu Dussehra Souvenir, 1974, pp. 2.

1561. Prasad, L. B. "Tyohar ke beech Santhal". *Vanyajati*, Vol. 19, No. 1, 1971 (January), pp. 29-32. [Hindi]

1562. Prasad, Narayan "Toda jati ke logon ke dharmik riti rivaaz". *Vanyajati*, Vol. 10, No. 2, 1962 (April), pp. 41-43. [Hindi]

1563. Pratapareddi, Suravaramu "Hinduvula pandugalu [microform] [On Hindu festivals]. 3rd ed. Karnulu: Balasarasvati Buk Dipo, 1953. xiv, 290 p. ; 18 cm. [Telugu]

1564. Pratt, J.B. "India and its faiths". New York, SBW Publishers, 1987.

1565. Prayojaka Sukhalala and Becaradasa "Paryushana-parvanam vyakhyano [microform]. [On Jaina festivals and rituals]. Amadavada, Jaina Sahitya Samsodhaka Karyalaya, 1930. xiv, 170 p. ; 18 cm. [In Gujarati]

1566. Premchand "Festival of Eid". New Delhi, National Book Trust, 1988. p. 32 : ill. p.

1567. Prior, L. F. Loveday (Lilian Faith Loveday) "Punjab prelude [microform] [Punjab Social life and customs]". London, John Murray, 1952. xii, 218 p. : map ; 22 cm.

1568. Priya, K. R. "The health care practices and associated rituals for the mother and the new born: A study among the Mukkuvas of Kerala". Man and Life, Vol. 36, No. 1-2, 2010 (Jan-June), pp. 103-110.

1569. Priyamvad "Budhe ka utsav". *Kathadesh*, Vol. 27, No. 12, 2007 (Feb.), pp. 34-42. [Hindi]

1570. Pundeer, S. R. "Sirmor ke utsav tyohar". *Somsi*, Vol. 12, No. 2, 1986 (April), pp. 49-64. [Hindi]

1571. Punia, Deep and Sharma, M. L. "Festivals in the folk-songs of Haryana: an anthropological analysis dealing with cultural aspects". *Folklore*, Vol. 31, No. 7-8, 1990, pp. 169-176.

1572. Punjab. Superintendent of Census Operations "Census of India 1971: Punjab fairs and festivals". Vol. xiii, pt. vii-B. [s.l.]: [s.n.] vi, p. 740 : plates p.

1573. Pupul Jayakar "The earth mother: legends, goddesses, and ritual arts of India". San Francisco, Harper & Row, 1990 xxx, 248 p., 32 p. of plates: ill. ; 21 cm.

1574. Purohit, M. L. "Rajasthani Vrat Kathayen". Bikaner, 1961. [Hindi]

1575. Purohit, Sunita "Untooti rahe parampara". *Kalavaarta*, Vol. 23, No. 107-08, 2004 (Jan.-June), pp. 75-76. [Hindi]

1576. Putman, John J. "Focus on India festivals across U.S. celebrate a diverse culture". *National Geographic*, Vol. 167, No. 4, 1985, pp. 460-461.

1577. Pym, Michael "The power of India". New York, London, G.P. Putnam's Sons, 1930, 317 p. front., plates, ports. 23 cm.

1578. Radha Devi, D. "Age at marriage in India: vision and reality. New Delhi: Serials Publications. 2006.

1579. Raghavan, Neeraja "Dasara in Mysore". *Discover India*, Vol. 12, No. 2, 1999, pp. 29-31.

1580. Raghunandana Bhattacarya "Grahayaga tattvam. [Rituals for worship of and sacrifice for the planets.; In Bengali script]. Calcutta, Sanskrit sahitya parisad, 1925. xx, 36 p. : front. ; 23 cm. [In: Sanskrit]

1581. Raghuramiah, K. Lakshmi "Dowry once a good custom, now a menace". *Dowry Custom (Vivekananda Kendra Patrika, Madras)* Vol. 2. No. 2. 1973, pp. 167-170.

1582. Raheja, Gloria Goodwin "The poison in the gift: ritual, prestation, and the dominant caste in a north Indian village". Chicago, University of Chicago Press, 1988, xiv, 286 p. ill. ; 23 cm.

1583. Rahul Peter Das "Problematic aspects of the sexual rituals of the bauls of Bengal". *Journal of the American Oriental Society*, Vol. 112, No. 3 (July - Sep., 1992), pp. 388-432.

1584. Rai, M. "Hamare kuch Prachin Lokotsava". Allahbad, 1953. [Hindi]

1585. Rai, Suresh Vrat "Dassera in Allahbad". *Ill. Weekly India*, Vol. 97, No. 40, Oct. 1976, pp. 36-37.

1586. Raikar, P. "Interpersonal attraction as a function of belief similarity and caste (india). Loyola University of Chicago). Pro Quest Dissertations and Theses, 1983., 299p., Online at, http://search.proquest.com/docview/303169812?accountid=43898.

1587. Raj, Selva J. and Harman, William P. "Dealing with deities: the ritual vow in South Asia". Albany : State University of New York Press, 2006, xix, 287 p. : ill., maps ; 24 cm.

1588. Raj, Selva J. "Shared vows, shared space, and shared Deities: vow rituals among Tamil Catholics in South India." In, 'Dealing with Deities: The Ritual Vow in South

Asia', eds. Selva J. Raj and William P. Harman, Albany: State University of New York Press. 2006. pp. 43-64.

1589. Rajagopalchar, K., "Marriage rites in Karnataka". In, 'Proceedings of the national seminar on 'Living customs and their ancient Indian sources', Edited by V. N. Jha, Pune, Centre of Advanced Study in Sanskrit, University of Poona, 1991, pp. 88-94.

1590. Rajalakshmi, N. S. "Festivals of early Travancore: a brief description". *Folklore*, Vol. 30, No. 12, 1989, pp. 272-278.

1591. Rajan, Rajendra "Fulaichi: festival of flowers". *Express Week,* Oct. 13, 1990, p. 1.

1592. Rajasthan. Superintendent of Census operations "Census of India 1961: Rajasthan- Fairs and Festivals". Vol. xiv, Pt. vii-B. [s.l.], [s.n.], 1966. p. 141.

1593. Rajendran, C. "The role of Napita in religious ceremonies and its sources". In, 'Proceedings of the national seminar on 'Living customs and their ancient Indian sources', Edited by V. N. Jha, Pune, Centre of Advanced Study in Sanskrit, University of Poona, 1991, pp. 37-43.

1594. Rajeshwari Pandharipande "Metaphor as ritualistic symbol". *Anthropological Linguistics*, Vol. 29, No. 3 (Fall, 1987), pp. 297-318.

1595. Raju, M. V. T. "Changing patten of entertainments during festival Nights in rural Andhra Pradesh". *Folklore*, Vol. 17, No. 1, 1975, pp. 34-37.

1596. Raju, P. Subbarama, Sudhakar, C. and Umamohan, Ch. "Chenchus and social transformation: A study of a primitive tribe in Kurnool district of Andhra Pradesh" *The Anthropologist*, Vol. 11, No. 3, 2009, 167-172.

1597. Ramacandran Cettiyar, C. M. "Enkal nattuppuram. [Customs, menners and festivities in and around Coimbatore]". Coimbatore, Kovai nilayappatippakam, n.d. p. illus.; 19 cm. [Tamil]

1598. Ramachandran, Bindu "Fertility concept in a ritual an anthropological explanation of "Pandal Pattu". *Stud. Tribes Tribals,* Vol. 2, No. 1, 2003, pp. 19-21.

1599. Ramachandran, Nirmala "Close of festival of India in USSR: Russians' interest in Carnatic music". *Sruti: South Indian Classsical Music and Dance Magazine,* Issue No. 48, 1988, pp. 45-46.

1600. Raman, A. S. "The culture heritage of South India". *East and West,* Vol. 8, No. 4, 1958, pp. 389-391.

1601. Raman, N. Pattabhi "Mad mad festival season". *Sruti: South Indian Classsical Music and Dance Magazine,* Issue No. 161, 1998, pp. 15-21.

1602. Raman, Pattabhi "The Madras festival season: Mostly more of the same". *Sruti: South Indian Classsical Music and Dance Magazine,* Issue No. 15, 1985, pp. 13-18.

1603. Raman, Tulsi. "Jila Shimla Pasubali, yage-tohar paramparaye". *Somsi*, Vol. 4, No. 2, April 1978, pp. 69-76. [Pahari Laguage]

1604. Raman, U. Vaidya "Symbolic festival celebrating Sri Krishna's Boyhoods pranks". In. Festivals in Indian Society, 2 Vols., Ed. Usha Sharma, A Mittal Publication, New Delhi, pp. 189-192.

1605. Ramapandi, K. "Koothandavar festival". *South Indian Folklorist,* Vol. 3, No. 1, 1999, pp. 107-113.

1606. Ramapandi, K. and Gurusamy, A. "Dusserah festival". *South Indian Folklorist*, Vol. 3, No. 1, 1999, pp. 115-124.

1607. Ramaswamy, S. "The pot boils over". *Discover India*, Vol. 7, No. 1, 1994, pp. 14-15.

1608. Ramkumar, Hari "Celebrating female energy: The festival of Kaliyoot" *The India Magazine*, Vol. 6, No. 9, 1986, pp. 20-27.

1609. Ramlal "Tapasya se arjit punji he Guru-Shishya parampara". *Kalavaarta*, Vol. 23, No. 107-08, 2004 (Jan.-June), pp. 55-56. [Hindi]

1610. Ramsankar, Basu "The "Soharai" festival of "Mundas" in Purulia". *Ethnoboatny*, Vol. 13, No. 1-2, 2001, pp. 140-141.

1611. Rana, T. S., Datta, Bhaskar and Rao, R. R. "Soor: A tradtional alcoholic beverage in tons valley, Garhwal". *Indian Journal of Traditional Knowledge,* Vol. 3, No. 1, 2004, pp. 59-65.

1612. Ranade, Ashok D. "Keertan: and effective communication". In, 'His on music and musicians of Hindoostan', New Delhi, Promil and Co., 1984.

1613. Randhawa, M. S. "The cult of trees and tree worship in Buddhist-Hindu sculpture". New Delhi, 1964.

1614. Rangarajan, M. R. "Pongal". *Our Cultural Fabric*, 1977, pp. 55-64.

1615. Rangey, Raghav "Samajik sansthayen aur riti rivaaz". Agra, Vinod Pustak Mandir, 1961, p. 211. [Hindi]

1616. Ranjan, Atmaram "Gasaee rotku ra tyohaar". *Himbharti*, Vol. 29, No. 109, 1997 (July-December), pp. 33-34. [Pahari language]

1617. Ranpatiya, Amar Singh "Gadyaar kshetra ka tyohar: Baso". *Somsi*, Vol. 3, No. 2, 1977 (April), pp. 53-58. [Hindi]

1618. Ranpatiya, Amar Singh, "Gaderan ka jaatra utsav". *Somsi*, Vol. 6, No.1, Jan 1980, pp. 18-29. [Pahari language]

1619. Ranpatiya, Amar Singh. "Gadyaar Chetra ka Tohar Baso". *Somsi*; Vol. 3, No.2, April, 1977, pp. 53-58. [Pahari language]

1620. Rao, K. N. "Kaal sarpa yoga: why such fright? Delhi: Vani Publications. 2003.

1621. Rao, P. Durga, Babu, M. Sudhakar & Rao, V. L. Narasimha "Persistent traditional practices among the Tribals of North Coastal Andhra Pradesh". *Studies Tribes and Tribals,* Vol. 4, No. 1, 2006, pp. 53-56.

1622. Rao, R. Narasinha "Festivals in medieval Andhradesa". In, 'Festivals in Indian Society, 2 Vols., Ed. Usha Sharma, A Mittal Publication, New Delhi, pp. 231-240.

1623. Rao, Renu Ananda "The Karaga festival". *The India Magazine,* Vol. 7, No. 12, 1987, pp. 66-72.

1624. Rao, S. Balachandra, "Tradition, science and society". Delhi, 1985.

1625. Rao, Shanta Rameshwar "The Legend of Manasa Devi". Madras: Orient Longman, 1977.

1626. Rao, Ursula "Ritual (AS) politics". *Man in India,* Vol. 89, No. 1-2, 2009 (Jan- June), pp. 173-188.

1627. Rao, V. Ramchandra "A mammoth meeting". *Discover India,* Vol. 8, No. 3, 1995, 78-79.

1628. Rappaport, Roy A. "Ritual, sanctity and cybernetics". *American Anthropologist,* Vol. 73, No. 1, 1971 (February), pp. 59-76.

1629. Rashid Ahmad Ansari "Kitab-i-tahrir-ul-mirat. [Manners and customs in Islam]". Agra, Matba-i-mufid-i-am, 1903. 172 p. ; 18 cm. In: Urdu.

1630. Ratan, Sushil Chand. "Buda ka Tohar". *Himprasat,* Vol. 13, No.10, Jan 1969, pp. 56-57. [Pahari language]

1631. Ratan, Sushil Chand. "Lohadi". *Himprasat,* Vol. 17, No.10, Jan. 1972, pp. 28-31. [Hindi]

1632. Rath, Saraju, "Secular customs of marriage in Orissa". In, 'Proceedings of the national seminar on 'Living customs and their ancient Indian sources', Edited by V. N. Jha, Pune, Centre of Advanced Study in Sanskrit, University of Poona, 1991, pp. 95-100.

1633. Rathod, Kamal Singh and Jain, Teena "Rajasthan ki janjatiya sanskrriti aur paramparayen". *Vanyajati,* Vol. 57, No. 2, 2009, pp. 26-31. [Hindi]

1634. Rau, Santha Rama "Home to India". New York, London, Harper & Brothers, 1945, 236 p.; 20 cm.

1635. Raval, J. S., Pandya, G. and Rathod, J, "Fairs and festivals of tribals in Gujarat". *Tribal Research and Training Centre, Gujarat,* 1982.

1636. Ray, Bidyut Lata "The car festival of lord Jagannatha as depicted in the Niladri-Mahodayam". *Haryana Sahitha Akademi Journal of Indological Studes*, Vol. 1, No. 1, 1986, pp. 154-167.

1637. Ray, Bidyut Lata "Jagannatha cult origin, rituals, Festivals, religion and philosophy: a critical study of sthala purana 'Niladri Mahodaya". Delhi, Kant Publications, 1998. xviii, 303 p.: Col. ill. p.

1638. Ray, Himanshu Prabha and Ravindranath, Sudha "The archaoelogy of ritual spaces: Satellite images and early Chalukyan temples". *Man and Environment*, Vol. 32, No. 1, 2007, pp. 89-101.

1639. Ray, Manas and Tat, Suparna "A study on the nature and structure of ritual language of the bauls of Birbhum, West Bengal". *Man and Life*, Vol. 29, No. 3-4, 2003, pp. 117-138.

1640. Ray, Nauvat "Kahar Jati aur Varnvyavastha [The Kahar Jati and the Varna Systems]". Firozabad, Agra, Fakirchand, 1920.

1641. Raya, Binaya Bhushana. "Socioeconomic Impact of Sati in Bengal and the role of Raja Rammohan Roy". Calcutta: Naya Prokash, 1987.

1642. Raya, Manmatha "Hamare kucha pracina lokotsava [microform] [On ancient folk festivals of India]. Manmatha Raya. 1. Samskarana. Ilahabada: Sahitya Bhavana, 1953. vi, 173 p. ; 19 cm. [Hindi]

1643. Raychaudhuri, Bikash "Fishing rituals of the marine fisher folk: of Jambudwip: a socio-cultural study". *Bulletin of The Anthropological Survey of India*, Vol. 17, No. 2, 1968 (April), pp. 83-109.

1644. Rebecca M. Brown "Abject to object: colonialism preserved through the Imagery of Muharram". *RES:*

Anthropology and Aesthetics, No. 43, Islamic Arts (Spring, 2003), pp. 203-217.

1645. Reddy, A. Munirathnam "On the role of ritual friendship in the mobility of wealth in the Viskhapatnam agency". *Man in India*, Vol. 53, No. 3, 1973 (July - Sept.), pp. 243-255.

1646. Reddy, B. Krishna "Mahabharata Yagnam in Rayalaseema: interaction between great tradition and little tradition". *Folklore*, Vol. 23, No. 5, 1982, pp. 102-104.

1647. Reddy, G. Linga "Holi" festival of Telangana area of Andhra Pradesh". *Folklore*, Vol. 18, No. 3, 1977, pp. 70-72, 82.

1648. Reddy, G. P. "Structural and functional change in the traditional rituals of a tribal village in Andhra Pradesh". *Vanyajati*, Vol. 19, No. 1, 1971 (January), pp. 8-21.

1649. Reddy, G. P. "A changing festival in Vanyajati". *Vanyajati*, Vol. 16, No. 3, 1968.

1650. Reddy, K Viswanadha "Ganga Jathara: a folk festival in a small city Tirupati and the neighbouring villages in Andhara Pradesh". *Folklore*, Vol. 17, No. 7, 1976, pp. 237-42.

1651. Reddy, K Viswanadha "Molakala Punnami: a folk festival in the Western region of Chitoor district of Andhra Pradesh". *Folklore*, Vol. 20, No. 3-4, 1979, pp. 76-82.

1652. Reddy, K. Viswanadha and Mukherjee, D. P. Rain "Cults and rituals in the Rayalaseema region of Andhra Pradesh". *Folklore*, Vol. 17, No. 1, 1975 (January), pp. 1-6.

1653. Reddy, N. S. "Rites and customs associated with marriage in a NorthIndian village". *The Eastern Anthropologist,* Vol. 9, No. 2, 1956, pp. 77-91.

1654. Reddy, P. Munirathnam "Little traditional festivals in an Andhra village: Vemur". *The Eastern Anthropologist,* Vol. 38, No. 2, 1985, pp. 169-171.

1655. Reddy, P. Munirathnam "Study of a Harijan caste deity festival: Mathamma Kolupu" *Journal of Social Research,* Vol. 25, No. 1, 1982, pp. 52-55.

1656. Reddy, P. Munirathnam and Suryanarayana, M. "Peddintlamma ferstival among the vaddis of Kolleru lake: A continuum of little and great traditions". *Man in India,* Vol. 68, No. 1, 1988, pp. 105-111.

1657. Reddy, S. Krishna "Involvement of Hindus in Muslim Religious Ritual: to maintain peace and harmony for national integration". *Folklore,* Vol. 31, No. 10-11, 1990 (October-Nov), pp. 215-216, 223.

1658. Reddy, V. K. "Marriages in ancient India". Gurgaon, Academic press, 1978.

1659. Reddy, V. Narayan "Ritual connected with the life-cycle of the Oddis: some accounts from Andhra Pradesh". *Folklore,* Vol. 29, No. 6, 1988 (June), pp. 131-137.

1660. Reddy, V. Narayan "Festivals of the Oddis: field note of a researcher" *Folklore,* Vol. 27, No. 9, 1986, pp. 187-191.

1661. Reghunathan, Sudhamahi "Diwali: When the stars come down to earth" *Discover India,* Vol. 6, No. 11, 1993, pp. 2-11.

1662. Rele, J. R. "Some aspects of family and fertility in India". *Population Studies,* Vol. 15, No. 3 (March, 1962), pp. 267-278.

1663. Rengarajan, La Su. "A story without an end". *Dowry Custom (Vivekananda Kendra Patrika, Madras)* Vol. 2. No.2. 1973, pp. 131-135.

1664. Reynolds, Holly Baker "The auspicious married woman." In, 'The Powers of Tamil Women, ed. Susan S. Wadley, Syracuse, NY: Maxwell School of Citizenship and Public Affairs, Syracuse University. 1980. pp. 35–60.

1665. Reynolds, Holly Baker "To keep the Tali Strong: women's rituals in Tamilnad, India". Ph.D. diss., University of Wisconsin, 1978.

1666. Rgvedi "Aryancya sananca pracina va arvacina itihasa [microform], [Hinduism Customs and practices]". Mumbai, Vhi. Prabna ani Kampani, [1916] xiv, 412 p. : ill. (some col.), maps ; 18 cm. [Marathi]

1667. Rgvedi "Aryona tahevarono pracina tatha arvacina itihasa [microform], [Fasts and feasts Hinduism]". Amadavada: Gujarata Puratattva Mandira, 1979 [1923] xvi, 588, [3] p. ; 19 cm. [Gujarati].

1668. Rice, Stanley "Hindu customs and their origins [microform]". With a foreword by Maharaja Gaekwar of Baroda. London, George Allen and Unwin, 1937. 219 p. ; 21 cm.

1669. Richard Schechner "The future of ritual". *Amerikastudien / American Studies*, Vol. 32, No. 1, (Theater In The U.S.A.), 1987, pp. 49-64.

1670. Rima Hooja "Icons, artefacts and interpretations of the past: early Hinduism in Rajasthan". *World Archaeology*, Vol. 36, No. 3, The Archaeology of Hinduism (Sep., 2004), pp. 360-377.

1671. Rinehart, Robin "Contemporary Hinduism: ritual, culture, and practice". Santa Barbara, Calif., ABC-CLIO 2004, ix, 448 p. : ill., maps ; 24 cm.

1672. Rivett-Carnac, J. H. "The snake symbol in India, especially in connection with the worship of Siva." *Journal of the Asiatic Society of Bengal*, Vol. 28, No. 1, 1879, pp. 17-30.

1673. Rizvi, B. R. "Religion and world-view of the Hill Korwa of Chhattisgarh (M. P.)". *Human Science*, Vol. 32, No. 3, 1983, pp. 157-168.

1674. Rizvi, S. N. H. "Uttarakhand ki seemant janjatiyon ke riti rivaz". *Vanyajati*, Vol. 56, No. 4, 2008, pp. 55-58. [Hindi]

1675. Rizwana "Current intrapartum care practices in india". University of New Hampshire). Pro Quest Dissertations and Theses, 2006, p. 64. http://search.proquest.com/docview/305279691? accountid =43898

1676. Robert Blust "The Origin of dragons". *Anthropos*, Vol. 95, No. 2, 2000, pp. 519-536.

1677. Robert Deliege "The myths of origin of the Indian untouchables". *Man, New Series*, Vol. 28, No. 3 (Sep., 1993), pp. 533-549.

1678. Robert Elgood "Hindu arms and ritual: arms and armour from India 1400-1865". Delft, Eburon, 2004. 312 p.: ill. (Chiefly col.), map; 31 cm.

1679. Robert L. Simon "Tyāgarāja and the South Indian Bhajana Sampradāya". *Asian Music*, Vol. 20, No. 1 (Autumn, 1988 - Winter, 1989), pp. 114-127.

1680. Robert P. Goldman "Karma, guilt, and buried memories: public fantasy and private reality in traditional India". *Journal of the American Oriental Society*, Vol. 105, No. 3, Indological Studies Dedicated to Daniel H. H. Ingalls (Jul. - Sep., 1985), pp. 413-425.

1681. Roberts, John M. Jr. and Chick, Garry "Culture and behaviour: Applying log-linear models for transitions between offices in a Mexican festival system". *Social Science Research*, Vol. 36, No. 1, 2007, pp. 313-328.

1682. Roheim, G. "Dying gods and puberty ceremonies". In, 'Internatioanal encyclopaedia of tribal religion' Vol. 7. Edited by S. M. Channa, New Delhi, Cosmo Publications, 2000, pp. 59-88.

1683. Rojevich, Tadhoosh, and Soni, Madan "Sahitya aur utsav dharmita". *Purvagrah*, Vol. 15, No. (1-2), 1989 (Sept.-Feb.), pp. 107-109. [Hindi]

1684. Rolf Groesbeck "Dhim, Kam, Cappu, Pottu: Timbral discourses and performances among temple drummers in Kerala, India". *Yearbook for Traditional Music*, Vol. 35, 2003, pp. 39-68.

1685. Romesh Chandra "Types and forms of marriage in a Kinnaur village". *Main in India*, Vol. LII, No. 2, April-june 1973, pp. 176-187.

1686. Rondo, J. "Mythology and believes of Si- donyi festival of the Tagins". *Resarun: Journal of the Directorate of Research,* Vol. 30, 2004, pp. 98-104.

1687. Rongmuthu, Dewansing, "Wangala the harvest festival of the Garos". *The monthly that informs North-Eastern spectrum and book supplement* Vol. 1. No. 11-12, Gauhati, 1977.

1688. Rongmuthu, Dewansing, "The matrilineal system in Meghalaya (An appreciation)". *The monthly that informs North-Eastern Spectrum and book supplement,* Vol. 1. No. 5, Gauhati, 1976.

1689. Rose, H. A. "Customary law regarding succession in the ruling families of Punjab hill states". *Indian Antiquary,* Vol. 34, 1905, pp. 266-267; 1906, pp. 233-291.

1690. Ross, E. Denison (Ed.) "An alphabetical list of the feasts and holidays of the hindus and muhammadans". Calcutta: Imperial Record Department, 1914.

1691. Rowena Robinson "Taboo or beiled consent? Goan Inquisitorial Edict of 1736". *Economic and Political Weekly,* Vol. 35, No. 27 (July 1-7, 2000), pp. 2423-2431.

1692. Roy, Arindam, Moktan, Bijoy and Sarkar, Prabir "Traditional technology in preparing legume-based fermented foods in Orissa". *Indian Journal of Traditional Knowledge,* Vol. 6, No. 1, 2007, pp. 12-16.

1693. Roy, B. C. "The Onge of Litttle Andaman and their customs and beliefs". *Folklore*, Vol. 25, No. 3, 1984 (March), pp. 45-52.

1694. Roy, Buddhadev "Marriage rituals and songs of Bengal: with staff notations". Calcutta: Firma KLM Private Limited, 1984. V, p. 34.

1695. Roy, Chaudhary, P. C. "Marriage in a mountain area". *Hindustan Times Magazine*, January 28, 1979, p. 2.

1696. Roy, Chaudhary, P. C. "Temples and legends of Himachal Pradesh". Bombay, 1981, p. 200.

1697. Roy, Debesh "Marriage rules and marriage rituals among the Kokna tribe of Maharashtra, *Man in India*, Vol. 75, No. 1, 1995 (March), pp. 25-35.

1698. Roy, Dilip Kumar "The Legend of Kumbha". In. 'Festivals in Indian Society', 2 Vols., Ed. Usha Sharma, A Mittal Publication, New Delhi, pp. 53-60.

1699. Roy, Dilip Kumar "The mythology of Kumbha". In. 'Festivals in Indian Society, 2 Vols., Ed. Usha Sharma, A Mittal Publication, New Delhi, pp.65-76.

1700. Roy, Dilip Kumar "Kumbha India's ageless festival". Bombay, Bharatiya Vidya Bhavan, 1955. xxviii, p. 204.

1701. Roy, Kumkum "The emergence of monarchy in North India, eighth—fourth centuries B.C.: as reflected in the Brahmanical tradition". New York, Oxford University Press, 1994, xii, 344 p. ; 23 cm.

1702. Roy, Nandini "Durga puja". *Our Cultural Fabric*, 1977, pp. 11-22.

1703. Roy, Sarat Chandra "Oraon religion and customs". Caclutta: Editions Indian, 1972. xiii, p. 303.

1704. Roy, Sarat Chandra, Rai Bahadur "Oraon religion and customs [microform]". With an introduction by T.C. Hodson. Calcutta: K.M. Banerjee, 1928. xvi, 418 p. : ill. ; 21 cm.

1705. Roy, Sarat Chandra, Rai Bahadur "The Oraons of Chota Nagpur [microform]: their history, economic life, and social organization". With numerous illustrations and a map, and an introduction by A.C. Haddon. Ranchi : Bar Library, 1915. xxi, 491, [1] p. : ill., map ; 17 cm.

1706. Rukbo, T. "Festival of the land of the rising sun". *Link*, Vol. 18, No. 32, 1076, pp. 42-44.

1707. Rymbai, R. T. "Festivals of Meghalaya". In, 'Festivals in Indian Society, 2 Vols., Ed. Usha Sharma, A Mittal Publication, New Delhi, pp. 153-158.

1708. Rymbai, R. T. "Festivals of Meghalaya". *Our Cultural Fabric*, 1977, pp. 36-39.

1709. Sabar, Bhubaneswar "Kitchen room of Chujtia Bhunjia tribe: An anthropological analysis". *Journal of Social Anthropology,* Vol. 7, No. 1-2, 2010, pp. 139-147.

1710. Sadhu, J. N. "Chamba festival of rain (Minjar Ka Mela)". *The Sunday Standard,* August 27, 1972, p. 4.

1711. Sadhu, J. N. "Festival of rain in Himachal Pradesh". *Patriot Sunday Magazine*. August 1973, p. 7.

1712. Sadhu, J. N. "Lavi trade fair: A glorious past". *Indian Express,* November 13, 1978, p. 6.

1713. Sagar, Sundar Lal, "Hindu culture and caste system in India". Uppal BK store, 1975.

1714. Sahajal, Vijay. "Himchal Devta ke sanga melo ka moja". *Navbharat Times Yearly* 1975, pp. 52-53. [Pahari Language]

1715. Sahay, S. "Perspective on Sati". *Telegraph,* January 26, 1988.

1716. Saheb, S. A. A. "Study of Nagore- e- sharief: A sacred complex in Chennai". *Journal of the Anthropological Survey of India,* Vol. 49, No. 2, 2000, pp. 41-54.

1717. Sahoo, P. C., "Living customs of Blackmagic in Orissa and their counterparts in the Vedas". In, Proceedings of the national seminar on 'Living customs and their ancient Indian sources', Edited by V. N. Jha, Pune, Centre of Advanced Study in Sanskrit, University of Poona, 1991, pp. 271-277.

1718. Sahu, Chaturbhuj and Dayal, N. "Cerumen types among tribal population of Bihar". *Indian Journal of Physical Anthropology and Human Genetics*, Vol. 11, No. 1-2, 1985, (April-August), pp. 95-98.

1719. Sakuntala Rao Sastri "The historical drama of Kaumudi-Mahotsava, or full-moon festival". *Journal of Indian and Budhist Studies,* Vol.4 , No. 2, 1956, pp. 590-588.

1720. Salaj Nag "Bamboo, rats and famines: famine relief and perceptions of British Paternalism in the Mizo Hills (India)". *Environment and History*, Vol. 5, No. 2 (June 1999), pp. 245-252.

1721. Samaddar, Arindam "Technology adoption and its impact of religious rituals". *The Eastern Anthropologist*, Vol. 63, No. 3-4, 2010 (July-Dec.), pp. 345-363.

1722. Sandal, Veenu "Capital celebrations". *Discover India*, Vol. 7, No. 12, 1994, pp. 71-77.

1723. Sangar, S. P. "Hindu festivals as reflected in the literature of Sur Das". In. 'Festivals in Indian Society, 2 Vols., Ed. Usha Sharma, A Mittal Publication, New Delhi, pp. 207-216.

1724. Sangari, Kumkum and Sudesh Vaid. "Sati in modern India: A report". *Economic and Political Weekley*, Vol. 16, No. 31, 1981. pp. 1284-1288.

1725. Sangari, Kumkum, "Perpetuating the myth". *Seminar* 342, 1988. pp. 24-30.

1726. Sani, Kaihrii "Customs and traditions of Aao Naga: Aao Dialect (Manipuri)". [S.l.]: Directorate Tribal Development Manipur, 1993. p. 86.

1727. Sankarananda, Mukhopadhaya "Austrics of India-their religion and tradition". K. P. Bagchi and company, Calcutta, 1975, pp. 75-76.

1728. Sankaranarayan, A. S. and Lakshmanan, K.K., "A tribal festival in Attapady, Kerala: An aspect of worship of nature as God". *Folklore*, Vol. 28, No. 10 October, 1987, p. 235-236.

1729. Sankarasuri Ghare "Srivratodyapanakaumudiprarambhah [microform] [Hindu rituals related to the fasting to be observed on the auspicious days]. Mumbai, Srivenkatesvara Presa, 1936. iii, 109 p.; 26 cm. [Sanskrit]

1730. Sanon, Arun "Festive India". New Delhi, Frank Bros & Co., 1987.

1731. Santhi, G. "Folk deities and festivals at Tamil Nadu: with special reference Puttu Mariyamman". *Folklore*, Vol. 29, No. 2, 1988, pp. 25-33.

1732. Santhi, G. "On the field study on village-Gods and festivals: a view of folklore teacher". *Folklore*, Vol. 30, No. 11, 1989, pp. 240-247.

1733. Santhi, G. "Serpent worship in Tamil Nadu: Some Observations – Fieldwork Report." *Folklore* Vol. 32, No. 5-6, 1991, pp. 85-90.

1734. Saraf, Samarendra "Hindu caste system and the ritual idiom". Delhi: Mittal Pulications, 1986. vii, p. 203.

1735. Saraf, Samarendra "The Hindu ritual purity-pollution complex". *The Eastern Anthropologist*, Vol. 22, No. 2, 1969, pp. 161-175.

1736. Saraf, Samarendra, "Hindu marriage and Dowry: A historical-sociological review". *Dowry Custom (Vivekananda Kendra Patrika, Madras)* Vol. 2, No. 2, 1973, pp.173-183.

1737. Saran, A. K. "Traditional thought: Towards as axiomatic appraoch-A book of reminers". Central Ist. of Higher Tibetan studies, 1996.

1738. Sarangi, A. T. "Concept of purity and inpurity in Orissa and its sources". In, Proceedings of the national seminar on 'Living customs and their ancient Indian sources',

Edited by V. N. Jha, Pune, Centre of Advanced Study in Sanskrit, University of Poona, 1991, pp. 218-224.

1739. Saraswat, K. S. and Pokharia, A. K. "On the remains of Botanical material used in fire- sacrifice ritualized during Kushana period at Sanghol (Punjab)". Pragdhara, Vol. 8, 1998, pp. 149-181.

1740. Saraswat, Sharda "Holi ka poranik mahatva". *Ojaswini*, 2007 (March), pp. 36-37. [Hindi]

1741. Saraswati, Baidyanath "Brahmanic ritual traditions in the crucible of time". Simla: Indian Institute of Advanced Study, 1977, xxii, p. 299.

1742. Saraswati, Baidyanath "Ritual language: A transanthropological perspective". *Man in India*, Vol. 62, No. 1, 1982 (March), pp. 1-18.

1743. Saraswati, Baidyanath "The ladakhi custom of cremation". *Man in India*, Vol. 47, No. 04, 1967 (Oct.-Dec.), pp. 263-270.

1744. Sardesai, Laxmanrao "Riti-rivajo ka qila todkar". *Samkaleen Bhartiya Sahitya*, Vol. 25, No. 114, 2004 (July-August), pp. 101-102. [Hindi]

1745. Sarita Sahay "The heavenly cow rupan and the festivals of ceremonial torture Gaigoheri: myth, rituals and sacrifice among the people of the Bhil tribe of western India". Accessed online at http://www.folklore.ee/folklore/Vol. 45/sahay.pdf

1746. Sarkar, A. "The impact of agricultural practices on environmental health: A comparative analysis in India". Queens University (Canada)). Pro Quest Dissertations and Theses, 2010. http://search.proquest.com/docview/853293566?accountid=43898

1747. Sarkar, Ajita, Biswas, Kishor and Das, A. P. "Ethnobotany of Kirat fesitival of magar community in Buxa Duar area of West Bengal, India". *Ethnobotany*, Vol. 22, No. 1-2, 2010, pp. 82-85.

1748. Sarkar, Amitabha and Dasgupta, Samira "Sustainable growth of population in relation to customary laws among the Abujh Maria". *Journal of Indian Anthropological Society,* Vol. 40, No. 2-3, 2005 (July/ Novembe), pp. 147-150.

1749. Sarkar, Benoy Kumar and Rakshit, Hemendra K. "The folk-element in Hindu culture; a contribution to socio-religious studies in Hindu folk-institutions". New Delhi, Oriental Books Reprint Corp.; exclusively distributed by Munshiram Manoharlal, 1972, xx, 312 p. 22 cm.

1750. Sarkar, R. M. "Women in tribal India through custom and traditions". *Folklore* Vol. 9. No. 1-2, December, pp. 458-467.

1751. Sarkar, R. N. "Hindu marriage act". New Delhi, 1956.

1752. Sarkar, Vatsala "The role of kinship rituals among Sindhis". *The Eastern Anthropologist,* Vol. 38, No. 4, 1985, pp. 337-345.

1753. Sarma, C. R. "Dowry custom among the Andhras". *Dowry Custom (Vivekananda Kendra Patrika, Madras)* vol.2. no.2. 1973, pp. 12-14.

1754. Sarma, Dimbeswar. "Religious fairs and festivals of Assam". *Assam Res Soc J.* Vol. 18, 1968, pp. 22-45.

1755. Sarma, Hemant Kumar "The Bhatheli festival of Assam". *Journal of Assam Res. Soc.* Vol. 18, 1968, pp. 17-22.

1756. Sarma, Madan M. and Dutta, Parasmoni "Baresahariya Bhaona: Community drama festival of Assam a living tradition". *Asian Theatre Journal,* Vol. 26, No. 2, 2009, pp. 303-319.

1757. Sarma, Viswanath Deva "The Hindu rituals". Calcutta: Viswa Jyotirvid Samgha, 1993, p. 82 : ill. P.

1758. Sastri, A. M. "Marriage forms under ancient Hindu law". Bombay, 1906.

1759. Sastri, Acarya Vahisha (Ed.) "Asli brahat brahaspativar vrat katha". Kanpur, Sri Krinshn Pustakalaya, 1975. [Hindi]

1760. Sastri, Gaurinath "Rituals and practices of tantra". New Delhi: Cosmo Publications, 2002, 3 Vols. p. 970.

1761. Sastri, Heramba Chatterji "The Authoritativeness of the customs as sources of Dharma: The attitude of the Dharmasastra". In, 'Proceedings of the national seminar on 'Living customs and their ancient Indian sources', Edited by V. N. Jha, Pune, Centre of Advanced Study in Sanskrit, University of Poona, 1991, pp.131-138.

1762. Sastri, S. M. Natesa "Holi and Kamandi". In, 'Festivals in Indian Society', 2 Vols., Ed. Usha Sharma, A Mittal Publication, New Delhi, pp. 87-91.

1763. Sastri, S. M. Natesa "The Hindu New Year's day". In, 'Festivals in Indian Society', 2 Vols., Ed. Usha Sharma, A Mittal Publication, New Delhi, pp. 101-102.

1764. Sastri, S. M. Natesa "The Mahasivaratri". In 'Festivals in Indian Society', 2 Vols., Ed. Usha Sharma, A Mittal Publication, New Delhi, pp. 83-86.

1765. Sastri, S. M. Natesa "The Mukkoti or Vaikuntha Ekadasi". In, 'Festivals in Indian Society, 2 Vols., Ed. Usha Sharma, A Mittal Publication, New Delhi, pp.181-185.

1766. Sastri, S. M. Natesa "The Onam feast in Malabar". In, 'Festivals in Indian Society, 2 Vols., Ed. Usha Sharma, A Mittal Publication, New Delhi, pp.161-164.

1767. Sastri, S. M. Natesa "The Vinayaka Chaturthi". In, 'Festivals in Indian Society, 2 Vols., Ed. Usha Sharma, A Mittal Publication, New Delhi, pp.149-152.

1768. Sastri, S. M. Natesa "The Dipavali". In 'Festivals in Indian Society, 2 Vols., Ed. Usha Sharma, A Mittal Publication, New Delhi, pp. 177-180.

1769. Sastri, Sukraraj, Vidyabhusan "Nitya karma vidhi". [On Hindu rituals]. Darjeeling, Hindu School, 1928. 24 p.; 17 cm. [In: Nepali]

1770. Sastri, T. R. Venkatarama "Monkeys and Serpents in the epics." *Journal of Oriental Research (Madras: Kuppuswami Sastri Research Institute)* Vol. 17, No. 4, 1946. pp. 233-37.

1771. Sastry, Shankara and Ravi Satry "Raahu Kethu Sarpa Dosha Nivarana Mantra. [Audio Recording]. Chennai: Music Syndicate. 2004. [Tamil]

1772. Satayarthi, D. "Giddha". Delhi: Navyug publishers, 1936.

1773. Sateesh "Mhare pradesa ra vishu". *Himbharti*, Vol. 17, No. 66, 1985 (June), pp. 63-65. [Pahari language]

1774. Sathe, Jayashree, "The serpent-workship and the living customs". In, Proceedings of the national seminar on 'Living customs and their ancient Indian sources', Edited by V. N. Jha, Pune, Centre of Advanced Study in Sanskrit, University of Poona, 1991, pp. 245-250.

1775. Satya, "Dowry: A diagnosis". *Dowry Custom (Vivekananda Kendra Patrika, Madras),* Vol.2. No.2. 1973, pp. 114-116.

1776. Satyanathan "Utsav manao mukti ka". *Samkaleen Bhatrtiya Sahitya,* Vol. 30, No. 146, 2009 (Nov.-Dec.), pp. 21-22. [Hindi]

1777. Sauter, J. A. (Johannes A.) "Among the Brahmins and Pariahs [microform]". Translated from the German by Bernard Miall. London, T. Fisher Unwin, 1924. 241 p.; 22 cm.

1778. Savarkar, Vinayak Damodar "Ksha kirane [microform] [India Social life and customs]. Avrtti 1. Pune, Godabole Grantha Bhandara, 1950. ii, 176 p. : ill. ; 18 cm. [In: Marathi].

1779. Sax, William S. "Mountain Goddess: gender and politics in a Himalayan pilgrimage". New York: Oxford University Press. 1991. p. 579.

1780. Saxena, Rajendra "Striyon ka sobhagya parv Gangor". *Chomasa*, Vol. 7, No. 24, 1991 (Nov.-Feb.), pp. 55-57. [Hindi]

1781. Sayal, Balwant "Sikh panth sidhant riti-rivaj aur itihas". Varanasi, Nagri Pracharini Sabha, p. 200. [Hindi]

1782. Schmiedchen, Annette "The ceremony of Tulapurusa: the Puranic concept and the epigraphic evidence". In, 'Script and image: papers on art and epigraphy'. Edited by Adalbert J Gail and Richard Soloman, Delhi, Motilal Banarasidass Publidsher, 2006.

1783. Schnepel, Burkhard "Corporations, personhood and ritual in tribal society: three interconnected topics in the Anthropology of Meyer fortes". *Journal of The Anthropological Society of Oxford: Jaso,* Vol. 21, No. 1, 1990, pp. 1-31.

1784. Schultes, R. E. and Hoffman, A. "Plants of the Gods: their sacred healing and Hallucinogenic power". Rochester, Healing Art Press, 1996.

1785. Schultes, R.E. and Hoffman, A. "Plants of the Gods". New York, McGrahill Book Company, 1979.

1786. Schulze, F. V. P. "The religion of the Kuvi Konds, their customs and their folklore", Madras, 1912.

1787. Schwalbe, Lydia icke "Agrarian rites of the Durga festival - an analysis of Bengal customs". *Journal of Indian Anthropological Society,* Vol. 28, No. 3, 1993 (November), pp. 285-288.

1788. Scott, Thomas "An essay on the mythological significance of tree and serpent worship". Mount Pleasant: Ramsgate, 1870.

1789. Seed, G. "The abolition of suttee in Bengal". *History*, October 1955, pp. 286-299.

1790. Sehoembucher, Elisabeth, "Gods, ghosts, and demons: possession in South Asia". In, 'Flags of fame: Studies in south Asian folk culture. Ed. Heidrun Bruckner, Lothar Lutze, and Aditya Malik, Delhi, Manohar 1993, pp. 239-267.

1791. Sehoembucher, Elisabeth. "Death as the beginning of a new life: Hero worship among a south Indian fishing caste". In, 'Ways of dying. Death and its meanings in south Asia'. Ed. Elisabeth Schoembucher and Claus Peter Zoller, Delhi, Manohar. 1999, pp. 162-178.

1792. Seitzinger, Thomas J., Jr. "Marriage practices, laws and social rules in India, China and Rome, 500BC—20AD". State University of New York Empire State College). ProQuest Dissertations and Theses, 2003., p.134. http:// search. proquest.com/docview/305213268? accountid= 43898

1793. Sekhar, Padhi Himansu "Stambhewari cult in Orissa". *Utkal historical Research, Journal,* Vol. VII, P.G. Department of History, Utkal university, Bhubaneswar, Orissa, 1996, pp. 26-36.

1794. Semwal, P. N. "Bishu fair of war dance: colourful life of the Himachal Pradesh". *Himachal Times (Dehradun).* Vol. 9, No. 27, pp. 23, 26.

1795. Sen Gupta, Sankar, ed. "Tree symbol worship in South Indian Civilization". Delhi, Oxford, 1965.

1796. Sen, A. C. "The Car festival of India". In, 'Festivals in Indian Society, 2 Vols., Ed. Usha Sharma, A Mittal Publication, New Delhi, pp. 131-140.

1797. Sen, Gertrude Emerson "Voiceless India". Westport, Conn., Greenwood Press 1971, 458 p. illus., map. 23 cm.

1798. Sen, Sudhir "Empty ritual". *Economic and Political Weekly,* Vol. 18, 27, 1983 (July), pp. 1169-1170.

1799. Seneviratne, H. L. "Rituals of the Kandyan state". Cambridge: Cambridge University Press, 1978. x, 190 p.: ill.; maps.

1800. Sengupta, N. "Evolution of Hindu marriage with special reference to rituals". Bombay, 1965.

1801. Sengupta, Padmini Sathianadhan "Everyday life in ancient India [microform]". London, Oxford University Press, 1950. viii, 203 p. : ill. ; 18 cm.

1802. Sengupta, S. "Tree symbols worship in India". Calcutta, India Publishers, 1965.

1803. Sengupta, Sankar "Holi of the Hindus and Jomshim of the Santals: assimilation and diffusion of ideas of the Great and Little". *Folklore*, Vol. 24, No.5, 1983, pp. 98-105.

1804. Sengupta, Sankar "Introduction to Indian fire festival: from the observation of Southern and Northern Indian Rites". *Folklore*, Vol. 25, No. 55, 1984, pp. 88-92.

1805. Sengupta, Sankar "Significance of Deepavali: a short note on the festival of light". *Folklore*, Vol. 28, No.12, 1987, pp. 295-296.

1806. Sengupta, Sankar "Social significance of Durga Puja in Bengal: some aspects of Agamani Songs". *Folklore*, Vol. 28, No.9, 1987, pp. 231-234.

1807. Sengupta, Sankar "The Fire Festival of North India: with special reference to Bengal". *Folklore*, Vol. 24, No.11, 1983, pp. 221-228.

1808. Sengupta, Sankar "The fire festival of North India: with special reference to Bengal". *Folklore*, Vol. 25, No. 2, 1984, pp. 32-40.

1809. Sengupta, Sankar "The fire festival of North India: with special reference to Bengal". *Folklore*, Vol. 25, No. 1, 1984, pp. 9-17.

1810. Seremetakis, C. Nadia "The last word: women, death and divination in Inner Mani". Chicago: University of Chicago Press. 1991.

1811. Seshadri, H. V. "Buddha Jayanti-Vaishakha Poomima". In, 'Festivals in Indian Society, 2 Vols., Ed. Usha Sharma, A Mittal Publication, New Delhi, pp. 3-6.

1812. Seshadri, H. V. "Guru Govind Singh Jayanti-Maargashira Shukla Saptami". In, 'Festivals in Indian Society, 2 Vols., Ed. Usha Sharma, A Mittal Publication, New Delhi, pp. 61-64.

1813. Seshadri, H. V. "Mahaveera Jayanti-Chaitra Shukla Trayodashi". In 'Festivals in Indian Society, 2 Vols., Ed. Usha Sharma, A Mittal Publication, New Delhi, pp.1-2.

1814. Seshadri, H. V. "Rakshaa Bandhan". In 'Festivals in Indian Society, 2 Vols., Ed. Usha Sharma, A Mittal Publication, New Delhi, pp. 139-142.

1815. Seth, Pepita "Honouring the deities of Trichur". *Discover India,* Vol. 2, No. 4, 1989, pp. 64-69.

1816. Seth, Pepita "Trichur Pooram: Mighty deities, majestic march". *Discover India*, Vol. 5, No. 5, 1992, pp. 52-59.

1817. Seth, Pepita "Trichoor Puram: Shaktishali devon ka shandar Jaloos". *Discover India,* Vol. 5, No. 5, 1992 (May), pp. 52-58. [Hindi]

1818. Setha, Kesava Ha. "Lagnavrata [microform] [Marriage customs and rites]". Vaghodiya : Manilala Mangalaji Kasivala, 1973 [1916] iv, 43 p. ; 21 cm. [Gujarati]

1819. Settar, S. "Inviting death: Indian attitude towards the ritual death". (Series: Monographs and theoretical studies in sociology and anthropology in honour of Nels Anderson, publication 28), New York, Brill, 1989, xxx, 324 p., xlix p. of plates : ill. ; 24 cm.

1820. Seunarine, J. F. "Reconversion to Hinduism through suddhi: A field study of the suddhi practice of the arya samaj in India and its implications for an understanding of modern Hinduism and for hindu-christian relations". Princeton Theological Seminary). Pro Quest

Dissertations and Theses 1975, p. 195, http://search.proquest.com/docview/302790025? accountid=43898

1821. Seymour, John "Around India". New York, Day [1954, 1953, 310 p. illus. 22 cm.

1822. Shah, Sudhir "Itihas ki smriti me: Naharshi kumbha banam utreni". *Sanskriti*, Vol. 27, No. 3, 1985 (July-Sept.), pp. 57-58. [Hindi]

1823. Shah, Sudhir "Kurmanchal ka mahan sanskritik-Etihasik parv: Utreni". *Chayanat*, Vol. 7-8, 1979 (Oct.-March), pp. 53-55. [Hindi]

1824. Shah, Sudhir "Parvatiya anchal me holi". *Chayanat*, Vol. 20, 1982 (Jan.-March), pp. 35-37. [Hindi]

1825. Shahani, V. N. "Dowry system". *Dowry Custom (Vivekananda Kendra Patrika, Madras)* Vol. 2. No. 2. 1973, pp. 73-74.

1826. Shaikh, Abdul Ghani "Festivals of Ladakh". In, 'Festivals in Indian Society, 2 Vols., Ed. Usha Sharma, A Mittal Publication, New Delhi, pp. 103-110.

1827. Shalya, Yashdev "Bhartiya parampara me nari ki asmita". *Unmeelan*, Vol. 18, No. 2, 2004 (July), pp. 169-177. [Hindi]

1828. Shamra, T. R. "Tribal customary law in India a preliminary statement". *Journal of Social Research*, Vol. 22, No. 2, 1979, pp. 1-38.

1829. Shamvaal, P. N. "Himachal kchhetra mein sati pratha: ek vivecan". *Somsi*, Vol. 5, No. 2, April 1979, pp. 1-6. [Hindi]

1830. Shanbhag, D. N. "Some typical Madhva customs and their sources". In, Proceedings of the national seminar on 'Living customs and their ancient Indian sources', Edited by V. N. Jha, Pune, Centre of Advanced Study in Sanskrit, University of Poona, 1991, pp.152-158.

1831. Sharad Chari "Ritual and urbanism. Reviewed work(s): Landscapes of Urban Memory: The Sacred and the Civic in India's High-Tech City by Smriti Srinivas". *Economic and Political Weekly*, Vol. 41, No. 32 (Aug. 12-18, 2006), pp. 3508-3510.

1832. Sharam, S.C. "Bharat ke Tyohar". New Delhi, 1963. [Hindi]

1833. Sharif, Jafar "Muslim festivals". In, 'Festivals in Indian Society', 2 Vols., Ed. Usha Sharma, A Mittal Publication, New Delhi, pp. 13-38.

1834. Sharma, Amar Chand. "Kullu ka Dhashara: Prachin sabayata va sanskriti ka muha bolta chatra". *Veer Pratap,* Oct. 14, 1975, p. 1. [Pahari Language]

1835. Sharma, Arvind, Ajit Ray, Alaka Hejib, and Katherine K. Young "Sati: historical and phenomenological essays". Delhi: Motilal Banarsidass, 1988.

1836. Sharma, B. R. "Fairs and festivals of the kinnaras of Western Himalaya". In, 'Fairs and Festivals of Indian tribes', Ed. by Robin David Tribhuwan, Discovery Publishing House, New Delhi, 2003, pp. 17-30.

1837. Sharma, Banshi ram "Kinnro ka pushpa pram". *Himprasta*, Vol. 25, No.1, July 1974, pp. 10-14. [Pahari Language]

1838. Sharma, Banshiram "Kennar chatriya vivah prathaye". *Himpratra*, Vol. 21, No. 3, June 1957, pp. 25-25; Vol. 21, No. 4, July 1950, pp. 41-44; Vol. 21, No. 5, Aug. 1975, pp. 52-66; Vol. 21, No.5, Sept. 1975, pp. 16-19; Vol. 21, No.7, Oct. 1975, pp. 32-37; Vol. 21, No. 8, Nov. 1975, pp. 17-20.

1839. Sharma, Bhanshiram "Vecetra prathayo ka desha: Kennor". *Hindustan Sunday*, Aug. 6, 1965, pp. 1-6. [Pahari Language]

1840. Sharma, Brahm Dev "Minjar fair: Recalling Chamba's past". *Express Week End*. August 4, 1990, p. II, c.1-8, illus.

1841. Sharma, Brij Narain "Holi and Dussehra". *Our Cultural Fabric,* 1977, pp. 23-29.

1842. Sharma, Brijendra Nath "Festivals of India. New Delhi, Abhinav Publications, 1978. Col. ill. p. 156.

1843. Sharma, Chandrakanta "Ude Gulal-abeer prem ras bares jamkar". *Sanskriti*, Vol. 27, No. 4, 1985 pp. 68-69. [Hindi]

1844. Sharma, Dilip. "Kullu aur mela". *Himbharti*, Vol. 6, No. 3, sept. 1974. pp. 91-93. [Pahari Language]

1845. Sharma, Dinesh C. "Rituals cause lead exposure and fish kill". *Frontiers in Ecology and the Environment*, Vol. 2, No. 10 (Dec., 2004), p. 510.

1846. Sharma, Duni Chand. "Tatta pani ka mela". *Himbharti*, Vol. 3, No. 3, Sept. 1971, pp. 12-15.

1847. Sharma, Duni Chandra "Tattapani kshetra me Gaoon ka prasidh tyohar mal". *Somsi*, Vol. 13, No. 3, 1987 (July), pp. 51-56. [Hindi]

1848. Sharma, H. "Vrata-Parichaya". Gorakhpur, Gita Press, 1963. [Hindi]

1849. Sharma, Kedar "Pangi Ghati va Jukaru Parv". *Somsi*, Vol. 21, No. 78, 1995 (December), pp. 82-84 [Hindi]

1850. Sharma, Krishna "Bhakti and the Bhakti movement: a new perspective". New Delhi, Munshiram Manoharlal Publisher, 1986.

1851. Sharma, Malti "Maharashtra ka mithbola parv maker Sankranti". *Chomasa*, Vol. 21, No. 64, 2004, pp. 120-122. [Hindi]

1852. Sharma, Murari "Rangon Me dooba Himachal ka Janjatiya parv". *Ojasvini*, 2008 (July), pp. 36-37. [Hindi]

1853. Sharma, N. C. "Kullu ke meloo aur utsavo ki ek jalak". *Himbharti*, Vol. 6, No. 3, Sept. 1974, pp. 87-90. [Pahari Language]

1854. Sharma, Narandra "Kullu ke Sanskar". *Somsi*, Vol. 4, No. 4, Oct. 1978, pp. 76-81. [Pahari Language]

1855. Sharma, Narandra. "Shimla/Kullu chatra faagali mela". *Somsi*, Vol. 3, No. 3, July 1977. pp. 65-67.

1856. Sharma, Preet "Karwa Choth". *Himbharti*, Vol. 16, No. 62, 1984, pp. 83-84. [Hindi]

1857. Sharma, Prem "Chamba ki Basoaa parampara". *Somsi*, Vol. 13, No. 3, 1987. pp. 88-92. [Hindi]

1858. Sharma, Pushpa "Jwalamukhi di Lohri". *Himbharti*, Vol. 17, No. 65, 1985, pp. 50-53. [Pahari Language]

1859. Sharma, R. C. "Polyandrous partnership in Himalayas". *Himalaya Kalpadrum (Simla)*. Vol.1, No.2-3, January 1965, pp. 18-23.

1860. Sharma, Rakash. "Vart parv, and tohar, Bhartiya Sanskriti samvardhan parisad". New Delhi, 2004. [Hindi]

1861. Sharma, Rameshswar Dutt "Pahari kshetra ke do vishisth tyohar". *Somsi*, Vol. 10, No. 4, 1984 pp. 62-64. [Hindi]

1862. Sharma, Ramsenihal "Bhartiya Toharon ka sanskritik nihitarth". *Sahitya Sagar*, Vol. 6, No. 3, 2007 (October), pp. 27-29. [Hindi]

1863. Sharma, S. P. "Fairs and festivals of India". New Delhi, Hindoology Books, September 2006. p. 146 : Coloured Illustrated p.

1864. Sharma, Sant Ram "Solan mela". Grishamotsav, 1979 Solan, pp. 28-29.

1865. Sharma, Satyapal. "Parvati Chetra mein sati pratha: ek Vivecan". *Somsi*, Vol. 3, No. 2, April 1977, pp. 34-37. [Pahari Language]

1866. Sharma, Shami "Himchal ka lok sanskritik parv seri ka tyohar". *Somsi*, Vol. 9, No. 3, 1983 (July), pp. 59-61. [Hindi]

1867. Sharma, Shiv Sakti. "Shivratri mela". Mandi Shivratri samarika, 1975, p. 3. [Hindi]

1868. Sharma, Surendra "Kangda me Rali Vivah". *Somsi*, Vol. 15, No. 2, 1989, pp. 68-69. [Hindi]

1869. Sharma, V. N. "Shrivrataraja". Bombay, 1963.

1870. Sharma, Vaidha "Kullu ghati mein jagat ka suprashidha jacholi mela". *Himprasta*, Vol. 22, No. 1, April 1976, pp. 30-21. [Pahari Language]

1871. Sharma, Vasudav "Mahaari suni lavlori jataro". *Himprasta*, Vol. 7, No. 1, March 1975, pp. 20-20. [Pahari Language]

1872. Sharma, Vasumati "Rathor Rajvansh ke Riti-Rivaaj 1600-1850." Jodhpur, Maharaja Mansingh Prakash Kendra, 2000, p. 192. [Hindi]

1873. Sharma, Veerendra "Bundel Sanskriti ke mool Aadhar Bugadkhand ke lok parv". *Chomasa*, Vol. 8, No. 26, 1991 (July), pp. 32-36. [Hindi]

1874. Shastri, Dakshina Ranjan "Origin and development of the rituals of ancestor worship in India". Calcutta, Book land. 1963, p. 399.

1875. Shastri, Gangadutt "Rohdu kshetra ka dev utsav pratishtha". *Somsi*, Vol. 24, No. 4, 1991, pp. 45-47.

1876. Shastri, Metra Nanda. "Besu ka parva". *Himprasta*, Vol. 17, No. 1, April 1971, pp. 15-17. [Pahari Language]

1877. Shastri, Purudhar "Busahar ka parva". *Himprasta*, Vol. 14, No. 3, June 1970, pp. 44-45. [Pahari Language]

1878. Shastri, Shrikantha "Hamare Parv aur Tyohar". New Delhi, 1900. [Hindi]

1879. Sheikh Abrar Husain "Marriage customs among Muslims in India: a sociological study of the Shia marriage customs". New Delhi, Sterling Publishers, 1976, x, 226 p. ; 23 cm.

1880. Shelabh "Utsav ke yeh Din". Ujjain, Metri Prakashan, 1985, 176 p. [Hindi]

1881. Sheorey, A. G. "Marriage: a sacrament or a bargain". *Dowry Custom (Vivekananda Kendra Patrika, Madras)* Vol. 2. No. 2. 1973, pp. 106-110.

1882. Sherring, Charles A. "Western Tibet and the Indian borderland: the sacred country of Hindus and Buddhists with an account of the government, religion and customs of its peoples". Delhi: Cosmo, 1974. xv, p. 376.

1883. Shesh, Arvind "Unmaad ke utsav me gum sawal". *Kathadesh,* Vol. 15, No. 2, 2011 (April), pp. 107-109. [Hindi]

1884. Shirur, T.M. "Dassera – another great Indian festival". Goa Today, Vol. 10, No. 4, 1975, p. 21.

1885. Shobhna Gupta "Festivals of India". New Delhi, Har-Anand Publications, 2002.

1886. Shrama, B.N. "Festivals of India", Abhinav Publication, New Delhi, 1978.

1887. Shri, Sita, "Can an Age old custom be abolished". *Dowry Custom (Vivekananda Kendra Patrika, Madras)* Vol.2. No.2. 1973, pp. 136-140.

1888. Shrivastava, O. P. L. "Bundelkhand kala me Shev parampara". *Puratan*, Vol. 6, 1989, pp. 176-178. [Hindi]

1889. Shrivastava, Rajkumar "Prayaag ka anokha parv: Dhedhiya'. *Chayanat*, Vol. 74-75, 1995, (July-Dec.), pp. 49-53. [Hindi]

1890. Shrivastava, Rishi Mohan "Jaware". *Chomasa*, Vol. 14, No. 44, 1997 (july-Oct.), pp. 149-150. [Hindi]

1891. Shrivastava, Veena "Pashchim Nimar ke aadivasiyon ke tyohar". *Vanyajati*, Vol. 18, No. 1, 1970 (January), pp. 34-35. [Hindi]

1892. Shroff, M. R. "Child nutritional status, feeding practices and womens autonomy in rural andhra pradesh, India".

The University of North Carolina at Chapel Hill). Pro Quest Dissertations and Theses, 2007, http://search.proquest.com/docview/304831585? accountid=43898

1893. Shukla, Hira Lal "Tribal heritage of Madhya Pradesh". New Delhi: B.R. Publishing Corporation, 1986.

1894. Shull, E. M. "Worship of the tiger-god and religious rituals associated with tigers among the Dangi hill tribes of the Dangs district, Gujrat state Western India". *The Eastern Anthropologist*, Vol. 21, No. 2, 1968, pp. 201-206.

1895. Shulman, David Dean "Tamil Temple Myths: Sacrifice and Divine Marriage in the South Indian Saiva Tradition. Princeton, N.J.: Princeton University Press, 1980.

1896. Shulman, David Dean "The Serpent and the Sacrifice: An Anthill Myth from Tiruvārūr." *History of Religions* Vol. 18, No. 2 (November 1978) 1978, pp. 107-137.

1897. Shuttleworth, H. L. H. "An inscribed metal mask discovered on the Occasion of the Bhunda Ceremony at Nirmand". *Acta Orientalia*, Vol.1, pp. 224-229, illus.

1898. Simha, Yatindramohan "Udisyar citra. [Life and customs in Orissa]". 3rd ed. Calcutta: Indian Book Club, 1920. ii, 314 p. ; 18 cm. [Bengali]

1899. Singer, Milton, "The great tradition of Hinduism in the city of Madras". Anthropology of Folk Religion (ed.) Leslie, Charles, Vintage Books, 1960.

1900. Singh, Ajitti, K., "Tribal festivals of Bihar a funtional analysis". New Delhi, Concept Publishing Company, 1982.

1901. Singh, Amarjeet "Changing context of political praxis and ritual realm: Chhatrapatis and chitpavans". *Contemporary India*, Vol. 4, No. 3, 2005, pp. 123-151.

1902. Singh, Brijendra "Phoolwalon ki sair". *Indian and Foreign Review,* Vol. 23, No. 3, 1985, pp. 16-18. [Hindi]

1903. Singh, Jai Kishan "Mahasoo ke riti rivaj". *Himbharti*, Vol. 23, No. 2-3, 1990, pp. 26-30. [Pahari language]

1904. Singh, Jasveer "Ukhyad, Geethal, Phuled ke geet". *Somsi*, Vol. 15, No. 3, 1989, pp. 45-49. [Hindi]

1905. Singh, Kulraj "Baisakhi of 1699 – the creation of Khalsa". *Sikh Review*, Vol. 23, No. 256, 1976, pp. 5-7.

1906. Singh, Madan Mohan "Ancient popular festivals in North-East India". In, 'Festivals in Indian Society, 2 Vols., Ed. Usha Sharma, A Mittal Publication, New Delhi, pp. 93-102.

1907. Singh, Maham "Nongkrem festival". *Seng Khasi magazine*, 1963. p. 1.

1908. Singh, Malvika "The festival at Avignon". *The India Magazine,* Vol. 5, No. 10, 1985, pp. 60-64.

1909. Singh, Mian Goverdhan "Festivals, fairs and customs of Himachal Pradesh". New Delhi, Indus Publishing Company, 1992. p. 128. ill. p.

1910. Singh, Mohan "Guramata gaurawata, athava, Guramata anusara wiwaha samsakara de lai waratamana waidaka-riti da pola jo gurabani, guramatta de pusataka, Hindu dharama shastram de pramanam ate yukatiam sahita guramata tom bhuliam ara guramata wirodhiam do bhrama di nawira [Marriage customs and rites, Sikh and Hindu]". 1908. ii, 97 p. ; 18 cm. [In: Panjabi]

1911. Singh, Mutum Bokul "A note on the inter-clan relationship in agricultural rituals and festival of the Tarao of Manipur". *Man in India*, Vol. 72, No. 3, 1992, pp. 331-341.

1912. Singh, P. "Burial practices in ancient India". Varansi, (U.P.) 1970.

1913. Singh, P. K. "The Maler: A restudy of nature-man spirit complex". Ph.D. Thesis submitted to the Deptt. of Anthropology, Ranchi University, Ranchi, 1984.

1914. Singh, Prabhat K. "Folk festivals of Jharkhand with special reference to the Kurmis". *Man in India*, Vol. 74, No. 4, 1994, pp. 359-369.

1915. Singh, Prabhat K. "The Tusu festival of Jharkhand: a reminiscent of the past". *Folklore*, Vol. 28, No. 5, 1987, pp. 110-114.

1916. Singh, Pratap "Jalrangon ka utsav". *Kala Samay*, 2004 (December- March), pp. 28-29. [Hindi]

1917. Singh, Rana P. B. "Ethno-geography of the sun Goddess festival, 'chhatha', in Bhojpur region, India: from locality to universality, *Man in India*, Vol. 89, No. 1-2, 2009, pp. 103-120.

1918. Singh, Ranjeet K. "Pando Janjati me parv-tyohar". *Vanyajati*, Vol. 24, No. 4, 1976, (October), pp. 11-15. [Hindi]

1919. Singh, Roop "Gavri ritual of the Bhils". *Folklore*, Vol. 17, No. 1, 1975, pp. 13-16.

1920. Singh, Roop G. "Ritual of the Bhils". *Folklore*, Vol. 17, No. 1, 1975 (January), pp. 13-16.

1921. Singh, S. B. "Fairs and festivals in rural India". Varansi, Tara Book Agency, 1989.

1922. Singh, Satyendra Pal "Santhalon ke parv-tyohar". *Vanyajati*, Vol. 37, No. 2, 1989 (April), pp. 01-04. [Hindi]

1923. Singh, T. R. "Some aspects of ritual purity and pollution". *The Eastern Anthropologist*, Vol. 19, No. 2, 1966, pp. 131-142.

1924. Singh, Trilochan "Baisakhi in Sikh history". *Sikh Review*, Vol. 23, No. 255, 1976, pp. 37-40.

1925. Singhal, Prabhat Kumar "Makar Sankranti ki dhoom". *Sanskriti*, Vol. 27, No. 1, 1985 (January-March), pp. 63-64. [Hindi]

1926. Singhi, N. K. and Joshi, R. "Folk, Faith and Fendalism". Jaipur, Rawat Publications, 1995.

1927. Sinha, A. C. "The annual festivals among the Santals". *Vanyajati*, Vol. 18, No. 2, 1970, pp. 84-98.

1928. Sinha, Avdhesh K. "Santhal Qabile me varshik tyohar". *Vanyajati*, Vol. 17, No. 3-4, 1969 (July-October), pp. 110-114. [Hindi]

1929. Sinha, B. "Encyclopaedia of Fairs and Festivals in India; with select rituals, vows, Holy cities, Temples and pilgrim centers". Delhi, Raj Publications, 2001, p. 256.

1930. Sinha, Binod Chandra "Serpent worship in ancient India. New Delhi, Books Today, 1979.

1931. Sinha, Binod Chandra "Tree worship in ancient India". (Series: Worship in India series, No. 1), New Delhi, Books Today, 1979, 103 p. 23, leaves of plates: ill. ; 22 cm.

1932. Sinha, Dilip "Sivaratri at Mandi". *The India Magazine*, Vol. 7, No. 4, 1987, pp. 20-27.

1933. Sinha, R. K. "Bhilala festivals and rituals". *Vanyajati*, Vol. 29, No. 2, 1981, pp. 18-28.

1934. Sinha, R. K. "Birth-rites and rituals among the Bhilala". *Vanyajati*, Vol. 32, No. 3, 1984 (July) , pp. 5-8.

1935. Sinha, R. P. N., "Fairs and festivals". *Illustrated Weekly India*. Vol. 89, No. 12, 24 March 1968, pp. 42-44.

1936. Sinha, S. C. "Changes in the cycle of festivals in a Bhumi village". *Journal of Social Research*. Vol. 01, 1958. pp. 38-42.

1937. Sinha, Surajit "Rituals and social organisation of deer hunting in a Bhumij village". *Bulletin of Bihar Tribal Research Institute,* Vol. 7, No. 1, 1965, pp. 1-3.

1938. Sinha, Surajit, Dasgupta, Biman Kumar and Banerjee, Hemendra Nath "Rituals in agriculture". *Bulletin of The Anthropological Survey of India,* Vol. 10, No. 1, 1961, pp. 29-35.

1939. Sinha, Surjit "Expression of santiments in the songs associated with the Karam festival of rural Manbhum

(Bihar, India)". *Man in India*, Vol. 37, No. 1, 1957, pp. 34-48.

1940. Sinha, Vivek R. "Dodda-Jatra: the grand religious procession". *The India Magazine*, Vol. 12, No. 8, 1992, pp. 58-73.

1941. Sirpati , Roy, "Customs and customay law in British India", Mittal Publication, 1986

1942. Sita "Banaile Phool: vraton aur parvon ki kathayen". Delhi, National Publishing House, 1970. [Hindi]

1943. Sita Anantha Raman "Popular pūjās in Public Places: lay rituals in South Indian temples". *International Journal of Hindu Studies,* Vol. 5, No. 2 (Aug. 2001), pp. 165-198.

1944. Sitalasahay "Hindu tyoharom ka itihas. Allahabad: Camd karyalay, 1936. x, 118 p. ; 19 cm. [Hindi]

1945. Sitaraman, Soumya "The festival of Kapali and Karpagambaal". *Discover India*, Vol. 12, No. 4, 1999, pp. 72-74.

1946. Sitvel, S. "Primitive science and festivals". London, 1942.

1947. Siv Datta Sarma, Aribam "Sradhanjali" [Rituals]. Imphal, The author, 1936. p. ; 18 cm. [In:Manipuri]

1948. Sivacarya, Aghora "Kriyakramajyotika. [Manual of rituals associated with the worship of Siva and allied deities]". Chidambaram, Arumukha Navalar sanatana granthavali Office, 1927. xl, 488 p. ; 24 cm.

1949. Sivananda Swami. "Hindu fasts and festivals and their philosophy". Rishikesh, The Sivananda Publication League, 1947.

1950. Sivaramakrishnan, M. "Reasoning about causality and treatment of childhood nutritional deficiencies in rural India: Role of indigenous knowledge and practices".

McGill University (Canada)). ProQuest Dissertations and Theses, 1991, p. 199, http://search.proquest.com/docview/250013244?accountid=43898

1951. Siwaswamy Aiyer, Sir P. S. "Evolution of hindu moral ideas". Calcutta: Calcutta university, 1935.

1952. Skfneer, Thomas, "The Suttee". In, 'The Oxford Book of Travel Verse', ed, by Kevin Crossley-Holland, Oxford: Oxford University Press, 1986, pp. 299-302.

1953. Smith, Brian K. "Reflections on resemblance, ritual, and religion". New Delhi, Oxford University Press, 1989. xiv, p. 265.

1954. Smith, Frederick M. "The self possessed: Deity and spirit possession in South Asian literature and civilization. New York: Columbia University Press, 2006.

1955. Smith, H. Daniel. "Impact of 'god posters' on Hindus and their devotional traditions". In, 'Media and the Transformation of Religion in South Asia. Ed. by Lawrence A. Babb and Susan S. Wadley, pp. 24-50. Philadelphia: University of Pennsylvania Press. 1995.

1956. Smith, Ian "Repeats of one ritual". *TLS : The Times Literary Supplement,* No. 4937, 1997 p. 21.

1957. Smith, Richard Saumarez "Rule by records: land registration and village custom in early British Panjab". Delhi, Oxford University Press, 1996, 451 p.: chiefly folded maps; 23 cm.

1958. Sobhanan, B. "Tiruvonam: a study based on folklore". *Folklore*, Vol. 22, No. 3, 1981, pp. 67-69.

1959. Soderblom, Nathan "Death and disposal of the dead: Parsi". *ERE*, Vol. 4, 1971.

1960. Sohar, Anada. "Sirmor ke Lok Jivan ki Jhaki: Mela ranuka". *Himprastra*, Vol. 23, No. 9, Dec. 1977, pp. 32-33. [Pahari Language]

1961. Solanki, Mangilal "Bhil Janjati ka utsav: Gal". *Chomasa*, Vol. 13-14, No. 42-43, 1997 (November-June), pp. 116-118. [Hindi]

1962. Solapurkar, G. R. "Religious rites and festivals of India". Varansi, Bhartiya Vidya Prakashan, 1990. viii, p. 329.

1963. Somadev "Kathasaritsagara". Bombay, 1915.

1964. Soni, Amit "Santal customary law: An anthropological perspective". *Journal of The Anthropological Survey of India,* Vol. 49, No. 4, 2000 (December), pp. 115-139.

1965. Soni, L. N. "Fairs and festivals of the Bhilala tribe". In, 'Fairs and Festivals of Indian tribes, Ed. by Robin David Tribhuwan, Discovery publishing house, New Delhi, 2003, pp. 74-82.

1966. Sontheimer, Gunther-Dietz "Pastoral deities in western India". Trans. Ann Feldhaus. New York, Oxford. 1989.

1967. Sophia Khanam Pathan "Featival cycle of Hindus in a Karnataka village". *Journal of Karnataka University*, Vol. 20, 1976, pp. 112-25.

1968. Spaak, Asha Narang "The "Rath Yatra" of Jagannath Puri". *Indian and Foreign Review*, Vol. 21, No. 18, 1984, pp.19, 22-23.

1969. Spencer, Cornelia & Lewis, Allen "Made in India; the story of India's people and of their gifts to the world". (Series: Borzol books for young people), New York, Knopf, 1953, 203 p. illus. 22 cm.

1970. Spenher, Dorothy, M. "The recruitment of shamans among the Mundas". *History of Religions*, Vol. 10, No.1, 1970. pp. 1-31.

1971. Spiro, G. Melford "Nats". In, 'Internatioanal encyclopaedia of tribal religion' Vol. 1. Edited by S. M. Channa, New Delhi, Cosmo Publications, 2000, pp. 269-85.

1972. Spolia, Kamala, "The dowry system the bane of our society". *Dowry Custom (Vivekananda Kendra Patrika, Madras)* Vol. 2, No. 2 1973, pp. 53-56.

1973. Spolia, Monika and Tribhuwan, Robin D. "Tribal fairs and festivals of Rajasthan". In, 'Fairs and Festivals of Indian tribes, Ed. by Robin David Tribhuwan, Discovery Publishing House, New Delhi, 2003, pp. 53-62.

1974. Spolia, Monika and Tribhuwan, Robin D. "Vaneshwar Fair". In, 'Fairs and Festivals of Indian tribes, Ed. by Robin David Tribhuwan, Discovery Publishing House, New Delhi, 2003, pp. 185-194.

1975. Sprreboom, M. and Heesterman, J. C. "The ritual of setting up the sacrificial fires according to the Vadhula School (Vadhulasrautasutra 1.1-1.4) Wien, Verlag der Osterreicheschen Akademie der Wissenschaften, 1989.

1976. Sradha "Ekodista". [Rituals translated from Sanskrit]". Varanasi: Hitaisi Co., 1950. 56 p.; 17 cm. [Sanskrit, Nepali]

1977. Srinivas, M. N. "Religion and society among the Coorgs of South India". Bombay, Asia Publishing House. 1965.

1978. Srinivasa, Smriti "The mouths of people, the voice of god: Buddhists and Muslims in a frontier community of Ladakh". Delhi ; New York : Oxford University Press, 1998, vi, 219 p. : ill., Maps ; 22 cm.

1979. Srivastava, N. P. "Fairs and festivals of the Dhelki Kharias: report of an anthropological field investigation". *Folklore*, Vol. 27, No. 10, 1986, pp. 208-211.

1980. Srivastava, Narayan Prasad "Chhat Parva: Ek Samiksha". *Journal of the Anthropological Survey of India*, Vol. 45, No. 1, 1996, pp. 67-76.

1981. Srivastava, S. K. "Spring festival among the Tharu". *The Eastern Anthropologist,* Vol. 2, No. 1, 1948, pp. 27-38.

1982. Srivatsan, R. "Conditions of visibility: writings on photography in contemporary India". Calcutta: Stree; Mumbai: Distributed by Popular Prakashan, 2000.

1983. Stanley, J. M. "Gods, ghosts and possession". In 'The experience of Hinduism: Essays on religion in Maharashtra'. Ed. Eleanor Zelliot and M. Berntsen, Albany, State University of New York Press. 1988, pp. 26-29.

1984. Stanley, John M. "Special time, special power". *Journal of Asian Studies,* Vol. 37, No. 1, 1977.

1985. Staal, Frits "Agni: the Vedic ritual of the fire altar". Berkeley, Asian Humanities Press, 1983.

1986. Stefan Fiol "Dual framing: locating authenticities in the music videos of Himalayan possession rituals". *Ethnomusicology*, Vol. 54, No. 1 Winter 2010, pp. 28-53.

1987. Stella, Kramrisch andYoung, M. H. de "Unknown India; ritual art in tribe and village". Philadelphia? 1968, 127 p. illus. (part col.) 31 cm.

1988. Stevenson, Sinclair "The rites of the twice born". 1920, reprint, New Delhi, Oriental Books Reprint Corporation, 1971.

1989. Stewart, John "Social counterpoint: the festival". *Journal of Anthropological Research,* Vol. 44, No. 1, 1988, pp. 87-91.

1990. Stocks, C. De Beauvoir "Sikkim customs and folklore". Delhi, Cosmo Publications, 1975. Iii, p. 189.

1991. Stork, Hélène "Mothering rituals in Tamil Nadu: Some magico-religious beliefs." In, 'Roles and Rituals for Hindu Women, ed. Julia Leslie, Delhi: Motilal Banarsidass. 1992. pp. 89-105.

1992. Stuart H. Blackburn "Death and deification: folk cults in Hinduism". *History of Religions*, Vol. 24, No. 3 (Feb., 1985), pp. 255-274.

1993. Stutchbury, Elizabeth. "Blood, fire and meditation: Human sacrifice and window burning in nineteenth century India". In, 'Women in India and Nepal, ed. by

Michel Allen and S. N. Mukherjee, Canberra: Australian National University Monographs on South Asia, number 8.

1994. Subhra and Chatterjee, Jayabrato "Durga: Wife and mother". *Discover India*, Vol. 7, No. 10, 1994, pp. 14-18.

1995. Subrahmanyam, T. V. "Ganesh Chathurthi from the medicinal angle". In, 'Festivals in Indian Society, 2 Vols., Ed. Usha Sharma, A Mittal Publication, New Delhi, pp. 143-148.

1996. Subrahmanyam, T. V. "The Navarathri Festival". In, 'Festivals in Indian Society, 2 Vols., Ed. Usha Sharma, A Mittal Publication, New Delhi, pp.165-171.

1997. Sukhbodhanad "Shabdateet Gyan: Jeevan me bhee utsav aur mrityu me bhee utsav". Banglore, Prasanna Trust, 2006, p. 221. [Hindi]

1998. Sukhwal, Ghanshayam "Parva, Utsav aur Jayantiyan". Udaipur, Rajasthan Prakashan Grih, 1999, p. 186. [Hindi]

1999. Sultan, Tariq "2nd international Roma festival a cultural pilgrimage". *Roma*, Vol. 8, No. 1-2, 1984, pp. 26-29.

2000. Suman, Hariprasad "Gaddi Janjati ke teej tyohar". *Somsi*, Vol. 2, No. 3, 1976 (July), pp. 49-52. [Hindi]

2001. Suman, Himprashad "Pavash parva-mijar mela". *Himprastra*, Vol. 6, No. 5, Aug. 1971, pp. 12-13. [Pahari Language]

2002. Suman, Himprashad. "Gadi janjati ke Tij-tohar". *Somsi*, Vol. 2, No. 2, July 1976, pp. 49-52. [Pahari Language]

2003. Sunder Rajan, Rajeswari. "The subject of Sati: pain and death in the contemporary discourse on Sati". *Yale Journal of Criticism* Vol. 3, No. 2, 1990, pp. 1-23.

2004. Surdam, W. E. "South Indian Saiva rites of initiation: "the diksavidhi" of aghorasivacaryas "kriyakramad-yotika" (India)". University of California, Berkeley). Pro

Quest Dissertations and Theses, 1984, p. 456, http://search.proquest.com/docview/303299698? accountid=43898

2005. Suryayyatara, Pramodcandra Bhattacharya. "Asamar lok utsav". Pra. Vol. 16, 1969, p. 108.

2006. Suzanne, Hanchett "Festivals and social relations in a Mysore village mechanics of two processions". *Economic and Political Weekly, special number* August 1972, p. 1517.

2007. Swami Satprakashananda "Folk festivals in India". *Midwest Folklore*, Vol. 6, No. 4 (Winter, 1956), pp. 221-227.

2008. Swami Sivananda "Hindu fasts and festivals". Shivanandanagar, the devine society, 1997. p. 92. Also available on http://www.dlshq.org/cgi-bin/store/commerce.cgi?keywords=es59

2009. Swamy, D Krishna "Kaarthikai Kuumbu: fire festival, an assessment of South Indian Rites". *Folklore*, Vol. 24, No. 7, 1983, pp. 136-144.

2010. Swamy, K. B. R. "Taking stock at Diwali time". *Discover India*, Vol. 11, No. 10, 1998, pp. 136-144.

2011. Swamy, Krishna "Kaarthikai Kuumbu: an Indian fire festival: an assessment of South Indian rites with reference to Tamil Nadu". *Folklore*, Vol. 24, No. 6, pp. 111-118.

2012. Swamy, Krishna "Kaarthikai Kuumbu: fire festival: an assessment of South Indian Rites". *Folklore*, Vol. 24, No. 9, 1983, pp. 179-187. Vol. 24, No. 10, 1983, 199-210. Vol. 24, No. 11, 1983, 229-231.

2013. Swamy, M. Sivakumara "Sources of Vratas in Karnataka". In, Proceedings of the national seminar on 'Living customs and their ancient Indian sources', Edited by V. N. Jha, Pune, Centre of Advanced Study in Sanskrit, University of Poona, 1991, pp. 139-145.

2014. Swanson, Guy E. "The birth of the Gods, the origin of primitive beliefs". Ann Arbor: The University of Michigan Press, 1960.

2015. Swayam, S. "Sites of ritual construction of identities: A fresh look at the memorial stones of Gujarat". *Man in India,* Vol. 84, No. 3-4, 2004 (July - Dec.) pp. 303-339.

2016. Tachikawa, Musashi "Puja and samskara". Delhi, Motilal Banarasidass Publishers, 2001.

2017. Tachikawa, Musashi, Bahulkar, Shrikant & Kolhatkar, M. "Indian fire ritual". Delhi, Motilal Banarasidass Publishers, 2001.

2018. Taft, Frances "From pardah to people". Jaipur, Rawat Publications, 2001.

2019. Tak, Raghubir Singh "Sacrament of 'Amrita' in Sikh society: an aspect of Baisakhi festival of the Khalsas". *Folklore*, Vol. 23, No. 6, 1982, 136-139.

2020. Tak, Raghubir Singh "Rituals in the seventh century Sikh Society". *Folklore*, Vol. 20, No. 1, 1979 January, pp. 1-6.

2021. Tak, Raghubir Singh "Ritualt in Sikh Society of the Seventheenth Century". *Folklore*, Vol. 22, No. 6, 1981 (June), pp. 122-127.

2022. Talimenla, and Tribhuwan, Robin D. "Festivals and fairs of the Nagas". In, 'Fairs and Festivals of Indian tribes, Ed. by Robin David Tribhuwan, Discovery Publishing House, New Delhi, 2003, pp.164-173.

2023. Talukdar, Morormi "Ritual associated with the subsistence economy: A case study of the Karbi of Kamrup district". *The Oriental Anthropologist*, Vol. 5, No. 1, 2005: 22-29.

2024. Tampy, K. P. Padmanabhan "Boat festivals of Kerala". In, 'Festivals in Indian Society', 2 Vols., Ed. Usha Sharma, A Mittal Publication, New Delhi, pp. 123-130.

2025. Tapp, Michael "Why ritual"? Edinburgh, Floris Books, 1978. p. 41.

2026. Tarlekar, G. H., "The relevance of the Upanayana, the Vivaha and the Antyesti Samskaras in modern times". In, 'Proceedings of the national seminar on 'Living customs and their ancient Indian sources', Edited by V.N. Jha, Pune, Centre of Advanced Study in Sanskrit, University of Poona, 1991, pp. 28-36.

2027. Tarlekar, Nalini, "Indian women in the Vedic, mediaval and the present age". In, 'Proceedings of the national seminar on 'Living customs and their ancient Indian sources', Edited by V. N. Jha, Pune, Centre of Advanced Study in Sanskrit, University of Poona, 1991, pp. 172-180.

2028. Tatacharya, Agnihotra Ramanuja, "No support to dowry from the tradition of Hinduism". *Dowry Custom (Vivekananda Kendra Patrika, Madras)* Vol. 2. No. 2. 1973, pp. 111-113.

2029. Tekam, Vijay Singh "Mawai Madai ki Chhaya me". *Vanyajati*, Vol. 18. No. 3, 1970 (July), pp. 58-65. [Hindi]

2030. Terwiel, B. J. "Tai funeral customs: Towards a reconstruction of archaic-tai ceremonies" *Anthropos: International Review of Ethnology and Linguistics*, Vol. 74, No. 3-4, 1979, pp. 393-432.

2031. Tewari, Laxmi G. "A splendour of worship woman's fasts, rituals, stories and art". New Delhi, Manohar, 1991. ix, p. 145 : ill. p.

2032. Tewari, Laxmi G. "Ceremonial songs of the Kanyakubja Brahmans". *Essays in Arts and Sciences*, Vol. 6, No. 1, 1977, pp. 30-52

2033. Thakara Singha "Guramata Hulasa [microform]: janama tom leke anta prayanta gurabani anusara singham de karaja karana di bidhi [On Sikh social and religious rituals]. Ammritasara: Wazira Hinda Praisa, 1898. ii, 80 p. ; 23 cm. [In Panjabi]

2034. Thakur, Balaram "Kullu ke mele: Ek Adhyayan". *Jan Sahitya,* Vol. 5, No. 5-7, May-July 1966, pp. 70-76. [Hindi]

2035. Thakur, Bhagat Singh "Bharmor ke tyohar". *Himprasth*, Vol. 14, No. 12, March 1970, pp. 18-20. [Pahari Language]

2036. Thakur, Devendra and Thakur, D. N. "Tribal life in India: customs, law and administration, women, education and development towards 2000 AD". New Delhi: Deep & Deep Publications, 10 Vols. 1994.

2037. Thakur, Hukumchand. "Kahaloor ki Jumba pratha". *Somsi*, Vol. 5, No.2, April 1979, pp. 72-74. [Pahari Language]

2038. Thakur, Laxman S. "Human sacrifice (Bhunda) in the Western Himalayas". *Punjab Historical Conference (Patiala), 17th Session,* October 8-10, 1982, pp. 27-32.

2039. Thakur, Mangal Chand. "Badagra ka devta tatha unke chahra". *Himpratra*, Vol. 22, No. 6, Sept. 1976, pp. 44-47. [Pahari Language]

2040. Thakur, Mangal Chandra "Badagra ka devta tatha uske Mele". *Himbharti*, Vol. 6, No. 2, June 1974, pp. 95-99. [Pahari Language]

2041. Thakur, Molu Ram. "Kullu ka Dhashara: Puraana sarir naya chahra". *Himprastra*, Vol. 22, No. 6, Sept. 1976, pp. 44-47. [Pahari Language]

2042. Thakur, Molu Ram. "Sulpoena in the existance of Kulu Gods". *Kulu Dussehra Souvenir*, 1976, pp. 40-48.

2043. Thakur, Puran Singh "Graoonjee Saaja". *Himbharti*, Vol. 25, No. 96, 1992, pp. 32-36. [Pahari Language]

2044. Thakur, Surat "Balon Panjo-Sagar Manthana ra tyohar". *Himbharti*, Vol. 30, No. 111, 1998 (July-December), pp. 17-19. [Pahari Language]

2045. Thakur, Surat "Kullu Janpada na Maagh". *Himbharti*, Vol. 21, No. 3, 1989 (September), pp. 62-64. [Pahari Language]

2046. Thakur, Vidha Chand. "Kullu ka ek Dharmik mela". *Himbharti*, Vol. 31, Sept. 1976, pp. 49-51. [Pahari Language]

2047. Thakur, Vidha Chand. "Maharasi parasar janmoustav sara paanju". *Himpratra*, Vol. 31, Sept. 1976, pp. 49-51. [Pahari Language]

2048. Thakur, Vidya Chandra "Kullu ka ek dharmik mela". *Himbharti*, No. 31, Sept. 1976, pp. 49-51. [Pahari Language]

2049. Thakur, Vidya Chandra "Mahrishi Parashar Janmotsava Sara Panju". *Himprasth*, Vol. 20, No. 11, February 1975, pp. 45-46. [Pahari Language]

2050. The Hindu "Dalits attacked for touching 'ceremonial umbrella". *The Hindu*, December 30, 2009.

2051. Thomas, F.W. "The mutual influence of the Mohammadans and Hindus". Deighten, 1892.

2052. Thomas, P. "Festivals and holidays of India". D.S. Taraporvala Sons and Co. Ltd., Mumbai, 1971.

2053. Thomas, Paul "Hindu religion, customs and manners; describing the customs and manners, religious, social and domestic life, arts and sciences of the Hindus". Bombay, D.B. Taraporevala Sons, 1960, xiii, 139 p. illus. 30 cm.

2054. Thomas, Paul "Hindu religion, customs and manners [microform]: describing the customs and manners, religious, social and domestic life, arts and sciences of the Hindus". Bombay, D.B. Taraporevala Sons & Co., [1948?] xiv, 161 p.: ill. ; 28 cm.

2055. Thompson, Edward John "Suttee; a historical and philosophical enquiry into the Hindu rite of widow-burning". London, G. Allen & Unwin, 1928, 165 p. front., plates. 20 cm.

2056. Thorat, S. S. "Certain social factors associated with the adoption of recommended agricultural practices by rural local leaders and ordinary farmers in India". Michigan State University). Pro Quest Dissertations and Theses, 1966, p. 133, acess online at, http://search.proquest.com/docview/302218742?accountid=43898

2057. Thurston, Edgar., & K. Rangachari "Omens and superstitions of Southern India". London: 1912.

2058. Tikkaku, Raj Indra. "Mandi mein Shivratri mela". Pancajagat, Vol. 1, No. 3, March 1962, pp. 44. [Pahari Language]

2059. Tilman, H. W. Harold William "The ascent of Nanda Devi [microform]". With a foreword by T.G. Longstaff. Cambridge, University Press, 1937. xiv, 235 p : ill., Maps; 22 cm.

2060. Tirodkar, M. "Adaptations of contemporary ayurvedic medical practice in urban India". The University of Chicago). Pro Quest Dissertations and Theses, 2005, p. 268. Access online at, http://search.proquest.com/docview/305413723?accountid=43898

2061. Tiwari, Ananta Sharan "Vedic myth, ritual and philosophy (A study of Dvaita Interpretation of the Veda by Madhva)". Delhi, Pratibha Prakashan, 2001. xviii, p. 344.

2062. Tiwari, Jagdish Narain "Disposal of the dead in the Mahabharata: a study in the funeral customs in ancient India".Varanasi, Kishor Vidya Niketan, 1979, p. 96.

2063. Tod, James "Annals and antiquities of Rajasthan, London: Routledge and Kegan, 1920.

2064. Tomar, Ramesh Chandra "Narvrat". *Chomasa*, Vol. 17, No. 52, 2000 (March-June), pp. 114-116. [Hindi]

2065. Tooker, Elisabeth Jane "Ritual, power and the supernatural: a comparative study of Indian religions in south western United States". Radcliffe College, 1958.

2066. Trawick Egnor, Margaret "Notes on love in a Tamil Family". Berkeley, University of California Press, 1990.

2067. Tribe, Walter H. "Serpent-worshippers of India." *Harper's Monthly Magazine* Vol. CII, No. DCXI (April), 1901. pp. 681-90.

2068. Tribhuwan, Robin D. "Medical world of the tribals: explorations in illness ideology, body symbolism and ritual healing". New Delhi, Discovery, 1998. xvii, p. 334.

2069. Tribhuwan, Robin D. "Bhima Shankar tribal fair". In, 'Fairs and Festivals of Indian tribes', Ed. by Robin David Tribhuwan, Discovery Publishing House, New Delhi, 2003, pp. 221-224.

2070. Tribhuwan, Robin D. "Devmogra and Asthamba Fairs". In, 'Fairs and Festivals of Indian tribes, Ed. by Robin David Tribhuwan, Discovery Publishing House, New Delhi, 2003, pp. 230-233.

2071. Tribhuwan, Robin D. "Festivals of selected tribes from South India". In, 'Fairs and Festivals of Indian tribes, Ed. by Robin David Tribhuwan, Discovery Publishing House, New Delhi, 2003, pp.174-184.

2072. Tribhuwan, Robin D. "The Mahalaxmi fair of tribals in South Gujarat and Western Maharashtra". In, 'Fairs and Festivals of Indian Tribes, Ed. by Robin David Tribhuwan, Discovery Publishing House, New Delhi, 2003, pp. 225-229.

2073. Tribhuwan, Robin D. "Tribal festivals in Maharashtra". In, 'Fairs and Festivals of Indian tribes, Ed. by Robin David Tribhuwan, Discovery Publishing House, New Delhi, 2003, pp. 83-94.

2074. Tribhuwan, Robin D. and Nayak, Kunj Bihari "Toranmal fir of the tribals from Satpuda Mountain ranges". In, 'Fairs and Festivals of Indian tribes, Ed. by Robin David Tribhuwan, Discovery Publishing House, New Delhi, 2003, pp. 214-220.

2075. Tribhuwan, Robin D. and Savilli, Laurence "Bohada: The mask festival of Bharsatmet". In, 'Fairs and Festivals of Indian tribes, Ed. by Robin David Tribhuwan, Discovery publishing house, New Delhi, 2003, pp.145-163.

2076. Tribhuwan, Robin D. and Tribhuwan, Preeti R. "An introduction to tribal fairs and festivals: Theoretical considerations". In, 'Fairs and Festivals of Indian tribes, Ed. by Robin David Tribhuwan, Discovery Publishing House, New Delhi, 2003, pp. 3-16.

2077. Tribhuwan, Robin David "Fairs and Festivals of Indian tribes". New Delhi, Discovery Publishing House, 2003. p. 233 : Col. ill. p.

2078. Tripathi, C. M. "Deeksha ki Bhartiya paramparayen". (2 Vols.) New Delhi, Prabhat Prakashan, 2009, p. 220. [Hindi]

2079. Tripathi, Harsh "Navratri in Gujarat". *Ill. Weekly India*, Vol. 96, No. 41, 12 Oct. 1975, p. 37.

2080. Tripathi, Hema and Rajput, Devi Singh "Customs and beliefs of Raika pastoralist of Rajasthan associated with camel husbandry". *Indian Journal of Traditional Knowledge*, Vol. 5, No. 2, 2006, pp. 284-286.

2081. Tripathi, R. P. "Hinduon ke Vrata, Parva aur Tyohar". Allahabad, 1971. [Hindi]

2082. Tripathi, Radhavallabh, "Sanjna of Malwa and its Puranic origin". In, 'Proceedings of the national seminar on 'Living customs and their ancient Indian sources', Edited by V. N. Jha, Pune, Centre of Advanced Study in Sanskrit, University of Poona, 1991, pp. 64-71.

2083. Tripathi, Suresh Chandra "Kanaui lok sahitya me samaj ka pratibinba". Delhi, Rupayana Prakashan, 1977. [Hindi]

2084. Tripathy, Biyot K. "Growth of mimetic forms from ritual to drama: classification and chronology by comparative reference". *Folklore*, Vol. 23, No. 10, 1982, (October), pp. 203-214.

2085. Tripura. Superintendent of Census Operations "Census of India 1961: Tripura-fairs and festivals". Vol. 26, pt. VII-B. Delhi, Manager of Publications, 1969. vii, p. 123.

2086. Troisi, J. "The Santal life cycle: rites and ceremonies". In, 'Internatioanal encyclopaedia of tribal religion' Vol. 7. Edited by S. M. Channa, New Delhi, Cosmo Publications, 2000, pp. 273-320.

2087. Troisi, J. "Tribal religion: religious beliefs and practices among the Santals". New Delhi, Manohar, 1979.

2088. Trumbull, Robert "As I see India". New York, W. Sloane Associates, 1956, 256 p. illus. 22 cm.

2089. Turner, Edith "Feast and festivals. In, 'Encyclopedia of Cultural Anthropology'. D. Levinson & M. Ember (eds.) New York: Henry Holt & Company, 1996. pp. 484–487.

2090. Turner, V. W. "The ritual process". *Minnesota*, Vol. 26, No. 1, 1973, pp. 104-107.

2091. Turner, Victor W. "Ritual process: structure and anti-structure". Middlesex, Penguin Books, 1969. xii, p. 204.

2092. Turner, Victor W. "Ritual, tribal and catholic". Worship, *Minnesota*, Vol. 50. No. 6, Nov. 1976, pp. 504-526.

2093. Tusell, Felix; Rau, Mercedes S. & Others "Hinduism: faith, festivals and rituals". Princeton, NJ, Films for the Humanities and Sciences, 2000, 1 videocassette (51 min.), sd., col.; 1/2 in.

2094. Tusell, Felix; Rau, Mercedes S. & Others "Islam: the five pillars of faith". Princeton, NJ, Films for the Humanities & Sciences, 2000, 1 videocassette (52 min.) : sd., col. ; 1/2 in.

2095. Uddin, Nizam "Kashmir ke parva or tyohar". *Sanskriti*, Vol. 27, No. 2, 1985, pp. 22-25. [Hindi]

2096. Underhill, M. M. "The Hindu religious year. Calcutta: Association Press, 1921. 194 p. ; 19 cm. also Published by Oxford University Press, London.

2097. Unithiri, N. V. P. "Customs relating to Niskramana Samskara in Kerala and their sources". In, 'Proceedings of the national seminar on 'Living customs and their ancient Indian sources', Edited by V. N. Jha, Pune, Centre of Advanced Study in Sanskrit, University of Poona, 1991, pp. 18-22.

2098. Upadhyay, Brahmabandhav "Brahmamrta". [Essays on Hindu religious festivals]. Calcutta : s.n., 1909- Vol. 1 (24 p.) ; 17 cm. [Bengali]

2099. Upadhyay, Brahmabandhav "Palparvan. [Essays on Hindu religious festivals of which all except two are taken from Brahmamrta]. Calcutta : Pravartak Publishing House, 1925. 40 p. ; 18 cm. [Bengali]

2100. Upadhyay, K. D. "Bhartiya Lok Vishwas". Allahabad, Hindustani Academy, 1991. [Hindi]

2101. Upadhyay, Sadhna Hemant, "Nimad ke Vrat or tyohar". *Chaumasa*, Vol. 15, No. 47, 1998, pp. 79-84. [Hindi]

2102. Upadhyaya, Uliyar Padmanabha "Bhuta worship: aspects of ritualistic theatre". Udupi, Regional Resources Centre for Folk Performing Arts, 1984, viii, p. 64.

2103. Upinder Singh "Cults and shrines in early historical Mathura (c. 200 BC-AD 200)". *World Archaeology,* Vol. 36, No. 3, The Archaeology of Hinduism (Sep., 2004), pp. 378-398.

2104. Upreti, Anand Ballabh "Prakriti ke Badalte Swaroop ke sath Jude Kumaon ke tyohar". *Sanskriti*, Vol. 27, No. 3, 1985, pp. 86-88. [Hindi]

2105. Usha Menon "Making Śakti: controlling (Natural) impurity for female (Cultural) power". *Ethos,* Vol. 30, No. 1/2 (March-June, 2002), pp. 140-157.

2106. Usha Shah, A. K. Pratinidhi and P. V. Bhatlawande "Perinatal mortality in rural India: Intervention through Primary Health Care. II Neonatal Mortality". *Journal of Epidemiology and Community Health (1979-),* Vol. 38, No. 2 (June, 1984), pp. 138-142.

2107. Usman, Mahomed. "Significance of Mohurram". In, 'Festivals in Indian Society, 2 Vols., Ed. Usha Sharma, A Mittal Publication, New Delhi, pp. 51-52.

2108. Uttar Pradesh. Deputy Superintendent of Census Operations "Census of India 1961: Uttar Pradesh fairs and Festivals". Vol. xv, Pt. vii-B. Delhi, Manager of Publication, 1966. p. 253 : plates p.

2109. Vaidha, Haimandra Lal "Mandi jila ka shaskratik pratik shivratri mela". *Himprasta*, Vol. 4, No. 12, Feb. 1959, pp. 8-9, 47. [Pahari Language]

2110. Vaidha, Kishori Lal "Himachal ki lokkala ke pratik shivratri ke shaskratik mela". *Panchagat*, Vol. 5, No. 2, Feb. 1996, pp. 16-18, 23. [Pahari Language]

2111. Vaidha, Kishori Lal "Janjatiya Chatra lahool mein sadiyoo ke utsav va parva". *Giriraj*, Vol.1, No. 14, Jan. 3, 1979, pp. 6-7. [Pahari Language]

2112. Vaidha, Prakash "Mandi jila mein vartra tatha tohar". *Himprasta*, Vol. 9, No. 6, Sept. 1963, pp. 46-47. [Pahari Language]

2113. Vaidya, Hemendra Lal "Colourful Kulu Dussehra fairs and Festivals". *Cultural Forum (Delhi),* Vol. 13, No. 3-4, July 1971, pp. 27-29.

2114. Vaidya, Hemnedra Lal "Himachal: The land of the colourful fairs and festivals". 32nd Indian Road Congress, Shimla 1969 Souvenir, pp. 35-41, illus.

2115. Vaidya, K. L. "Cultural heritage of the Himalayas". Delhi, 1977, p. 183.

2116. Vaidya, K. L. "Winter festival of Lahual". Lahaul and Spiti Tribal fair, 1976, pp. 16-18.

2117. Van Buitenen, J. A. B. "Pravargya: an ancient Indian iconic ritual described and annotated". Poona, Deccan College Postgraduate and Research Institute, 1968. p. 159.

2118. Van den Bosch, Lourens P. "Pilgrimage, prestige and protest: On the origin of recent sati temples in India". In, 'The Sacred centre as the focus of political interest". ed. Hans Bakker, Groningen: Egbert Forsten, 1992.

2119. Van Der Veer, Peter "Gods on earth: the management of religious experience and identity in a north Indian pilgrimage centre". *London Schools of Economics, Monographs on Social Anthropology, No. 59,* London, Athlone Press, 1988.

2120. Varadappan, Sarojini, "Dowry custom". *Dowry Custom (Vivekananda Kendra Patrika, Madras)* Vol. 2. No. 2. 1973, pp. 59-60.

2121. Varma, M. C. "Kullu ke Mela aur utsav ki ek ek jalak". *Himbharti*, Vol. 6, No. 3, Sept. 1974, pp. 87-90. [Pahari Language].

2122. Vartak, V. D., Gadgil, M. "Dev Rahati: An ethnobotanical study of the forests preserved on Grounds of religious beliefs". *Abstract, Proceedings, Indian Science Congress, No.* 60, 1973. p. 341.

2123. Vashisth, Sudarshan "Kullu Ka utsav Darpon Kahika". *Somsi*, Vol. 6, No. 4, 1980, pp. 93-95. [Hindi]

2124. Vashisth, Sudarshan "Parva-Utsav". New Delhi, Suhani Books, 2007, p. 192. [Hindi]

2125. Vashistha, Amarnath. "Vilashpur ra mela nalvaadi hor tisare shaan". *Himbharti*, Vol. 2, No. 3, Sept. 1970, pp. 97-93. [Pahari Language]

2126. Vashistha, Chandramani. "Himalaya ke mela aur tohar". *Himbharti*, No. 26-27, June-Sept. 1975, pp. 82-84. [Pahari Language]

2127. Vashistha, Sudarshan "Kullu ka kahiya mela, jisme noda Marta hai". *Danik tribute Sunday*, July 20, 1980, p. 7.

2128. Vasudeva Ratha "Smrtiprakasa. [Manual of the religious calendar and orthodox rituals]. Calcutta, Asiatic Society of Bengal, 1912. 96 p. ; 22 cm. [In: Sanskrit]

2129. Vaswani, K. N. "Stray thoughts on the thoughless dowry custom". *Dowry Custom (Vivekananda Kendra Patrika, Madras)* Vol. 2. No. 2. 1973, pp. 188-192.

2130. Vathita, Gutam "Kagadye cha holi". *Himbharti*, Vol. 8, No. 29, March 1976, pp. 21-28. [Pahari Language]

2131. Vatuk, Ved Prakash "Studies in Indian folk traditions". New Delhi : Manohar, 1979, 221 p. ; 23 cm.

2132. Vaudeville, Charlotte and Dalmia, Vasudha "Myths, saints, and legends in medieval India". Bombay, Oxford University Press, 1996, 334 p. : ill., map ; 23 cm.

2133. Veena Poonacha "Rites de passage of Matrescence and social construction of motherhood: Coorgs in South India". *Economic and Political Weekly,* Vol. 32, No. 3 (Jan. 18, 1997), pp. 101-110.

2134. Venkatalakshmi, V. "Customs and beliefs pertaining to menarche in north arcot district of Tamil Nadu". *Journal of Indian Anthropological Society*, Vol. 20, No. 1, 1985 (March), pp. 43-49.

2135. Venkateswar, Sita "Development and ethnocide: colonial practices in the Andaman Islands". (IWGIA document, 111.), Copenhagen, IWGIA, Somerset, N.J., Distribution in North America, Transaction Publishers, 2004, 264 p. : ill., map ; 25 cm.

2136. Verghese, I. "The Kota". *Bulletin of the Anthropological Survey of India,* Vol. 18, No. 2, 1969, pp. 103-182.

2137. Verghese, Jamila "Christmas star-easter moon". *Our Cultural Fabric*, 1977, pp. 1-10.

2138. Verma "Aadi (Minyong) tyohar: Manoranjan ke aadhar". *Vanyajati*, Vol. 31, No. 2, 1983 (April), pp. 1-3. [Hindi]

2139. Verma "Bihar ka ek tantric lokotsav: Jhinjhiya". *Chayanat*, Vol. 85, 1998 (April-June), pp. 49-52. [Hindi]

2140. Verma "Jonsar Babar me mele aur tyohar". *Vanyajati*, Vol. 26, No. 1, 1978 (January), pp. 15-21. [Hindi]

2141. Verma "Sama-Chakeva: Mithila ka anupam lok parv". *Chayanat*, Vol. 86, 1999 (June), pp. 91-99. [Hindi]

2142. Verma, Siddeshwar. "Customs as reflected in North Western Himalayan languages". *Indian Linguistics (India)*, Annual 29, Vol. 68, pp. 87-89.

2143. Vickers, Topham "Clay deities". *Ceremic Review*, Issue No. 213, 2005, pp. 48-51.

2144. Vidyarnava, Rai Bahadur Chandra "The daily practices of Hindus containing morning and midday duties". 1918 Reprint, New York, AMS Press, 1974.

2145. Vidyarthi, L. P. "The Maler: the study of nature man spriti complex of a hill tribe". Bookland Pvt. Ltd. Calcutta. 1963.

2146. Vidyarthi, Lalita Prasad and Rai, Binay Kumar "The tribal culture of India. New Delhi: Concept Publishing Company, 1985.

2147. Vinayak Chaturvedi "The making of a peasant King in colonial Western India: the case of Ranchod Vira". *Past and Present*, No. 192, 2006, (Aug.), pp. 155-185.

2148. Vinod Mishra, T. K. Roy and Robert D. Retherford "Sex differentials in childhood feeding, health care, and nutritional status in India". *Population and Development Review,* Vol. 30, No. 2, 2004 (June), pp. 269-295.

2149. Vir, Ram Chander "Sati parampara, Jvalant Jyoti Sikhaya". Virat Nagar, Rajasthan: Pac Khand Pith, 1986.

2150. Virel, Andre "Ritual and seduction: the human body as art". New York, New English Library, 1980, p.191 index.

2151. Virginius Xaxa "Politics of language, religion and identity: tribes in India. *Economic and Political Weekly,* Vol. 40, No. 13 (March 26 - April 1, 2005), pp. 1363-1370.

2152. Virmani, Shabnam. "The spirit of Sati lives on". *Times of India,* September 12, 1987.

2153. Vishveshvaranand, Jash "Ancient Indian spring festival". *Indological Jouranl,* Vol. 10, No. 1-2, 1972, p. 102.

2154. Vizenor, Gerald Robert "Tribal scenes and ceremonies". Minneapolis, Nodin Press, 1976, 191 p. : ill. ; 22 cm.

2155. Vogel, J. Ph. "Indian Serpent-Lore or the Nāgas in Hindu Legend and Art". New Delhi: Asian Educational Services. 1995.

2156. Von Furer-Haimendorf, Christoph and Von Furer-Haimendorf, Elizabeth "The Gonds of Andhra Pradesh: tradition and change in an Indian tribe". London, Boston, George Allen & Unwin, 1979, x, 569 p., [6] leaves of plates: ill., map (on lining papers) ; 24 cm.

2157. Vyas, Madan Lal "Guru-shishya parampara: Kal aur aaj". *Kalavarta,* Vol. 23, No. 107-08, 2004 (January-June), pp. 48-50. Error! Not a valid link.

2158. Vyas, Shyam Manohar "Manbhavan Gangor". *Ojasvani,* 2002 (March), pp. 43 [Hindi]

2159. Wadley, Susan S. "Hindu women's family and household rites in a North Indian village." In, 'Women in India: two perspectives', eds. Doranne Jacobson and Susan S. Wadley, New Delhi: Manohar, 1995, pp. 157-170.

2160. Wadley, Susan S. "Collecting popular traditions". *South Asia Library Notes and Queries* No. 1, 1978a. pp. 4-6.

2161. Wadley, Susan S. "Shakti: power in the conceptual structure of Karimpur religion". Chicago: Department of Anthropology, University of Chicago 1975.

2162. Wadley, Susan S. "Text in context: oral traditons and he study of religion in Karimpur". In, 'American Studies in the Anthropology of India', Edited by Sylvia Vatuk, New Delhi, Manoharlal, 1978.

2163. Wadley, Susan S. "Vrats: transformers of destiny." In, 'Karma: An Anthropological Inquiry', eds. E. Valentine Daniel and Charles F. Keyes, Berkeley: University of California Press. 1983. pp. 147-62.

2164. Wadley, Susan S. "Women and the Hindu tradition". *Signs*, Vol. 3, No. 1, Women and National Development: The Complexities of Change (Autumn, 1977), pp. 113-125.

2165. Waghorne, Joanne Punzo "Diaspora of the Gods: modern Hindu temples in an urban middle class world. New York: Oxford University Press, 2004.

2166. Waghorne, Joanne Punzo and Cutler, Norman (Ed.) "Gods of flesh, gods of stone: the embodiment of divinity in India". Chambersberg, PA, Anima Publication, 1985.

2167. Walker, Anthony "The dairymen priests among the Todas". In, 'Internatioanal encyclopaedia of tribal religion' Vol. 6. Edited by S. M. Channa, New Delhi, Cosmo Publications, 2000, pp. 171-194.

2168. Walter Hutchinson "Customs of the world: a popular account of the manners, rites and ceremonies of men and women in all countries". Delhi: Concept Publishing House, 1912-14. 2. Vols., xxiv, p. 1209 ; plate's p.

2169. Watson, Jane Werner & Andersen, Susan "India celebrates!" (Series: An Around the world holiday book), Champaign, Ill.: Garrard, 1974, 96 p.: ill. (Part col.) ; 24 cm.

2170. Welbon, Guy R and Glenn, E. Yucom "Religious festivals in South India and Srilanka" See (Preface), Manohar Publications, New Delhi, 1982.

2171. Werblowsky, R. J. Zwi "Funerary rites and customs". In, 'Encyclopaedia Britannica, Vol. 9, Allen Kent, London. 1970.

2172. Werner Menski "Sati: a review article". *Bulletin of the School of Oriental and African Studies, University of London,* Vol. 61, No. 1, 1998, pp. 74-81.

2173. Westermarkk, E. "History of human marriage", 3 Vol., 5th Edn, Macnimllan, London, 1924.

2174. Wheelock, Wade T. "Mantra in Vedic and tantric ritual". In, 'Mantra, Edited by Harvey P. Alper, Albany, State University of New York Press, 1989.

2175. White, David Gordon "The alchemical body: siddha traditions in medieval India". Chicago, University of Chicago Press, 1996.

2176. Whitehead, George "In the Nicobar islands; the record of a lengthy sojourn in islands of sunshine and palms amongst a people primitive in their habits and beliefs and simple in their manner of living, with a description of their customs and religious ceremonies and an account of their superstitions, traditions and folklore". London, Seeley, Service & Co., 1924, 276 p. front., plates, map. 22 cm.

2177. Whitehead, Henry "The village gods of south India". (Series: Religious life of India.), London, New York, H. Milford, Oxford University Press; [etc.] 1916, 172 p. xv pl. 18 cm. Reprint, Delhi, Sumit Publications, 1976.

2178. Wilkins, W. J. "Hindu mythology". Delhi, Delhi Book Store, 1972.

2179. Wilkinson, Philip "Illustrated dictionary of religions: rituals, beliefs, and practices from around the world". New York, DK Publisher, 1999, 128 p.: ill. (Some col.) ; 29 cm.

2180. William A. Noble "Nilgiri dolmens (South India)". *Anthropos*, Vol. 71, No. 1-2, 1997, pp. 90-128.

2181. William S. Sax "Village daughter, village Goddess: residence, gender, and politics in a Himalayan pilgrimage". *American Ethnologist*, Vol. 17, No. 3 1990, (August), pp. 491-512.

2182. Williams, Raymond Brady (Eds.) "A sacred trread: modern transmission of Hindu traditions in India and abroad". Chambersberg, Anima Publications, 1991.

2183. Willigen, John Van and Channa, V. C. "Law, custom, and crimes against women: The problem of dowry death in India". *Human Organization*, Vol. 50, No. 4, 1991 (Winter), pp. 369-377.

2184. Willis, Michael "The archaeology of Hindu rituals: temples and the establishment of the Gods". Cambridge, Cambridge University Press, 2009.

2185. Wilson, Guy R. "Introduction to Hindu festivals". In, 'Festivals in Indian Society, 2 Vols., Ed. Usha Sharma, A Mittal Publication, New Delhi, pp. 21-26.

2186. Wilson, Guy R. and Glenn E Yocum, "Religious festivals in South India and Sri Lanka". Delhi, Manohar Publisher, 1982, p. 341.

2187. Wilson, H. H. "Snake workship in Kashmir". In, 'Festivals in Indian Society', 2 Vols., Ed. Usha Sharma, A Mittal Publication, New Delhi, pp. 115-116.

2188. Wiser, W. H. "The Hindu Jajmani system". Lucknow, Lucknow Publishing House, 1936.

2189. Wilson, H. H. "The religious festivals of Hindus". *Journal of the Royal Asiatic Society*, Vol. 9.

2190. Wolf, Richard K. "The black cow's footprint: time, space, and music in the lives of the Kotas of south India". Urbana, University of Illinois Press, 2006, xv, 313 p., (16) p. of plates: ill., maps; 23 cm. + 1 sound disc (digital; 4 ¾ in.)

2191. Wolk, B. "The supernatural horror in folk-superstitions and customs of the Slavic peoples". *Folklore*, Vol. 20, No. 8 (232), 1979 (August), pp. 162-178.

2192. Wood, V. J. G. "Customs and manners of the uncivilized race of men". Delhi, Swati Publications, 1989. In 2. Vols. (viii, 774; viii, p. 864); plates p.

2193. Woodruff, John "Sakti and sakta" Madras, Ganesh Publishers, 1987.

2194. Woodruff, John, "The serpent power". Madras, Ganesh Publishers, 1992.

2195. Yadav, Leeladhar "Holi: Bundeli lok sanskriti me". *Sanskriti*, Vol. 25, No. 4, 1983 (October-December), pp. 30-32. [Hindi]

2196. Yadav, Ramcharan "Loparv Tesu Vivah". *Chomasa*, Vol. 18, No. 57, 2002, (November-February), pp. 44-45. [Hindi]

2197. Yael Bentor "Interiorized fire rituals in India and in Tibet". *Journal of the American Oriental Society*, Vol. 120, No. 4, 2000, (Oct. - Dec.), pp. 594-613.

2198. Yang, Anand A. "Sacred symbol and sacred space in rural India: community mobilization in the anti-cow killing riot of 1893". *Comparative Studies in Society and History,* No. 22, 4 October 1980, pp. 576-96.

2199. Younger, Paul "Playing host to deity: festival religion in the South Indian tradition". New York, Oxford University Press, 2002, vii, 189 p.: ill. ; 25 cm.

2200. Younger, Paul "Ritual life of the Natarajan temple". Marg, Vol. 55, No. 4, 2004, pp. 25-33.

2201. Yuko Nishimura "South Indian wedding rituals. A Comparison of Gender Hierarchy". *Anthropos* Vol. 91, No. 4-6, 1996, pp. 411-423.

2202. Zavos, John "Defending Hindu Tradition: Sanatana Dharma as a symbol of orthodoxy in colonial India". *Religion* 13, 2001, pp. 109-123.

2203. Ziffren, A. "Human effort and "destiny": A study of beliefs among the Tamil people of south India (literature, women, and phenomenology)". The University of

Wisconsin - Madison). Pro Quest Dissertations and Theses, 1984, 447p. Access online at, http://search.proquest.com/docview/303315366? accountid= 43898

2204. Zimmer, Heinrich "Myths and symbols in Indian art and civilization". Bollingen Series 6, ed. Joseph Campbell. Princeton, NJ: Princeton University Press, 1992.

2205. Zuess, Evan M. "Meditation on ritual". *Journal of the American Academy of Religion*. Vol. 43, No. 3, 1975, pp. 517-31.

2206. Zuesse, Evan M. "Ritual". In, 'The Encyclopedia of Religion'. Edited by M. Eliade, New York, MacMillan Publishing Company, New York, 1987, pp. 405–422.

Subject/Keywords Index

A

Aali aaye Linga 1428
Abode 326
Abolition 568-69, 1789
Aboriginal festival 1334
Absent Lord 147
Abujh Maria 1748
Actorhood 1528
Adibasis 170, 901, 1431
Adilabad District 45
Adi-puran 122
Adis 92, 100, 1503
Adivasi 393, 566, 584, 805, 1891
Adolescent Health 337
Adoption 1721, 2056
Adoration 121
Adyera Gambhira 1439
Aesthetics1363, 1644
Affair 182
Age 18, 21, 1069, 1578, 1887
Aghara Ritual 725
Aghori 1484
Agni 1985
Agricultural practices 1746, 2056
Agricultural rituals 349, 1911
Agro-ecosystem 828
Ajmere Urs 28
Ajodhya hills 349
Akti parv 760
Alcoholic beverage 164
Aligning rituals 77
Allahbad 1584-85, 2100
Alpona, Bengal 368
Altruistic Suicide 676
Amavasya 1352
Ambiguously 214
Ambivalence 620-21
Amrita 2019
Anatomy 433, 530
Ancestor 914, 1119, 1415, 1874
Ancient India 13, 36, 133, 137, 153, 167, 242, 262, 304, 364, 381, 389, 449, 452, 483, 486, 502, 525, 669, 700, 831, 860, 892, 904-05, 928-30, 936, 1057, 1064, 1100, 1117, 1190, 1223, 1240, 1249, 1260, 1317, 1350, 1441, 1443, 1447, 1468, 1474, 1498-99, 1511, 1539, 1589, 1593, 1631, 1658, 1717, 1738, 1761, 1801, 1830
Ancient Manners 521
Andaman 529, 1693, 2135

Andhradesa 1622
Anklet 132
Anthill 434, 871
Anthropological Explanation 1598
Ants 1299
Antyesti Samskaras 2026
Apa Tanis 350-51
Apocryphal 1106
Aravallis 326
Archaeological 23, 461
Archaeology 183, 335, 636, 829, 1482, 1670, 2184
Archaic-tai Ceremonies 2030
Armour 1678
Arms 1678
Art and Ritual 300, 630, 895-96, 946
Artefacts 1670
Articulation 1418
Arunachal Pradesh 92, 350-51, 574, 579, 1172, 1231
Arya Samaj 1820
Ascetics 147, 1484
Assam 110, 114, 249, 287, 298, 399, 457, 466, 718-19, 738, 788, 857, 1303, 1305, 1366, 1754-56
Assertion 805
Asthamba Fairs 2070
Asur Festivals 1076
Atharavaveda 154
Attapady, Kerala 1728
Auspicious 194, 306, 1664, 1729
Austrics 1727
Autumn 1519
Avignon 1908
Ayurvedic 669, 1538, 2060
Azadirachta Indica 17

B

Badagra 2039, 2040
Baha festival 1149
Bahu 508
Baisakhi 1905, 1924, 2019
Baithan ki Holi 244
Bal Kalyan 979
Ballads 513
Baluvu 891
Bamboo 1720
Bandana festival 266, 1277, 1284, 1317
Banjara Samaj 1472
Barber 1511
Baresahariya Bhaona 1756
Baru Puja 1516
Baruni 60, 695
Bastar 218, 476, 607, 889, 900, 1313,
Bathing 693
Bauls 477, 1583, 1639,
Beads 603
Beauti 125
Beheading 549
Belief(s) 95, 170, 230, 271, 303, 308, 331, 360, 406, 418, 448, 666, 718, 876, 894, 900, 901, 1206, 1216, 1220, 1239, 1255, 1299, 1303, 1375, 1386, 1406, 1431, 1483, 1501, 1528, 1551, 1693, 1991, 2014, 2080, 2087, 2122, 2134, 2176, 2179, 2203
Bengal 15, 129, 166, 172, 176, 179-80, 190, 192, 251, 254, 259, 264-65, 170, 293, 368, 381, 470, 482, 497, 554, 654, 656-57, 662, 800, 853, 908, 934, 959, 960, 985, 1003, 1049, 1103, 1159, 1160,

1177, 1214, 1263, 1267-68, 1294-96, 1311, 1313, 1315, 1371-73, 1386, 1408, 1419-20, 1432, 1439, 1535, 1583, 1639, 1641, 1694, 1747, 1787, 1789, 1806-09, 2128
Bengali Cooking 179
Beshakhi 745
Besu ka parva 1876
Betrothal rites 1046
Bhadraloks 1311
Bhadu Festival 959
Bhaona 1366, 1756
Bharsatmet 2075
Bhatheli Festival 1755
Bhatinda 709
Bhil 61, 255, 307, 550, 658, 790, 806, 1046, 1047, 1144, 1187, 1342, 1359, 1745, 1919-20, 1961
Bhilala Festivals 1933, 1934, 1965
Bhojonavidhi 669
Bhojpur Region 1917
Bhumi Village 1936, 1937
Bhuta 125, 1340
Bihu 156, 249, 255, 287, 788
Binjhal festival 1445
Bir Babas 419
Bird Refugia 498
Birhor 09
Birjhias 267
Birth 186, 337, 679,
Bishu fair 937, 995
Bissenpour 521
Black cow's footprint 2190
Blackmagic 1717
Blood 638
Bo Tree 1392
Boat(s) 600, 2024
Boat Festivals 2024
Bodana 1190, 1539
Bodos 193, 298, 457
Body 33, 203, 275, 501, 1084, 1102, 1328, 1545, 2068, 2150, 2175
Body Adorned 501
Bohada 2075
Bonded Labour 1499
Boro 193, 754
Boro aiyen 193
Botanical(s) 1518, 1739
Botor 456
Boundaries 416, 501
Breastfeeding 1107
Bride(s) 113, 730, 860, 1085
British Paternalism 1720
British rule 1423
Buddhists 336, 381, 446, 927, 1194, 1550, 1613, 1882, 1978
Buffalo fight 515
Bull Vaulting 187
Bundelkhand 149, 559, 762
Burashavar 1287
Burial 23, 215, 461
Buried Memories 1680
Burning 429, 490, 629, 823-24, 1165, 1228, 1343, 1401, 1993, 2055
Buxa Duar area 1747

C

Camphor Flame 661
Capital celebrations 1722
Car festival 06, 254, 1636, 1796
Care Practices 1568, 1675
Carnivals 600
Carving 1467
Caste(s) 60, 76, 206, 227, 228, 473, 639, 729, 815, 975, 1131,

1202, 1295, 1322, 1369, 1405, 1407-08, 1411, 1582, 1586, 1655, 1713, 1734, 1791,
Cattle 449, 819, 1195, 1323
Causality 1950
Cauth Candra Puja 924
Cēkkilār 849
Celebration 285, 387, 426, 562, 898, 1144, 1722
Celestial Umbrella 365
Centenary festival 81
Ceremonies 21, 101, 159, 183, 205, 258, 396, 420, 437, 440, 510, 544, 559, 568, 763, 781, 837, 855, 859, 1271-72, 1365, 1400, 1408, 1490-91, 1508, 1511, 1593, 1682, 2030, 2086, 2154, 2168, 2176
Chaitra 138, 1018
Chalukyan Temples 1638
Chamba 222, 233-34, 792, 909, 1369, 1710, 1840, 1857
Chandigarh 344, 950, 1351
Change 135, 280, 301, 573, 593, 692, 724, 729, 766, 803, 867, 872, 919, 1150, 1221, 1237, 1308, 1648, 1936, 2156, 2164
Changing festivals 373
Charak festival 697
Chattisgari ritual 145
Chenchus 1596
Chhat Parva 1917, 1980
Chhau Dances 1018
Chhos Kor 519
Childhood 1950, 2148
Chitoor, Andhra Pradesh 1651
Chodas 622
Chota Nagpur 1152, 1705
Christians 206, 874, 1820
Chroes 1201
Chujtia Bhunjia 1709
Churah 301
Circus 295
Civilization 1037, 1286, 1795, 1954, 2204
Clan 599, 1911
Classical 75, 1298
Classsical Music 75
Clay Deities 2143
Coastal 1035, 1038, 1621
Cobra 988, 1080
Cochin 791
Co-existing 894
Cognition 473
Coimbatore 1597
Colour(s) 201, 220, 289, 794, 859, 1081, 1290, 1332, 1552
Coloured Rice 794
Communities 76, 823
Complementarily 343
Compromise 343
Conceptions 434
Conference 327, 428, 1482, 2038
Confrontation 291, 343
Conservation 359, 497, 1031
Consumption 1417
Contemporary 165, 191, 288, 366, 472, 692, 1139, 1341, 1448, 1671, 1982, 2003, 2060
Contentious Traditions 1179
Continuity 08, 135, 416, 724, 1237
Cosmology 9, 1463
Courtyard 270
Couvade 989
Cradle Tales 1355
Craving 279
Creativity 240
Crime(s) 1170, 2183
Crooked Stalks 1461
Cuddapah District 52

Cultivating 985, 1461
Cultivating Virtue 1461
Cultural anthropology 1004, 2089
Cultural Ecology 447, 819, 1195
Cultural Heritage 62, 108, 184-86, 2115
Culture shock 1042
Customary Law(s) 91, 193, 225, 241, 1157, 1176, 1187, 1188-89, 1243, 1265, 1312, 1342, 1500, 1689, 1748, 1964
Cuttack 206, 484
Cycle Rituals 101, 1128, 1936, 1967, 2086

D

Dahashara Kullu 200
Daily Rituals 133, 284, 335, 744, 976, 2144
Dairymen Priests 2167
Dalit(s) 66, 872, 1210, 2050
Dalkhai Ritual 1425
Dance-Dramas 89, 152, 155, 369, 457, 466-67, 551, 567, 1018, 1079, 1794
Dancers 126
Dangi hill tribes of the 1894
Dangs district, Gujrat 1894
Danguria Tharu 584
Daroi Gonds 184-86
Darœan 589
Dasa Pratha 1499
Dayamayi maa 538
Death 04, 199, 215, 542, 620-21, 644, 678, 687, 822, 836, 839, 879, 922, 957, 997, 1036, 1038, 1086, 1279, 1285, 1298, 1343, 1485-87, 1489, 1550, 1791, 1810, 1819, 1959, 1992, 2003, 2183
Death Customs 215, 542
Death- Ritual 199, 620, 621, 1279, 1285, 1298
Deeksha 2078
Deepawali 63, 80
Deities 195, 251, 615, 809, 1039-40, 1160, 1198, 1348, 1587-88, 1731, 1815-16, 1948, 1966, 2143
Demon 202, 585, 849, 1035, 1197, 1406, 1790
Deodha Dance 466-67
Desert Places 493, 955
Destiny 454, 2163, 2203
Dev Rahati 2122
Deva Sharif 1448
Devadasi 1336
Deval 508
Devgarh 401
Devi 783, 805, 1062, 1328, 1625, 2059,
Devmogra 2070
Devotion 433, 812, 849, 1370, 1536
Devotional Life 1955
Dharma 688, 868, 885, 1193, 1336, 1761, 2202
Dharmic Fallacy 357
Dhelki Kharias 1970
Dialectics 488
Diasporic Contexts 195
Dictionary 390, 2179
Dignity 1245-46
Diksavidhi 2004
Dimasa Kachari 698
Dimension(s) 213, 1038, 1285, 1289, 1410
Dipa-Garbha 892
Dirges 407
Discursive Practices 227-28
Disease 282

Disposal 221, 438, 771, 882, 839, 859, 1059, 1550, 1959, 2062
Divine 148, 431, 585, 589, 1026, 1028-29, 1086, 1109, 1329, 1895
Divine Hierarchy 148
Diwali 198, 562, 717, 898, 1661, 2010
Doctrine 492
Documents 217, 2135
Dodda-Jatra 1940
Dohada 279
Dowry custom 69, 76, 273, 363, 367, 464, 511-12, 1058, 1186, 1753, 2120,
Domestic Sanitation 487, 795, 1014, 1128, 1212, 1400, 1406, 2053-54
Drama 89, 134, 572, 802, 1719, 1756, 2084
Draupadinam Cira 506
Dravidan Gods 594
Dravidian Ritual 1531
Drummers 1684
Drums 1365
Duonia Monastery 1147
Durgapuja 176-77, 258, 960, 1061, 1062, 1432, 1702, 1787, 1806, 1994
Dusk 155
Dussehra Festival 64, 481, 840, 1146, 1390, 1476, 1480, 1533, 1554, 1560, 1841, 2113

E

Easter Parade 1523
Eastern India 479, 647, 1161, 1277, 1415
Eastern wisdom 948
Eclipse Ritual 784-85, 807
Ecological Perspective 38, 349, 1349
Ecology 11, 447, 499, 819, 1195, 1328, 1426
Economic 226, 978
Economy 257, 767, 903, 2023
Ellaiyamman 410
Emancipatory Mythography 410
Emotion 105, 341, 1370
Encounters 417, 1036
Encyclopedia Britannica 612
Enkal Nattuppuram 1597
Epic(s) 131, 1770
Eternal Lord 134
Ethnic Symbols 159
Ethno crchaeological 1280
Ethno botanical 360, 1177, 2122
Ethno–geography
Ethno-anemology 1463
Ethnobiological 1426
Ethnobotany 190, 382, 1747
Ethnocide 2135
Ethnographic Study 178, 1419
Ethnography 408, 411, 735, 1137
Ethno-sociological 1367
Etiquette 1025, 1042
Events 472
Everyday Healing 214
Evidence 300, 461, 870, 1139, 1782
Evil 302, 536, 971, 1192, 1319, 1394, 1544
Experiencing Siva 417

F

Faag Literature 149
Fair(s) 43-55, 65, 82, 238, 285-86, 314, 317, 328, 337, 344-47, 555, 561, 583, 656, 681, 757-58, 775, 797, 841, 972,

983, 1007-8, 1021-22, 1076-79, 1141, 1172, 1181, 1262-63, 1304, 1313, 1360-61, 1399, 1547-47, 1572, 1542, 1635, 1712, 1754, 1794, 1836, 1840, 1863, 1909, 1921, 1929, 1935, 1965, 1973-74, 1979, 2022, 2069, 2071-77, 2085, 2108, 2113-14, 2116,
Faiths 314, 317, 476, 783, 1370, 1515, 1526, 1564, 1567, 1926, 2093-94
Fame 310, 649
Family 16, 241, 619, 766, 794, 880, 914, 973, 1002, 1039, 1307, 1325, 1412, 1462, 1662, 2066, 2159
Family law 241
Famines 1720
Fanatical 849
Farmers festivals 261, 1252, 2056
Fasts 315, 475, 505, 775, 1218, 1314, 1362, 1520, 1667, 1949, 2008, 2031
Feasts 14, 505, 643, 1218, 1314, 1362, 1667, 1690, 1766, 2089,
Feeding Skulls 1214
Feeds 226
Female Bridegroom 730
Female Infanticide 340
Female Power 434
Feminine 226, 1028-29
Fendalism 1926
Fertility 209, 1137, 1327, 1516, 1598, 1662
Festival of Lights 63, 80
Festive Cuisine 862
Fiction 279
Fierce Gods 1245-46
Fighting 1319
Fire-Walking 318
Fishing Rituals 1643
Five 1426, 2094
Flags 310, 649, 1790
Flates 111
Flowers 1149, 1214, 1341, 1591,
Fluid Signs 455
Flute 1027
Fly a Kite 1133
Folk Art 602, 945, 1109, 1329
Folk Cults 13, 1085, 1992
Folk festival 259, 456, 695, 940, 1444, 1642, 1650, 1651, 1914, 2007
Folk-Deity 129
Folkloric 157, 293, 784, 844, 1105, 1224, 1299
Folk-Superstitions 2191
Food 180, 861, 1112, 1219, 1485, 1692
Forests 566, 1221, 1463, 2122
Frightening visitors 1319
Fulaichi Festival 1591
Fun 246
Funeral customs 489, 715, 2030, 2062
Funeral priests 1488
Funeral Ritual (Dak Vidhi) 698, 1507

G

Gadaba festivals 1256
Gaddi Janjati 2000
Gaj Samaroh 1082
Gambling 765
Ganapati 994, 1242
Ganesh festival 877
Ganga Jathara 1650

Ganga Sagar mela 353
Gangasagar 1381
Ganges River 34
Gangor 1459, 1477, 1780, 2158
Ganikas 1289
Ganjifas 765
Garasia tribes 225
Garba 892, 1227
Garhwali Bagpipes 56
Gariband 1310
Garo(s) 290, 324, 617, 1187-89, 1305, 11307, 1337, 1687
Gauri and Ganesh 779
Gavri Ritual 1919
Gaya, Bihar 1066
Gender 165, 291, 430, 634, 662, 808, 975, 1085, 1102-03, 1143, 1217, 1379, 1779, 2181, 2201
Genealogies 323
Geography 922, 1917
Germany 195, 1196
Ghosts 644, 1340, 1488, 1790, 1983
Ghotul 606
Gift 655, 1208, 1582, 1969
Glass 309, 1026
Glimpses 382, 1282
Goa(n) 36, 431, 538, 1017, 1370, 1691, 1884
Godaba 465
Godavari District 48, 54
Goddess 20, 180, 195, 202, 204, 258, 272, 435, 517, 534, 535, 592, 614, 631, 635, 731, 738, 809-11, 816, 914, 915, 961, 1028, 1043, 1120, 1162, 1214, 1267, 1328, 1372, 1408, 1540, 1573, 1779, 1917, 2181, Holi 223, 244, 246, 422, 1209, 1332, 1353, 1647, 1740, 1762, 1803, 1824, 1841, 2130, 2195
Goomsur 567
Gora Puja 1153
Graha santi 86
Grass-roots 432
Graveyard Petitions 407
Great Tradition 229, 1646, 1899
Grhya Sutras 106, 390
Gudhi Padava 1498
Guga Naumi 646
Gujarat 705, 732, 757-58, 1155, 1167, 1182, 1304, 1334, 1556, 1635, 2015, 2072, 2079
Guntur District 46
Gurkhas 1385
Guru Govind Singh Jayanti 1812

H

Hajong Marriage Customs 1164
Handbook 196, 744
Haridwar 299, 987
Harijan 1655
Harmony 476, 1278, 1657
Harvest festival 572, 779, 1090, 1687
Haryana 1571
Hasi Khusi Ka Parv 980
Haunting Melodies 1458
Head-Hunting 857
Heat 145, 201, 297, 1034
Hebrews 302
Hemis 152, 1234-35
Henna 1288
Heretic tradition 477
Hçwisi Pūjā 104
Hijarā 1297
Hill 111, 340, 349, 474, 567, 635, 666, 978, 1043, 1184, 1257,

1373, 1422, 1508, 1673, 1689, 1720, 1894, 2145
Himachal Pradesh 68, 117, 388, 515, 684, 840-41, 951, 1000, 1369, 1711, 1794, 1909,
Himalayan 485, 610, 801, 998, 1367, 1779, 1986, 2142, 2181
Hindoo 07, 143, 586, 702
Hindu belief 22
Hindu Culture 34, 168
Hindu Deity 415, 417
Hindu Exogamy 986
Hindu Law 171, 934, 943, 1758
Hindu Manners 1
Hindu Marriage 69, 135, 299, 430, 570, 808, 1236-37, 1254, 1736, 1751, 1800
Hindu New year 138
Hindu Samskaras 1453
Hindukush 1143
Ho 11401, 1244, 1275-76, 1278, 1279, 1281
Holy Cow 640, 1048, 1138
Honeymoons 1288
Hopi 281
Hor 527
Horse 1536
Hos 370, 1280
Householders 334, 1239, 1487
Hum log 308
Human Community 24, 1426
Human Destiny 454
Human Sacrifice 280, 340, 494, 568-69, 666, 820, 2038
Humanity 1473
Hunting Festival 276, 1151
Husband Hunting 681, 1262
Hyderabad 706, 1022, 1171, 1302
Hymn(s) 450, 846

I

Iconic 410
Iconographies 429
Iconography 816, 895
Icons 399, 410, 1466, 1558, 1670, 2117
Illustrated Guide 303, 1220
Images 146, 450, 800, 1043, 1517, 1638
Immanence 1417
Impact 372, 1152, 1641, 1721, 1746, 1955
Incomparable India 278
Indian folklore 81
Indian Mythology 116
Indian Ritual(s) 02-03, 109, 262, 596, 723, 773, 831, 1350
Indian Village(s) 468, 531, 537, 556, 646, 1043, 1245, 1545, 1653, 2159
Indological 229, 1680
Indus 489, 797, 1482, 1909
Industry 17
Inequality 1245-46
Innovation 416, 1119
Instrument 533
Intangible Cultural Heritage 184-86
Integrated Pest Management 17
Intent 414, 642
Interaction 591, 685, 1286, 1646
Intrapartum 1675
Invisible Custom 637
Isattul Hasanat 1301
Islami 706, 1301, 1493, 1644,
Island Ecology 11

J

Jaad Bhotia Janjati 759

Jagar Utsav 902, 921, 1017
Jagrata 1198
Jain rite of Worship 852
Jain ritual 137
Jaina Canonical Mythology 194
Jainism 630
Jaipur Virasat festival 240
Jajmani system 210, 741, 742, 814, 2188
Jallikattu 187
Jamatia tribe 1176
Jambudwip 1643
Jatakarma 486
Jatapus ritual 1559
Jaunsaris 764
Jettatura 1544
Jewish Community 791
Jhagde ki Phagen 398
Jhala Rajput 931
Jhampan 327
Jharkhand 371, 1151, 1914-15
Jhauba 285
Jhunjhunu Mela 10
Juangs 603, 1079, 1257
Jubbal State (Simla) 480
Jumbo Jamboree 1456
Jyotisma Ritual 283

K

Kaal Sarpa Yoga 1620
Kaarthikai Kuumbu 2009, 2011, 2012
Kabir Panth 1131
Kabui Nagas 1516
Kachari 754
Kadu Kuruba 891
Kagada Ghati 1198
Kagadye cha Holi 2130
Kahamtis of Assam 718
Kahar Jati 1640
Kalahandi 1136, 1250
Kalakshetra 89
Kalam elluttu 946
Kalaviveka 934
Kali 166, 369, 756, 1027, 1179, 1215, 1313
Kalidasa 1064
Kaliyoot 1608
Kalptaru 1248
Kaman festival 920
Kamar tribe 557, 1310
Kameng 509
Kandali Utsav 1449
Kang-Dali 375
Kangra Rajputs 334
Kaniyan 941
Kaniyas, Karnataka 516
Kansa Indian death customs 542
Kanya Kubja 1013, 2032
Kapali 1945
Karaga festival 1623
Karakam 332
Karam Festival 460
Karbala 1536
Karbi 114, 456, 2023
Karimnagar District 55
Karma 79, 194, 454, 1680, 1769, 2163
Karnataka 08, 242, 516, 861-62, 891, 1060, 1589, 1967, 2013
Karpagambaal 1945
Kartik Snan 397
Kashmir 90, 463
Kasi 1487
Kennar chatriya 1838
Keral ka bada din 356
Ketu 338, 491
Khalasa 71, 87, 136
Khammam District 44, 50
Khandesh 1518

Khari Song 457
Khariya Janjati 263
Kherai 754
Khohdi 527
Khuksi 458
Kikur 456
Kings 147
Kingship 164
kinship 16, 290, 465, 571, 654, 836, 906, 1148, 1306, 1379, 1752
Kirat fesitival 1747
Kisans 267
Kitchen room 1709
Knowledge 304, 881, 1219, 1950
Kodavas 675
Kodungallur festival 1068
Kokna tribe 1697
Kolam 1109, 1191, 1329
Kolhan Area 1285
Koli festival 690
Konda Reddis 230
Koothandavar festival 1605
Kora 172, 1515
Koraput, Orissa 465
Korivi 1526
Korku 1506
Kota 729, 2126, 2190
Krishna 47, 246, 647, 1607
Kriyakramajyotika 1948
Kshatriya 1537
Kudmis 1277
Kugti village 1369
Kuki customary law 91
Kukite Chondan 91
Kullu Janpad 200, 329, 684, 1390, 1440, 1834, 1844, 1853-55, 1870, 2034, 2041, 2045-46, 2048, 2121, 2123, 2127
Kulpali 10
Kumbh 514, 833, 881, 1099, 1698-1700, 1822
Kurmis 1284, 1914
Kurnool 1596
Kushana Period 1739
Kuvi Kandha, Orissa 178, 1786

L

Labyrinth Ritual 1108
Ladakh 62, 301, 818, 1356, 1743, 1826, 1978
Ladakhi custom 1743
Lai Haraoba 275
Landscapes 1228, 1831
Lao hill tribes 1184
Lavi Mela 911
Laws of Manu 459
Legal Aspects 511
Legend 19, 560, 898, 915, 1422, 1508, 1573, 1625, 1696, 1698, 2132, 2155
Legitimacy 164
Lepchas 746
Lesser Known Dances 369
Life-Cycle 1417, 1659
Lingayats 385
Linguistic 709, 1278
Little traditional 1654
Living Customs 137, 153, 167, 242, 381, 389, 452, 483, 486, 502, 525, 669, 892, 936, 1063, 1065, 1190, 1223, 1249, 1468, 1474, 1593, 1717, 1738, 1761, 1774, 2026-27, 2082
Living Manners 1443
Lodhas 265, 554
Lohadi 234, 670, 792
Lohri 151, 527, 694, 1858
Lokparva 32

Lord Jagannatha 06, 1636
Lord Krishna 246, 647
Lord of Obstacles 427
Lore 157, 252, 293
Losar Tyohar 759
Love 111, 337, 628
Low-country 21
Lushai Customs 510, 1490

M

Maa Manikeswari 1136
Maaghi 547
Maargashira Shukla Saptami 1812
Mad festival 1601
Madhva customs 1830, 2061
Madhya Pradesh 559, 561, 900, 1479, 1893
Madras festival 75, 1602
Magar community 1747
Magic 153, 1410, 1465
Magico-religious 170, 271, 900, 901, 1431, 1991
Maha Sivaratri 139
Mahabharata 313, 1084, 1646, 2062
Mahadevi 435, 1540
Mahalaxmi fair 2072
Mahaliathal 1437
Maharashtra-fairs 347
Mahare Kuthaha 394
Mahasivaratri 1764
Mahaveera Jayanti 1813
Mahbubnagar District 51
Mahua 1310
Maibis 275
Maidenhood 21
maithil Brahmin 1158
Malabar 513, 648, 740, 1232, 1766
Malva village 1202
Malwa 2082
Mammoth 1627
Mamulia 778
Manasāmangala 291
Mandi 72, 151, 239, 354, 670, 672, 694, 944, 972, 977, 982-83, 1169, 1867, 1932, 2058, 2109, 2112
Mangoes 1102
Manipur 91, 1181, 1483, 1726, 1911
Mantras 106, 381, 926, 1055, 1771, 2174
Manu 459, 1300
Marathi Pradesh 144
Mare Puja 466, 467
Marhatta Brahmin 520
Maria Murder 604
Marine Fisher folk 1643
Māriyamma(n) 434, 1513, 1731
Marriage customs 206, 352, 652, 737, 791, 854, 1164, 1288, 1302, 1430, 1532, 1879
Marriage System 114
Martha History 1005
Martyr 883
Marwar(i) 59, 1326
Mask dance 152
Masked festival 1238
Masks 57, 152, 1897, 2075
Mass 1529
Matamma Tradition 635
Mate selection 385
Mathura 231, 834
Matrilineal System 1337, 1688
Mauritius 386
Mayamo Marriage rituals 1467
Medak District 53
Medhi 449
Medical anthropology 411

Medical ritual 154
Medicine 17, 153
Medieval India 383, 496, 750, 2132, 2175
Medieval Society 513
Meditation 1993, 2205
Mediterranean Area 359
Mediumship 412
Meghalaya 1688, 1707-08
Mejar 70, 952
Mela 10, 60, 70, 117, 236, 238-39, 353, 671, 739, 745, 833, 881, 902, 911, 951, 977, 1098, 1110, 1144, 1175, 1287, 1448, 1471, 1710, 1844, 1846, 1855, 1864, 1867, 1870, 1960, 2001, 2046, 2048, 2058, 2109-10, 2121, 2125-27
Mela Jagara 902
Mela Markand 238
Meliaceous Plants 17
Memoires 180
Menarche 2134
Meo of Northern India 906, 1493
Meriah system 474
Mesoamerican 437
Metal Mask 1897
Metamedical Discourse 227-28
Metaphor 1467, 1594
Meyer Bratakatha 1316
Midnapur, West Bengal 264, 268
Milan Parv-Basoya 235
Mimetic 2084
Mind 1520, 1545
Minjar fair 400, 1840
Miracle Plays 834
Mirani Sindhuri 1171
Mishing 1045
Mithun 1516
Mizo Hills 1720
Modernization 261, 1150
Mohurram 2107
Molakala Punnami 1651
Mongoose 504
Monkeys and Serpents 1770
Monpa 519
Moonless Night 1347
Mopin 92, 1357
Moral Responsibility 454
Mortuary Practices 185, 554, 1280
Mother 434, 592, 614, 656-57, 731, 915, 1043, 1260, 1306, 1373, 1568, 1573, 1991, 1994
Motifs 116, 1064
Mountain 1695, 1779, 2074
Mourning 678
Movement 432, 463, 479, 695, 1115, 1850
Mudras 1032
Muggu 1022
Mukkoti 1765
Mukkuvas, Kerala 1568
Munda(s) 190, 372, 460, 1247, 1410, 1415, 1610, 1970
Muniappans 1437
Munnakakkanni 1433
Murals 631
Muria Religion 25, 606
Murtipuja 425, 939
Music Rituals 680
Musical tradition 56
Muslim 16, 29, 96, 214, 241, 315, 624, 1225, 1408, 1536, 1658, 1833, 1879, 1978
Mussulmauns 26, 1222
Mustached brides 1085
Mutilation 221

Mylapore Festival 1056
Myoko Festivals 350-51
Mysore Village 748, 2006
Mythological 549, 799, 1220, 1788
Myth-Ritual Complex 1381
Myths 205, 421, 605, 607, 701, 896, 1050, 1395, 1397, 1677, 1895, 2132, 2204

N

Nadars 66
Nadu Veedu 1462
Nag Panchami 33, 1080, 1083
Naga Customs 843
Nagarattar 1379
Nagbansi 599
Nagore-e-Sharief 1716
Naked Nagas 667
Nalgonda District 49
Nalkantha, Gujarat 705
Nalwari fair 238, 1021
Namasudra community 60
Namdev tradition 1387
Nanda Raj Jat Yatra 956

Napita 1593
Narrative 20, 277
National Integration 1657
Nats 1971
Nature 109, 721, 848, 1063, 1321, 1415, 1639, 1728, 1913, 2145
Navagrahas 374
Nāyanārs 849
Nayars 1222, 1465
Nazeer Akbaraabadi 1180
Neem 17, 37
NEFA 100
Nepal(i) 79, 86, 98, 518, 598, 727, 1016, 1101, 1769, 1976, 1993
Netarhat 267
Nicobar Islands 529, 1464, 2176
Nilgiri 566, 2180
Nine Planets 374
Nishis 553, 574
Niskramana 2097
Nitya Karma Vidhi 1769
Nomadic 9, 227-28
Non-conformist's 273
Nongkrem Festival 1907
Non-Vedic Rituals 453
Northern Orissa 1283
Nuakhai Tradition 1496
Nyishis 1172
Nyokum Yullo 553

O

Observation 26, 257, 598, 1222, 1279, 1733, 1804
Oddis 1659-60
Omens 856, 1468, 1892, 2057
Onam 865, 942, 1087-88, 1427, 1766, 1958
Onge 1693
Oracles 746
Oral Performance 277
Oraon Religion 1703-05
Ordinary Farmers 2056
Orthodox 432, 2128
Orthodoxy 2202
Osakothi Ritual 631
Oscillating 496

P

Pagan Sacrifice 150
Pageant 76
Pahari Bhasa 119, 962
Painted Prayers 858
Painting 631, 1505
Palm 1467, 2176
Palparvan 2099

Pambin Tullal 1363
Pandal Pattu 1598
Pangi 301, 1849
Paniyas 1514
Paraber Anginay 270
Parade 1081, 1383, 1523
Paraiyars 410
Parampara 12, 78, 93, 103, 526, 540-41, 563, 682, 893, 968, 992, 1000, 1154, 1226, 1377, 1452, 1575, 1603, 1609, 1633, 1827, 1857, 1888, 2071, 2149, 2157
Pardah 2018
Parental Beliefs 894
Parhaiya 10701
Parsee Festivals 316, 1271
Parturition 230
Parv 94, 99, 144, 235, 760, 777, 893, 979-80, 1009, 1018, 1030, 1045
Past 483, 578, 1117, 1315, 1468, 1670, 1712, 1840, 1915
Pastoral Deities 1966,
Patang 1133
Patra Pooja 696
Patterns 342, 767, 1184
Pauri Bhuiyas 276
Peasant Ritual 619
Pēcum Teyvam 1433
Perfection 446
Performance 196, 211, 275, 277, 990, 1118, 1387, 1684
Performing Vows 195
Periya Purāam 849
Persistence 257
Phenomenology 410, 2203
Philosophical 110, 260, 490, 2055
Phool Yatra 247
Phoolwalon Ki Sair 1902
Phulkari 709
Physical 771, 1418, 1559
Physical Phenomena 1559
Pilgrimage 34, 232, 439, 485, 588, 595, 625, 881, 957, 991, 1296, 1779, 1999, 2118-19, 2181
Planet Śani 1037
Plants 17, 158, 170, 245, 539, 559, 623, 696, 718, 900-01, 1066, 1386, 1431-32, 1784-85
Pods 985
Poetry 111, 433
Poison 1582
Pollution 1014, 1735, 1923
Polyandry 05, 480, 978, 1481, 1530
Pomo Indians 183
Pongal 1020, 1071, 1324
Pooja Parva 144
Popular Entertainments 196
Possession 25, 411-12, 628, 722, 735, 1363, 1406, 1529, 1790, 1954, 1983, 1986
Post-funeral Ritual 698
Pot Boils 1607
Potter 1362, 1507
Praise 105, 508
Pravargya 846, 2117
Prayag Raj 881
Prayers 296, 458
Pregnant 279
Primitive 438, 822, 1430, 1596, 1946, 2014, 2176
Primordial Mound 871
Prodigious 194
Property Rights 1379
Propinquity 385
Prose 735
Puberty 21, 1110, 1682
Puja 104, 169, 177, 250, 258, 321, 361, 391, 403, 466-67, 597,

701-02, 953, 1049, 1153, 1313, 1380, 1419, 1421, 1432, 1516, 1702, 1806, 1943, 2016
Punerary Customs 608
Punjab 344-45, 463, 583, 826, 1567, 1689, 1739
Punjab Prelude 1567
Puranic Beliefs 448
Puranic Tale 98
Purity 648, 1014, 1735, 1738, 1923
Purulia 190, 1177
Puruottama Ketra 963
Puttu Mariyamman 1731

Q

Quaint marriage Customs 1430

R

Raas 12
Rabhas 458
Rāhu 491, 1470
Rāhu-Ketu 491
Rain 1457, 1710
Rainbow colours 1332
Rajaparba 209
Rajasthan 164-65, 223, 226, 242, 377, 401, 422, 720-22, 1183, 1326, 1434-35, 1574, 1592, 1633, 1670, 1973, 1998, 2063, 2180, 2149
Rajbanshi (Rajbansi) 479
Rajput Elite 165
Raksabandhana 936
Rāku Pakavān 339
Rali 237, 528, 1868
Ram Mohun Ray 436
Ramayana 158
Rath rathni ra mela 236
Rath Yatra 236, 1968
Rationale 174
Rebellion 976, 1422
Reconversion 1820
Refugee Monastery 336
Regeneration 428, 1486
Relics 498
Religious
Renovation Ritual 660
Reproductive 1429
Republic Day 197
Rg-veda 106
Rice 219, 794, 1415
Riddle Hymn 846
Rising Sun 1706
Riti Rivaaz 401, 1562, 1615
Ritual Arts 915-16, 1573
Ritual Hand Poses 1032
Ritual Healing 227, 228
Ritual Practice 212
Ritual Theory 212
Ritual Transforms 413
Ritualistic approach 58
Ritualistic ceremony 98
Ritualistic Theatre 1017, 2102
Ritual-motifs 1064
Rivers 31, 121, 626, 1096
Roma festival 35, 950, 964, 1069, 1999
Rongali Bihu 156
Rowdy Songs 407
Rural Debt 641
Rural India 113, 916, 1329, 2119, 1950, 2106
Rural Integration 371
Rural Manbhum 1939

S

Sacrament 1455, 1881, 2019
Sacred Bath Ceremony 1381

Sacred days 253
Sacred Groves 189, 498
Sacred India 97, 847
Sacred waters 34
Sacrifice 150, 280, 340, 428, 430, 434, 471, 494, 568-68, 582, 587, 666, 820, 831, 848, 885, 905, 1211, 1423, 1426, 1580, 1739, 1745, 1895, 1993, 2038,
Sahagamana 1223
Saintly Householders 1239
Saints 334, 1054
Sakta Pithas 306-07, 587, 615, 774
Sal-Blossom festival 1309
Salient features 544
Samanvit Prayas 540
Sanatana Dharma 2202
Sanghol (Punjab) 1739
Sanjna 2082
Sankaracharya 18
Sanskar 329, 1156, 1455, 1854
Sanskrit inscriptions 167
Sanskritik Virasat 1326
Santal 1326
Santal society 112, 1150, 1312
Sapindikarana 1036
Saptmatrika worship 1466
Sarbojonin Durgotsab 169
Sarguja 749
Sarhul festival 269
Sati 10, 15, 59, 217, 357, 383, 428-30, 436, 459, 490, 526, 629, 676, 686, 820, 823, 825, 876, 899, 914, 954, 1179, 1253, 1261, 1315, 1343, 1401, 1442, 1641, 1715, 1724, 1829, 1835, 1865, 2003, 2118, 2149, 2152, 2172
Sati worship 59
Satluj ghati 160
Satpuda Mountain 2074
Sattriya 362
Saturn 1037
Saundarya Lahari 961
Sauria Paharia 1077
Savage society 1170
Scheduled Caste 60
Scriptual System 389
Season 75, 179, 907, 1079, 1173, 1426, 1601-02
Secret 307, 311, 326
Secular 502, 1100, 1147, 1632
Self –Sacrifice 1211
Semen 33
Semiotic approach 295
Sensuality 216
Serpent
Serpent lore 252
Serpent Worship 157, 399, 466, 627, 703, 1178, 1232, 1402-03, 1733, 1788, 1930
Severed Head 832
Sex 33, 225, 297, 337, 1532, 2148
Sexism 436
Sexual Rituals 1583
Sexual Symbol 1318
Shabdateet Gyan 1997
Shadi 1302
Shamanism 1462
Shantiniketan 173
Sherdukpen 519
Sherpa 1414
Shia 492, 1879
Shimla 65, 117, 346, 1603, 1855, 2114
Shinto aspects 1194
Shivratri 72, 798, 972, 982-83, 1169, 1867, 2058, 2109

Shraddh Ritual (Pindadan) 1066
Shravani Parv 99
Shri Satyanarayana 137
Shrine, Shahul Hamid 1348
Si-Donyi festival 1686
Sickness 297
Siddavesa 274
Siddha 2175
Siddis 352
Sign Language 933
Sikhism Rituals 87, 136
Sikkim 1990
Singhbhum 1140
Sinhalese 21, 1110, 1391
Sins 1488
Sipi ka Mela 1471
Siri Myth 1529
Sirmor 395, 913, 1570, 1960
Skanda-Kumāra 1482
Slavic Peoples 2191
Slovenly Woman 1362
Smallpox 592, 628, 1043, 1372
Smarta ritual 321
Snake Worship 2187
Snakes 293, 327, 432, 731, 738, 1224, 1672, 2187
Social Bodies 1418
Social Change 3,1, 766, 919
Social Contents 262, 1350
Social Custom 298, 383, 1386
Social Hierarchy 406
Social Institution 384, 1315
Social life 469, 1011, 1057, 1567, 1778
Social Mobility 576
Social Movements 479
Social Organisation 459, 1937
Social Reforms 686
Social Theory 1300
Social Transformation 1596
Socio-cultural 386
Socioeconomic Impact 1641
Socio-ethical 511
Sociology 1087, 1819
Soharai 190, 1610
Sojourn 2176
Solan 119, 1864, 1961
Solar Contagion 1105
Solung 100
Sonbhadra 1009
Songs 90, 113, 123, 246, 407, 875, 959, 1089, 1571, 1694, 1806, 1939, 2032
Soor 1611
Sorrows 721
Soul 294
South Kanara 124
Southern Kerala 241
Spirit 124, 411-12, 722, 735, 1913, 1954, 2152
Spirit Cult 124
Spiritual Ecstasy 294
Spitit 167
Splash of Colour 289
Split Goddess 435
Split Mothers 434
Spring 42, 156, 188, 348, 422, 639, 1203, 1981, 2153
Sradha Paddhati 687
Sradhanjali 1947
Sri Lanka 786, 2186
Sri Rama Navami 141
Srinivasamangapuram 680
Stambhewari Cult 1793
Stars 804, 1661
Stirring Beats 1382
Stratification 1556
Structure 473, 642, 742, 794, 814, 826, 867, 1005, 1294, 1298, 1391, 1411, 1420, 1527, 1639, 2091, 2161
Suata 777
Subansiri 1450

Submission 291
Suddhi 1820
Suicide 604, 676, 1127
Sukharpuda 1441
Suliya Jatra 1444
Sun 252, 716, 904, 1403, 1706, 1917
Superstitions 333, 843, 1384, 1406, 2057, 2176, 2191
Suppression 474
Sur Das 1723
Suskar-Kinnar 888
Sustainability 566
Suvasin 452
Svetambar Jain Temples 425
Swati Tirunal Festival 1354
Swinging 1457
Symbol 109, 146, 159, 203, 330, 410, 576, 588, 614, 772, 780-81, 1318, 1594, 1672, 1795, 1802, 2198, 2202, 2204
Syncretism 476, 1276, 1278, 1281
Synthesis 476, 550

T

Tagino 1686
Tai-Ahom 719
Taking Meals 1443, 1476
Tales 131, 1355, 1535
Tamia 562
Tamil Diaspora 416
Tamil Tradition 277
Tanaha 355
Tanks 1535
Tantra Asana 1293
Tantric Religion 260
Tarao of Manipur 1911
Tarnetar fair 681, 1262
Tatta Pani, Mela 1846
Tatti re Mela 117
Taziadari 224
Teez tyohar 119, 2000
Teleological Study 1503
Televangelism 24
Telgu Speaking 207
Terminology 290
Thakurnagar 695
Thanks Giving Ceremony 1284
Tharu 393, 584, 1981
The Quran 623,
Theatre 799, 1017, 1756, 2102
Theyya Kavu 127
Theyyams 990
Tîccanni 875
Tirupati 1650
Tiruvonam 1958
Todas 2167
Toleration 167
Tongue 1387
Tons Valley 1611
Topographies 105
Torana 449
Toranmal Fir 2074
Tortoise 1512
Toys 1538
Traditional 18, 110, 157, 245, 293, 355, 359, 573, 639, 692, 744, 861, 867, 945, 1041, 1101, 1105, 1224, 1299, 1376, 1458, 1515, 1621, 1648, 1654, 1680, 1692, 1737
Traditional Reserves 359
Traditional Technology 1692
Transformation 08, 432, 816, 1596, 1955
Transgenderism 297
Transgression 291
Transience 1417
Travancore 05, 1590
Travels 68, 847, 1496, 1952

Tree 17, 37, 39, 251, 627, 703, 721, 772, 844, 1130, 1219, 1259, 1266-67, 1392, 1447, 1482, 1613, 1788, 1795, 1802, 1931
Tree marriage 844
Tribal
Tribal marriage 225
Tribal Pujas 250
Tribal Rituals 101, 1415
Tribal Societies 101
Trichur 1383, 1815, 1816
Trichur Pooram 1383, 1816
Trinkaus Mortuary 1207
Tripura 250, 1176, 2085
Trocadero 387
Tulapurusa 1782
Tulu Oral Traditions 412
Turmeric 586
Tusu Festival 1283, 1915
Typical 242, 1830

U

Udaipur 224-25, 377, 1183, 1998
Udisyar Citra 1898
Untouchables 1677
Upanayana 502, 2026
Urali 715
Urban 532, 700, 795, 933, 1831, 2165, 2190
Utsav 173, 233, 358, 921, 1045, 1067, 1142, 1248, 1449, 1569-70, 1618, 1683, 1776, 1853, 1875, 1880, 1883, 1916, 1961, 1997-8, 2005, 2011, 2121, 2123-24
Uttar Kashi 102

V

Vadhula School 1975
Vaikuntha Ekadasi 1765
Vaishnava 1537
Vajrayogini 601
Vaneshwar Fair 1974
Varkaris 1238
Varna Systems 1640
Varnvyavastha 1640
Vart 1860
Vasant 173, 348
Vasava Bhil 790
Vāstu yāg 703
Vedic Funeral customs 489
Vedic Rituals 108, 379, 390, 451, 453, 507, 726, 1985
Veneshwar Mela 1144
Vernacular 634
Vertigo 25
Vesasraya Bidhi 688
Victor Turner's Theory 330
Village Daughter 2181
Vinayaka Chaturthi 659, 1767
Violence 66, 448
Violent 849
Virgin 655, 735, 1537,
Virgin birth 735
Viskhapatnam agency 1645
Vistas 157, 294, 784, 844, 1105, 1224, 1299
Visual 878
Vivah 163, 222, 329, 381, 974, 1838, 1868, 2026, 2196
Vivahasaskara 405
Vow 195, 809, 1348, 1504, 1587-88, 1929
Vratas 242, 2013

W

Wangala 1687
War Dance 1794
Warangal District 43

Warlis 445
Wealth 1545, 1645
Wedding 503, 544, 1047, 1517, 1541, 2201
Wedding Rites 113, 1047
Widow Burning 490
Wife 508, 905, 1038, 1994
Wild Animals 11
Wisdom 306, 601, 692, 948, 1349
Womanhood 291, 626, 795, 1379
Women
Wood 1349
World of Gracias 326
Worship Pattern 458
Worshiping Śiva 496
Writings 1982
Wynad, Kerala 1514

Y

Yaga 415, 703,
Yalman's 1110
Yellamma 297
Youth 1338

Z

Zebu 640, 1048

Title Index

1,500 Witness 'Sati' ritual. 1442
2nd international Roma festival a cultural pilgrimage. 1999

A

A brief survey on the festivals of Nalkantha area of Gujarat. 705
A cattle festival. 1323
A century of Toda studies. reviewed work(s): The Toda of South India: A New Look 609
A changing festival in Vanyajati.1649
A comparative analysis of the Jajmani system. 210
A critique of Yalman's interpretation of Sinhalese Gill's puberty ceremonial. 1110
A custom law and procures: a reference book. 1185
A day in the life of India. 1241
A descriptive study of the dramatic function and significance of the clown during Hopi Indian public ceremony. 281
A dictionary of the Vedic rituals based on the Śrauta and Grhya Sūtras. 390
A family in India. 880
A festival to sita: in praise of the devoted wife, the ideal bahu, the wronged woman, at Deval. 508
A Jajmani system of North India: Its structure, magnitude, and meaning. 814
A Kerala village temple festival: rituals and folk art forms as communications of traditional culture. 945
A mammoth meeting. 1627
A manual of Hindu marriage. 299
A Marhatta Brahmin ambassador explains hindu

manners and customs. 520
A marriage to India. 462
A non-conformist's view of the dowry custom. 273
A note on customs of naming and south Indian genealogies. 323
A note on Hajong marriage customs. 1164
A note on important festivals among the major tribals of West Bengal. 192
A note on rural debt and control of ceremonial expenditure in India. 641
A note on the festivals of mediaeval Bengal: in the light of Bengali literature and folklore. 1159
A note on the inter-clan relationship in agricultural rituals and festival of the Tarao of Manipur. 1911
A note on the Rajbanshi (Rajbansi) of Eastern India with special reference to Social Movements.479
A Pagan Sacrifice. 150
A phulkari from Bhatinda.. 709
A physiological explanation of unusual behaviour in ceremonies involving drums. 1365
A program for collection of material on the customs and rituals associated with childbirth. 1126
A promise fulfilled. 1525
A rite for the Suvasin and the Vedic Puranic tradition. 452
A sacred trread: modern transmission of Hindu traditions in India and abroad. 2182
A Santal Jaher: Rituals and biodiversity conservation. 1031
A search in secret India. 311
A short cultural geography of death and the dead. 922
A short history and ethnology of the cultivating Pods. 985
A short note on polyandry in Jubbal State (Simla). 480
A short note on the Festival of the Jhargram sub-division, Midnapur, West Bengal, 264
A splash of colour. 289
A splendour of worship woman's fasts, rituals, stories and art. 2031
A story without an end. 1663
A study of a social institution in Indian villages. 384
A Study of syncretism in the Ho rituals and festivals. 1276
A study of the festivals of the Kisans and Birjhias of Netarhat. 267
A Study of the Origin of Ratha Yātrā in the Puruottama Ketra. 963
A study of village through ritual analysis. 256

A study on the nature and structure of ritual language of the bauls of Birbhum, West Bengal. 1639
A study on the ritual actions in Ho festivals. 1244
A temple festival of Māriyamma. 1513
A tribal festival in Attapady, Kerala: An aspect of worship of nature as God. 1728
A view of nature of the Munda people in eastern India: rice, ancestor and nature. 1415
A village where Dalits can't wear footwear or ride bikes. 1210
Aadi (Minyong) tyohar: Manoranjan ke aadhar. *2138
Aali aaye Linga. [Hindi]. 1428
Aanad or ullas ka parv Pongal. [Hindi]. 1071
Abject to object: colonialism preserved through the Imagery of Muharram. 1644
Aboriginal festivals in Gujarat. 1334
Above the forest: a study of Andamanese ethno-anemology, cosmology, and the power of ritual. 1463
Absent lord: ascetics and kings in a Jain ritual culture. 147
Adaptations of contemporary ayurvedic medical practice in urban India. 2060
Adup Perukku of adoration of the rivers. 121
Adyera Gambhira [microform] : Bangalara dharmma o samajika itihasera eka adhyaya [Account of Gambhira festival of Bengal]. 1439
Aesthetics and power in Pambin Tullal: A possession ritual of rural Kerala. 1363
Afterword: the mysteries and communities of Sati. 823
Age at marriage in India: vision and reality. 1578
Aging, gender and widowhood: perspectives from rural West Bengal. 1103
Agni: the Vedic ritual of the fire altar. 1985
Agrarian rites of the Durga festival - an analysis of Bengal customs 1787
Agricultural rituals of the Santals of Ajodhya hills: Techno - ecological perspective. 349
Ahnika-paddhati [microform]: daily routine for princes. [Hinduism Rituals], 335
Aise manaee Jati he Chamba me Lohdi. [Hindi]. 909
Akhti. [Hindi]. 776
Akti parv. [Hindi]. 760
Aligning rituals. 77
Alpona: ritual decoration in Bengal. 368
Amar bihu. [On Bihu - a national festival of Assam]. [Assamese] 249

Among the Brahmins and Pariahs [microform 1777
An abode in the Aravallis: the secret world of Gracias. 326
An alphabetical list of the feasts and holidays of the hindus and muhammadans. 1690
An annual festival of the Hos 370
An appraisal to the marriage system of the Karbis of Assam. 114
An area of darkness. 1335
An essay on the mythological significance of tree and serpent worship. 1788
An Ethnobotanical envision into Santhali festivals in Purulia district, West Bengal. 1177
An ethnographic account of the religious practice in a Tibetan Buddhist refugee monastery in northern India. 336
An ethnographic study of the Kuvi Kandha of Orissa. 178
An Indian affair. 182
An inscribed metal mask discovered on the Occasion of the Bhunda Ceremony at Nirmand. 1897
An introduction to tribal fairs and festivals: Theoretical considerations. 2076
Anatomy of a ritual. 530
Ancient Hindu marriage law and scriptures. 1254
Ancient Indian folk cults. 13
Ancient Indian rituals and their social contents. 262
Ancient Indian rituals and their social contents. 1350
Ancient Indian spring festival. 2153
Ancient manners of the Indian still existing in Bissenpour. 521
Ancient popular festivals in North-East India. 1906
Ancient promises. 1258
Anjali's prospects: class mobility in urban India 532
Annals and antiquities of Rajasthan. 2063
Annual festivals of the Lodhas of west Bengal. 265
Annual hunting festival of the Pauri Bhuiyas: and significance of the annual hunt among the Tribes of Cent. 276
Another autumn in Kashmir. 1519
Another reason: science and imagination of modern India. 1557
Anthills, split mothers, and sacrifice: conceptions of female power in the Mariyamman tradition. 434
Ants and folk-beliefs in South India. 1299
Apni mahan paramparaon ko khokar hi ham deen-heen bane hen. [Hindi]. 78

Archaeological evidence on cremation and post-cremation burial in India. 461
Around India. 1821
Art and rituals: 2500 years of Jainism in India. 630
Art: regional traditions the temple of Jagannatha architecture sculpture painting ritual. 1505
Articulation of physical and social bodies in Kerala. 1418
Artthamulla Inthu Matam. [Tamil]. 970
Arunachal Pradesh: Apa Tanis and Myoko festivals. 350
Arunachal Pradesh: Apa Tanis and Myoko festivals. 351
Aryancya sananca pracina va arvacina itihasa [microform], [Hinduism Customs and practices]. 1666
Aryona tahevarono pracina tatha arvacina itihasa [microform], [Fasts and feasts Hinduism]. 1667
As I see India. 2088
Asamar lok utsav. 2005
Asauc nirnay. [Religious rituals in verse]. [Nepali] 1016
Asli brahat brahaspativar vrat katha. 1759
Asokan Pillars: a reassessment of the evidence. Part 5, Symbolism, Burmington Magazine, 870
Aspects of culture and customs of Arunachal Pradesh. 579
Aspects of social customs of the Bodos. 298
Aspects of speech in Vedic ritual. 451
Assam valley [microform]: beliefs and customs of the Assamese Hindus. 1303
Assamese marriage customs: Pre-nuptial. 737
Asur festivals. 1076
At the Trocadero: A celebration of India. 387
Atha Pratistha sangraha prarambhah [microform]. [Hinduism Rituals]. [Sanskrit] 130
Auspicious wisdom: the texts and traditions of Srividya Sakta Tantrism in South India. 306
Austrics of India-their religion and tradition. 1727
Avadhi vrat kathayen. [Avadhi]. 1451

B

Baadiya ra mela. [Pahari Language].739
Baba: the Santhal Sal-Blossom festival. 1309
Badagra ka devta tatha unke chahra. [Pahari Language]. 2039
Badagra ka devta tatha uske Mele. [Pahari Language]. 2040
Baisakhi in Sikh history. 1924

Baisakhi of 1699 – the creation of Khalsa. 1905
Baithan ki Holi. [Hindi]. 244
Bal Kalyan ka puneet parv Ahoi. 979
Balikaon ka parv 'Suata. [Hindi].777
Balon Panjo-Sagar Manthana ra tyohar. [Pahari Language]. 2044
Baluvu: a ritual among Kadu Kuruba tribe of Karnataka. 891
Bamboo, rats and famines: famine relief and perceptions of British Paternalism in the Mizo Hills (India). 1720
Banaile Phool: vraton aur parvon ki kathayen. [Hindi]. 1942
Banaras: cosmos and pilgrimage in the Hindu imagination. 588
Bandana festival of Kudmis of eastern India. 1277
Bandana Parab: a thanks giving ceremony of the Kurmis. 1284
Bangles, sacred trees, and fertility: interpretations of the Indus 576 script relating to the cult of Skanda-Kumāra. 1482
Barahon mahine ke sampurna vrat aur tyohar. [Hindi] 231
Baresahariya Bhaona: Community drama festival of Assam a living tradition. 1756
Barsat ke teen tyohar. [Hindi]. 545
Baruni Mahamela: A religious festival of a scheduled caste (Namasudra). 60
Baruni: a folk festival of Thakurnagar: organised by the Namasudra community for onward movement. 695
Bastar-Lok (Kala-Sanskriti Prasangha). 889
Beads among the Juangs of India. 603
Beating out the cash for a dowry. 1549
Beauti and the Bhuta. 125
Because it gives me peace of mind: rituals fasts in the religious lives of Hindu Women. 1520
Being Vaishnava, becoming Kshatriya: culture, belief, and identity in north India, 1800-1940. 1537
Beliefs and practices related to parturition among the Konda Reddis of Andhra Pradesh. 230
Beliefs are concerning human sacrifice among the Hill Reddis. 666
Bengali cooking: seasons and festivals. 179
Bengali customs and traditions. 657
Besu ka parva. [Pahari Language]. 1876
Betrothal rites among the Bhil, of North-Western Central India. 1046

Bhadu festival of West Bengal: a glance of the pattern of Bhadu songs. 959
Bhakti and its publics. 1388
Bhakti and the Bhakti movement: a new perspective. 1850
Bhaona: the ritual play of Assam. 1366
Bharat ke Tyohar. 1832
Bharatvarsh me vivah evam parivaar. [Hindi]. 974
Bharmor ke tyohar. [Pahari Language]. 2035
Bhartiya Lok Vishwas. [Hindi]. 2100
Bhartiya parampara me nari ki asmita. 1827
Bhartiya Samajik paramparaon me manvadhikaron ki shashavat anugunj. [Hindi]. 563
Bhartiya Toharon ka sanskritik nihitarth. [Hindi]. 1862
Bhartiya Vratotsava. [Hindi]. 376
Bhil Janjati ka utsav [Hindi]. 1961
Bhil Janjati ke samajik sanrachna evam unke riti rivaj. [Hindi]. 806
Bhil tribal festivals. 61
Bhilala festivals and rituals. 1933
Bhils of Ratanmal: an analysis of Western India community. 1359
Bhils: between social self-awareness and cultural Synthesis. 550
Bhima Shankar tribal fair. 2069
Bhojonavidhi: a living custom as reflected in Ayurvedic treatises. 669
Bhuta worship: aspects of ritualistic theatre. 2102
Bihar ka ek tantric lokotsav: Jhinjhiya. [Hindi]. 2139
Bihu aru tar prakrtik citra. [On Bihu, the festival of Assam] 788
Bihu: festival of Assam. 287
Birth and associated rituals of the Daroi Gonds: A study on intangible cultural heritage. 186
Birth rituals of the Ho tribe. 1275
Birth-rites and rituals among the Bhilala. 1934
Bishu fair of war dance: colourful life of the Himachal Pradesh. 1794
Blood, fire and meditation: Human sacrifice and window burning in nineteenth century India. 1993
Blood, milk and coconuts: A study of intra-cultural ritual variation. 638
Boat festivals of Kerala. 2024
Boats, boat builders and carnivals: The Kerala regatta. 600
Bodana-Motana. 1539
Bohada: The mask festival of Bharsatmet. 2075

Bonded Labour or Dasa Pratha. 1499
Borders & beliefs: ethics, actor hood, and the India Pakistan conflict. 1528
Bori dek [microform]. [Manners and customs]. [Konkani]. 1199
Boro Aiyen: customary law of Bodos. 193
Botor Kikur: a folk festival of the Karbis for Rair. 456
Brahmamrta. [Essays on Hindu religious festivals]. [Bengali] 2098
Brahmanic ritual traditions in the crucible of time. 1741
Bsoaa: ek vivechan. [Hindi]. 118
Buda ka Tohar. [Pahari language]. 1630
Buddha Jayanti-Vaishakha Poomima. 1811
Budhe ka utsav. [Hindi]. 1569
Buffalo fight of Himachal Pradesh. 515
Bundel Sanskriti ke mool Aadhar Bugadkhand ke lok parv. [Hindi]. 1873
Bundeli Lokotsava Mamulia. [Hindi]. 778
Bundeli sanskriti ka prateek Mamuliya. [Hindi]. 768
Bundelkhand kala me Shev parampara. [Hindi]. 1888
Bundelkhand me Fago ke vividh roop. [Hindi]. 762
Burashavar ka Mela. [Hindi]. 1287
Burial customs as an Archaeological source. 23
Burial practices in ancient India. 1912
Busahar ka parva. [Pahari Language]. 1877

C

Can an Age old custom be abolished. 1887
Capital celebrations. 1722
Carving the palm: The role of metaphor in Mayamo marriage rituals. 1467
Caste and ritual in a Malva village. 1202
Caste and ritual in an Andhra Village. 1322
Caste status and ritual observances in a west Bengal Village. 1295
Cauth candra puja. [Moon worship ritual in the 4th day of Bhadra observed in Mithila]. 924
Celebrating female energy: The festival of Kaliyoot 1608
Celebrating republic day. 197
Celebration of life: Festivals in Jhauba. 285
Celebration on Diwali among the Gonds of Tamia. 562
Celvam kolikkum cina vastu. [Tamil] 1320
Census of India 1961: Andhra Pradesh fairs and festivals Adilabad District 45
Census of India 1961: Andhra Pradesh Fairs and Festivals Cuddapah District. 52

Census of India 1961: Andhra Pradesh Fairs and Festivals East Godavari District. 54
Census of India 1961: Andhra Pradesh fairs and festivals Guntur District. 46
Census of India 1961: Andhra Pradesh fairs and festivals Karimnagar District 55
Census of India 1961: Andhra Pradesh fairs and festivals Khammam District. 44
Census of India 1961: Andhra Pradesh fairs and festivals Krishna District. 47
Census of India 1961: Andhra Pradesh fairs and festivals Mahbubnagar District. 51
Census of India 1961: Andhra Pradesh Fairs and Festivals Medak District 53
Census of India 1961: Andhra Pradesh fairs and festivals Warangal District. 43
Census of India 1961: Andhra Pradesh-Fairs and Festivals Khammam District. 50
Census of India 1961: Andhra Pradesh-Fairs and Festivals Nalgonda District. 49
Census of India 1961: Andhra Pradesh-Fairs and Festivals West Godavari District 48
Census of India 1961: Gujarat-fairs and festivals. 758
Census of India 1961: Gujarat-Fairs and festivals. 757
Census of India 1961: Himachal Pradesh-fairs and festivals. 841
Census of India 1961: India-study of customary rights and living and working conditions of scavengers in two towns. 864
Census of India 1961: India-Ugadi the New Year's festival of Andhra Pradesh, 866
Census of India 1961: Kerala-fairs and festivals of Kerala Statements. 1007
Census of India 1961: Kerala-Fairs and festivals of Kerala. 1008
Census of India 1961: Kerala-Onam a festival of Kerala. 865
Census of India 1961: Madras fairs and festivals. 1141
Census of India 1961: Maharashtra - fairs and festivals in Maharashtra.l 286
Census of India 1961: Manipur-fairs and festivals. 1181
Census of India 1961: Pondicherry State Fairs and Festivals. 1546
Census of India 1961: Pondicherry-Fairs and Festivals. 1547
Census of India 1961: Rajasthan- Fairs & Festivals. 1592

Census of India 1961: Tripura-fairs and festivals. 2085
Census of India 1961: Uttar Pradesh fairs and festivals. 2108
Census of India 1971: Punjab fairs and festivals. 1572
Ceremonial songs of the Kanyakubja Brahmans. 2032
Ceremonies customs and colour: behind the veil. 859
Ceremonies observed by low-country Sinhalese: A girl attaining the age of puberty or maidenhood. 21
Ceremonies of the Pomo Indians. 183
Ceremony and social structure in 19th centuary Punjab. 826
Certain social factors associated with the adoption of recommended agricultural practices by rural local leaders and ordinary farmers in India. 2056
Cerumen types among tribal population of Bihar. 1718
Chaitra parva rituals chhau dances. 1018
Chaitra Vishu: the Hindu new year day. 138
Chamba festival of rain (Minjar Ka Mela). 1710
Chamba ka lokpriva lohadi nitya shastri adhan. 234
Chamba ka lokpriya utsav. [Hindi] 233
Chamba ki Basoaa parampara. [Hindi]. 1857
Chamba ki Lohadi. [Pahari Language].792
Chamba ki vivahik prampraye. [Hindi]. 222
Change and continuity in Hindu marriage rituals. 1237
Change and continuity in Indian religion. 724
Changes in customs and practices among some lower agricultural castes of the of the Kotah state. 729
Changes in the cycle of festivals in a Bhumi village. 1936
Changing context of political praxis and ritual realm: Chhatrapatis and chitpavans. 1901
Changing economic, social and ritual relationships in a modern South Indian village. 793
Changing festivals of the Santals in Jharkhand. 373
Changing patten of entertainments during festival Nights in rural Andhra Pradesh. 1595
Changing religion and ritual in a Vasava Bhil community impacted by involuntary resettlement. 790
Character, manners and customs of the people of India; and of their institutions, religion and civil. 564

Chenchus and social transformation: A study of a primitive tribe in Kurnool district of Andhra Pradesh 1596
Chhat Parva: Ek Samiksha. 1980
Chhos kor: the festival of the monpa and the sherdukpen 519
Child nutritional status, feeding practices and womens autonomy in rural andhra pradesh, India. 1892
Children protecting Deities and rituals of Bengal: a study. 1160
Children's appropriation of their teacher's beliefs about the purpose of reading: An exploratory study in an Indian setting. 1501
Chodas ka mahaparva. [Hindi]. 622
Christmas star-easter moon. 2137
Circus and culture: A semiotic approach. 295
Clan and some customs of the Nagbansi. 599
Clay deities. 2143
Close of festival of India in USSR: Russians' interest in Carnatic music. 1599
Co-existing in two cultures: Parental beliefs and childrens activities in an Indian immigrant community. 894
Collecting popular traditions. 2160
Colour and heat in a south Indian ritual. 201
Coloured rice, symbolic structure in Hindu family festivals. 794
Colourful Kulu Dussehra fairs and Festivals. 2113
Comment: the continuing invention of the Sati tradition.1401
Community, discourse and critique in Jnaneswar. 1114
Concept of purity and inpurity in Orissa and its sources. 1738
Conditions of visibility: writings on photography in contemporary India. 1982
Confrontation, transgression, and submission: ideals of womanhood in the Manasāmangala. 291
Connected places: region, pilgrimage, and geographical imagination in India. 625
Conservation ethos in local traditions: The West Bengal heritage. 497
Construction practices in traditional dwellings of Kerala, india. 1041
Contemporary Hinduism: ritual, culture, and practice. 1671
Contemporary Indian architecture at the Festival of India. 366
Contemporary Indian tradition, 288

Contemporary marriage practices in north India: evidence from three Uttar Pradesh villages. 1139
Contentious traditions: the debate on SATI in colonial India. 1179
Continuities and changes: Interrelationships of ritual and social dance contexts in Dubrovnik-area villages. 573
Corporations, personhood and ritual in tribal society: three interconnected topics in the Anthropology of Meyer fortes. 1783
Cradle tales of Hinduism. 1355
Creating new myths: post - puja reflections. 701
Cremation and liberation: therevision of a Hindu ritual. 495
Crime and custom in savage society. 1170
Critical events: an anthropological perspective on contemporary India. 472
Crooked stalks; cultivating virtue in South India. 1461
Cult of Bongaism, linguistic synthesiis and religious syncretism in the Ho society 1278
Cult of the tree deities of Bengal. 251
Cults and rituals in the Rayalaseema region of Andhra Pradesh. 1652
Cults and shrines in early historical Mathura (c. 200 BC-AD 200). 2103
Cults, customs, and superstitions of India; comprising studies and sketches of interesting peculiarities in the beliefs, festivals and domestic life of the Indian people 1406
Cultural Anthropology: The Science of Custom. 1004
Cultural heritage of Ladakh. 62
Cultural heritage of the Himalayas. 2115
Cultural significance of fairs. 583
Cultural significance of fairs. 583
Culture and behavior: Applying log-linear models for transitions between offices in a Mexican festival system. 1681
Culture and customs of India. (Culture and customs of Asia.), 835
Culture and power: legend, ritual, bazaar, and rebellion in a Bengali society. 1422
Culture and the arts festival of the twentieth century. 873
Culture in India. 755
Culture shock: a guide to customs and etiquette. 1042
Current intrapartum care practices in india. 1675

Custom of Gudhi Padava and its sources. 1498
Customary law as the corner - stone of legal framework. 1265
Customary law of marriage among the Jamatia tribe of Tripura. 1176
Customary law of the Kangra district (excluding Kulu). 1243
Customary law regarding succession in the ruling families of Punjab hill states. 1689
Customary law, dispute and litigation among the Garos. 1187
Customary laws among the Gond of Madhya Pradesh. 1500
Customary laws, marriage among Bhils. 1342
Customary rites and festivals in Santal society. 1312
Customs and beliefs of Raika pastoralist of Rajasthan associated with camel husbandry. 2080
Customs and beliefs pertaining to menarche in north arcot district of Tamil Nadu. 2134
Customs and customay law in British India 1941
Customs and manners of the uncivilized race of men. 2192
Customs and taboos observed by east women from pregnancy to childbirth. 1166
Customs and traditions of Aao Naga: Aao Dialect (Manipuri). 1726
Customs as reflected in North Western Himalayan languages. 2142
Customs at the time of taking meals in Maharashtrian families. 1474
Customs of a few Naga Tribes: some accounts derived from the old files. 1093
Customs of sati: Probable causes of its origin. 1253
Customs of the world: A popular account of the manners, rites and ceremonies of man and women in all countries 837
Customs of the world: a popular account of the manners, rites and ceremonies of men and women in all countries. 2168
Customs regarding hospitality and their sources. 1249
Customs relating to Niskramana Samskara in Kerala and their sources. 2097
Customs relating to the selection of Bride in Maharashtra and their Ancient Sources. 860
Customs, rites and ceremonies. 396

D

Dahashara kullu ka. [Hindi] 200
Daily life in ancient India: from 200 BC to 700 AD 133

Daily rituals: Rekha Rodwittiya's rebellion. 976
Dalits attacked for touching 'ceremonial umbrella. 2050
Dance festival with a difference. 551
Dancers and festivals of India: Selection system under scrutiny. 126
Dancing for themselves: folk, tribal and ritual dance of India. 1019
Darsan: seeing the divine image in India. 589
Das karma paddhati. [On Hindu rituals]. [Sanskrit]. 79
Das Patsahiam de Gurparab. [Religious festivals]. [Panjabi] 1010
Dasara in Mysore. 1579
Dashara in Bastar: a study of Raja tribal relationship. 1333
Dassera – another great Indian festival. 1884
Dassera in Allahbad.1585
Dealing with deities: the ritual vow in South Asia. 1587
Death and cosmogony in Kasi. 1487
Death and deification: folk cults in Hinduism. 1992
Death and disposal of dead: Hindu. 839
Death and disposal of dead: Introduction and primitive. 822
Death and disposal of dead: Jaina. 879
Death and disposal of the dead: Buddhist. 1550
Death and disposal of the dead: Parsi. 1959
Death and kinship in Hinduism: structural and functional Interpretations. 836
Death and the digestion: the symbolism of food and eating in North Indian mortuary rites. 1485
Death as the beginning of a new life: Hero worship among a south Indian fishing caste. 1791
Death customs: an analytical study of burial rites. 215
Death in Banaras. 1489
Death ritual and social structure in classical antiquity. 1298
Death ritual of the Ho: a study in Kolhan Area. 1285
Death rituals of the Ho tribe: An anthropological observation. 1279
Deeksha ki Bhartiya paramparayen. [Hindi]. 2078
Deepawali: The festival of lights 80
Deepawali: The festival of lights. 63
Defending Hindu tradition: Sanatana Dharma as a symbol of orthodoxy in colonial India. 2202
Depression beliefs in Northern India and the United States: A cross-cultural study. 1375

Description of the character, manners and customs of the people of India. 543
Desert places. 493
Determination of seasons and equinoxes in Old India and related festivals. 1173
Deuri Janjatiyo ke Dharmik evam Samajik parvotsav. [Hindi]. 993
Dev Rahati: An ethnobotanical study of the forests preserved on Grounds of religious beliefs. 2122
Development and ethnocide: colonial practices in the Andaman Islands. 2135
Development of domestic rites. 487
Devmogra and Asthamba Fairs. 2070
Dewali. 999
Dhagon ka tyohar Rakshabandhan [Hindi]. 546
Dharma and Moksa. 868
Dharmasastra, custom, 'real law' and 'apocryphal' smritis. 1106
Dharmik Samskara va nityakarma. [Hindi]. 392
Dharmik sanskritik, etihasik evam naitik paramparaon ka prateek raksha bandhan parv. 893
Dhim, Kam, Cappu, Pottu: Timbral discourses and performances among temple drummers in Kerala, India. 1684
Dialectics of Hindu ritualism [microform] 488
Diaspora of the Gods: modern Hindu temples in an urban middle class world. 2165
Die Flambierte Frau: Sati in European Culture. 629
Dimension of religion, magic and festivals of Indian tribe: the Munda. 1410
Dipa-Garbha to Rasa-Garba an enchanting evolution of a fascinating festival Navaratri. 892
Disposal of dead. 1059
Disposal of the dead and physical types in ancient India. 771
Disposal of the dead by mutilation in spiti. 221
Disposal of the dead in the Mahabharata: a study in the funeral customs in ancient India. 2062
Disuasendra in Santhal Society. 555
Divarala ki sati. 954
Diwali: The legend and its celebration. 898
Diwali: Then and now. 198
Diwali: When the stars come down to earth 1661
Diwari Mahotsav. [Hindi]. 770
Dodda-Jatra: the grand religious procession. 1940
Does Tantric ritual empower women? renunciation and domesticity among female Bengali Tantrikas. 1212

Domestic worship and the festival cycle in the South Indian city of Madurai. 1128
Domesticity and difference/ woman and men: religious life in medieval Tamil Nadu. 1413
Dowries from Kutch: a women's folk art tradition in India: [exhibition and catalogue]. 602
Dowry and inheritance. 191
Dowry custom among the Andhras. 1753
Dowry custom barbarous and anti-Hindu. 363
Dowry custom. 2120
Dowry in Hindu marriage as a social scientist sees it. 570
Dowry old order and the new. 380
Dowry once a good custom, now a menace. 1581
Dowry system - a social evil. 1192
Dowry system today. 1494
Dowry system. 1825
Dowry: A diagnosis. 1775
Dowry: Scourge on society. 1058
Dowry : An obsolete custom. 923
Draupadinam cira [microform] 506
Dravidan gods in modern Hinduism. 594
Dreams and omens among the Nagas. 856
Dual framing: locating authenticities in the music videos of Himalayan possession rituals. 1986
Dugra puja: with notes and illustration. 702
Durga Aagman Samaroh. 1061
Durga Pooja: Devi ki shaktishali Talwar. 1062
Durga puja yesterday, today and tomorrow, 177
Durga puja. 1702
Durga: Wife and mother. 1994
Durgapuja in Bengal. 176
Durgotsava. 181
Dussehra of Kulu. 64
Dusserah festival. 1606
Dying before the Mahabharata war: Martial and transsexual body-building for Aravan 1084
Dying gods and puberty ceremonies. 1682
Dying the good death: the pilgrimage to die in India's Holy City. 957

E

Eastern wisdom: the philosophies and rituals of the East. 948
Eclipse ritual in South India. 784
Eclipse ritual in south India. 785
Eclipses in Hindu life and thought. 807
Ecology and rituals in tribal areas. 499
Economic base of polyandry in the hill region of India-conflicting values and their socio-economic implications. 978
Economic development and peasant marriage in South India. 613
Economy and persistence of rituals: Observation in two settings. 257

Education and the beliefs of popular Hinduism; a study of the beliefs of secondary school boys in central provinces, India, in regard to nineteen major beliefs of popula 1216

Effects of hum log, a television soap opera, on pro-social beliefs in india. 308

Ekodista. [Rituals translated from Sanskrit]. [Sanskrit, Nepali] 1976

Empty ritual. 1798

Encountering Kali: in the margins, at the centre, in the west. 1215

Encyclopaedia of fairs & festivals in India; with select rituals, vows, Holy cities, Temples and pilgrim centers. 1929

Encyclopaedia of Puranic beliefs and practices. 448

Enkal nattuppuram. [Customs, menners and festivities in and around Coimbatore]. 1597

Essays in Indian folklore. Papers presented to the centenary festival of Rai 81

Essays on the ritual of social relations. 712

Ethnobiological analysis from myth to science: XII. Pancha Yajnya (five sacrifices)-A welcome episode of the Human community for rainy season exhibited through fes 1426

Ethnobotanical folk practices and beliefs of the Ao Nagas in Nagaland, India. 360

Ethnobotany of Kirat fesitival of magar community in Buxa Duar area of West Bengal, India. 1747

Ethnobotany on the 'Soharai' festival of 'Mundas' in Purulia district West Bengal. 190

Ethno-geography of the sun Goddess festival, 'chhatha', in Bhojpur region, India: from locality to universality, 1917

Ethnography of fertility and birth. 1137

Everyday healing: Hindus and others in an ambiguously 559

muslim place. 214

Everyday life in ancient India [microform]. 1801

Everyday life in early India. 590

Evolution of Hindu marriage with special reference to rituals. 1800

Evolution of hindu moral ideas. 1951

Experiencing Siva: encounters with a Hindu deity. 417

Exploring tho roots of villago Hinduism in South Asia. 829

Expression of santiments in the songs associated with the Karam festival of rural Manbhum (Bihar, India). 1939

F

Faag literature in Bundelkhand. 149

Facets of Mandi Shivratri festival. 1169

Fairs and festivals in rural India. 1921

Fairs and festivals of Bengal. 656

Fairs and festivals of India. 1863

Fairs and festivals of India. 328

Fairs and festivals of India. 82

Fairs and festivals of Indian tribes. 2077

Fairs and festivals of Madhya Pradesh, Cenus of India. 1954 Elementary forms of the religious life 561

Fairs and festivals of Punjab. 345

Fairs and festivals of the Bhilala tribe. 1965

Fairs and festivals of the Dhelki Kharias: report of an anthropological field investigation. 1979

Fairs and festivals of the kinnaras of Western Himalaya. 1836

Fairs and festivals of tribals in Gujarat. 1635

Fairs and festivals of West Bengal. Alipore, (West Bengal)1263

Fairs and festivals, Chandigarh. 344

Fairs and festivals, Shimla. 346

Fairs and festivals. 1935

Fairs and festivals. 65

Fairs in the tribal Bihar. 1078

Faith is all! emotion and devotion in a Goan Sect. 1370

Faiths, fairs & festivals of India. 317

Faiths, fairs and festivals of India. 314

Family and land in peasant ritual. 619

Family and marriage in Lahul Valley. 1325

Family and social changes in India. 766

Family law and customary practices of Muslims in Southern Kerala. 241

Family spirits and deities among the Santals and associated rituals. 1039

Family, kinship and marriage among muslims in India. 16

Far from peaceful: Nadars join the orgy of violence with thevars; dalits continue to suffer. 66

Farmers festivals: A case from eastern Orissa. 1252

Farmers rituals and modernization: a sociological study. 261

Fasting, a lesson in restraint. 1358

Fasting, feasting. 505

Fasts, feasts, and the slovenly woman: Strategies of resistance among North Indian potter women. 1362

Feast and festival. 643

Feast and festivals. 2089

Feasting and fasting: the Vrata tradition and its significance for Hindu women. 1218

Featival cycle of Hindus in a Karnataka village. 1967

Female initiation rites on the Malabar coast (Curl Bequest prize essay for 1953). 740

Feminine feeds in Rajasthan district. 226

Fertility concept in a ritual an anthropological explanation of Pandal Pattu. 1598
Fertility decline in Tamil Nadu: Social capillarity in action? 1327
Festival and emerging social reality: Perspectives on the Idu Mishimis of Arunachal Pradesh. 1231
Festival colours. 1290
Festival of art. 1475
Festival of colours. 220
Festival of colours: introducing the primary and secondary colours. 1552
Festival of Eid. 1566
Festival of India. 714
Festival of India: 1985-86. 67
Festival of India: in the United states 1985-1986. 83
Festival of Mahaliathal and Muniappans. 1437
Festival of rain in Himachal Pradesh. 1711
Festival of the 63 Saints. 1054
Festival of the desert. 955
Festival of the land of the rising sun. 1706
Festival of the Nishis of Arunachal Pradesh. 574
Festivals and fairs of the Nagas. 2022
Festivals and holidays of India. 2052
Festivals and sacred days. 253
Festivals and social relations in a Mysore village mechanics of two processions. 2006
Festivals Himachal Pradesh. 68
Festivals in Indian society. 84
Festivals in medieval Andhradesa. 1622
Festivals in the folk-songs of Haryana: an anthropological analysis dealing with cultural aspects. 1571
Festivals. 305
Festivals of ancient India as gleaned from the Indian Literature-Festival as an important aspect of social life. 1057
Festivals of early Travancore: a brief description. 1590
Festivals of India. 1842
Festivals of India. 1886
Festivals of India. 674
Festivals of India. 699
Festivals of India. 1885
Festivals of India. 863
Festivals of India. 1044
Festivals of India. 85
Festivals of India: A theoretical consideration. 1360
Festivals of Kameng: a few selected. 509
Festivals of Ladakh. 1826
Festivals of Meghalaya. 1707
Festivals of Meghalaya. 1708
Festivals of repentance, a study of Mahashivratri. 1129
Festivals of Sauria Paharia. 1077
Festivals of selected tribes from South India. 2071
Festivals of Subansiri. 1450
Festivals of the Chroes. 1201
Festivals of the goddess Bhagavati in Kerala. 517

Festivals of the Oddis: field note of a researcher. 1660
Festivals on an all India basis. 713
Festivals, fairs and customs of Himachal Pradesh. 1909
Festivals, fairs and customs of the Himachal Pradesh. 797
Festivals, fairs and fasts of India. 775
Festivals, rituals and ethnicity among east Indians in Trinidad. 325
Festivals: a sociological approach. 580
Festive India. 1730
Festive rituals. 1134
Fetivals and legends of South India. 19
Fierce gods: inequality, ritual and the politics of dignity in a South Indian village. 1246
Fierce Gods: Inequality, ritual, and the politics of dignity in a South Indian village. 1245
Fighting evil and frightening visitors. 1319
Finding one's place in the text: A look at the theological treatment of caste in traditional India. 639
Fire sacrificial plants. 539
Fire-walking the tribal way. A rejoinder. 318
Fishing rituals of the marine fisher folk: of Jambudwip: a socio-cultural study. 1643
Flags of fame: studies in South Asian folk culture. 310
Flowers and festivals. 1341
Flowers in the Santal festival: an interpretation of Baha festival. 1149
Fluid Signs: Being a Person in the Tamil Way. 455
Focus on India festivals across U.S. celebrate a diverse culture. 1576
Folk belief behind a festival: A case study in Midnapur. 268
Folk dance in the season of fairs and festivals amongst Juangs. 1079
Folk deities and festivals at Tamil Nadu: with special reference Puttu Mariyamman. 1731
Folk festivals in India. 2007
Folk festivals of Bengal. 259
Folk festivals of Jharkhand with special reference to the Kurmis. 1914
Folk icons and rituals in tribal life. 1558
Folk religion of Bengal. 470
Folk rituals of eastern India. 1161
Folk, faith and fendalism. 1926
Folklore, cultural performances, and popular entertainments: A communication-centered handbook. 196
Food of the Gods: the search for the original tree of knowledge. 1219
Forests, people and state: continuities and changes. 1221
From dawn to dusk they dance with joy. 155
From material to deity: Indian rituals of concecration. 596

From pardah to people. 2018
From ritual to ceremony: death ritual in Hindu North India. 199
From the margins of Hindu marriage: Essays on gender, religion, and culture. 808
From transience to immanence: consumption, life-cycle and social mobility in Kerala, South India 1417
Fruitful journeys: The ways of Rajasthani pilgrims. 720
Fruits of worship: practical religion in Bengal. 1371
Fulaichi: festival of flowers.1591
Funeral rites (Antyesti) and secular practices. 1100
Funeral ritual (Dak Vidhi) in Potter community: of Maharastra and its importance. 1507
Funerary rites and customs. 2171
Further comparative notes on the Hijara of India. 1297
Furthering their own demise: How Kansa Indian death customs accelerated their depopulation. 542

G

Gadaba festivals. 1256
Gaddi Janjati ke teej tyohar. [Hindi]. 2000
Gaderan ka jaatra utsav. 1618
Gadi janjati ke Tij-tohar. [Pahari Language]. 2002
Gadyaar Chetra ka Tohar Baso. [Pahari language]. 1619
Gadyaar kshetra ka tyohar: Baso. 1617
Gaj Samaroh ki rangeen shobha. [Hindi]. 1082
Ganesa and the Ganesa festival in Maharashtra: a study in Hindu religious celebration. 426
Ganesa: Lord of obstacles, Lord of beginnings. 427
Ganesh Chathurthi from the medicinal angle. 1995
Ganesh Chaturthi: When the lord comes to town. 1522
Ganga Jathara: a folk festival in a small city Tirupati and the neighbouring villages in Andhara Pradesh. 1650
Ganga Sagar mela: A tryst with the truth [Hindi]. 353
Gangor: vevahik such aur sampannata ka parv. [Hindi].1459
Ganikas in early India: its genesis and dimensions. 1289
Ganjifas, the tradition of gambling in India. 765
Garba. 1227
Garhwali Bagpipes: syncretic processes in a North Indian regional musical tradition. 56
Garo and Khasi-A comparative study in matrilineal systems. 1337
Garo Avuncular authority and matrilineal cross-cousin marriage. 324
Garo customary laws and practices: a sociological study. 1189

Garo customary laws and practices: sociological study. 1188
Garo family. 1307
Garo kinship terminology, 290
Gasaee rotku ra tyohaar. 1616
Gavri ritual of the Bhils. 1919
Gender, kinship and property rights: Nagarattar womanhood in South India. 1379
Ghosts, greed and sins: the occupational identity of the Benaras funeral priests. 1488
Ghosts: life and death in North India. 644
Giddha. 1772
Glass and cultural tradition in India. 309
Goa ki dayamayi maa. [Hindi]. 538
Gods and ghosts Teyyam and bhuta rituals. 1340
Gods in the Bazaar: the economies of Indian calendar art. 897
Gods of flesh, gods of stone: the embodiment of divinity in India. 2166
Gods on earth: the management of religious experience and identity in a north Indian pilgrimage centre. 2119
Gods, ghosts and possession. 1983
Gods, ghosts, and demons: possession in South Asia. 1790
Gogo: history, customs and traditions. 1270
Gonda janpad ke Danguria Tharu aadivasiyon ke riti-rivaj. [Hindi]. 584
Goomsur, the late war there-the Khonds or Hill tribes. 567
Gora Puja evam Deepavali parv. [Hindi]. 1153
Gorkha sampraday me Dashahra utsav. [Hindi]. 1142
Graha santi. [Rituals]. [Nepali]. 86
Grahayaga tattvam. [Rituals for worship of and sacrifice for the planets.; [Bengali]. 1580
Graoonjee Saaja. [Pahari Language]. 2043
Great tradition and little traditions: Indological investigations in cultural anthropology. 229
Grhya Mantra aur unka Viniyoga. [Hindi]. 1055
Growth of mimetic forms from ritual to drama: classification and chronology by comparative reference. 2084
Guardians of Tamil Nadu: folk deities, folk religion, and Hindu themes. 1196
Guests at God's wedding: celebrating Kartik among the women of Benares. 1541
Guga naumi. 646
Gujarat and the Gujaratis [microform]: pictures of men and manners taken from life 1167
Gujarat's tribal fairs. 1304
Guramata gaurawata, athava, Guramata anusara wiwaha samsakara de lai warata mana waidaka-riti da pola jo gurabani, guramatta de pusataka, Hindu dharama shas 1910

Guramata Hulasa [microform]: janama tom leke anta prayanta gurabani anusara singham de karaja karana di bidhi [On Sikh social and religious rituals]. 2033
Guramata prakasha, arathata, Guramryada karana di bidhi [microform]. [Sikhism Rituals]. 87
Gurkhas: their manners, customs and country. 1385
Guru Govind Singh Jayanti-Maargashira Shukla Saptami. 1812
Guru-shishya parampara: Kal aur aaj. [Hindi]. 2157

H

Hair like snakes and mustached brides: crossed gender in an Indian folk cult. 1085
Hamare kuch Prachin Lokotsava. [Hindi]. 1584
Hamare kucha pracina lokotsava [microform] [On ancient folk festivals of India]. 1642
Hamare Parv aur Tyohar. [Hindi]. 1878
Hamare riti-rivaaz. 1351
Happy married life in ancient India. 1269
Harvest festivals in honour of Gauri and Ganesh. 779
Hasi Khusi Ka Parv: Teez. 980
Having become a God, he should sacrifice to the Gods. 582
Heat and control of Chattisgari ritual. 145
Hemis ka Parv: dusht aatmaon ki parajay. [Hindi]. 1235
Her body, her story: situating the Maibis in the ritual-performance of Lai Haraoba. 275
Here is India. 1006
Hierarchy of marriage alliance in South Indian kinship. 571
Himachal ka pahari Jubal: Beshakhi ke mela mein nacati talvar. [Hindi]. 745
Himachal kchhetra mein sati pratha: ek vivecan. [Hindi]. 1829
Himachal ke riti-rivaaj. [Hindi]. 912
Himachal ke ye mela. [Hindi]. 1175
Himachal ki lokkala ke pratik shivratri ke shaskratik mela. [Pahari Language]. 2110
Himachal pradesh ka ek pramparik purav: Kullu dasahara. 681
Himachal Pradesh ka prasedha renuka mela. 951
Himachal Pradesh ki samajik paramparayen. [Hindi]. 1000
Himachal: A land of fairs and festivals. 983
Himachal: The land of the colourful fairs and festivals. 2114
Himachali lokparampara me parv evam tyohar. 1075
Himalaya ke mela aur tohar. Himbharti, No. 26-27, June-Sept 1975. 82-84. [Pahari Language]. 2126

Himalayan district of Kooloo, Lahul and Spiti. London, 1871. 381. 801
Himalayan pilgrimage. Delhi, 1961. 103 485
Himchal Devta ke sanga melo ka moja. [Pahari Language]. 1714
Himchal ka lok sanskritik parv seri ka tyohar. [Hindi]. 1866
Hindoo holiday: an Indian journal. 7
Hindu acarara bicara. [On the Hindu customs and manners]. [Oriya]. 1509
Hindu and Mohammadan festivals. 1321
Hindu and Sikh wedding ceremonies: with salient features of Hindu and Sikh rituals. 544
Hindu arms and ritual: arms and armour from India 1400-1865. 1678
Hindu caste system and the ritual idiom. 1734
Hindu character. 1344
Hindu culture and caste system in India. 1713
Hindu culture custom and ceremony. 168
Hindu customs and their origins. 1534
Hindu exogamy [microform]. 986
Hindu fasts and festivals. 2008
Hindu fasts and feasts. 1314
Hindu fasts and festivals and their philosophy. 1949
Hindu festivals (Parvani). 1424
Hindu festivals and scriptures. 969
Hindu festivals as reflected in the literature of Sur Das. 1723
Hindu festivals throughout the year. 677
Hindu festivals. 312
Hindu Goddesses: vision of the divine feminine in the Hindu religious tradition. 1028
Hindu holidays and ceremonials with dissertations on origin, folklore, and symbols [microform]. 780
Hindu holidays and ceremonials. 782
Hindu holidays and ceremonies with dissertations on origin, folklore and symbols. 781
Hindu holidays and ceremonies. 763
Hindu holidays. 1052
Hindu ki Divya Sati Parampara evam Vartaman Sandarbh. [Hindi]. 526
Hindu law and customs. 943
Hindu life and customs. 734
Hindu mannars and customs. 1
Hindu manners, customs and ceremonies. 565
Hindu marriage act. 1751
Hindu marriage and Dowry: A historical-sociological review. 1736
Hindu marriage in continuity and change. 135
Hindu Marriage: More is meant than mere ritual. 69
Hindu method of tribal absorption, 292

Hindu mythology. 2178
Hindu myths. 1397
Hindu myths: A sourcebook translated from the Sanskrit. 1395
Hindu Nationalism, untouchable reform, and the ritual production of a South Indian Village. 531
Hindu Parv Mimansa. [Hindi]. 1097
Hindu religion, customs and manners; describing the customs and manners, religious, social and domestic life, arts and sciences of the Hindus. 2053
Hindu religion, customs and manners [microform]: describing the customs and manners, religious, social and domestic life, arts and sciences of the Hindus. 2054
Hindu rites in modern Tamil literature. 668
Hindu rites of food, 1012
Hindu Samskaras. 1453
Hindu Samskara-samajik tatha dharmik adhyayan [Hindi]. 1454
Hindu Sanskaras: Socio Religious Study of the Hindu Sacraments. 1455
Hindu scriptual system and economic development in India. 389
Hindu society and rituals. 1023
Hindu teoharon ki asliyat aur un ki jughrafiyai kaifiyat [microform] [On Hidu festivals]. 1492
Hindu tyoharom ka itihas. [Hindi]. 1944
Hindu women's family and household rites in a North Indian village. 2159
Hindu customs and their origins [microform]. With a foreword by Maharaja Gaekwar of Baroda. 1668
Hindu-Buddhist festivals of Nepal. 927
Hinduism: experiments in the sacred. 1033
Hinduism: faith, festivals and rituals. 2093
Hinduization of tribal deities in Orissa: The 'Sakta and Saiva typology. 615
Hinduon ke Vrata, Parva aur Tyohar. [Hindi]. 2081
Hinduvula pandugalu [microform] [On Hindu festivals]. [Telugu]. 1563
Historical Studies in the Cult of the Goddess Manasa: A Socio-Cultural Study. 1162
History of human marriage, 2173
History of Rahu and Ketu. 1470
History of the rise and progress of the operations for the suprression of human sacrifice and female infanticide in the hill tracts of Orissa. Selections from the records of 340
History of the Tantric religion: a historical, ritualistic and philosophical study. 260
Holi and Dussehra. 1841

Holi and Kamandi. 1762
Holi festival of Telangana area of Andhra Pradesh. 1647
Holi ka poranik mahatva. [Hindi]. 1740
Holi of the Hindus and Jomshim of the Santals: assimilation and diffusion of ideas of the Great and Little. 1803
Holi: Bundeli lok sanskriti me. [Hindi]. 2195
Holi: rangon ka tyohar. [Hindi]. 1353
Holi: The festival of rainbow colours. 1332
Holi-er in spring. 1203
Holy cow! the apotheosis of Zebu or why the cow is sacred in Hinduism. 1048
Holy Cow! The apotheosis of Zebu, or why the cow is sacred in Hinduism. 640
Holy Cow: an Indian adventure. 1138
Home to India. 1634
Honouring lord Venkateshwara. 882
Honouring the deities of Trichur. 1815
Horse of Karbala: Muslim devotional life in India. 1536
Hosting the divine: The Kolam in Tamil Nadu. 1109
Hosting the divine: The Kolam in Tamil Nadu. 1329
How Dalits have changed the mood at Hindu funerals: A view from South India. 872
Human effort and destiny: A study of beliefs among the Tamil people of south India (literature, women, and phenomenology). 2203
Human sacrifice (Bhunda) in the Western Himalayas. 2038
Human sacrifice in history and today. 494
Hunting festival of the tribal people of Jharkhand. 1151

I

Icons, artefacts and interpretations of the past: early Hinduism in Rajasthan. 1670
Identities and utility of botanicals used in religious worship and festivals in Khandesh region of Maharashtra. 1518
Identity and divinity: Boundary crossing Goddesses in medieval South India. 1120
Identity and symbols of sustenance: explorations in social mobility of medieval South India. 576
Illustrated dictionary of religions: rituals, beliefs, and practices from around the world. 2179
Images from Vedic hymns and rituals. 450
Imapct of pilgrim tourism at Haridwar. 987
Impact of Brahminical culture on the Tribes of Chotanagpur, Indian Festival - a case study. 1152

Impact of 'god posters' on Hindus and their devotional traditions. 1955
Impact of some Hindu rituals among the Mundas of Midnapore. 372
Important Parsi Festivals. 984
In Amma's healing room: gender and Vernacular Islam in South India. 634
In an Indian village. 468
In pursuit of rituals. 917
In the image of fire: Vedic experience of the heat. 1034
In the Nicobar islands; the record of a lengthy sojourn in islands of sunshine and palms amongst a people primitive in their habits and beliefs and simple in their manner. 2176
In the time of trees and sorrows: nature, power, and memory in Rajasthan. Durham, NC, Duke University Press. 2002. 721
Incomparable India [microform] : tradition, superstition, truth. 278
India and its faiths. 1564
India celebrates a festival of science in the USA. 1438
India celebrates! 2169
India fairs and festivals. 1399
India unveiled. 115
India. The people. 967
India: A cultural voyage Chapt. On festivals: Accents on truer lights. 1345
India: a primary source cultural guide. 552
India: now and through time. 673
India: past into present. 578
India: specially published for the festival of India in the. S. S. R. 88
India's silent revolution. 632
Indian caste customs. 1405
Indian death rituals: the enactment of Ambivalence (India, Hinduism, Brahmin). 621
Indian death rituals: the enactment of ambivalence. 620
Indian embers. 1092
Indian fire ritual. 2017
Indian pilgrimage. 439
Indian ritual and belief: the keys of power. 2
Indian Serpent-Lore or the Nagas in Hindu Legend and Art. 2155
Indian village. 556
Indian women in the Vedic, mediaval and the present age. 2027
India's sacred cattle and cultural ecology. 447
India's social heritage [microform]. 1404
Indigenous forest use practices and sustainability: A case study of the adivasis of the nilgiri biosphere region, south India. 566
Influence of Kali Puja festival on tribals of West Bengal. 1313
Instrument and purpose; studies on rites and rituals in South India. 533

Inter caste marriage in Kugti village, upper Budl Nadi Brahmaur Tehsil, Chamba district, Himachal Pradesh, India. 1369

Interiorized fire rituals in India and in Tibet. 2197

International Roma festival reportage. 964

Interpersonal attraction as a function of belief similarity and caste (india). Loyola University of Chicago). 1586

Interpretation of dream through the eyes of moderns and ancients. 1065

Introduction to Hindu festivals. 2185

Introduction to Indian fire festival: from the observation of Southern and Northern Indian Rites. 1804

Invisible custom: public lectures as ceremonials. 637

Inviting death: Indian attitude towards the ritual death. 1819

Involvement of Hindus in Muslim Religious Ritual: to maintain peace and harmony for national integration. 1657

Isattul hasanat. [On some Islamic customs]. [In: Tamil] 1301

Islam in India, or, the Qanun-i-Islam [microform]: the customs of the Musalmans of India. 884

Islam: the five pillars of faith. 2094

Islami taqarib. [Essays on Islamic festivals]. [Urdu] 706

Islamic revival in modern India: The case of the Meos. 1493

It is the custom in this village. 30

Itihas ki smriti me: Naharshi kumbha banam utreni. 1822

J

Jagannatha cult origin, rituals, Festivals, religion and philosophy: a critical study of sthala purana 'Niladri Mahodaya. 1637

Jagar Utsav: ek manovishleshan. [Hindi]. 921

Jagmagaati Amavasya. [Hindi]. 1352

Jaina iconography: the tirthankara in Jaina scriptures art and rituals. 895

Jaipur virasat festival explores different mediums of creativity. 240

Jallikattu in Tamil Nadu: Bull vaulting. 187

Jalrangon ka utsav. [Hindi]. 1916

Jananasauca and Maranasuca: The past and present practice. 483

Janjatiya Chatra lahool mein sadiyoo ke utsav va parva. [Pahari Language]. 2111

Jatapus ritual and belief concerned with the physical phenomena. 1559

Jaware. [Hindi]. 1890
Jesuit narration of manners and customs in south India. 522
Jewels of authority: women and textual tradition in Hindu India. 1510
Jhagde ki phagen. [Hindi]. 398
Jhampan: A conference of snake charmers. 327
Jhunjhunu Mela in Kulpali. [Hindi]. 10
Jila Shimla Pasubali, yage-tohar paramparaye. [Pahari Laguage]. 1603
Jivata tahevaro [microform]. 966
Join the Easter parade. 1523
Jonsar Babar me Magh tyohar. [Hindi]. 947
Jonsar Babar me mele aur tyohar. [Hindi]. 2140
Journey's end: death and mourning. 678
Jumbo jamboree. 1456
Juthe sutak nirnay. [On Hindu customs] [Nepali]. 518
Jwalamukhi di Lohri. [Pahari Language]. 1858

K

Kaagada ke Mukhaya sanskar. [Hindi]. 1156
Kaal sarpa yoga: why such fright? 1620
Kaarthikai Kuumbu: an Indian fire festival: an assessment of South Indian rites with reference to Tamil Nadu. 2011
Kaarthikai Kuumbu: fire festival, an assessment of South Indian Rites. 2009
Kaarthikai Kuumbu: fire festival: an assessment of South Indian Rites. 2012
Kagada Ghati main Jagrata. [Hindi]. 1198
Kagadye cha holi. [Pahari Language]. 2130
Kahaloor ki Jumba pratha. [Pahari Language]. 2037
Kahar Jati aur Varnvyavastha [The Kahar Jati and the Varna Systems]. 1640
Kalakshetra: festival of dance-dramas. 89
Kalam elluttu: Art and ritual in Kerala. 946
Kalaviveka. [treatise on Hindu law & rituals]. [Sanskrit]. 934
Kalptaru ki utsav leela: Ramkrishan Paramhans. 1248
Kanaui lok sahitya me samaj ka pratibinba. [Hindi]. 2083
Kandali utsav: Barahven sal phir. [Hindi]. 1449
Kangda me Rali Vivah. [Hindi]. 1868
Kang-Dali. 375
Kangde de Janane parv tyohar (Pahari Bhasa). [Pahari Language]. 1030
Kaniyan: ritual performers of Tamil Nadu, South India. 941
Karam festival in a Munda village. 460

Karama: A Binjhal festival-its socio-religious significance. 1445
Karma and control: The prodigious and the auspicious in Jaina canonical mythology, 194
Karma, guilt, and buried memories: public fantasy and private reality in traditional India. 1680
Karnataka janajivana [microform]. 1060
Kartik Snan. [Hindi]. 397
Karwa Choth. [Hindi]. 1856
Kashmir ke parva or tyohar. [Hindi]. 2095
Kathasaritsagara. 1963
Keertan: and effective communication. 1612
Kennar chatriya vivah prathaye. 1838
Keral ka bada din. [Hindi]. 356
Ketu Pakavan. [Tamil].338
Khairo barkat ki shadi vagherah. [Marriage customs]. [Urdu]. 1302
Khalasa dharama shasatra samsakarabhaga, arathata, Guru ke sikham lai guramata anusara janama tom laike anta prayanta de samskaramdi bidhi [microform] 136
Khari song and dance of the Bodos of Assam: a festival of farewell and well-coming a New Year, 457
Khariya Janjati ke vishwas, mele aur tyohar. [Hindi]. 263
Kherai- the national festival of the Boro - Kachari. 754
Khichadi Ri Saji. (Pahari Bhasa) 962
Khuksi: the folk-festival of the Rabhas, an outline of the worship pattern. 458
Kinnnor ke tyohar mele. [Hindi]. 1364
Kinnro ka pushpa pram. [Pahari Language]. 1837
Kinship and ritual in Bengal: anthropological essays. 654
Kinship and rituals among the Meo of Northern India: locating sibling relationship. 906
Kishano ka mela: Mejar. [Hindi]. 70
Kitab-i-tahrir-ul-mirat. [Manners and customs in Islam]. 1629
Kitchen room of Chujtia Bhunjia tribe: An anthropological analysis. 1709
Kodavas their customs and culture. 675
Koeshur rof. [Anthology of songs for marriage festivals]. [In: Kashmiri] 90
Kolhon ke ullasmaya tyohar. [Hindi]. 1251
Koli festival among the Kolies. 690
Kond rituals practices and prayers. 296
Koothandavar festival. 1605
Kora religious belief: A fusion of traditional tribal faith and Hinduism. 1515

Korivi: A festival of faith. 1526
Korku Janjati ke parv. [Hindi]. 1506
Krityakalpataru, Rajadharama kanda. 248
Kriyakramajyotika. [Manual of rituals associated with the worship of Siva and allied deities]. 1948
Krtyakalpataru [microform]. [Hinduism Rituals]. [In: Sanskrit] 1094
Ksha kirane [microform] [India Social life and customs]. [In: Marathi] 1778
Kuki customary law: Kukite Chondan (Kuki) 91
Kullu aur mela. [Pahari Language]. 1844
Kullu Dussehra: devtaon ki shradhanjali. [Hindi]. 1390
Kullu ghati mein jagat ka suprashidha jacholi mela. [Pahari Language]. 1870
Kullu janpad mein vivah sanskar sambandhi sabdo ka shanskratik dharatal. [Hindi]. 329
Kullu Janpada na Maagh. [Pahari Language]. 2045
Kullu ka Dhashara: Prachin sabayata va sanskriti ka muha bolta chatra. [Pahari Language]. 1834
Kullu ka Dhashara: Puraana sarir naya chahra. [Pahari Language]. 2041
Kullu ka ek dharmik mela. [Pahari Language]. 2048
Kullu ka ek Dharmik mela. [Pahari Language]. 2046
Kullu ka kahiya mela, jisme noda Marta hai. 2127
Kullu ka prasidha devoustav dashahara. [Pahari language]. 1440
Kullu Ka utsav Darpon Kahika. [Hindi] 2123
Kullu ke Mela aur utsav ki ek ek jalak. [Pahari Language]. 2121
Kullu ke mele: Ek Adhyayan. [Hindi]. 2034
Kullu ke meloo aur utsavo ki ek jalak. [Pahari Language]. 1853
Kullu ke Sanskar. [Pahari Language]. 1854
Kulu Dussehra becomes international festival. 1480
Kulu Dussehra, than and now'. 1560
Kulu Dussehra. 1533
Kulu Dussehra. 1476
Kulu Dussehra. 840
Kulu's Dussehra tradition. 1146
Kuluyi utsav, Tyohar or parv. [Hindi]. 1067
Kumbh parv ka vegyanik vishleshan. [Hindi]. 1099
Kumbha India's ageless festival. 1700
Kumbha-why did they come. 514
Kurmanchal ka mahan sanskritik-Etihasik parv: Utreni. 1823
Kuttannavar: The divine lives of a severed head. 1086
Kuttum kutiyattavum [microform]. [In: Malayalam]. 41

L

Labyrinth ritual in South India: Threshold and tattoo designs. 1108
Ladakh: Gods and mortals behind the Himalaya. 818
Lagnavrata [microform] [Marriage customs and rites]. 1818
Lahaul ke tyohar tatha mele. [Hindi]. 162
Lahol mein Vivah pratha. [Hindi]. 163
Lal Mandi ri lohri. [Hindi]. 694
Language of symbols: a project on south Indian ritual decorations of a semi-permanent nature. 109
Lao hill tribes: traditions and patterns of existence. 1184
Lavi Mela. 911
Lavi trade fair: A glorious past. 1712
Law, custom, and crimes against women: The problem of dowry death in India. 2183
Let's go fly a kite (Aao Patang udayen). [Hindi]. 1133
Life beyond death. 4
Little traditional festivals in an Andhra village: Vemur. 1654
Living customs of Blackmagic in Orissa and their counterparts in the Vedas. 1717
Living customs regarding Jatakarma. 486
Living manners at the time of taking meals in Orissa and their sources. 1443
Local festivals of Ladakh. 1356
Lohadi. [Hindi] 1631
Lokaranjanam [microform]. 733
Lokotsava: Gangore. [Hindi]. 1477
Lokparva: Sama-Chakeba. [Hindi]. 32
Loparv Tesu Vivah. [Hindi]. 2196
Love me two times.' from smallpox to AIDS: contagion and possession in the cult of Sitala. 628
Lushai custom: a monograph on lushai customs and ceremonies. 1491
Lushai customs and ceremonies. 510

M

Maa Manikeswari-the Tutelary deity of Kalahandi. 1136
Maaghi. [Hindi]. 547
Machong among the Garos of Assam, 1305
Mad mad festival season. 1601
Made in India; the story of India's people and of their gifts to the world. 1969
Madhya Pradesh: lok Sanskrit aur Sahitya. [Hindi]. 1479
Magic and medicine. 153
Magico-religious beliefs about plants among Adibasis of Bihar. 1431
Magico-religious beliefs about plants among some adibasis of India. 170
Magico-religious beliefs about plants among the tribal of Bastar, Madhya Pradesh. 900

Maha Sivaratri. 139
Mahaari suni lavlori jataro. 1871
Mahabharata Yagnam in Rayalaseema: interaction between great tradition and little tradition. 1646
Mahabharata. 313
Maharashtr me banjara samaj ka teej parv. [Hindi]. 1472
Maharashtra ka mithbola parv maker Sankranti. [Hindi]. 1851
Maharashtra-fairs and festivals in Maharashtra. 347
Maharasi parasar janmoustav sara paanju. [Pahari Language]. 2047
Mahare kuthaha. [Pahari language] 394
Mahasoo ke riti rivaj. [Pahari language] 1903
Mahasu-mela aur tohar. [Hindi]. 1098
Mahasuvi Lok-Kavya me pushp-tyohar ki mahima. [Hindi]. 1001
Mahatmya. [On observation of rituals]. [In: Nepali] 598
Mahaveera Jayanti-Chaitra Shukla Trayodashi. 1813
Mahrishi Parashar Janmotsava Sara Panju. [Pahari Language]. 2049
Mahua: A trai-complex in the kamar tribe of gariband 1310
Mak' Monre (Mak' Mode)-A Santal Festival in Calcutta: A study in tradition and change. 1308
Makar Sankranti ki dhoom. 1925
Making Sakti: controlling (Natural) impurity for female (Cultural) power. 2105
Making virtuous daughters and wives: an introduction to women's Brata rituals in Bengali Folk religion. 1213
Man and god in art and ritual: a study of iconography, architecture and ritual action as primary evidence of religious belief and practice. 300
Man and Mongoose in Indian Culture 504
Manamukha Sudhara [micro-form]. [In: Panjabi]. 71
Manbhavan Gangor. [Hindi]. 2158
Mandan-Hidatsa myths and ceremonies. 205
Mandi aari shivratra (mela). 239
Mandi Janpad me Lohri ka tyohar. [Hindi]. 151
Mandi jila ka shaskratik pratik shivratri mela. [Pahari Language]. 2109
Mandi jila mein vartra tatha tohar. [Pahari Language]. 2112
Mandi ka Lohadi. [Pahari language] 670
Mandi ka prashidha va pramparik Shivratri mela [Hindi]. 977
Mandi ka Shar tohar. [Pahari language] 672

Mandi ki Shivratri.[Hindi]. 72
Mandi mein Shivratri mela. [Pahari Language]. 2058
Mandi-Rivalsar re mele tuhaar. [Pahari Language]. 354
Manners and customs of Hindus. 523
Mantra and other constituents of Tantric practice. 845
Mantra in Vedic and tantric ritual. 2174
Mantra: hearing the divine in India. 431
Manu: A study in Hindu Social theory. Ganesh & Co.' Madras, 1937. 1300
Marathi Pradesh ke lokgeet aur Pooja Parva. [Hindi]. 144
Mare puja and Deodha dance of Assam: a note on a type of serpent worship. 466
Mare puja and deodha dance. 467
Maria murder and suicide. 604
Marriage and family in India. 1002
Marriage and family in India. 973
Marriage are simpler quieter. 1553
Marriage custom and Vivaha Mantras of the Bengalee Buddhists. 381
Marriage customs among Muslims in India: a sociological study of the Shia marriage customs.1879
Marriage customs among the christians of clean caste origin in Cuttack town of Orissa. 206
Marriage customs of Khonds. 652
Marriage customs of the Siddis. 352
Marriage customs of the world. 854
Marriage customs of the world: from henna to honeymoons. 1288
Marriage forms under ancient Hindu law. 1758
Marriage in a mountain area. 1695
Marriage practices of the Sikhs: a study of intergenerational differences. 958
Marriage practices, laws and social rules in India, China and Rome, 500BC-20AD. 1792
Marriage rites in Karnataka. 1589
Marriage rites, customs and ceremonies of the World. 855
Marriage rituals and songs of Bengal: with staff notations. 1694
Marriage rules and marriage rituals among the Kokna tribe of Maharashtra. 1697
Marriage rules in Bengal. 1003
Marriage, Dowry system and their implications. 707
Marriage, hierarchy and identity in ideology and practice: An anthropological study of Jhala Rajput society in western India, against a historical background, 1090-199. 931

Marriage: a sacrament or a bargain. 1881
Marriages in ancient India. 1658
Martha history, structure, and ritual. 1005
Marwar Ki Sanskritik Virasat. [Hindi]. 1326
Masti aur umangon bhara, Christmas dhoop me khila. Hindi]. 1521
Mate selection, age at marriage and propinquity among the lingayats of India. 385
Mawai Madai ki Chhaya me. [Hindi]. 2029
Medhi and the Torana. 449
Medical anthropology and the ethnography of spirit possession. 411
Medical ritual in the Atharavaveda tradition. 154
Medical world of the tribals: explorations in illness ideology, body symbolism and ritual healing. 2068
Medieval Indian society, state and social custom: Sati as a case study. 383
Meditation on ritual. 2205
Mejar ek Vijaya Prava. 952
Mela Jagara. 902
Mela kutha. [Pahari language] 671
Mela Markand. 238
Men wearing masks: issues of description in the analysis of ritual. 57
Mera Gao: Tatti re mela. [Hindi]. 117
Mesoamerican and Indian fire gods and ceremonies. 437
Metaphor as ritualistic symbol. 1594
Meyer bratakatha. [Bengali]. 1316
Mhachala ri lohri hor Khohdi. [Pahari Language]. 527
Mhare pradesa ra vishu. [Pahari language]. 1773
Milan parv-Basoya. [Pahari Language] 235
Mind, body and wealth; a study of belief and practice in an Indian village. 1545
Minjar fair. 400
Minjar fair: recalling Chamba's past. 1840
Minute on Sati. 217
Mirani Sindhuri. [Account of the life and customs of Sindhis during the reign of Mirs who ruled Sind before the advent of the British]. 1171
Mishing Janjatiyon ke paramparagat dharmik utsav evam parv. [Hindi]. 1045
Modern India and the west: a study of the interaction of their civilization. Oxford University Press, 1286
Modern Indian kingship: tradition, legitimacy and power in Rajasthan. 164
Modernization and ritual: Identity and change in Santal Society. 1150
Mohurrum: Requiem to a martyr. 883

Molakala Punnami: a folk festival in the Western region of Chitoor district of Andhra Pradesh. 1651
Monkeys and Serpents in the epics. 1770
Monks and miracles: religious symbols and images of origin among Osval Jains. 146
Monograph on Lushai customs and ceremonies. 1490
Mopin festival in Arunchal Pradesh. 1357
Mopin: a festival of Adis of Arunachal Pradesh. 92
More harvest festival dramas of Tibet. 572
Mortuary customs in Southern India. 1229
Mortuary practices of the Daroi Gonds: A study of their intangible cultural heritage. 185
Mortuary practices of the Hos: an Ethno archaeological study. 1280
Mortuary practices of the Lodhas of West Bengal. 554
Mother Goddes in central India. 1260
Mother Goddess and snake worship. 731
Mother in law marriage and kinship Organisation. 1306
Mothering rituals in Tamil Nadu: Some magico-religious beliefs. 1991
Motifs in Indian mythology. 116
Mountain Goddess: gender and politics in a Himalayan pilgrimage. 1779
Movement to suppress the custom of femaale infanticide in the Punjab and Kashmir. 463
Muddle and Mystery in a passage to India. 938
Mudras: the ritual hand poses of the Budha priests and the Shiva priests of Bali. 1032
Muhammadan festivals. 752
Munda janjati ka dharmik parv-tyohar. [Hindi]. 1247
Munnakakkanni: Oru Pecum Teyvam. Tinakaran, [Tamil]. 1433
Murals for goddesses and gods: the tradition of Osakothi ritual painting in Orissa, India. 631
Murtipuja in Svetambar Jain temples. 425
Museums and the festivals of India: the search for a rationale. 174
Music and temples: a ritualistic approach. 58
Music rituals of Srinivasamangapuram. 680
Music the soul of spiritual ecstasy. 294
Muslim festivals and fasts. 315
Muslim festivals. 1833
My Divali. 850
My India. 423
My rituals and my gods: Ritual exclusiveness in medieval India. 751

Myth, ritual and religion. 1104
Mythologies of the world: the illustrated guide to mythological beliefs and customs. 1220
Mythology and believes of Si-donyi festival of the Tagins. 1686
Myths and reality. 1050
Myths and symbols in Indian art and civilization. 2204
Myths of Hindus and the Budhists. 421
Myths of middle India. 605
Myths, religion and ritual of the Kamars. 557
Myths, saints, and legends in medieval India. 2132

N

Nadu Veedu rituals and family shamanism in Tamil society: A cult institution of hinduism. 1462
Nag Panchami: Bhay or Bhakti. [Hindi]. 1083
Nag Panchami: snakes, sex, and semen 33
Nag Panchami: The day of the cobra. 1080
Naga cult in Orissa. 1446
Naga Mandala: play with a Cobra. 988
Naga worship in Kerala. 1543
Nag-Pañchami. 663
Nāka Pañcami Pūjai. [Tamil]. 918
Nāka Pañcami! Karuna Pañcami! 1206
Nalwari fair, its unique importance. 1021
Name taboos and rigid performativity. 633
Nanda Raj Jat Yatra. 956
Narvrat. [Hindi]. 2064
Nats 1971
Navagrahas (Nine Planets). 374
Navratri in Gujarat. 2079
Navroze. 869
Nazeer Akbaraabadi aur basant ke tyohar. [Hindi]. 1180
Need for consolidating the gains of Chandigarh Roma festival. 950
Neem in sociocultural life in South Asia. 17
Neem tree: a review. 37
Negotiating relationships with the Goddess.809
New beginnings: celebrating birth. 679
Night of Mandaan. 1469
Night of the growing dead: A cult of Virabhadra in coastal Andhra. 1035
Nilgiri dolmens (South India). 2180
Nimad ke Vrat or tyohar. [Hindi]. 2101
Nirjan me utsav. [Hindi].358
Nitya karma vidhi. [On Hindu rituals]. [In: Nepali] 1769
No one cries for the dead: Tamil dirges, rowdy songs, and Graveyard petitions. 407
No support to dowry from the tradition of Hinduism. 2028
Nongkrem festival. 1907

Note on magico-relious beliefs about plants among Lodhas of Midnapur, West Bengal. 1386
Notes on love in a Tamil Family. 2066
Notes on some popular festivals in ancient India: with special reference to Pali literature. 1317
Notes on the customs and beliefs in Spiti. 331
Novena and Navaratri. 1555
Nuakhai: a tradition of Western-Orissa: oath-taking to live a peaceful and happy life. 1497
Nutrient composition of traditional festival foods of North Karnataka. 861
Nyokum Yullo: A festival of the Nishis 553
Nyokum: The festival of the Nyishis of Arunachal Pradesh. 1172

O

Obscure religious cults. 478
Observation on the mussulmauns of India: descriptive of their manners, customs, habits, & religious opinions made during a Twelve Year residence in their immediate. 26
Observations on the Mussulmauns of India. 1222
Of faith and sacrifies: The village of Devi Dhura. 783
Of piety and gaiety. 1051
Offering flowers, feeding skulls: Popular Goddess worship in West Bengal. 1214
Old deccan days. 651
Omens and superstitions of Southern India. 2057
Omens: past and present. 1468
On Dussehra festival. 481
On gomukh and Indian customs and manners. 524
On hindu belief. 22
On the banks of the Ganga: when wastewater meets a sacred river. 31
On the cult of Jujube tree. 1266
On the cult of tree Goddess in Eastern Bengal. 1267
On the ethnographic study complex Bengali pujas festivals. 1419
On the field study on village-Gods and festivals: a view of folklore teacher. 1732
On the meaning of Sakti to women in Tamil Nadu 593
On the remains of Botanical material used in fire-sacrifice ritualized during Kushana period at Sanghol (Punjab). 1739
On the road: a Maharashtrian pilgrimage. 991
On the role of ritual friendship in the mobility of wealth in the Viskhapatnam agency. 1645
On the uses of turmeric in Hindoo ceremonial. 586
Onam. 942
Onam: The festival of fraternity 1088

Onam: the national festival of Kerala. 1427
Oracles and dreams among the Lepchas. 746
Oral performance: narrative and ritual in Tamil tradition. 277
Oraon religion and customs [microform]. 1704
Oraon religion and customs. 1703
Origin and antiquity of the custom of sati in ancient India. 1261
Origin and development of the rituals of ancestor worship in India. 1874
Orisa (Orisha) tradition in Trinidad. 665
Other people's rituals: ritual eclecticism in early medieval Indian religious. 750
Our Hindu friends [microform]. [On the rites and practices]. 1024
Our women are free: gender and ethnicity in the Hindukush. 1143
Oxford University papers on India. 723

P

Padmanabha. 1233
Pagi ki phool yatra. [Hindi]. 247
Pahado mein Shivratri. [Pahari Language]. 798
Pahari kshetra ke do vishisth tyohar. [Hindi]. 1861
Painted myths of creation: Art and rituals of an Indian tribe. 896
Painted prayers: women's art in village India. 858
Palkhi Sohala. [Marathi]. 1368
Palparvan. [Essays on Hindu religious festivals of which all except two are taken from Brahmamrta]. 2099
Pañcaturya Nada and the Hewisi Puja. 104
Panchavadyam, thyambaka, percussion of Kerala: From stirring beats to soft and fragile notes. 1382
Pando Janjati me parv-tyohar. [Hindi]. 1918
Pandugu Kathalu. [Stories of religious festivals]. [In: Telugu]. 1095
Pangi Ghati va Jukaru Parv. [Hindi]. 1819
Paraber Anginay: In the court-yard of festivals in Bengali. 270
Parampara aur aadhunikta. [Hindi]. 992
Parampara itihas bodh aur sanskriti. [Hindi]. 1154
Parampara me vikas ke naye aayaam. 541
Parampara. [Hindi]. 1226
Paramparaon me chipe tark. [Hindi]. 93
Paramparik prasang gunjte geet. [Hindi]. 1460
Paraya hota parampara ka saaj. [Hindi]. 682

Parenting children with visual impairments in rural south India: Exploring contexts of maternal beliefs and behavior. 878
Parsee Festivals. 316
Participation of the Telgu speaking immirgrants in the religious activities of the host society. 207
Parva, Utsav aur Jayantiyan. [Hindi]. 1998
Parvati Chetra mein sati pratha: ek Vivecan. [Pahari Language]. 1865
Parvatiya anchal me holi. [Hindi]. 1824
Parva-Utsav. [Hindi] 2124
Paryushanaparvanam vyakhyano [microform]. [On Jaina festivals and rituals]. 1565
Pashchim Nimar ke aadivasiyon ke tyohar. [Hindi]. 1891
Pastoral deities in western India. 1966
Pattan Ghati (Lahul) ke kuch mukhya mele tyohar. [Hindi]. 161
Patterns of religious observance in three villages in Rajasthan. 342
Pavash parva-mijar mela. [Pahari Language]. 2001
Peddintlamma ferstival among the vaddis of Kolleru lake: A continuum of little and great traditions. 1656
People at the Kodungallur festival: A phtographer's portfolio. 1068
Peoples of India. 708
Performance. 211
Performativity in ritual: The mianmin case. 683
Performing of northern Kerala. 649
Performing vows in diasporic contexts: Tamil hindus, Temples, and Goddesses in Germany. 195
Perinatal mortality in rural India: Intervention through Primary Health Care. II Neonatal Mortality. 2106
Perpetuating the myth. 1725
Persistent traditional practices among the Tribals of North Coastal Andhra Pradesh. 1621
Perspective on Sati. 1715
Phoolwalon ki sair. [Hindi]. 1902
Phransana jagavikhyata navalakathakara Viktara Hyugoni amara krti La mijharebala [microform]. 851
Pictures of Indian life [microform]. Foreword by Rash Behary Ghose, 704
Pilgrimage as a source of knowledge: The Kumbh mela of Prayag Raj 1989. 881
Pilgrimage in the Hindu tradition: a case study of West Bengal. 1296
Pilgrimage in the Indian tradition. 232
Pilgrimage, prestige and protest: On the origin of recent sati temples in India. 2118

Plants associated with Durga puja ceremony in West Bengal. 1432
Plants in Patra Pooja: notes on their identity and utilization. 696
Plants in religious cultural beliefs of the Kahamtis of Assam (India). 718
Plants of Ramayana. 158
Plants of the Gods. 1785
Plants of the Gods: their sacred healing and Hallucinogenic power. 1784
Plants of the Quran. 623
Plants: traditional worshipping. 245
Play, symbolism, and ritual: a study of Tamil Brahmin women's rites of passage. 581
Playing host to deity: festival religion in the South Indian tradition. 2199
Plnats in folk religion and mythology. 382
Political organization and customary laws of the Bhotia of Uttaranchal. 1157
Politics of language, religion and identity: tribes in India. 2151
Polyandrous partnership in Himalayas. 1859
Polyandry in the Himalayas. 1481
Pongal. 1614
Pongal: Shubh or sumangal. 1020
Pongal: The blessings of the pot that boiled over. 1324
Poorvani Ra Bishu (Pahar Bhasa). [Pahari language]. 995
Popular pujas in Public Places: lay rituals in South Indian temples. 1943
Post-funeral ritual in a Dimasa Kachari village. 698
Pox and the terror of childlessness: images and ideas of the smallpox Goddess in a North Indian village. 1043
Prachalit Riti-Rivaj tatha yog evam tantra. 928
Pracina Hindamam sanghajivana [microform 1155
Prakrati ke sang Hulsane ka parv. [Hindi]. 94
Prakriti ke Badalte Swaroop ke sath Jude Kumaon ke tyohar. [Hindi]. 2104
Pravargya: an ancient Indian iconic ritual described and annotated. 2117
Prayaag ka anokha parv: Dhedhiya'. [Hindi]. 1889
Pregnancy rituals amongst the Rajput elite in contemporary Rajasthan: Anthropology and the world of women. 165
Primitive rites of disposal of the dead, with special reference to India. 438
Primitive science and festivals. 1946
Principal Hindoo religious festivals of Southern India. 143

Problematic aspects of the sexual rituals of the bauls of Bengal. 1583
Problems of ritual in general. 1124
Proceedings of the national seminar on living customs and their ancient Indian sources. 930
Puja [microform] [Hindu rituals]. [In Marathi] 403
Puja and samskara. 2016
Puja in society. 1421
Puja Vidhana.[Hindi]. 953
Puja. 391
Puja: a study in Smarta ritual. 321
Punerary customs in Bastar state. 608
Punjab prelude [microform] [Punjab Social life and customs]. 1567
Purification of the sacred bundles, a ceremony of the Pawnee. 1125
Purity and violence: sacred power in the Teyyam worship of Malabar 648
Purusartha cintamanih. [Treatise on the Hindu festivals, their rituals and calendar]. [Sanskrit] 131
Puspunei: a festival of the Juangs: of the hills of Keonjhar district of Orissa. 1257
Put a bag over her head!': Beheading mythological women. 549

Q

Quaint marriage customs of a primitive people. 1430

R

Raahu Kethu Sarpa Dosha Nivarana Mantra. [Audio Recording]. 1771
Raas ki manchiya parampara aur uska vartmaan swaroop. [Hindi]. 12
Raghukul Riti Sadaa. [Hindi]. 120
Rajaparba: The festival of fertility cult in Orissa. 209
Rajasthan Bhils. 377
Rajasthan ke riti rivaaz: Devgarh thikane ka manavshastriya adhyayan. [Hindi]. 401
Rajasthan ke sahariya ke riti rivaaz. [Hindi]. 1434
Rajasthan ki aadim jaatiyon me tyohar aur pritibhoj. [Hindi]. 1435
Rajasthan ki Holi. [Hindi]. 223
Rajasthan ki janjatiya sanskrriti aur paramparayen. 1633
Rajasthan Ki Sanskritik parampara. [Hindi]. 1377
Rajasthani Vrat Kathayen. [Hindi]. 1574
Rajput ceremonial interactions as a mirror of a dying Indian state system, 1820-1947. 591
Raksabandhana.936

Raksha bandhan: prem aur suraksha ki pratigya. [Hindi] 1200
Raksha Bandhan: The bond of protection. 1205
Rakshaa Bandhan. 1814
Raku Pakavan. [Tamil]. 339
Rali. 237
Ram Mohun Ray on sati and sexism. 436
Rangon Me dooba Himachal ka Janjatiya parv. [Hindi] 1852
Rath rathni ra mela. [Pahari Language] 236
Rathor Rajvansh ke Riti-Rivaaj 1600-1850. [Hindi] 1872
Reaf the harvest and rejoice. 1090
Reasoning about beliefs: A human specialization? 1551
Reasoning about causality and treatment of childhood nutritional deficiencies in rural India: Role of indigenous knowledge and practices. 1950
Reconstructing the split Goddess as Sakti in a Tamil Village. 435
Reconversion to Hinduism through suddhi: A field study of the suddhi practice of the arya samaj in India and its implications for an understanding of modern Hindui. 1820
Reflections on resemblance, ritual, and religion. 1953
Regional variation in Matrka conventions. 1230
Relationship of modernity and childrearing practices among Guajarati Hindu families living in India. 1502
Religion against the self: ethnography of Tamil rituals. 408
Religion and magic among the Nayars. 1465
Religion and public memory: a cultural history of Saint Namdev in India. 1389
Religion and society among the Coorgs of South India. 1977
Religion and world-view of the Hill Korwa of Chhattisgarh (M.P.). 1673
Religion of Manipur: beliefs, rituals and historical development. 1483
Religions of the world: the illustrated guide to origins, beliefs, traditions and festivals. 303
Religiosity, economy and patterns of Hindu marriage in India. 767
Religious attributes of Bhils. 1183
Religious belief and social change: aspects of the development of Hinduism in British Guiana. 919
Religious beliefs and practices of North India during the early mediaeval period. 1255
Religious beliefs and rituals: cross cultural studies. 95
Religious beliefs and social hierarchy in Tamil Nadu, India. 406

Religious ceremonies, ordeals amd legends about Oriya infiltration in Kondh Hill. 1508
Religious fairs and festivals of Assam. 1754
Religious festivals and caste system in India during 19th century. 1407
Religious festivals in South India and Sri Lanka. 2186
Religious festivals in South India and Sri Lanka. 786
Religious festivals in South India and Srilanka 2170
Religious festivals of Parhaiya: A tribal community of Jhakhand. 1070
Religious rites and festivals among the tribes of Orissa. 208
Religious rites and festivals of India. 1962
Religious rites and riots: From community Identity to communalism in North India, 1870-1940. 650
Religious vows at the Shrine of Shahul Hamid. 1348
Re-membereing the tradition: Bhaktivinoda Thakura's Sajjantosani and the construction of a middle class Vaisnava sampradaya in 19th centuary Bengal. 662
Repeats of one ritual. 1956
Representing Hinduism: The construction of religious traditions and National identity. New Delhi, Sage Publications, 1995. 444
Rethinking the public sphere: The Ganapati festival and media competitions in Mumbai. 994
Re-viewing the religion of the Paraiyars: Ellaiyamman as an Iconic symbol of collective resistance and emancipatory mythography 410
Rhythm and intent: ritual studies from South India. 414
Rhythm and Intent: ritual studies from South India. The play of the Gods: Locality, Ideology, Structure and Time in the Festivals of a Bengali Town. 642
Rice rituals of Orissa. 219
Rights, roles and reciprocity in Hindu dharma. 1193
Risk, ritual and performance. 1118
Rites and ceremonies of the Indians of the Southwest. 420
Rites and customs associated with marriage in a North Indian village. 1653
Rites and rituals: media of rural integration. 371
Rites de passage of Matrescence and social construction of motherhood: Coorgs in South India. 2133
Rites of passage in Shanti Nagar. 645
Ritial and speculation in early Tantrism: studies in honour

of Andre Padoux. Albany, State Uiversity of New York Press, 1992. 743
Riti-rivajo ka qila todkar. Hindi]. 1744
Ritual and sensuality. 216
Ritual (AS) politics. 1626
Ritual action of political reaction: the invention of Hindu nationalist processions in India during the 1980s. 128
Ritual and belief of Jaunsaris. 764
Ritual and cosmology of the Birhor: A nomadic hunting and gathering tribe in India. 9
Ritual and emotions. 341
Ritual and music in South India: Syrian Christian Liturgical Music in Kerala. 874
Ritual and religion among Muslims in India. 29
Ritual and religion among Muslims in India. 96
Ritual and religion in the making of humanity. 1473
Ritual and routine objects. 769
Ritual and secular role of a Duonia monastery. 1147
Ritual and seduction: the human body as art. 2150
Ritual and the constitution of social structure. 1527
Ritual and urbanism. Reviewed work(s): Landscapes of Urban Memory: The Sacred and the Civic in India's High-Tech City by Smriti Srinivas. 1831
Ritual art of India. 1291
Ritual associated with the subsistence economy: A case study of the Karbi of Kamrup district. 2023
Ritual circles in a Mysore village 748
Ritual connected with the life-cycle of the Oddis: some accounts from Andhra Pradesh. 1659
Ritual enactments in Hindi Mythological': Betab's Mahabharat in Parsi theatre. 799
Ritual experts (Siampi) in Paite society. 736
Ritual friendship in Chhattisgarh. 558
Ritual friendship in santal society 112
Ritual healing: Metamedical discourse and discursive practices of a south Indian nomadic sub – caste. 227
Ritual healing: Metamedical discourse and discursive practices of a south Indian nomadic sub – caste. 228
Ritual in a Theyya Kavu. 127
Ritual in an oscillating universe: worshiping S´iva in medieval India. 496
Ritual kinship in Orissa. 1148
Ritual language: A transanthropological perspective. 1742
Ritual life and communication. 1163

Ritual life of the Natarajan temple. 2200
Ritual of the Bhils.1920
Ritual polity and economy: The transactional network of an imperial temple in Medieval South India. 903
Ritual pollulation as a integrator of caste and religion. 815
Ritual practices among the Kaniyas of Karnataka. 516
Ritual process: structure and anti-structure. 2091
Ritual purity and pollution in relation to domestic sanitation. 1014
Ritual releasing of wild animals threatens island ecology. 11
Ritual representation of political change: The case of the Puri king. 803
Ritual rights: the gender indications of Adhikara. 1217
Ritual songs and folksongs of the Hindus of Surinam. 123
Ritual structure of a village in West Bengal, India. 1294
Ritual theory: ritual practice. 212
Ritual transforms a Myth. 413
Ritual value of Paddy in Bengal. 482
Ritual, knowledge, and being: Initiation and Veda study in ancient India. 304
Ritual, narrative and the continuum: Anthropology of a Goddess festival. 20
Ritual, power and the supernatural: a comparative study of Indian religions in south western United States. 2065
Ritual, sanctity and cybernetics. 1628
Ritual, tribal and catholic. 2092
Ritual. 612, 2206
Ritual. In, 'International Encyclopedia of Social Sciences'. 1111
Ritual: perspectives and dimensions. 213
Ritualistic theatre of Goa: with special reference to Jagar. 1017
Ritualizing on the boundaries: continuity and innovation in the Tamil diaspora. 416
Rituals and practices of tantra. 1760
Rituals and ritual power of the broken people: A debate over strategies. 1548
Rituals and social organisation of deer hunting in a Bhumij village. 1937
Rituals cause lead exposure and fish kill. 1845
Rituals in agriculture. 1938
Rituals in maring social life. 469
Rituals in the seventh century Sikh Society. 2020
Rituals of protection in a Muslim community. 624
Rituals of the Kandyan state. 1799
Rituals. The New Encyclopedia Britannica. 1524

Ritualt in Sikh Society of the Seventheenth Century. 2021
Rivers in Hindu mythology and ritual. 1096
Rohdu kshetra ka dev utsav pratishtha. 1875
Role of Barber in the religious ceremonies. 1511
Role of plants in differents religious ceremonies common to Bundelkhand region of Madhya Pradesh. 559
Role of ritual in the Hindu marriage. 1236
Roles and rituals for Hindu women. 1121
Roma festival comes of age. 1069
Roma festival. 35
Rongali Bihu: The heady songs of spring. [Hindi] 156
Rule by records: land registration and village custom in early British Panjab. 1957
Rural protests as reflected in the ritual songs: analysis of the Teyyam cult of Kerala. 1089

S

Saach Jaatar va Jukaru tyohar. [Hindi]. 910
Sacrament of 'Amrita' in Sikh society: an aspect of Baisakhi festival of the Khalsas. 2019
Sacred bath ceremony and myth-ritual complex at Gangasagar. 1381
Sacred folk festivals of Tamil Nadu. 940
Sacred grove relics as bird refugia. 498
Sacred groves and conservation: The Comparative History of traditional reserves in the mediterranean area and in South India. 359
Sacred India. 97
Sacred marriage of Maturai: myth, ritual, and devotion in a South Indian temple. 812
Sacred space, sacred time: India's Maha Kumbh Mela draws millions 833
Sacred symbol and sacred space in rural India: community mobilization in the anti-cow killing riot of 1893. 2198
Sacred trees of Tamilnadu. 39
Sacred waters: a pilgrimage up the Ganges river to the source of Hindu culture. 34
Sacrifice and regeneration in the ritual of Sati. 428
Sacrifice dowry for Dharma. 885
Sacrifice: Its nature and function. 848
Sacrificed wife/ sacrificer's wife: women, ritual, and hospitality in ancient India. 905
Sacrificial death and the macrophages ascetic. 1486
Sacrificing the Mithun: Baru puja: fertility rite of the Kabui Nagas. 1516

Sacrificing women: A study of ritualized practices among women volunteers in India. 1264
Sade rasama riwaja [microform]. [Panjabi]. 887
Sahitya aur utsav dharmita. [Hindi]. 1683
Saintly householders: religious beliefs and practices among the Varkaris of Maharashtra, India. 1239
Saints and householders: a study of Hindu ritual and myth among the Kangra Rajputs. 334
Sakta-tantra: sacred sound as the Goddess. 204
Sakti and sakta Madras. 2193
Sama-Chakeva: Mithila ka anupam lok parv. [Hindi]. 2141
Samaj Nirman aur Lolkotswa. [Hindi]. 761
Samajasastravarila vyakhyane, athava, Hindusamajantila kahi caliritince samajasastradrshtya vivecana [microform].243
Samajik sansthayen aur riti rivaaz. 1615
Samanvit prayas hi parampara ko bachayenge. [Hindi]. 540
Sampradayik Sadbhav ke aadhar: Bharat ke Vividh tyohar. 1072
Samskaradarsa [microform] [Hinduism Rituals]. [Marathi]. 1116
Sanjna of Malwa and its Puranic origin. 2082
Sanskrit inscriptions and the spitit of religious toleration. 167
Sanskritik samanvaya ki lokdharmi parampara. 968
Santal customary law: An anthropological perspective. 1964
Santal rituals and Agro-ecosystem. 828
Santhal Jajjati dwara Manaye Janevala parv 'Sohray evam Geet'. 1074
Santhal Qabile me varshik tyohar. 1928
Santhalon ke parv-tyohar. [Hindi]. 1922
Sapindikarana: the Hindu rite of entry into heaven. 1036
Saptmatrika worship and sculptures: an iconological interpretation of the conflicts and resolutions in the storied Brahmanical Icons. 1466
Sarbojonin Durgotsab in Calcutta: a preliminary report of the pujas in 1969. 169
Sarguja: Aadivaasiyon ke Vrat aur tyohar. [Hindi]. 749
Sarhul festival at Netarhat, Bihar. 269
Sastyabdisanti: Its origin and nature extent today. 1063
Sati and social reforms in India. 686
Sati as a social institution in Bengal. 1315
Sati as altruistic Suicide in India. 676

Sati as profit versus Sati as a spectacle: The public debate on Roop Kanwar's death. 1343
Sati in eighteenth century Bengal. 15
Sati in modern India: A report. 1724
Sati Just a form of human sacrifice. 820
Sati or Murder. 899
Sati parampara, Jvalant Jyoti Sikhaya. 2149
Sati worship and marwari public identity in India. 59
Sati, sacrifice, and marriage: The modernity of tradition. 430
Sati: A historical, social and philosophical enquiry into the Hindu rite of widow burning. 490
Sati: a review article. 2172
Sati: historical and phenomenological essays. 1835
Sati: Political paralysis. 876
Sati: The blessing and the curse. 825
Sati: the Dharmic fallacy. 357
Satluj ghati ri Shivraatar. [Pahari Language] 160
Sattriya from ritual to performing art. 362
Satyanarayan brata katha. [Puranic tale relating to ritualistic ceremony]. [In: Nepali] 98
Saurashtrana Sumara [microform] [In: Gujarati] 1182
Science of social organisation or the Laws of Manu in the light of Atmavidya 3 Vols. 459
Secular customs in the Upanayana ceremony. 502
Secular customs of marriage in Orissa. 1632
Seeking Mahadevi: constructing the Identities of the Hindu Great Goddess. 1540
Self sacrifice' versus 'Self interest': a non-historicist reading of the history of women's rights in India. 1211
Serpent worship and manasa icons in Assam. 399
Serpent worship in ancient India. 1930
Serpent worship in Kerala. 157
Serpent worship in Malabar. 1232
Serpent worship in Tamil Nadu: Some Observations – Fieldwork Report. 1733
Serpent worship in Western India: The Naga-panchami holiday as it is now observed; serpent worship, the Nagas and Sarpas. 1178
Serpent-worshippers of India. 2067
Seven Hindu Goddesses of spritual transformation: the iconography of the Saptamatrikas. 816
Sex differentials in childhood feeding, health care, and nutritional status in India. 2148

Sonbhadra ke Janjatiya parv [Hindi]. 1009
Songs for the bride: wedding rites of rural India. 113
Soor: A tradtional alcoholic beverage in tons valley, Garhwal. 1611
Source of Indian tradition. 827
Sources of Vratas in Karnataka. 2013
South Indian customs. 142
South Indian festivals. 140
South Indian festivities [microform]. 886
South Indian festivities. 890
South Indian Saiva rites of initiation: the diksavidhi of aghorasivacaryas kriyakramadyotika (india). 2004
South Indian wedding rituals. A Comparison of Gender Hierarchy. 2201
Special time, special power. 1984
Spirit cult festivals in South Kanara. 124
Spirit possession and spirit mediumship from the perspective of Tulu oral traditions. 412
Spirit possession perceived and performed in rural Rajasthan.722
Spirits, politics and rituals in the history of Nicobar islands. 1464
Spring festival among the Tharu. 1981
Sraddhaprayoga [microform] [Sraddha Hindu rite]. [Marathi] 404
Sradha paddhati. [Religious rituals after death]. [Manipuri]687
Sradhanjali [Rituals]. [In:Manipuri]. 1947
Sri Rama Navami. 141
Srivratodyapanakaumudi-prarambhah [microform] [Hindu rituals related to the fasting to be observed on the auspicious days]. 1729
Stambhewari cult in Orissa. 1793
Sthala Vrikshas of Tamilnadu. 38
Stories about posts: Vedic variations around the Hindu Goddess. 272
Stratification among tribals in Gujarat. 1556
Stray thoughts on the thoughless dowry custom. 2129
Striyon ka sobhagya parv Gangor. 1780
Structural and functional change in the traditional rituals of a tribal village in Andhra Pradesh. 1648
Structure and cognition: aspects of Hindu caste and ritual. 473
Studies in Indian folk traditions 2131
Studies in Puranic records on Hindu rites and customs. 789
Studies in the rites and rituals of Hindu marriage in ancient India. 364
Study of a Harijan caste deity festival: Mathamma Kolupu 1655

Study of Nagore- e- sharief: A sacred complex in Chennai. 1716
Study of polyandry. 1530
Suffering and healing in Trinidadian Kali worship . 756
Suicide in the Hindu tradition: varieties, propriety and practice. 1127
Sukharpuda: Custom and it's sources. 1441
Suliya Jatra: a folk festival of Kondhs: A survey. 1444
Sulpoena in the existance of Kulu Gods. 2042
Superstitions of the Santals. 333
Surisarvasvam. [Manual of Brahmanic rituals]. [Sanskrit] 747
Suskar-Kinnar kaa prasida tohar. [Pahari Language]. 888
Sustainable growth of population in relation to customary laws among the Abujh Maria. 1748
Suttee; a historical and philosophical enquiry into the Hindu rite of widow-burning. 2055
Swati Tirunal festival in Trivandrum: Interesting new features. 1354
Swinging in the rain. 1457
Symbolic festival celebrating Sri Krishna's Boyhoods pranks. 1604
Symbolism in the marriage ceremonies of different nations. 1272
Syncretism in the Ho rituals and festivals: A study. 1281
Synthesis of tribal region and hindu cults in Bastar 476

T

Taboo or beiled consent? Goan Inquisitorial Edict of 1736. 1691
Tai funeral customs: Towards a reconstruction of archaic-tai ceremonies 2030
Tai-Ahom religion and customs. 719
Taking stock at Diwali time. 2010
Tales, tanks, and temples: The creation of a sacred center in Seventeenth-Century Bengal. 1535
Talking about Love and Sex in Adolescent health fairs in India. 337
Tamba kaiten hvai rimthim. (On traditional customs, culture and folkloro of Tamang people). 1101
Tamil Nadu: confrontation, complementarily, compromise. 343
Tamil Temple Myths: Sacrifice and Divine Marriage in the South Indian Saiva Tradition. 1895
Taming the fever Goddess: transforming a tradition in Southern India. 810
Tanaha: A traditional festival of Car Nicobar. 355

Tantra asana. 1293
Tantric visions of the divine feminine; the Ten Mahàvidyàs. 1029
Tantric way: art, science, ritual. 1292
Tantrik vichar parampara ke vedik aadhar. [Hindi]. 1452
Tapasya se arjit punji he Guru-Shishya parampara. 1609
Tarnetar fair: Let's go husband hunting. 681
Tarnetar fair: Out on a husband hunt 1262
Tatta pani ka mela. 1846
Tattapani kshetra me Gaoon ka prasidh tyohar mal. [Hindi]. 1847
Teacher taught relationship past and present. 1117
Technology adoption and its impact of religious rituals. 1721
Teej hi Tyohar [Hindi]. 996
Televangelism reconsidered: Ritual in the search of human community. 24
Temple festivals. 932
Temple Healing. 965
Temples and legends of Himachal Pradesh. 1696
Text in context: oral traditons and he study of religion in Karimpur. 2162
Tharu Aadivasiyon ki pujaa evam tyohar. [Hindi]. 393
The abolition of suttee in Bengal. 1789
The Adì-puran festival. 122
The After life in Indian tribal belief. 618
The Aghara ritual of Vaikhanasas. 725
The Aghori ascetics of Benaras. 1484
The Ajmer Urs. 28
The alchemical body: siddha traditions in medieval India. 2175
The Anatomy of devotion: The life and poetry of Karaikkal Ammaiyar. 433
The Andaman and Nicobar Islands in the Twentieth Century: A Gazetteer. 529
The 'Anna Kali' of Bengal. 166
The annals of rural Bengal. 853
The annual festivals among the Santals. 1927
The archaeology of Hindu rituals: temples and the establishment of the Gods. 2184
The archaeology of religious ritual. 636
The archaoelogy of ritual spaces: Satellite images and early Chalukyan temples. 1638
The archetypal actions of ritual: a theory of ritual illustrated by the Jain rite of worship. 852
The ascent of Nanda Devi [microform] 2059
The Assamese Bihu festival. 255
The Asur. 1122
The auspicious married woman. 1664
The Authoritativeness of the customs as sources of Dharma: The attitude of the Dharmasastra. 1761

The awakening of spring: Holi in Rajasthan. 422
The Bandana festival of midnapore. 266
The bauls and their heretic tradition. 477
The Bhadraloks of Bengal. 1311
The Bhakti movement in India: a critical introduction. 1115
The Bhatheli festival of Assam. 1755
The Bir Babas of Banaras: an analysis of a folk deity in North India. 419
The birth of the Gods, the origin of primitive beliefs. 2014
The black cow's footprint: time, space, and music in the lives of the Kotas of south India. 2190
The Blessing and the curse, the burning of wives in India. 824
The body adorned: dissolving boundaries between sacred and profane in India' art. 501
The Brahmans, theists, and Muslims of India [micro-form]: studies of goddess-worship in Bengal, caste, Brahmaism and social reform. 1408
The Brahmin tradition. 867
The brightest moonless night. 1347
The broken world of sacrifice: an essay in ancient indian ritual. 831
The camphor flame: Popular Hinduism and society in India. 661
The Car festival of India. 1796
The car festival of lord Jagannatha as depicted in the Niladri-Mahodayam. 1636
The car festival of lord Jagannatha. 6
The Car festival of West Bengal. 254
The case of the severed head. 832
The ceremonial friendship among the tribal people of Andhra Pradesh, 1274
The ceremony of Tulapurusa: the Puranic concept and the epigraphic evidence. 1782
The changed mother, or what the smallpox Goddess did when there was no more smallpox. 592
The changind Brahmana: association and elites among the Kanya Kubja of North India. 1013
The changing face of Kattavarayan. 1197
The Charak festival in India: A review and a case study from Delhi . 697
The coming of the Devi: Adivasi assertion in Western India. 805
The concept of rituals in modern sociological theory. 1330
The concept of time in Vedic ritual. 507

The cult of Jagannath and the regional tradition of Orissa. 616
The cult of Manasa in Bengal. 908
The cult of trees and tree worship in Buddhist-Hindu sculpture. 1613
The cultural ecology of India's sacred cattle. 819
The cultural ecology of India's sacred cattle. 1195
The culture heritage of South India. 1600
The custom of burning human effigies of straw on the last day of the Bengali month Kartik (October-November) - in some parts of Bengal. 1165
The custom of couvade. 989
The custom of marriage and its longevity in modern society. 1113
The custom of polyandry as practised in Travancore. 5
The custom of Sahagamana, some early references. 1223
The daily evening and morning offering (Agnihotra) according to the Brahmanas. 284
The daily practices of Hindus containing morning and midday duties. 2144
The dairymen priests among the Todas. 2167
The Dalkhai ritual of Western Orissa 1425
The Daroi Gonds of central India: A study on their intangible cultural heritage. 184
The Dasara at Mysore. 753
The dead: Shinto aspects of Buddhist ritual. 1194
The Devadasi, Dharma and the state. 1336
The development of perfection: The interiorization of Buddhist ritual in the eighth and ninth centuries. 446
The Dipavali. 1768
The divine and the demonic: supernatural affliction and its treatment in North India. 585
The divine hierarchy: popular Hinduism in central India. 148
The Dohada or craving of pregnant women: a motif in Hindu fiction. 279
The dowry cult. 1186
The dowry custom. 367
The dowry system in India. 1273
The dowry system the bane of our society. 1972
The Durga Puja. 1380
The Dusshehra festival of Bastar: Understanding secularization and universalization. 218
The earth as Goddess Bhu Devi: Toward a theory of 'Embedded ecologies' in folk Hinduism. 1328
The earth mother: legends, goddesses, and ritual arts of India. 1573
The earth mother: Legends, ritual art, and goddesses of India. 915

The earther drum: an introduction to the ritual arts of rural India. 916
The economic aspects of tribal rituals: a case study of Paniyas in Wynad district of Kerala. 1514
The elementary forms of religious life, 611
The emergence of monarchy in North India, eighth-fourth centuries B.C.: as reflected in the Brahmanical tradition. 1701
The encounter never ends: A return to the field of Tamil rituals. 409
The eternal Ganga. 1145
The ethnography of a South Indian God: virgin birth, spirit possession, and the prose of the modern world. 735
The evil eye among the Hebrews. 302
The evil eye and bewitchment in a peasant village. 536
The evolution of religious life and social life of man. 1011
The female bridegroom: a comparative study of life-crisis rituals in South India and Sri Lanka. 730
The festival at Avignon. 1908
The festival of a Voyage to the island of Bali held at Cuttack. 484
The festival of India: its import and perspectives. 73
The festival of India: its import and perspectives. 74
The festival of Kapali and Karpagambaal. 1945
The festival of Rali. 528
The Festivals in the History and Culture of the Khasi. 1135
The Fire Festival of North India: with special reference to Bengal. 1807
The fire festival of North India: with special reference to Bengal. 1808
The fire festival of North India: with special reference to Bengal. 1809
The first series of government measures for the abolition of human sacrifice among the Khonds. 568
The folk-element in Hindu culture; a contribution to socio-religious studies in Hindu folk-institutions. 1749
The formation of puja ceremony. 597
The fun and frolic of Holi songs: a note of the festival in areas associated with Lord Krishna. 246
The funeral customs of the Urali. 715
The future of ritual. 1669
The Ganesh festival. 877
The Garos, their customs and mythology. 617
The gift of a virgin: women, marriage, and ritual in a Bengali society. 655
'The gifts, forms and functions of exchange in Archaic 1208

The Goddess and her powers: the tantric identites of the Saundarya Lahari. 961
The Goddess and the demon: A local South Indian festival in its wider context. 202
The Goddess of snakes in medieval Bengali literature, Part II. 535
The Goddess of Snakes in medieval Bengali literature. 534
The Goddess Sitala and epidemic smallpox in Bengal. 1372
The Gods at play: Vertigo and possession in Muria religion. 25
The Gods of India: their history, character and worship. 1416
The Gonds of Andhra Pradesh: tradition and change in an Indian tribe. 2156
The great tradition of Hinduism in the city of Madras. 1899
The Grihya-sutras: rules of Vedic domestic ceremonies. 1400
The health care practices and associated rituals for the mother and the new born: A study among the Mukkuvas of Kerala. 1568
The heavenly bodies in Hindu ritual. 320
The heavenly cow rupan and the festivals of ceremonial torture Gaigoheri: myth, rituals and sacrifice among the people of the Bhil tribe of western India. 1745
The Hemis festival. 1234
The Hill of flates: life, love and poetry in tribal India: a portrait of the Santal. 111
The Himalayan Beas basin: A study in Habitat. 998
The Hindu hearth and home. 1015
The Hindu Jajmani system. 2188
The Hindu Jajmani system: A case of economic particularism. 741
The Hindu law of marriage and stridhana. 171
The Hindu New Year's day. 1763
The Hindu religious year. 2096
The Hindu ritual purity-pollution complex. 1735
The Hindu rituals. 1757
The Hindu woman [microform]. 424
The historical aspect of some Himalayan customs 610
The historical drama of Kaumudi-Mahotsava, or full-moon festival. 1719
The Ho: a glimpse of tribal life in transition. 1282
The Holi festival among the Indians of Fiji. 1209
The hour of the Goddess: memoires of women, food and rituals in Bengal. 180
The iconographies of Sati.429
The impact of agricultural practices on environmental health: A comparative analysis in India.1746

The Indian eye on English life or rambles of a pilgrim reformer [microform]. 1168
The interpretation of ritual. 1091
The Invention of tradition. 842
The Jagra festival. 1123
The Jajmani system of North India: Its structure, magnitude and meaning. 742
The Jettatura and the evil eye. 1544
The Jyotisma ritual: Jaiminia Brahmana, 1, Introduction translation and commentary. 283
The Kaman festival among the Tamilian estate labourers in Ceylon. 920
The Karaga festival. 1623
The keys of power: a study of Indian ritual and belief. [Microform], 3
The Khonds-abolition of human sacrifice. 569
The Kolam tradition: A tradition of figure-drawing in southern India expresses mathematical ideas and has attracted the attention of computer science. 1191
The Konds: human sacrifice and religious change. 280
The Kora in the Pull of Hindu: great tradition. 172
The Kota. 2136
The Kulu beat, Dussehra with a difference. 1554
The ladakhi custom of cremation. 1743
The Ladies of lord Krishna: rituals of middle-aged women in eastern India. 647
The language of sacrifice. 471
The last word: women, death and divination in Inner Mani. 1810
The leaf and the flame. 1495
The Legend of Kumbha. 1698
The Legend of Manasa Devi. 1625
The life of women in a village of North India: a survey of role and status. 1132
The living custom of Bodana and its ancient Indian sources. 1190
The mad Madras season of 1999-2000: An update. 907
The Madras festival season: Mostly more of the same. 1602
The Madras festival season: Too much and too little. 75
The Mahalaxmi fair of tribals in South Gujarat and Western Maharashtra. 2072
The Mahasivaratri. 1764
The Maithil Brahmin festival of Jursital. 1158
The making of a peasant King in colonial Western India: the case of Ranchod Vira. 2147
The Maler: A restudy of nature-man spirit complex. 1913
The Maler: the study of nature man spriti complex of a hill tribe. 2145
The Manasa images of Bengal. 800

The Mandala s an image of man 773
The Mantrartha chandrodaya [microform] [Hindi, Mantras for the rituals in Hinduism]. 926
The marriage customs of the Jewish community of Cochin. 791
The marriage of tree in South India. 1130
The marriage rites of the Bhils. 658
The marriage ritual among the Nagar Brahmins of Gujarat. 732
The mask dances of Hemis. 152
The masked festival: disguise or affirmation? 1238
The matrilineal system in Meghalaya (An apprecia-tion). 1688
The meaning and etymology of puja. 361
The medieval society of Kerala as reflected to the customs and practices of the Ballads of North Malabar. 513
The mela of Deva Sharif. 1448
The miracle plays of Mathura. 834
The Mirrir as ritualized aggres-sion. 322.
The mouths of people, the voice of god: Buddhists and Muslims in a frontier community of Ladakh. 1978
The Mukkoti or Vaikuntha Ekadasi. 1765
The Muria and their ghotul. 606
The mutual influence of the Mohammadans and Hindus. 2051
The Mylapore festival. 1056
The mythology of Kumbha. 1699
The myths of origin of the Indian untouchables. 1677
The Naga cult. 175
The Nagas: a contribution to the history of serpent worship. 1402
The naked Nagas [microform]. 667
The naming of names' in Indian folk belief. 664
The Nationalization of Hindu traditions: Bhartendu Harishchandra and 19th centuary Benaras. 443
The nature and significance of ritual. 1331
The Navarathri Festival. 1996
The Newars: An ethno-sociologi-cal study of a Himalayan community. 1367
The Nuakhai tradition of West Orissa. 1496
The Onam feast in Malabar. 1766
The Onge of Litttle Andaman and their customs and beliefs. 1693
The Oraons of Chota Nagpur [microform]: their history, economic life, and social organization. 1705
The Origin of dragons. 1676
The origin of popular supersti-tions and customs. 1384

The origin of the Ganapati cult. 1242
The origins of evil in Hindu mythology. 1394
The Pageant of marriage-through dowry and no dowry (Customs of different castes and communities). 76
The painted world of the Warlis: art and rituals of the Warli tribes of Maharashtra. 445
The play of the gods: locality, ideology, structure and time in the festivals of a Bengali town. 1420
The poison in the gift: ritual, prestation, and the dominant caste in a north Indian village 1582
The politics of reproductive ritual. 1429
The popular religion and folklore of Northern India. 441
The position of women in Vedic ritual. 379
The pot boils over. 1607
The power of India 1577
The Pratice of collective enterprise. 929
The propriety of Confucius: A sense of ritual. 787
The Rahu-Ketu Myth. 491
The Rath Yatra of Jagannath Puri. 1968
The ravenous hyenas and the wounded sun: myth and ritual in ancient India. 904
The recruitment of shamans among the Mundas. 1970
The relevance of the Upanayana, the Vivaha and the Antyesti Samskaras in modern times. 2026
The religion of the Kuvi Konds, their customs and their folklore. 1786
The religious and cultural bases for breastfeeding practices among the Hindus. 1107
The religious ceremonies and customs of the Parsees. 1271
The religious festivasl of Hindus. 2189
The renovation ritual in a South Indian temple: The 1995 Kumbhabhieka in the Minaki Temple, Madurai. 660
The Rg-veda mantras in their ritual setting in the grhya sutras. 106
The Rites of passage, 691
The rites of the twice born. 1988
The ritual accessories of Teyyam 1339
The ritual murder. 981
The ritual of bathing. 693
The ritual of setting up the sacrificial fires according to the Vadhula School (Vadhulasrautasutra 1.1-1.4) 1975
The ritual pragmatics of a Vedic Hymn: The Riddle Hymn and the Pravargya Ritual. 846
The ritual process. 2090
The ritual sutras. 727
The ritual world of Pocahontas. 711

The role of kinship rituals among Sindhis. 1752

The role of Napita in religious ceremonies and its sources. 1593

The roots of tantra. 817

The sacred anthill and the cult of the Primordial Mound. 871

The sacred marriage of a hindu goddness. 813

The sacred marriage of the Hindu Goddess. 811

The sacrifice of human being: British rule and the Konds of Orissa. 1423

The sacrifice of religion, and the Sakta Pithas. 587

The Santal life cycle: rites and ceremonies. 2086

The Santal: a tribe in search of a great tradition. 1409

The Santals and Disease. 282

The Santals: religion and rituals. 378

The secret of the three cities: An introduction to Hindu Sakta Tantrism. 307

The self possessed: Deity and spirit possession in South Asian literature and civilization 1954

The Serpent and the Sacrifice: An Anthill Myth from Tiruvarur. 1896

The Serpent as a folk-deity in Bengal. 129

The Serpent as sexual symbol. 1318

The serpent power. 2194

The serpent-workship and the living customs. 1774

The significance of head-hunting in Assam. 857

The Sikhs, their religious beliefs and practices. 418

The simple guide to customs and etiquette in India. 1025

The Siri myth and ritual: a mass possession cult of South India. 1529

The sirmur marriage, with an intro. by H.H. Mandi. 944

The snake in the grass-roots movement: Orthodox texts and the preservation and transformation of snake worship rituals. 432

The snake symbol in India, especially in connection with the worship of Siva. 1672

The sociology of Onam. 1087

The Soharai festival of Mundas in Purulia. 1610

The spirit of Sati lives on. 2152

The spring -festival of India. 188

The structure of Hindu caste values, a preliminary study of hierarchy and ritual defilement, ethnology. 1411

The structure of Sinhalese healing rituals. 1391

The subject of Sati: pain and death in the contemporary discourse on Sati. 2003

The sun and the serpent lore. 252

The Sun and the serpent: a contribution to the history of serpent worship. 1403

The supernatural horror in folk-superstitions and customs of the Slavic peoples. 2191
The suppression of the Meriah system among the hill tribes of Orissa. 474
The Suttee. 1952
The Svetambar Murtipujak Jain Mendicant. 939
The sword and the flute. Kali and Krisna: dark visions of the terrible and the sublime in Hindu mythology. 1027
The symbolic merger of body, space and cosmos in Hindu Tamil Nadu. 203
The symbolic representation of death. 997
The symbolism of black and white babies in the myth of parental impression 548
The tale of an Anklet: an epic of South India: the Cilappatikaram of Inako Anika. 132
The Tanjore Mahratta Principality in Southern India; The Land of the Chola the Eden of the South. 838
The tongue makes a good book: history and performance in the Namdev tradition in Maharashtra. 1387
The tool box approach of the Tamil to the Issues of moral responsibility and human destiny. 454
The traditional of religion in Assam: a philosophical study. 110
The tribal culture of India. 2146
The tribe 'Santals' and their sacred groves rituals. 189
The Trichur Pooram: A ritual, a ceremony and a parade. 1383
The Tusker Parade: Colour and pageantry. 1081
The Tusu festival of Jharkhand: a reminiscent of the past. 1915
The two 'lds. 27
The value of rituals. 1112
The vastu yaga and its bearing upon tree and serpent worship in India. 703
The village gods of south India. 2177
The village mother in Bengal. 1373
The 'Vinayaka Chaturthi' festival and hindutva in Tamil Nadu. 659
The Vinayaka Chaturthi. 1767
The way of the ancestors: Custom, innovation, and resistance. 1119
The wedding of the eternal Lord and Spouse-In a new act of the drama of the world. 134
The worship of Mahaganapati according to the Nityotsava. 319
The Yaga: a fire ritual in South India. 415
This beautiful India: Himachal Pradesh. 388
Through the looking glass: divine madness in the Hindu religious tradition. 1026

Through the year in India. 1398
Ticcanni. [Audio Recording[. [Tamil] 875
Tiruvonam: a study based on folklore. 1958
To be happy': ritual, play, and leisure in the Bengali Dharmaraj puja. 1049
To keep the Tali Strong: women's rituals in Tamil Nadu, India. 1665
Toda jati ke logon ke dharmik riti rivaaz. Hindi]. 1562
Toiling without rights: Ho women of Singhbhum. 1140
Toki Parab: a Kondh-Paraja festival of Kalahandi. 1250
Topographies of the self: Praise and emotion in Hindu India. 105
Toranmal fir of the tribals from Satpuda Mountain ranges. 2074
Tortoise in the Vedic mythology and ritual. 1512
Totemism among the Khonds. 653
Toward a theory of public ritual. 40
Toward an understanding of the Muggu: Threshold drawings in Hyderabad. 1022
Toys, Ayurvedic texts and ritual. 1538
Tracking the Goddess: religion, community, and identity in the Durga Puja Ceremonies of 19th century Calcutta. 258
Tradition and transformation: continuity and ingenuity in the temples of Karnataka. 8
Tradition in modern India. 830
Tradition of South India: Karakam. [Audio recording]. 332
Tradition, modernity and the landscapes of belief and ritual: Nirmal Verma's The burning bough and U.R. Anantha Murthy's why not worship in the Nude? 1228
Tradition, science and society. 1624
Traditional age of Sankaracharya and the Maths. 18
Traditional and contemporary life: Hormeneufica of perennial wisdom and social change. 692
Traditional cultures in South-East Asia. 1376
Traditional festive cuisine of North Karnataka. 862
Traditional technology in preparing legume-based fermented foods in Orissa. 1692
Traditional themes and haunting melodies. 1458
Traditional thought: Towards as axiomatic appraoch-A book of reminers. 1737
Traditions and customs in Indian society. 1073
Traditions from India. 1174

Traditions of non-caste Hinduism: the Kabir Panth. 1131
Transgenderism and the cult of Yellamma: heat, sex, and sickness in South Indian ritual 297
Travel and travelers in India, A.D. 1400-1700. 1396
Travels through sacred India. 847
Tree and serpent worship. 627
Tree marriage. 844
Tree symbol worship in India. 772
Tree symbol worship in South Indian Civilization. 1795
Tree symbols worship in India. 1802
Tree worship in ancient India. 1931
Tree worship in ancient India. 1447
Trees in the religion and folklore of the Konda Reddi of South India. 1259
Tribal customary law in India a preliminary statement. 1828
Tribal customs law and justics: a teleological study of Adis. 1503
Tribal fairs and festivals of Rajasthan. 1973
Tribal festivals in Kalhandi, Orissa. 1361
Tribal festivals in Maharashtra. 2073
Tribal festivals of Bihar a funtional analysis. 1900
Tribal gods and festivals in central India. 575
Tribal heritage of Madhya Pradesh. 1893
Tribal heritage: A study of the Santals. 442
Tribal legends and customs and tribal history. 560
Tribal life in India: customs, law and administration, women, education and development towards 2000 AD. 2036
Tribal marriage and sex relations: customary laws of marriage in bhil and Garasia tribes. 225
Tribal myths of Orissa. 607
Tribal pujas and festivals in Tripura. 250
Tribal religion: religious beliefs and practices among the Santals. 2087
Tribal rituals: life cycle rituals and ceremonies in tribal societies. 101
Tribal scenes and ceremonies. 2154
Trichoor Puram: Shaktishali devon ka shandar Jaloos. 1817
Trichur Pooram: Mighty deities, majestic march. 1816
Trinkaus mortuary ritual and mortuary remains. 1207
Tusu festival of the Kudumis of Northern Orissa: Origin and Causes. 1283
Two under the Indian sun. 716
Tyagaraja and the South Indian Bhajana Sampradaya. 1679

Tyohar ke beech Santhal. [Hindi]. 1561
Types and forms of marriage in a Kinnaur village. 1685

U

Udaipur ki Taziadari. [Hindi]. 224
Ude Gulal-abeer prem ras bares jamkar. [Hindi]. 1843
Udisyar citra. [Life and customs in Orissa]. [Bengali] 1898
Ukhyad, Geethal, Phuled ke geet. [Hindi]. 1904
Under the Bo tree. 1392
Under the celestial umbrella. 365
Unknown India [microform]: a pilgrimage into a forgotten world. 595
Unknown India: ritual art in tribe and village. 1053
Unknown India; ritual art in tribe and village. 1987
Unmaad ke utsav me gum sawal. 1883
Untooti rahe parampara. [Hindi]. 1575
Upari Mahasoo kshetra me Bishu ka tyohar. [Hindi]. 937
Urban and Rural Sign Language in India. 933
Urban morals in ancient India [microform]. 700
Use of ritual-motifs by Kalidasa. 1064
Utsav key eh Din. [Hindi]. 1880
Utsav manao mukti ka. 1776
Utsavon Ka samajshastra. [Hindi]. 1378
Uttar Kashi ke riti rivaz. 102
Uttarakhand ki Jaad Bhotia Janjati me 'Losar tyohar' ka mahatwa. [Hindi]. 759
Uttarakhand ki seemant janjatiyon ke riti rivaz. 1674

V

Vaikhanasa daily worship: according to the handbook of Atri, Bhrgu, Kashyapa, and Marici. 744
Vajrayogini: her visualizations, rituals and forms: a study of the cult of Vajrayogini in India Boston. 601
Vaneshwar Fair. 1974
Variety of Theyyams of Kerala: some descriptive notes about the performance and performer. 990
Vart parv, and tohar, Bhartiya Sanskriti samvardhan parisad. [Hindi]. 1860
Vasant Panchami: The spring festival through the ages. 348
Vasant Utsav at Shantiniketan 173
Vasantotsava: the spring festivals of India: texts and traditions. 42
Vecetra prathayo ka desha: Kennor. [Pahari Language]. 1839
Vedic funeral customs and Indus valley culture. 489

Vedic myth, ritual and philosophy (A study of Dvaita Interpretation of the Veda by Madhva). 2061
Vedic ritual: the non-Solemn rites. 726
Vedic rituals. In, 'The cultural heritage of India'. 108
Velaikkari. [On social customs]. Tamil]. 1346
Veneshwar mela: a Bhil celebration. 1144
Vesasraya bidhi. [Rituals regarding Sannyas dharma]. [Manipuri]. 688
Victory of good over evil. 971
Victory to the mother: the Hindu Goddess of Northwest India in myth, ritual, and symbol. 614
Vilashpur ra mela nalvaadi hor tisare shaan. [Pahari Language]. 2125
Village daughter, village Goddess: residence, gender, and politics in a Himalayan pilgrimage. 2181
Village Deities of the Santal and associated rituals. 1040
Violent and fanatical devotion among the Nāyānārs: A study in the Periya Purāam of Cēkkilār 849
Visnuism and Sivaism: a comparison. 728
Vist India Year 1991: Sportlight on culture. 710
Visu's sleep mahisa's attack. Durga's victory: Conceptss of royalty in a sacrificial drama 802
Vivahasaskara [microform]. Marathi, Sanskrit]. 405
Vividha-Tirtha-Kalpa. 935
Voiceless India. 1797
Vows and festivals in early medieval inscriptions of Northern India. 1504
Vrat aur tyohar. [Hindi]. 689
Vrata-Parichaya. [Hindi]. 1848
Vrataraja vratotsava-manjari [microform] [Hindu fast and festivals]. 475
Vrats: transformers of destiny. 2163
Vyavahar vijnan. Darbhanga [Social customs of Mithila] [Maithili]. 925

W

Wandering from 'Hills to Valleys' with the Goddess: protection and freedom in the Matamma tradition of Andhra. 635
Wangala the harvest festival of the Garos. 1687
Water and womanhood: religious meaning of rivers in Maharashtra. 626
Water, wood, and wisdom: ecological perspectives from the Hindu traditions. 1349
Ways to Shiva: life and ritual in Hindu India 949
We're from India. 1478
Wedding ceremonies: ethnic symbols, costume, and rituals. 159
Wedding etiquett. 503

Wedding rites among the Bhil of North-Western Central India. 1047
Western Tibet and the Indian borderland: the sacred country of Hindus and Buddhists with an account of the government, religion and customs of its peoples. 1882
When a wife dies first: The Musivayanam and a female Brahman ritualist in Coastal Andhra. 1038
When Paris went to town: The festival of India opens. 1374
When stars displace the gods: The folk culture of cinema in Tamil Nadu.804
White saris and sweet Mangoes: aging, gender, and body in North India. 1102
Whither the Indian village: culture and agriculture in 'rural' India. 537
Why ritual? 2025
Why we celebrate. 1204
Winter festival of Lahual.2116
Woman as tribute, woman as flower: images of Woman in weddings in North and South India. 1517
Womanhood in the making: domestic ritual and public culture in urban South India. 795
Women and the Hindu tradition. 2164
Women and the sacred in ancient Tamil Nadu 821
Women at work: ritual and cultural identity among Smarta Brahmans of Madras. 796
Women in the Saiva/Sakta ethos. 774
Women in the temple, the palace, and the family: The construction of women's identities in pre-colonial Tamil Nadu.1412
Women in tribal India through custom and traditions. 1750
Women's live, women's rituals in the Hindu tradition 1542
Women's stories, women's symbols: A critique of Victor Turner's theory of liminality 330
Women's right to perform religious rites. 525
Work, ritual, biography: a Muslim community in North India. 1225
Worship of the tiger-god and religious rituals associated with tigers among the Dangi hill tribes of the Dangs district, Gujrat state Western India. 1894

Y

Yajna tattva prakasa [microform]. [Hinduism Rituals]. 402
Yog ki pawan punya parampara. [Hindi]. 103
Yogini cult and temples: a tantric tradition. 500
Youth and status in Tamil Nadu, India. 1338

Glossary of Terms

A

Adharma - Irreligion, unrighteousness. Demerit vice, wrong action in the Mimamsa; in the same, the potency that produces misery; the principle of rest on immobility in Jainism.

Advaita - Non-dualist, monism.

Agama - That which has come down, sacred scripture accepted by sectarian schools.

Agarbatti - Incense-stick.

Ahimsa - Non-injury, non-violence.

Ajnana - Ignorance, nescience, the unconscious as a positive entity for the Advaitins.

Akasa - Space, ether, the source and substratum of sound.

Akhyati - Non-cognition, the nature of illusion according to the Mimamsa of Prabhakara; note the difference from anupalabdhi with is also translated as non-cognition as well as non-apprehension.

Alayavijnana - The storehouse of ideas, instinct, impression, and all other form of consciousness.

Ali-ai-ligang - Ligand or the Ali-ai-ligand is the most important festival of the Misings of Assam.

Amongmong festival - One of the most important festivals of Sangtam Nagas of Tuensang district, Nagaland is the 'Amongmong Festival' that occurs in the first week of the month of September.

Ampidorung festival - This is performed by the Adis of Arunachal Pradesh.

Anekantavada - The doctrine of the Jainism that contrary alternatives can all be true, but from different point of view.

Anivacanjya - The inexplicable, mainly in terms of contradictories like being and non-being 'is' and 'is not'.

Annkuta Day - The day after Diwali, the first day of the waxing fortnight of Kartika is called Annkuta the 'Mountain of Food'.

Antakharana - Inner instrument; for the Nyaya-Vaisesika, it is mans, which is called by them the inner sense organ; for the Sankhya-Yoga and the Vedanta, it include manas, ahamkara, and buddhi, and citta also for the Advaita.

Anu - Atom; the smallest visible particle for Kumarila and the Carvaka.

Anumana - Inference, generally the deductive syllogism.

Aoling Monyu festival - This is the festival observed by the Konyak of Nagaland, celebrated by the end of the month of March.

Apa Tanis - A tribes of Arunachal Pradesh (India)

Appayya Jayanti - Sri Appayya Jayanti is celebrated in South India in the month of October.

Aran festival - This is observed by the Adis of Arunachal Pradesh and is a New Year festival.

Arin Uyu festival - This festival is observed by the Hill Miris of Arunachal Pradesh.

Artha - Wealth, one of the four values of life.

Arthi (Arthi) - Funeral pyre.

Asat - Non being, nonexistence.

Asatkaryavada - The doctrine of the Nyaya-Vaiseika that the effect had no being before it is born.

Ashram - Religious school and hostel.

Atman - Self, spirit, that which manifests itself as the 'I'; when written as 'Atman', it means the Brahman also.

Atmid -'am-ness'; this not egoism, but a state reached when the ego is transcended; also the impurity called egoist.

Avanimulam - This festival of Tamil Nadu is associated with the life of Manikava-Cakar.

Avatar - (avatar, Skt. avatara) - Divine "descent", i.e., incarnation in another form.

Avidya - see ajnana.

Avyakta - Unmanifested, the unmanifest, used as synonym for Prakrti by the Sankhya.

Ayurvedic - Science of life.

B

Baba - The Santhal Sal-Blossom festival.

Baiko festival - Originally this festival occurred in the Assamese month of either Bohag or Jeth.

Baisakhi - This is the first day of the 'Vikrama' calendar of the Hindus and is about fifty years older than the Christian era.

Balangni Mutairenal - This festival is observed by the Tribals of Tripura.

Baluvu - A Ritual among Kadu Kuruba Tribe of Karnataka.

Bania - Member of one of the castes (jati) that comprise the Hindu merchant or trading classes.

Baraat - Marriage procession.

Barat festival - This is a colourful festival of Assam observed by the Tiwas.

Basant Panchami - It heralds the advent of spring. In the North, Basant Panchami is a spring festival when people wear yellow garments and fly kites. This is a Hindu festival that is celebrated in honors of Saraswati.

Basgo Gompa (Leh) - The Maitreya represents the Buddha of the future; this temple site dedicated to the Maitreya serves the Tibetan Buddhist Diaspora as a symbol of hope and faith.

Bas-Puja - Bas-Puja or the bamboo worship is still current in the Golapara regions and also among the Rabhas and the Hajongs as well as the Bodo-Kacharis of Assam.

Bateswar Cattle Fair - This is big fair that is held at Bateswar in Agra district.

Behdeinkhalam festival - Celebrated annually at Jowai in Jaintia hills by Jaintias that falls in the month of July.

Bel Tree - Wood apple, sacred to Shiva.

Bhadrakali Aman temple festival - This festival is held in the month of May-June. It is a eleven day festival held in the temple near Pondicherry in glory of Uma, the consort of Lord Shiva.

Bhadu Utsav - This is a fertility festival observed in the districts Purulia, Bankura West, Burdwan West and Birbhum of West Bengal.

Bhadu - A Festival of West Bengal.

Bhagavad Gita - "Song of the Glorious one", a Sanskrit poem (final redaction ca. 1st c. C.E.) forming part of the Mahabharata, in which Krishna discusses matter of ultimate significance with Arjuna.

Bhagoria - The Tribals of Western Madhya Pradesh observe 'Bhagoria' functions with traditional gaiety and enthusiasm on the occasion of Holi festival.

Bhajan Gopha (Nadia) - This is situated in village Phulia in the district Nadia of West Bengal.

Bhajan - Religious song.

Bhakti - Devotion, love.

Bhangrotu Nalari Fair - This is an important cattle fair held in the Mandi region of Himachal Pradesh that play a significant role in the life of the people of that region.

Bhaona - The ritual play of Assam.

Bharatiya Sanskrti - Indian culture.

Bharwada - This is a tribal observed by the Vartis, Koli tribes of Dadra and Nagar Haveli.

Bhat - Caste group who have the traditional occupation of being minstrels and genealogers.

Bhatheli/Sori/Suwari/Parwa - This festival is prevalent in the old district of Kamrup and Goalpara of Assam and is basically a magical rite associated with fertility-cult.

Bhed - Difference.

Bhedabheda - Difference cum identity; identity in difference.

Bhekuliar-biya - This means "marriage of frogs" current in many parts of Assam.

Bhibhuti - (Vibhuti) - Ashes, a religious symbol, especially associated with the Shiva worship.

Bhokta - Enjoyer (of the fruit of actions).

Bhrama - Illusion hallucination.

Bhunda/Shant/Bhoj Festival - These are some unique festivals of Himachal Pradesh. Like the Kumbh of Allahabad or Haridwar.

Bhuta - Element.

Bihu - A festival of Assam (India).

Bishu Fair - One of the most important fairs of Himachal Pradesh is Bishu or Bisvoa fair, the fair of spring season or say Baisakhi.

Bodhi Tree - Bodhi tree (pipal on ficus religiosa) plays an important part in every Buddhist family.

Bodhi - Enlightenment, gnosis, knowledge, wisdom.

Bodhisattva - One whose being is enlightenment, one on the way to nirvana.

Botor Kikur - A folk festival of the Karbis for Rair.

Brahman - (Brahmin), the ever-growing, the ever-increasing; the power of sacrifice which increases thus, the power of incantations, sacrifice; incarnations; the supreme spirit. From the Upanishads onwards, the word means the supreme spirit and in some systems evens the personal God.

Brahmans - The rituals texts of the Veda, its second part. The word means also the priest who recites the texts at the sacrifice. It means members of the first cast also.

Buddha Jayanti - Buddha is the Sanskrit term, from Buddhi, 'relating to intellect or undersign' and hence 'relating or belonging to the Buddha or to Buddhism.

Buddhi (bodhi) - Consciousness in the Nyaya-Vaisesika; reason in the Sankhya-Yoga and the vedanta; in the Sankhya ect., citta, Sankara and Mahat are its synonyms; in the Advaita of Sankara, citta is sometimes distinguished from Buddhi and given a higher place and Mahat is equated of Mahan Atma of te Katha Upanisad, Cosmic reason or Logos. See manas and ahamkara. Buddhi should not be translated by the same English word in all the systems.

Burhwa Mangal - Since the 1920's the Burhwa Mangal, an emblem of the great days of Hindu princely culture, has disappeared. This was a festival of boats.

C

Chachaban festival - This is held at the end of the successful harvesting and observed by the Wancho of Arunachal Pradesh.

Chachai festival - This is observed by the Wanchos of Arunachal Pradesh at the time of the sowing of millet and paddy seeds in the fields.

Chagramichawa festival - This is the spring festival observed by the Tiwars of Assams region that falls in the month of Phagun.

Chaliho Festival - This is the festival of the Sindhis that occur in the month of Asad (June-July).

Challiwan Festival - This is celebrated by the Noctes of Arunachal Pradesh.

Chandi Mela - Every year in the month of Agrahayan on Shukla Astami-Navami, the worship of Goddess Chandi is held at Barisa, 24 Parganas, West Bengal.

Chapchar Kut - This festival of spring occurs in the month of March or April. The festival is usually observed in Mizoram.

Chatri - A stele stone, or pavilion to honour the memory of a Sati.

Chetrali Festival - This is observed in Himachal Pradesh. The festival is also known as Chetra.

Chhat Festival - The festival of Chhat in honors of the Sun god is observed in large parts of Bihar and eastern Uttar Pradesh.

Chheshu Festival - This festival is held in Monasteries of Himachal Pradesh in the Lahaul region.

Chhos Kor - The festival of the monpa and the sherdukpen.

Chita - Funeral pyre.

Chmkara - Ego.

Chomangkan Festival - Though a death-rite, Chomangkan has today assumed the status of a festival observed by the Karbis of Assam.

Customary Maher - The amount of meher generally prevalent in a society or family.

D

Darsana - Sight, seeing, vision, view, system, school, philosophy.

Dashera-Jeth - This commemorate the birthday of Ganga, goddess of the Ganges.

Dechhang Festival - In Lahaul and Spiti district of Himachal Pradesh this festival is observed in the middle of Paus (December-January).

Deepavali (Diwali) - A Hindu Festival of light.

Deo-Uthan Ekadashi - This Hindu festival is observed in the month of October-November.

Deva (dev) - God.

Devdasi - Temple dancing girl and prostitute.

Dhan-Teras - Falls in the month of Kartika (October-November).

Dharma Patni - Wife according to Hindu religious mandate.

Dharma - Merit, virtue, right action and the potency that produces pleasure and happiness in the Mimamsa; the principle of motion in Jainism; law duty; the Buddhism the doctrine of Buddha, nature, category, quality and ultimate reality.

Dharmakaya - The body of law; the cosmic body of Buddha, somewhat corresponding to the Logos of Heraclitus.

Dhauli - Dhauli hill on the bank of the river Days is a little away from the main road to Puri/Konark from Bhubaneshwar. Capital of Orissa.

Dheki-Pota Ceremony - Means the "erecting of the husking peddles" prevalent in different parts of Assam.

Dhobi - Washer man (low caste).

Dholak - Drum.

Dhoti (dhoty) - (Lungee), Long Muslim skirt worn by men.

Doljatra - Doljatra is observed by the followers of the Vishu cult in Bengal.

Draupadi Amman festival - In the month of Adi (July-August). In many parts of South India, women's rituals take place and are participated by different castes and communities.

Dree Festival - Apatanis of Arunachal Pradesh celebrate this seasonal festival every year for three days in the month of July.

Dukha - Pain, suffering, misery.

Durga Ashtami - In Rajasthan, there is a grand festival of flowers in glory of Gouri (Parvati or Durga, wife of Isvara (or Shiva).

Durga Puja - Annual autumn festival in celebration of the great goddess Durga.

Dvaita - Dual, dualism.

Dvaitin - Dualist.

F

Fung-glin Festival - A wellknown festival celebrated by the Mijis of Arunachal Pradesh.

G

Ganga Jathara - A folk festival in a small city Tirupati and the neighboring villages in Andhara Pradesh.

Gangaur - This Rajasthani festival falls in the month of March/ April and is held about a fortnight after Holi in honors of Parvati, the consort of Lord Shiva.

Garya-Bandhana Parab - This is primarily a festival of Ahirs of Purulia district of West Bengal.

Gauna - Ceremony marking the time of bridebegins to live with her husband and his extended family as distinct from the wedding itself.

Gauri Puja - Gauri Puja is observed by prepubescent Gujaraṭi girls who keeps partial fast to get an ideal husband.

Gitchi Pong festival - This is celebrated by the Garos of Meghalaya before the sowing of the seeds.

Goch-lowa - This is an agricultural rite observed in Assam.

Govardhana Puja - The motive/purpose of Govardhana Puja is the protective ritual for calamities. The day after Diwali-the first day of the waxing fortnight of Kartika, in North India.

Gram Devi - Before harvesting of crops, this festival is performed by all tribes of Dadra and Nagar Haveli.

Gujar (gujjar) - Herdsman caste, sometime agriculturists as well.

Guna - Quality, attribute.

Gurparab - The birth anniversaries of the ten gurus, spiritual teachers or preceptors of Sikhism are observed as holy days, but those of Nanak and Govind Singh the first and the last are celebrated as festivals.

Guru Purnima - In honour of Vyasmuni, who is revered as the supreme Guru, Guru Purnima is observed on the full-moon day in the month of Asad (July-July).

Guru - A holy man.

H

Hadaga Festival - This is a festival of cultivation celebrated in the month of September-October in Maharashtra state.

Halda Festival - This is a New Year festival in Lahaul region of Himachal Pradesh and deity Shiskar Apa (Goddess of wealth) is worshipped.

Hanuman Jayanti - This festival occurs on the full-moon day in the month of Chaitra (March-April) in honour of Hunuman who is known for his devotion to Lord Rama.

Harijan - Beloved of God (lit.). One of the depressed classes.

Hilo Festival - This is a significant festival of the Hill Miris of Arunachal Pradesh.

Holi - A Hindu festival of colors.

Holla Mohalla - In Punjab, particularly at Anandpur Sahib, just a day after Holi, Holla Mohalla is observed by a sect of the Sikh community and stages mock battles with ancient weapons.

Hudum Puja - Hudum Puja is observed in the Goalpara region of Assam and is associated with the fertility cult.

J

Jahez (dahez) - Dowry.

Jamshed Navroz - This is celebrated in the month of March in Maharashtra and Gujarat, a New Year's Day for the Parsi followers of the Fasli calendar.

Jiya - Soul, the living.

Jnana - Consciousness, knowledge.

Jwalamukhi Festival - This is observed in Kangra valley of Himachal Pradesh twice a year in a April and October.

Jyoti - Light, luminescence.

K

Kaarthikai Kuumbu - Fire Festival, an assessment of South Indian Rites.

Kala (kaal) - Time.

Kalam Elluttu - Art and ritual in Kerala.

Kali Puja - Kali the goddess is the Shakti of Siva. She is called by the names including Sati, Parvati, Durga, Uma, Bhavani.

Kama - Passion, lust, love, desire, pleasure, enjoyment.

Kangra Fair - An import fair is held in the Kangra valley of Himachal Pradesh at Jawalamukhi in the month of April.

Kans Ka Mela - Kans ka mela is held in the month of Karti (October-November) in Mathura and Fatehpur Sikri in Agra.

Karam/Jaoma Puja - This is an agricultural festival observed in the Purulia district of West-Bengal.

Karma - action, movement.

Karwa Chouth - Falls in the month of Kartik (October-November) and married women observe vigorous fast.

Ker Festival - Just after a fortnight of Kharchi-puja, on the first Tuesday or Saturday, Ker festival is celebrated in Tripura.

Kerunnyi or Thekranyi festival - This is the festival of Angamis of Nagaland and a two-day pennie (suspension of domestic business) is associated with the festival.

Kevala - Alone, pure.

Kharchi Puja - This festival is also known as 'Chaturdash, or Chaudda-Devata Puja' and is observed in the Tripura state.

Khau Festival - In the month of February, falls the Khau festival observed by the Mijis of Arunachal Pradesh.

Khilunyie Festival - This harvest festival of eight days is observed by the Angamis of Nagaland.

Khuksi - the folk-festival of the Rabhas, an outline of the worship pattern.

Kim Kut - This is a harvest festival of Mizoram when the first crop other than paddy in the field is reaped and offerings are made to the reaped crop. On the occasion the Mizos offer food ceremonially to their dead relatives.

Kliyuga - The shortest, the most deeply degenerated era of world time

Kojagir Harvest festival - The festival is celebrated with great enthusiasm in Maharashtra and some other regions on the full-moon day in the month of Ashwin (September-October).

Kolattam - Marching song, dance.

Koli Diali - Koli Diali is celebrated in Kulu in honour of a Devi named Hirma.

Krsna - Moment, instant.

Kshtriya - Second main caste of Hindus (sprung from the arms and body of Brahma).

Kul - Clan, lineage.

Kuldevi - Goddess of a clan, lineage.

Kusha - A kind of grass often prescribed for usage in Vedic and Hindu ceremonies.

L

Lai Haraoba Festival - This festival is the most vibrant and colourful festival of the Manipur valley. This is a socio-religious festival. The meaning of the term 'Lai Haraoba' is the 'Pleasure of the gods'.

Lambara Festival - In the South of India, the nomadic tribes are known as Banjaras and Lambaras. The Lambaras festival occurs in the month of Phalguna (February-March) and is similar to Holi festival.

Laudongli Festival - This is observed at the end of the successful harvesting, celebrated by the Wanchos of Arunachal Pradesh.

Linga (skt.) - The 'emblem' of Shiva, often specially his erect phallus.

Lohri - The night before Makara Sanktranti is celebrated as Lohri in northern India when bonfires are lit and Agni, God of Fire is worshipped.

M

Mahabhutas - The gross elements, as distinct from Suksmabhutas, the subtle elements.

-Mahajan - The moneylender.

Mahamagam-Festival - Once in twelve years - Mahamagam festival is observed at Kumbakonam (Tamil Nadu).

Maho-ho Festival - This is observed in the individual district of Kamrup, Assam and is a seasonal festival.

Maih-Kheda Festival - This is a seasonal festival prevalent in Darrang. District of Assam to turn the buffaloes out from the Paddy-fields.

Mak' Monre - (Mak' Mode) A Santal Festival in Calcutta.

Makara Sankranti - On the fourteenth of January, either in the month of Pausha or Magha, falls the winter solstic in the India calendrical reckoning. This is the day when the sun begins its northern course (Uttarayana), thus marking the beginning of what one might call the "waxing" half of the year.

Mamita Festival - This festival is observed in the Tripura state by the tribals like Jamatia, Tripura and Noatia.

Manasa Puja -This Puja is mainly confined to Bengal and parts of Bihar, Orissa and Assam.

Mandir - Temple.

Manipur-Festival - The state of Manipur is divided into two tracts-the hills comprising of five districts and the plains with three districts. It is bounded by Upper Burma on east, the China hills of Burma on south-east, Nagaland on the north, Assam on west and Mizoram on south and south-West. Notable festivals of Manipur are Dol-Jatra, Lai Haraoba, Heikru Hitongba, Rasa Leela, Chieraoba, Ningol, Chak-Kouba, Rath-Jatra, Kut, Lui-Ngai-Ni, Gang Ngai and Id-ul-Fitr of Muslims and Christmas of the Christians of the region.

Mantra - A prayer, a text.

Markandeya Fair - This is the most important religious fair of Bilaspur district of Himachal Pradesh.

Ma-Sati-Kal - (Tamil ma sati kal) great sati stone.

Mata - Mother.

Math - Charitable dispensary.

Mauni Amawas - It falls usually in the month of January-February. This is a minor holiday Hindu, observing "Mauni Amawas' do not speak to anyone until they have performed the ablutions prescribed for the occasion.

Maya - The inexplicable power of the brahman; illusion, nescience; the principle of the cosmic unconscious, as distinct from avidya or ajnana; which is the principle of the individual Unconscious, the unconscious being in either case positive, not negative.

Medam-Me-Phi - Though is the death-rite of the Tai-Ahoms of Assam state, but is observed publicity in the style of a festival in which oblations are offered to the dead and sacrifices to the Gods.

Mehndi Myrtle-leaf paste used to produce a red dye - henna.

Mela Festive gathering, fair.

Mirani Sindhuri - Account of the life & customs of Sindhis during the reign of Mirs who ruled Sind before the advent of the British.

Mithya - false.

Miu Festival - Miu is a colourful festival observed by the Khiamngans of the district of Tuensang, Nagaland. This festival is associated with the sowing of the seeds.

Moksha (Moks) - Release from the cycle of birth and rebirth (samsara) emancipation, liberation, salvation.

Molakala Punnami - A folk festival in the Western region of Chitoor district of Andhra Pradesh.

Mopin Festival - This is the biggest festival of the Adis, particularly of the Gallongs, a sub-tribe of Adix of Arunachal Pradesh.

Mopin - A festival of Arunchal Pradesh.

Mukhota - Mask.

Murti - Image, statue especially of a deity.

Myoko - A tribes of Arunachal Pradesh (India).

N

Naga Festival -The Konyak Nagas of the India-Burma border have a "spring festival". In this Naga festival, the theme is the fertility of the field and the central formula runs.

Nagaland Festival - The festivals of Nagaland appear to be agricultural in colour and tone, though are linked with their traditional religious beliefs.

Nagoor Kanduri - This festival is celebrated in the state of Tamil Nadu at Nagoor.

Nai - The Barbar caste.

Naina Devi Festival - This is celebrated in Nainital, Uttar Pradesh in the month of September at the Shrine of Naina Devi.

Naknyu Lum Festival - This six-day festival of the Chang Nagas of the Tuensang district falls in the month of August.

Namangchole - Namanchole aims at the worship of the corn deity with the offerings of rice grains and animal sacrifice.

Nama-rupa - Name and form, mind and matter.

Nandi Bull, vehicle of Shiva.

Nari - Women.

Nauka-Vihar - (Float Festival) the birth anniversary of Tirumalavi Nayak, the 17th century under of Madurai is observed as 'Nauka-Vihar', the great floating festival at Madurai.

Nawala Festival - This is a festival of the Gaddi tribes inhabiting the valleys of Kangra, Chamba and some parts of Mandi and Kullu of Himachal Pradesh.

Neem Tree - Temple tree evergreen, bearing white flowers.

Ngadah Festival - This harvest festival of nine day is celebrated by the Rengmas of Nagaland.

Ngovi Festival - This festival of Angami usually falls in the month of April (the month of Kera).

Nirvana - Liberation from Sansara, quietude, salvation.

Nitya - Eternal.

Nompu - This is a votive act which was undertaken by the girls of Southern India. In the Tamil month of Tai (January-February).

Nonyu Festival - This is 12 days long festival celebrated by the Phoms of the district of Tuensang, Nagaland with great fanfare.

Nuakhia - Most significant festival of Sambalpur, Bolangir, Sundargarh, Kalahandi of the Western Orissa and some areas of Phulbani is Nuakhia.

Nyokum Yullo - A festival of the Nishis.

Nyokum - The festival of the Nyishis of Arunachal Pradesh.

O

Onam - This is the harvest festival of Kerala falling in the month of September.

P

Paceti Festival - Paceti or Pacati is a festival observed in Darrang district of Assam.

Pajjushana - This festival of Jainism fall in the month of Bhadrapada commencing with the thirteenth day of the dark half of Bhadrapada and ending after eight days on the fifty day of the bright half of Bhadrapada.

Panchakalyanakas - Jainas celebrate Panchakalyanakas.

Panchayat - Literally 'council of 5' in a less official way.

Paramartha - The ultimate, the absolute.

Paramatman - The supreme spirit.

Parasnath - Parasntha, a hill beak in Bengal is the main centre of Jaina worship in the eastern India.

Parinama - Change, substantial transformation, transformation of being, evolution; opposed to vivarta.

Parvati - Wife of Shiva, and a subsequent incarnation of Sati.

Paryaya - In Jainism quality.

Pather-Ka-Khel - There is a fair held at Halog, about 30 kms from Shima on the 2nd day of Diwali, The most striking feature of this fair is the Pather-Ka-Khal and the venue is the 'Khel-Ka-Chaunra.

Pativrata - Women who is bound by vows she has taken to protect her husband, a women devoted to her husband.

Pavitra van - Sacred Groves.

Pawl Kut - This is a harvest festival observed in Mizoram in the month of December.

Peepal - A sacred tree.

Pethuri Festival - This festival is also called "Pracha Amavasya' observed on the new moon of Sravana in glory of the 64 Yogini or female attendants of the goddess Durga.

Phagli Festival - This is the most significant event of the Pattan valley of Himachal Pradesh.

Pig Festival -(Nicobar Island) Feasts and festivals are an important part of the Nicobar culture.

Poalak-Le- Festival - This is observed by the Wanchos of Arunachal Pradesh.

Pola Festival - This is an agricultural celebrated in Maharashtra state in the month of July-August.

Pongal - A major harvest festival in Pongal in the southern states. In this big event, cattle are gaily decorated and feed on "Pongal", a sweet preparation of rice, as a symbolic gesture of veneration. Spring festival.

Po-Rag Festival - This is one of the most significant festivals prevalent among Mising society in Assam.

Pradhana - The primary, a synonym for Prakrt in the Sankhya.

Prajna - Knowledge, wisdom, gnosis; usually a synonym for buddhi.

Prakrti - The principle of primeval matter in the Sankhya; the Advaitin equate it to Maya.

Pramana - Measure, standard, the means of cognition.

Prameya - The object of cognition.

Prattyasamutpada - Dependent origination, origination as occasioned by the cause, in which the cause does not become the effect.

Pratyaka - Perception.

Pudgala - The person, the individual, the psycho-physical individual; ordinarily the body.

Puine Festival - This is observed by the Adis of Arunachal Pradesh and is basically a serpent rite.

Puja - The standard form of Hindu worship, in which various goods, honors, and services are offered to a deity present in an image form.

Pumple Festival - This is observed by the hill Miris of Arunachal Pradesh annually wishing good crops.

Puranas - Myths A.D. 400 – A.D. 800.

Purohit - Priests.

Purusa - Man, person, atman, Brahman.

Pusa-Parav - Pusa-parav or the festival of Pusa or Tushu Puja is observed by the tea garden communities of Assam at the time of Magh Bihu.

Pushkar Mela - Pushkar Mela of Rajasthan falls in the month of October/November.

Puttu Mariyamman - Folk Deities and Festivals at Tamil Nadu with special reference.

R

Rajas - The attribute of activity in the Sankhya.

Rakhi Purnima - This festival is celebrated on the full moon day (Rakhi Purnima) of the Hindu month Shrvan (July-August).

Rakshaa Bandhan - A Festival in Indian (Hindu) Society.

Rali Festival - Rali is a very significant festival of clay models observed in the Kangra valley with great enthusiasm.

Ramnavami - This festival falls in the month of Chitra (March-April). On the ninth day the birthday of Lord Rama is celebrated by Hindu everywhere.

Ramzan/Roja - It was in 622 CE, Prophet Mohammad (peace be upon him) migrated to Madina and saw the Jews fast.

Ras Lila Festival - This festival occurs on the full-moon day of the month of Agrahayana and is a very significant festival of Manipur.

Ratha (rath) - Temple cars.

Ratha Yatra - In Orissa, the most popular of the numerous festivals celebrated round the year is the 'Ratha Yatra' festival in the sacred city of Puri. This is the grand culmination of a number of celebrations spread over the summer and the monsoon months.

Rishi - A sage.

Rong Ker Festival - This festival is observed by the Karbis of Assam.

Rongchugala or Gindigala Festival - This festival of the Garos of Meghalaya is celebrated before the starting of harvest.

Ronglo Festival - This is a harvest festival which is celebrated in connection with the harvesting of millet Ronglo is observed by the Noctes of Arunachal Pradesh.

S

Sabda - Sound, word.

Sadhu - (Sanyasi) Hindu ascetic. Holy man.

Saharaj-Parav -In the month of Kati, the tea-garden communities of Assam-celebrate Suhari-parav or Garaya-Puja.

Sair Festival - This is most important festival in the Kangara valley celebrated every year on the first day of Asoj (September).

Sakila Festival - This is observed by the Wanchos of Arunachal Pradesh at the time of the sowing or millet and paddy seeds in the fields.

Sakshi - Witness, the higher atman that only observes the lower atman, but does not act or enjoy.

Sali - Sister-in-Law

Samfang Festival - This festival is celebrated before the sowing by the Tangsas of Arunachal Pradesh.

Sanjhi - This is a festival of Vraja, Fifteen days after Janamashtami occurs the birthday of his beloved Radha.

Sanskara - Life cycle ritual of passage.

Sanskriti - Culture.

Saral Visha - This is celebrated at Courtallam (Tamil Nadu) during July-August. As part of this festival, cultural programmes are organized.

Sat - Being, Existence.

Sati Dharma - Abode of sati.

Sati Pratha - The practice, custom or "system" of Sati.

Sati - Literally 'one who possesses sat' by extension, depending on one's point of view, a widow burned with her husband or the practice of wife of widow burning.

Satkaryavada -The doctrine that the effect had being even before it is born.

Sattva - The attribute to transparence or purity in the Sankhya.

Satya Narayan Vrat - This is observed in all parts of India during Sankranti or Purnima of any month in honour of Lorad Vishnu or Narayan.

Satya - True, real, existent.

Sejuti Vrat - This is observed by the unmarried girls for happiness and prosperity. They pray of cherished husband and children.

Shah - Noble, ruler.

Shakti (Sakti) - A principal in the composition of the cosmos that is understood to be intrinsically female. Force, energy, power.

Shava - (sav, sava) Corpse.

Shimgo (Holi festival) - Kunbis or Curumbins as they were called by the Portuguese, are a semi-tribal agricultural community that mainly inhabits the interior rural areas of Goa and are known for their folk dance 'Kunbinach'.

Shiva - One of the great goddess of Hindus.

Shradh - Death ceremony.

Skandha - Aggregate.

Smriti - Memory, the remembered, the epics and ethical codes.

Soharai - festival of Mundas in Purulia.

Soor - A tradtional alcoholic beverage in tons valley, Garhwal.

Sraddhaprayoga - Hindu rite.

Sruti - Hearing, ear, that which is heard, scripture, Veda.

Stupa - Tumulus most familiar in the Buddhist contexts where it enshrines relics or books.

Sudra - Lowest (4th) caste of Hindus (sprung from the feet of Brahma).

Suhag Marital good fortune.

Sunya - Vasana, smell, fragrance, impression, samskara. Void. Empty, Vacuous.

Swarg lok - Heaven, in a sense no more clearly defined than the English translation implies.

Swastik - Cross with bent arms (freemasonry).

Syadavada - The doctrine that 'it can be'. The doctrine of 'Let it be so', not its relation to anekantavada and nayavada. The doctrine that reality is the void, that it has no determinate essence that it is neither being nor non-being.

T

Taash-(Ganjifas), the tradition of gambling in India.

Tamas- Darkness, inertia, opaqueness.

Tanaha-A traditional festival of Car Nicobar.

Tanmattas-Subtle elements.

Tattva-The true, the real, category.

Teej-Teej is a very important festival for Rajasthani women. But this religious function is also observed in Eastern Uttar Pradesh and large parts of North India.

Teeiri Festival-Celebrated by the Sindhi women all over the country, both married and unmarried in the month of Shravana (July-August)

Teppon-This is observed in Tamil Nadu by ladies when prayers are offered to the family deities and icons of deities are carried out in a procession accompanied by music.

Terhunyi Festival-This is a significant occasion for Angami Nagas of Nagaland.

Thadari Festival-This is the festival of Sindhi women all over the country in honour of goddess Shitala.

The Hemis Festival - According to the Tibetan calendar, the great annual festivals held in the villages of Ladakh takes place in winter, with the exception of Thseshu held at Hemis in summer.

Therine Festival-This is the festival of the Chakhesang of Nagaland and is confined only to paddy huakinf.

Thirthamukh Mela-Also known as Dambaru Mela. Dambaru is at the source of the Gumati River in the sub-division of Amarpur of Tripura.

Tika-Forehead ornaments.

Trishul-Trident (weapon of emblem of Shiva and various goddesses).

Tsokum Festival-This is a colourful observed by the Khiamngans of the district of Tuensang, Nagaland and is connected with harvesting.

Tulsi-Basil, Sacred to Vishnu.

Tusu Festival-"Tusu" is a harvest festival of Bengal that is celebrated with great enthusiasm in Purulia, Bankura, Medinipur to Dhalbum, Singhbhum etc.

Tyohar-Festival.

U

Udni-In certain region of North India, the upper part of the traditional women's grab.

Unakuti Mela-This fair is held in hilly region of Kailasahar sub-division of the territory of Tripura state.

Upanishad-Writing 600 B.C.

Upvas-Fasts.

Urs of Ajmer Sharif - This is a great festival held annually at Ajmer, Rajasthan.

Urs of Hazrat Khwaja Nizamuddin Aulia - The Urs of Nizamuddin Aulia (1238-1324) is celebrated at the shrine of the saint every year in Delhi on the 17th of Rabi-ul-Awwul.

V

Vaikasi-Visaka - Vaikasi is the second Tamil month which corresponds to the English month May-June.

Vallamkali Festival - This is celebrated in Kerala, the Vallamkali or Boat race in typical of this region.

Vamangani - One possessing the left hand part (of a common body) i.e. a wife in relation to her husband.

Vaman-Janma Festival - It falls on the twelfth day of bright half of the month of Bhadra and is celebrated in Manipur valley to mark the birthday of Vamana.

Vatakunnatham - This temple festival is observed in Kerala in honour of Lord Shiva and a procession of temple elephants marks the occasion.

Vedas - Sacred hymns 1500 B.C.

Vijnana - A synonym for buddhi, consciousness, manas.

Vikalpa - Conceptual form or formation, image or image formation on the mind, separation, analysis (as opposed to samkalpa), determinant.

Vina (veena) - Musical instrument.

Vivah (shadi) - Marriage.

Vivarta - Change in form only, assuming a form without change of being, transformation of the material cause without affecting its being.

Vrat - Vow, especially a vow undertaken by women for the welfare or her husband of family, usually involving some form of fasting.

Vyavahara - Activity, customary activity, conventionality, empirically, pragmatics.

W

Wangala Festival - For Garos in Meghalaya, Saljong is the God of Fertility.

X

X'Mas/Christmas - The most widely known festival in the Christian calendar is the Christmas day that falls on 25th

December. This day is observed as the birthday of Jesus Christ.

Y

Yagna (yajna) -Sacrifice, in the Vedic mode; in modern times, a broader class of ceremonial and ritual acts so named to designate its continuity with of equivalency to Vedic sacrifice.

Yama Dvitiya -This festival is observed in honour of Lord Yama, the God of Death as also Chitragupta, who is said to have come out of the body of the creator Brahma, who then appointed him as judge in Samayamini, the capital city of Lord Yama.

Yaosang Festival - This festival is observed in the Manipur valley and is somewhat similar to the Holi festival. The Yaosang falls on the full-moon day of month of Lamdra (Phalgun) and lasts for five days.

Z

Zanana - Women's quarter; thence, women attached to a royal household and typically kept in seclusion.